# PRACTICAL EXPERIENCE ASSIGNMENTS

To Accompany

# ADMINISTRATIVE OFFICE MANAGEMENT

Eleventh Edition

**B. Lewis Keeling**
Professor Emeritus
Bucks County Community College
Newtown, Pennsylvania

**Norman F. Kallaus**
The University of Iowa
Iowa City, Iowa

---

**Consulting Editor**
**Dr. Sharon Massen**
Clarks Summit, PA

**Software Consultant**
**Marly Bergerud**
Saddleback Community College

**South-Western Educational Publishing**

ISBN: 0-538-71128-0

3 4 5 6 7 8 BN 02 01 00 99 98 97

Printed in the United States of America

I(T)P
International Thomson Publishing
South-Western Educational Publishing is a division of International Thomson Publishing Inc. The ITP trademark is used under license.

# *To the Student*

*Practical Experience Assignments* is designed to help you become personally involved and to participate more directly in your study of administrative office management. The different kinds of assignments simulate on-the-job experiences often found in offices of all size. The assignments, which complement your textbook and your instructor's presentation, will make you more aware of administrative management principles, policies, and practices. Of course, these assignments do not substitute for actual office experience; but by studying and completing them, you will add to your professional development.

In designing *Practical Experience Assignments,* I have followed the organization pattern of the Eleventh Edition of *Administrative Office Management* by Keeling and Kallaus, which is published by South-Western Educational Publishing. Thus, the chapter titles are the same as those in *Administrative Office Management* and appear in the same sequence. However, the study guides and projects in *Practical Experience Assignments* may also be used by students who are working with another office management textbook.

Now let's take a look at the layout of *Practical Experience Assignments.*

**Highlights of the Chapter** To introduce each chapter, I present a brief summary of the corresponding chapter in the Eleventh Edition of *Administrative Office Management.* By reading these introductory paragraphs, you will get a little "flavor" of the chapter.

**Section A** The opening part of each chapter of *Practical Experience Assignments* consists of self-test review questions. By answering these objective questions you will be able to check your understanding of the material contained in each chapter of the textbook. You will find the answers to the review questions at the back of this book.

**Section B** The second part of each chapter of *Practical Experience Assignments* contains the following kinds of projects:

*Self-Analysis.* These projects call upon you to look ahead to your career as an office supervisor or office manager. In these situations, you have an opportunity to assess yourself as a potential manager, to evaluate your leadership style, and to reflect upon your philosophy of management.

*Field Research.* The research projects take you individually or as a member of a group of students into the offices of your firm, a company in the community, or your campus offices. There you will investigate how the organization has dealt with certain office activities such as a feasibility study, the office environment, reprographic processes, newly emerging work schedules, and the flow of information processing. Following your on-the-job research, your instructor may ask you to prepare an oral or written report of your findings.

*Quantitative Analysis.* Several projects make use of quantitative analysis in solving problems dealing with capital expenditure analyses (payback period, average rate of return, and net present value), cost recovery (depreciation) and its effect on cash flow, and evaluating wage and salary survey data by means of the least squares conversion method. (None of these projects requires any more mathematics than the algebra you studied in high school or college.)

*In-Basket and Incident.* Throughout this book, but especially in the "In-Basket" projects, office incidents are described—many of which were faced by me. Drawing upon your study of office management and the experiences you have gained up to now, you will have an opportunity to make decisions and find solutions that will be mutually acceptable to the office employee and you as manager.

*Computer Hands-On.* The Computer Hands-On activities are new to this edition. Working with a computer, you will have an opportunity to complete assignments involving word processing, spreadsheet analyses, and graphic representation of quantitative information.

*Readings.* A variety of readings, drawn from office management journals and business periodicals, have been included to supplement your study of office management. Following each article is a list of questions to be answered. Some of the questions are answered within the readings, while others ask you, "What if you were . . .?" or "What would you do if . . .?"

*Crossword Puzzles.* A new feature in this edition are the crossword puzzles presented at the end of Chapters 5, 12, 20, and 23. Most of the clues in each puzzle are based upon Glossary items appearing within the four parts of the accompanying textbook. Solutions to the crossword puzzles are given at the back of this workbook.

*Comprehensive Case Problem.* The Comprehensive Case at the end of this workbook is divided into four parts that tie in with the corresponding parts of the textbook. Thus, you may solve each part after you have finished your study of that portion of the textbook. The case problem may be assigned in lieu of a term report, or portions of the case may be used for class discussion and oral reporting.

Good luck as you begin your study of office management. I hope that your experiences in completing *Practical Experience Assignments* will be as profitable as those of my students. To all of them I express my thanks for the contributions they made to the development of this publication.

B. Lewis Keeling
Newtown, Pennsylvania

# Contents


| | | Page |
|---|---|---|
| ***Chapter 1*** | | |
| ***Managing Offices in Our Global Economy*** | | ***1*** |
| Project 1–1 | Selecting a New Office Manager | 3 |
| Project 1–2 | Office Management References in Your Library | 5 |
| Project 1–3 | Field Research: The Office Manager—The Job, Responsibilities, and Personal Characteristics | 6 |
| Project 1–4 | Investigating the Outlook for Administrative Support Occupations | 8 |
| Project 1–5 | Understanding the Fundamental Differences in Management Styles among European Managers | 9 |
| Project 1–6 | Computer Hands-On: Learning About Diversity | 12 |
| ***Chapter 2*** | | |
| ***Applying Basic Management Principles*** | | ***13*** |
| Project 2–1 | Analyzing the Span of Control | 15 |
| Project 2–2 | A Philosophy of Office Management | 16 |
| Project 2–3 | Measuring Your Effectiveness as a Manager | 17 |
| Project 2–4 | Preparing an Organization Chart of the Administrative Office Management Function | 18 |
| Project 2–5 | Computer Hands-On: Preparing an Organization Chart and Estimating Weekly Salaries and Annual Sales | 21 |
| ***Chapter 3*** | | |
| ***Developing Problem-Solving Skills*** | | ***23*** |
| Project 3–1 | Brainstorming in the Classroom | 25 |
| Project 3–2 | How Creative Are You? | 25 |
| Project 3–3 | Integrating Two Cultures to Form a Decision-Making Process | 28 |
| ***Chapter 4*** | | |
| ***Administering Office Systems*** | | ***31*** |
| Project 4–1 | Shopping for a New Payroll System | 33 |
| Project 4–2 | Let's Debate | 37 |
| Project 4–3 | Calculating the Annual Depreciation Expense of a Computer System | 37 |
| ***Chapter 5*** | | |
| ***Communicating in the Office*** | | ***39*** |
| Project 5–1 | Selecting Media for Downward Communication | 41 |
| Project 5–2 | Removing Communication "Static" from a Business Report | 42 |
| Project 5–3 | Computer Hands-On: Reporting on the Reduction of Communication Costs | 44 |
| Project 5–4 | Fighting the Fog in Written Communication | 45 |

Project 5–5 Communicating Without Words .... 47
Project 5–6 Computer Hands-On: Reporting the Costs of Written Communications .... 48
Project 5–7 Making Yourself Understood Among Global Cultures .... 49
Crossword Puzzle 1 .... 52

***Chapter 6***
***Recruiting and Orienting the Workforce*** .... ***55***

Project 6–1 Computer Hands-On: Writing a Letter of Application .... 57
Project 6–2 Completing the Application Form .... 57
Project 6–3 "Please Be Seated. . ." The Interview .... 62
Project 6–4 Back to That Application .... 65
Project 6–5 Computer Hands-On: Writing a Help-Wanted Ad .... 66
Project 6–6 Which Fork Do I Use? .... 66
Project 6–7 Field Research: Determining the Access to Your Office by Applicants and Employees with Disabilities .... 67

***Chapter 7***
***Supervising the Office Staff*** .... ***69***

Project 7–1 Computer Hands-On: An In-Basket Problem .... 71
Project 7–2 What Is Your Leadership Style? Your Followership Style? .... 73
Project 7–3 How Safe Is My Job? .... 74

***Chapter 8***
***Training, Appraising, and Promoting Office Personnel*** .... ***79***

Project 8–1 Field Research: The Office Manager's Education and Training .... 81
Project 8–2 On-the-Job Training—Role Playing .... 81
Project 8–3 Computer Hands-On: Designing an Employee Appraisal Form .... 85
Project 8–4 Preparing for a Three Months' Assignment in Madrid .... 86
Project 8–5 Training About Foreign Cultures .... 87

***Chapter 9***
***Analyzing Office Jobs*** .... ***89***

Project 9–1 Computer Hands-On: Editing a Questionnaire and Preparing a Job Description .... 91
Project 9–2 Job Evaluation: The Ranking Method .... 93
Project 9–3 Job Evaluation: The Job Classification Method .... 93
Project 9–4 Job Evaluation: The Factor-Comparison Method .... 95
Project 9–5 Job Evaluation: The Point-Factor Method .... 96

***Chapter 10***
***Administering Office Salaries*** .... ***103***

Project 10–1 Investigating the Wage Gap Between Salaries Paid Women and Men .... 105
Project 10–2 Field Research: Management Reaction to Salary and Benefits Programs .... 106
Project 10–3 Computer Hands-On: Using the Least Squares Method to Compare Salaries Paid with Community Wage Curve .... 108
Project 10–4 Field Research: Studying a Union Contract .... 113
Project 10–5 Administering Salary Programs in Japan .... 114

***Chapter 11***
***Providing Employee Benefits*** .... ***117***

Project 11–1 Planning a Broader Offering of Employee Benefits .... 119
Project 11–2 Establishing an Educational Assistance Program .... 120
Project 11–3 Viewing the Organization from the Bottom .... 123

**Chapter 12**
**Examining Workplace Issues** . . . . . . . . **125**

Project 12–1 "Hey, How Would You Handle This One?" . . . . . . . . 127
Project 12–2 Field Research: Investigating Office Practices That May "Get Out of Hand" . . . . . . . . 129
Project 12–3 Hiring a Vice President's Daughter . . . . . . . . 130
Project 12–4 Field Research: Evaluating a New Work Schedule . . . . . . . . 133
Project 12–5 Snooping Electronically . . . . . . . . 133
Crossword Puzzle 2 . . . . . . . . 137

**Chapter 13**
**Managing Office Space** . . . . . . . . **141**

Project 13–1 Field Research: Determining the Availability and Cost of Office Space . . . . . . . . 143
Project 13–2 Planning a Layout for the Business Department Offices . . . . . . . . 144
Project 13–3 Computer Hands-On: Revising the Layout for an Open Office Area . . . . . . . . 146
Project 13–4 Computer Hands-On: Expanding the Storage Capacity of a Records Center . . . . . . . . 146
Project 13–5 Revising a Proposed Layout for an Overseas Office . . . . . . . . 147
Project 13–6 Taking Inventory of *Your* Office . . . . . . . . 149

**Chapter 14**
**Planning an Ergonomically Sound Office Environment** . . . . . . . . **151**

Project 14–1 Field Research: Evaluating the Office Environment . . . . . . . . 153
Project 14–2 Using Three-Dimensional Drawings in Planning an Office Layout . . . . . . . . 155
Project 14–3 Avoiding the Sick Building Syndrome . . . . . . . . 163

**Chapter 15**
**Selecting Office Furniture and Equipment** . . . . . . . . **165**

Project 15–1 Calculating the Purchase Price of Office Furniture and the Annual Depreciation Expense . . . . . . . . 167
Project 15–2 Selecting New Filing Equipment. . . . . . . . . 168
Project 15–3 Field Research: Surveying Users of Office Furniture . . . . . . . . 169
Project 15–4 Capital Budgeting—A Tool of Planning (Payback Period) . . . . . . . . 170
Project 15–5 Break-Even Analysis . . . . . . . . 171

**Chapter 16**
**Automating the Office** . . . . . . . . **177**

Project 16–1 Meeting the Information Needs of Executives . . . . . . . . 179
Project 16–2 Field Research: Investigating the Services Provided by a Data Service Center . . . . . . . . 182
Project 16–3 Computer Hands-On: Automating a Payroll Accounting System . . . . . . . . 183
Project 16–4 Field Research: Learning About a Computerized Banking System . . . . . . . . 185

**Chapter 17**
**Understanding Text/Word Processing Systems** . . . . . . . . **187**

Project 17–1 Inputting on the Dvorak Keyboard . . . . . . . . 189
Project 17–2 Computer Hands-On: Creating Input . . . . . . . . 192
Project 17–3 Field Research: Reporting on a Text/Word Processing System . . . . . . . . 194
Project 17–4 Field Research: Determining the Cost Effectiveness of Word Processors . . . . . . . . 195

**Chapter 18**
**Distributing Information: Telecommunication and Mailing Systems** . . . . . . . . **197**

Project 18–1 Getting Acquainted with the Telephone Directory . . . . . . . . 199
Project 18–2 Field Research: The Telephone Switchboard Operator . . . . . . . . 200
Project 18–3 Depreciation Methods and Their Effect on Cash Flow . . . . . . . . 203
Project 18–4 Reorganizing the Mailing Center . . . . . . . . 205

*Chapter 19*
***Managing Records*** . . . . . . . . . . . . . . . . . . . . . . . . . . . . . . . . . . . . . . . . . . . . . . . . . . ***207***

Project 19–1 Computer Hands-On: Designing a Combination Employee and Property Pass . . . . . . . . . . 209
Project 19–2 Reorganizing the Records Management System . . . . . . . . . . . . . . . . . . . . . . . . . . . . . 210
Project 19–3 Calculating Clerical Savings Resulting from Redesigning a Purchase Order Form . . . . . . 213
Project 19–4 Converting to Electronic Forms . . . . . . . . . . . . . . . . . . . . . . . . . . . . . . . . . . . . . . . . . 214

*Chapter 20*
***Managing Microimage and Reprographic Systems*** . . . . . . . . . . . . . . . . . . . . . . . . . . . . . . . ***217***

Project 20–1 Field Research: Office Copying Processes . . . . . . . . . . . . . . . . . . . . . . . . . . . . . . . . . 219
Project 20–2 Determining the Average Rate of Return . . . . . . . . . . . . . . . . . . . . . . . . . . . . . . . . . . 221
Project 20–3 Reducing the Misuse of Copiers . . . . . . . . . . . . . . . . . . . . . . . . . . . . . . . . . . . . . . . . 222
Crossword Puzzle 3 . . . . . . . . . . . . . . . . . . . . . . . . . . . . . . . . . . . . . . . . . . . . . . . . . . . . . . . . . . 224

*Chapter 21*
***Improving Administrative Office Systems*** . . . . . . . . . . . . . . . . . . . . . . . . . . . . . . . . . . . . . ***227***

Project 21–1 Field Research: Charting the Flow of a Purchase Requisition . . . . . . . . . . . . . . . . . . . . 229
Project 21–2 Constructing a PERT Chart for Scheduling a Conference . . . . . . . . . . . . . . . . . . . . . . . 230
Project 21–3 Integrating Human Resources and Payroll into One Information System . . . . . . . . . . . . 233
Project 21–4 Installing a New System Could Put Your Job on the Line . . . . . . . . . . . . . . . . . . . . . . 236
Project 21–5 Preparing a Forms Distribution Chart . . . . . . . . . . . . . . . . . . . . . . . . . . . . . . . . . . . . 238

*Chapter 22*
***Improving Office Productivity*** . . . . . . . . . . . . . . . . . . . . . . . . . . . . . . . . . . . . . . . . . . . . . . ***239***

Project 22–1 Measuring Work and Setting Standards: Direct Observation and Wristwatch Desk Audit . . . . . . . . . . . . . . . . . . . . . . . . . . . . . . . . . . . . . . . . . . . . . . . . . . . . . . . . . 241
Project 22–2 Computer Hands-On: Using Work Sampling to Determine Standard Times . . . . . . . . . . . 242
Project 22–3 Calling Upon the TD to Monitor and Control ERT by Establishing an RTP . . . . . . . . . . . 245
Project 22–4 Field Research: Examining Office Productivity Improvement Programs . . . . . . . . . . . . . 246
Project 22–5 To Downsize or Not to Downsize? . . . . . . . . . . . . . . . . . . . . . . . . . . . . . . . . . . . . . . 248

*Chapter 23*
***Budgeting Administrative Expenses*** . . . . . . . . . . . . . . . . . . . . . . . . . . . . . . . . . . . . . . . . . . ***251***

Project 23–1 Preparing an Operating Budget . . . . . . . . . . . . . . . . . . . . . . . . . . . . . . . . . . . . . . . . . 253
Project 23–2 Field Research: Investigating the Preparation of the Administrative Expenses Budget . . . . . . . . . . . . . . . . . . . . . . . . . . . . . . . . . . . . . . . . . . . . . . . . . . . . . . . . . . 254
Project 23–3 Computer Hands-On: Analyzing a Budget Performance Report . . . . . . . . . . . . . . . . . . . 257
Crossword Puzzle 4 . . . . . . . . . . . . . . . . . . . . . . . . . . . . . . . . . . . . . . . . . . . . . . . . . . . . . . . . . . 258

***Comprehensive Case for Critical Thinking*** . . . . . . . . . . . . . . . . . . . . . . . . . . . . . . . . . . . . . ***261***

***Answers to Section A • Review Questions*** . . . . . . . . . . . . . . . . . . . . . . . . . . . . . . . . . . . . . ***271***

***Solutions to Crossword Puzzles*** . . . . . . . . . . . . . . . . . . . . . . . . . . . . . . . . . . . . . . . . . . . . . . ***275***

1

# MANAGING OFFICES IN OUR GLOBAL ECONOMY

Sitting in our offices today, we can obtain information with lightning speed from our associates, customers, and suppliers not only locally and nationally but also globally. With the innovations that are emerging, many of us no longer are restricted to hearing a voice at the end of the telecommunications network—we can now see each frown or smile on the caller's face. Along with the challenges of the new technologies have come new "people" problems that require today's administrative managers to be adept at understanding and appreciating the cultural and ethnic diversity of their office employees.

Historically, administrative managers have taken different approaches in managing people and handling the information processing activities. Over the years, schools of management thought have emerged, with each emphasizing a somewhat different approach to understanding the process of management. As a student of office management, you may not find specific solutions to your problems within the contributions of any one of these schools. However, each school will provide you with certain underlying principles that can serve as guidelines for action and for a better understanding of the information management concept.

## SECTION A • REVIEW QUESTIONS

**Directions:** Indicate your answer to each of the following questions by circling "Yes" or "No" in the Answers column.

| | Answers | |
|---|---|---|
| 1. Do most administrative office managers have the same job responsibilities? | Yes | No |
| 2. Do administrative office managers have a company-wide responsibility for managing the information cycle? | Yes | No |
| 3. In a management information system, do automated machines perform all the activities in the information cycle? | Yes | No |
| 4. Do most office managers require more technical skills than human skills? | Yes | No |
| 5. Do most small firms provide clear-cut paths of promotion to the position of office manager? | Yes | No |
| 6. To achieve the C.A.M. designation, must the candidate have at least three years of management experience? | Yes | No |
| 7. Can administrative office management be viewed as *both* a science and an art? | Yes | No |
| 8. Has today's rapid technological change decreased the demand for intuitive managers? | Yes | No |
| 9. Were the earliest approaches to the study of management concerned mostly with production processes? | Yes | No |
| 10. Did Taylor believe that workers could be motivated by financial means, such as piecework systems? | Yes | No |
| 11. Did Weber view a bureaucracy as a form of organization that relies mainly upon managerial intuition? | Yes | No |
| 12. Was Leffingwell instrumental in applying the principles of scientific management to office work? | Yes | No |

13. Is Follett looked upon as the first management author to state clearly the several functions of management? .......... Yes No
14. Did the Hawthorne studies conclude that changes in the work environment had significant long-term effects upon worker productivity? .......... Yes No
15. Does Maslow's hierarchy of needs maintain that after our lower-level needs are satisfied, they no longer serve as motivating factors? .......... Yes No
16. Since the needs patterns of workers are alike, can the office manager effectively use one single approach to motivate workers? .......... Yes No
17. Does Herzberg look upon the quality of supervision as an example of a hygienic factor? .... Yes No
18. Is *decision making* defined as the making of a conscious choice between two or more alternative courses of action? .......... Yes No
19. Would you expect to find statistical tools and techniques used in a program of total quality management (TQM)? .......... Yes No
20. Are a firm's administrative office system and its subsystems completely independent of other systems? .......... Yes No

**Directions:** In the Answers column, write the letter of the person's name in Column 1 that is most often associated with each item in Column 2. Some of the names may be used more than once.

## Part I

| Column 1 | Column 2 | Answers |
|---|---|---|
| **A** Fayol, Henri | 1. Developed the Five Principles of Effective Work ........ | 1. _____ |
| **B** Follett, Mary Parker | 2. Viewed each worker as a separate economic person motivated by financial needs .......... | 2. _____ |
| **C** Gilbreth, Frank and Lillian | 3. Saw group organization as the new method in politics and the basis for future industrial systems .......... | 3. _____ |
| **D** Leffingwell, William H. | 4. Father of office management .......... | 4. _____ |
| **E** Taylor, Frederick W. | 5. Formulated the first comprehensive theory of management . | 5. _____ |
| **F** Weber, Max | 6. Father of scientific management .......... | 6. _____ |
| | 7. Developed an organization design known as bureaucracy .. | 7. _____ |
| | 8. Used motion pictures to study and improve motion sequences | 8. _____ |

## Part II

| Column 1 | Column 2 | Answers |
|---|---|---|
| **A** Deming, W. Edwards | 1. Researched the effects of physical environment upon worker output | 1. _____ |
| **B** Drucker, Peter F. | 2. Developed motivation theory based upon hierarchy of needs ..... | 2. _____ |
| **C** Herzberg, Frederick | 3. Introduced management by objectives (MBO) .......... | 3. _____ |
| **D** Juran, Joseph M. | 4. Pioneer in statistical analysis and quality management .... | 4. _____ |
| **E** Maslow, Abraham | 5. Examined American companies having Theory Z management styles | 5. _____ |
| **F** Mayo, Elton | 6. Developed Theories X and Y to describe dual nature of worker behavior .......... | 6. _____ |
| **G** McGregor, Douglas | | |
| **H** Ouchi, William | 7. Formulated the motivation-hygiene theory .......... | 7. _____ |

## SECTION B • PROJECTS

# Project 1–1 • Selecting a New Office Manager

As you complete this project dealing with the selection of an office manager, you will be critically analyzing questions such as these:

1. What personal characteristics am I looking for?
2. Should the office manager be male or female?
3. If the applicant is over 40 years of age, is he or she "too old to cut the mustard"?
4. How much of a salary increase over the applicant's present earnings must I offer to attract the jobseeker?
5. How important is an advanced degree?
6. Shall I search mainly for a married person with dependents to support?

Here is the background information you will need in order to select the best applicant:

TOPS IN KAN Beef Products is located in a combined meat-packing plant and office building in Kansas City, Missouri. The fourth floor of the building, soundproof and air-conditioned, is used for the administrative and operating offices. All accounting, credit, and human resources work and office services are provided in one large office area. The present office force is shown in Table 1–1.

**Table 1–1**
**OFFICE PERSONNEL AT TOPS IN KAN**

| Department or Service | Men | Women | Age Range (yrs.) |
|---|---|---|---|
| Accounting | 6 | 2 | 24 to 45 |
| Credit | 1 | 1 | 30 to 40 |
| Human Resources | 1 | 2 | 30 to 50 |
| Data Entry | 4 | 8 | 20 to 55 |
| Reprographics | 2 | 1 | 20 to 40 |
| Mailing | 0 | 6 | 19 to 60 |
| Records Management | 1 | 10 | 18 to 45 |
| Word Processing | 0 | 30 | 20 to 30 |

Bonnie Harrow, the present office manager, is 53 years old. She has been with the firm for 30 years but has decided to retire at the end of next month because of ill health. Although it is the company's policy to promote from within whenever vacancies occur, in this instance the company president has decided to select someone from outside the organization in order to rejuvenate and update the administrative office systems. The president feels that as a result of Harrow's long tenure, the office work has gotten in a "rut."

The starting salary of the new office manager will be $32,000. Harrow has been receiving an annual salary of $34,500. It is expected that the new office manager's salary will be increased to $36,000 within three to four years.

Applicants for the position have been narrowed down to three candidates. Table 1–2 summarizes the personal data obtained from the candidates' applications and other information volunteered during their interviews.

**Table 1–2**
**PERSONAL DATA OF CANDIDATES FOR OFFICE MANAGEMENT POSITION**

| Factor | Rose Carrera | Michael Hun | Jeffrey Berg |
|---|---|---|---|
| Age and marital status | 35 yrs., divorced | 36 yrs., single | 41 yrs., married |
| Number of dependents | 1 child | None | Wife and 2 children |
| Education | Two years at university evening school (secretarial science, credit management, human resources management) | College graduate, B.S.; accounting major, computer science minor | Community college associate degree; 3 yrs. college evening division (marketing, accounting, computer systems) |
| Experience | Administrative assistant to company president, 5 yrs.; credit manager, 7 yrs. to present | Junior accountant, 1 yr.; head bookkeeper, small retail store, 1 yr.; office manager, textile office—10 employees, 4 yrs.; employment agency, owner and manager, 8 yrs. to present | Yeoman, U.S. Navy, 4 yrs.; office manager, metal manufacturing, 4 yrs.; payroll manager, fuel oil distributor—22 employees, 10 yrs. to present |
| Annual salary | $29,900 | $31,000 | $32,500 |
| Professional organizations | Professional Secretaries International (PSI) | National Association of Temporary Services (NATS); American Management Association (AMA) | American Payroll Association (APA) |
| Reasons for desiring change | Well satisfied with present position; just "shopping around" | Plagued by problems of small business ownership; looking for greater long-term security and stability | No opportunity for advancement; personality conflict with CEO |

**Directions:** The president of the company has asked you to help select the new office manager by answering each of the following questions:

1. Which of the three candidates do you recommend be employed? Why?

2. For what reasons have you rejected the two other candidates?

*Name* ______________________________ *Date* ______________________ 

## Project 1–2 • Office Management References in Your Library

During your study of office management, you may be assigned case reports, research projects, or term papers for which library research will be needed. The journals listed below may aid you in locating references pertaining to the field of office management. These journals will be of value to you not only during your collegiate career but also on the job as you continue your lifelong career of education. If you are presently employed, you may wish to recommend that your company subscribe to one or more of these journals.

**Directions:** For each of the journals you find in your school's library, complete the form by recording the information requested.

| Name of Journal | Publisher | Frequency of Publication | Annual Cost of Subscription | Storage: Microimage or Bound Volumes |
|---|---|---|---|---|
| *Business Week* . . . . . . . . | | | | |
| *Computerworld* . . . . . . . | | | | |
| *Datamation* . . . . . . . . . . | | | | |
| *Forbes* . . . . . . . . . . . . . . | | | | |
| *Fortune* . . . . . . . . . . . . . | | | | |
| *Harvard Business Review* . | | | | |
| *HR Focus* . . . . . . . . . . . . | | | | |
| *Inc.* . . . . . . . . . . . . . . . . | | | | |
| *InfoWorld* . . . . . . . . . . . | | | | |
| *Journal of Applied Psychology* . . . . . . . . . . . | | | | |
| *Managing Office Technology* . . . . . . . . . . | | | | |
| *Monthly Labor Review* . . . | | | | |
| *Nation's Business* . . . . . . | | | | |
| *The New York Times* . . . . | | | | |
| *Office Systems* ('94 and following years) . . . . . . | | | | |
| *Personnel Journal* . . . . . . | | | | |
| *Supervisory Management* | | | | |
| *Training* . . . . . . . . . . . . . | | | | |
| *The Wall Street Journal* . . | | | | |

## Project 1–3 • Field Research: The Office Manager—The Job, Responsibilities, and Personal Characteristics

At your place of employment or in a company within your community, arrange for an interview with the person who is responsible for the office management activities. The purpose of this interview is to learn about the nature of work performed by the office manager, his or her level of responsibility, and some of the office administrator's personal characteristics.

**Directions:** During your interview, gather information that will enable you to complete the form below and on page 7 so that at a later date you can present a short written or oral report summarizing your conversation with the office administrator.

---

Title of the office administrator's position: ____________________

Level of position within the firm:

_______ Top Management
_______ Middle Management
_______ Supervisory or Operating Management

Title of manager or company officer to whom the office administrator reports: ____________________

Number of employees for whom the office administrator is responsible: ____________________

Highest level of formal education completed by the office administrator:

_______ High school diploma
_______ Junior or community college (associate degree)
_______ Vocational/secretarial school
_______ University (bachelor's degree)
_______ University (master's degree)
_______ Other: ____________________

Annual salary range:

_______ less than $25,000
_______ $25,000 to $35,000
_______ over $35,000

Professional organizations in which the office administrator holds membership: ____________________

____________________

____________________

____________________

Is the office administrator a Certified Administrative Manager? ____________________

Other certification? ____________________

____________________

Other comments: ____________________

____________________

____________________

Name ______________________ Date ______________

| Area of Responsibility | ✔ |
|---|---|
| Human resources (recruiting, interviewing, orienting, training, retraining, appraising, promoting, terminating) . . . . . . . . . . . . | |
| Administrative systems and procedures (analyzing and revising procedures and methods) . . . . . . . . . . . . . . . . . . . . . . . | |
| Analyzing jobs, preparing job descriptions and job specifications, and evaluating jobs | |
| Measuring work and setting standards . . . | |
| Budgetary control (preparing budgets, evaluating performance, analyzing variances) . | |
| Records management (filing, storage, retrieval, disposal) . . . . . . . . . . . . . . . . . . . | |
| Written communications (letters and reports, word processing, desktop publishing) . . . | |
| Oral communications (with employees and with public) . . . . . . . . . . . . . . . . . . . . . | |
| Telecommunications (telephone, facsimile services, data communications) . . . . . . . | |
| Office layout and design . . . . . . . . . . . . . . | |

| Area of Responsibility | ✔ |
|---|---|
| Forms design and control . . . . . . . . . . . . . | |
| Micrographics . . . . . . . . . . . . . . . . . . . . . | |
| Reprographics . . . . . . . . . . . . . . . . . . . . . | |
| Mailroom services . . . . . . . . . . . . . . . . . | |
| Purchasing (office supplies, machines and equipment, furniture) . . . . . . . . . . . . . . . | |
| Computer systems . . . . . . . . . . . . . . . . . . | |
| Administering office salary program and employee benefits . . . . . . . . . . . . . . . . . . | |
| Accounting (financial record keeping, reporting, and control) . . . . . . . . . . . . . . | |
| Other: ______________________ | |
| ______________________ | |
| ______________________ | |
| ______________________ | |
| ______________________ | |
| ______________________ | |

What does the office administrator look upon as his or her most difficult task?

______________________________________________________________________

______________________________________________________________________

______________________________________________________________________

______________________________________________________________________

______________________________________________________________________

______________________________________________________________________

______________________________________________________________________

______________________________________________________________________

______________________________________________________________________

______________________________________________________________________

______________________________________________________________________

______________________________________________________________________

______________________________________________________________________

## Project 1–4 • Investigating the Outlook for Administrative Support Occupations

Each day administrative office managers work with persons holding administrative support jobs. In this project, you will learn more about several administrative support jobs, the holders of which may report directly to the administrative office manager or to an office supervisor, depending upon the size of the organization.

Workers in the administrative support group include those who prepare and keep records; operate office machines and equipment; arrange schedules and make reservations; collect, distribute, or account for money, material, mail, or messages; or perform similar administrative duties. While administrative support jobs are located in virtually all industries, they are concentrated in the fast-growing service, trade, and finance sectors. Because of this concentration, these jobs are expected to grow rapidly.

**Directions:** Consult the latest *Occupational Outlook Handbook,* published by the U.S. Department of Labor, to learn about (1) the nature of the work; (2) working conditions; (3) employment; (4) training, other qualifications, and advancement; (5) job outlook; and (6) earnings for support jobs, such as the following:

Adjusters, investigators, and collectors
Bank tellers
Bookkeeping, accounting, and auditing clerks
Brokerage clerks and statement clerks
Claim representatives
Clerical supervisors and managers
Collection workers
Computer and peripheral equipment operators
Hotel and motel clerks
Mail clerks and messengers
Personnel clerks
Receptionists
Secretaries
Telephone, telegraph, and teletype operators
Typists, word processors, and data-entry keyers

Present your findings in a short oral or written report, as requested by your instructor.

Name ____________________ Date ____________________ 

# Project 1–5 • Understanding the Fundamental Differences in Management Styles Among European Managers

For the American company that is entering foreign operations, it is vital that the firm consider management style when selecting the appropriate local managers. Further, the firm must consider the ethnic mix of the workforce that will be managed because some regional management styles may be more compatible than others.

**Directions:** After you have read the following article, complete the exercise at the end.

Since the economic unification of Western Europe was announced in 1985, American business executives have been bombarded with advice on how to manage successfully in a market with 12 countries, 360 million consumers and significant business potential. Most of this advice, however, has focused on shaking hands, presenting business cards, and other niceties of foreign etiquette.

To manage successfully in Europe, however, American companies and their executives need to know more than protocol. There are fundamental differences between American and European companies in corporate structure, management style, and employee rights. Unless American executives understand these differences, they will have little chance of operating successfully abroad.

## A World of Difference

As a result of cultural traditions and political/economic disparities, management style—the manner in which an executive relates to employees and makes decisions—varies widely throughout Europe. In Europe, it is generally true that the farther north you go, the more participative the management style. It is often said that in Sweden, managers don't tell employees what to do—they *convince* them, and it is easier to find workers' councils and consensus management in Germany and Scandinavia than in Italy and Spain.

Corporate structure, generally legally mandated, can greatly influence a company's management style. In Germany, for example, management structure is tightly controlled by law. Corporations are run by management committees (*Geschäftsleitung*) whose members rotate top decision-making responsibility and have clear lines of command to appropriate employee groups within the company.

Executives in Germany tend to have extensive technical training and oftentimes higher degrees, especially in engineering-related businesses. German managers will rarely move out of their special field and will hold almost every management position within the relevant division or group before reaching the senior management level.

In France, most corporations are very much a one-person show, with a single *président directeur général* (PDG) holding both chairman and CEO responsibilities. PDGs often are graduates of one of the country's elite *grandes écoles* (technical universities), and they are expected to be not only brilliant technical planners, but also equally adept at industry, finance, and government.

People skills, however, often are not part of their portfolio. French companies typically have management hierarchies that discourage informality, reinforce a sense of "us" and "them" and lead to difficult labor relations—a constant in France.

British companies tend to be more similar to American companies. They typically have a board of management that can be led by a nonoperating chairman, while company operations are run by a managing director or CEO. Future managers are recognized young and often are rotated through various departments in the company for a broad—but not always thorough—overview of operations. High-level British executives, however, often tend to be aloof and somewhat out of touch with their company's workers. Often a wide gulf exists between management and labor, probably a holdover from Britain's long-standing class system.

## Who's Right for the Job?

To motivate and manage its overseas workforce, it is crucial that an American company expanding abroad consider management style in selecting an appropriate local executive, in addition to functional and geographical responsibilities. It is also important to consider the ethnic mix of the workforce that the executive will manage, because particular national styles are more compatible than others. Swedes may be frustrated by French executives who

---

Source: "Management in Europe: More Than Just Etiquette" by Donald R. Utroska. Reprinted, by permission of the publisher, from *Management Review* (November, 1992). 

don't believe in consensus management. Hierarchical Germans may not blend well with more emotional Italian executives. British executives are well respected for their financial and accounting skills, but they may not have the language skills to function effectively as general managers outside of the United Kingdom. In some cases, the best selection may be an American with international work experience.

To increase harmony among national cultures, some companies look for "Euromanagers," who speak several different languages and are at home in a variety of cultures. Not surprisingly, these individuals are difficult to find at all but the most senior executive levels. As an alternative, executives from Belgium, Holland or Switzerland are also considered good "blenders." Because of their small size, these countries have been forced over the years to become international, and most of their executives have good language skills and flexible management styles.

Many American companies are startled when their European executives request special allowances for cars, clubs and even housing—in addition to their salary and bonus. Since personal income taxes in most European countries are significantly higher than in the United States, the compensation packages of most European executives are designed to minimize taxes. In contrast with a typical American compensation package where base salary and incentive bonus are primary elements, nontaxable items like stock grants and perquisites can comprise 20 percent to 40 percent of a top European executive's compensation package.

Perquisites aren't necessarily reserved just for top executives; even lower-level managers typically have club memberships and company cars. In status-conscious Europe—particularly France, Germany and the United Kingdom—executive rank clearly is indicated by the executive's type and model of automobile. A mid-level manager might drive an Audi, but only a top executive would have a Mercedes or Jaguar.

American executives who think U.S. workers have it too easy would be stunned by the rights and benefits granted to European employees. In virtually every country in Europe, employee benefits like healthcare and pensions are significantly more generous than in the United States. Costs for pension plans and healthcare average 35 percent to 40 percent of the employee's base salary and are typically borne by the company.

Most European workers (including professionals, lower-level managers, salespeople and clerical people) are unionized, and unions continually press their case for higher wages, more vacation and greater benefits packages. Although unions and corporations are on friendly terms in Switzerland, in some countries like Sweden, unions can bypass employers entirely and negotiate wage increases directly with the government, which then issues near-mandatory "guidelines" to corporations.

#### Productivity vs. Playtime

Maintaining a high level of productivity in the face of employee vacations and holidays is a challenge, even for the most seasoned European manager. Four to six weeks of vacation is typical and there are an average of 12 civic and religious holidays per year in most Western European countries. More employee downtime results from *Kur*, an additional seven- to 10-day fully paid health retreat that is popular among German-speaking employees.

These frequent vacations and holidays—and the fact that they occur at different times all over Europe—can frustrate American companies that are used to a consistent, nonstop flow of business.

Productivity-conscious Americans also can be frustrated by workday rituals that are commonplace throughout Europe. In addition to a 60- to 90-minute lunch period and 15 minutes of day-end cleanup time, employees—from plant workers to secretaries to managers—take 20-minute morning and afternoon breaks, often with beer or wine. As a result, a nine-hour workday typically yields only seven hours of productive work.

U.S. companies are used to hiring and keeping employees based on their effectiveness and performance on the job. This is not necessarily the case in Europe. Everybody—from secretaries to CEOs—has a contract that virtually guarantees permanent employment, no matter what the company's financial condition or business objectives. Once individuals have been hired, it is not easy for a manager to fire them—no matter how bad their job performance.

#### Womb to Tomb

Dismissing an employee for poor performance is possible, but the costs can be significant. Several years ago, a major American pharmaceutical company operating in Sweden attempted to fire an alcoholic employee who had not responded to treatment programs and other company-paid assistance. It took more than two years to get him off the payroll, during which time the employee came to work drunk, was completely incoherent by the end of the day and annoyed other workers in the process.

In some socialist countries like France, Belgium and the United Kingdom, the only grounds for immediate dismissal are criminal behavior. Laying off or dismissing employees following acquisitions, management change or restructuring—standard practice in the United

States—is extremely difficult in Europe, and thus rarely occurs.

All terminated employees expect—and receive—significant severance packages that might be considered extravagant in the United States. Typically, terminated employees are given three months' notice, during which time they collect full salary and benefits and are free to look for another job. An executive would receive at least one year's salary plus one month's pay for every year he or she had been with the company. In addition, the company has to pay all accumulated vacation pay. If a company does not adhere to these unwritten guidelines, it risks being dragged into labor court—a special tribunal established to hear employee rights cases—and forced to defend its decision. Generally, the courts find in favor of the dismissed employee.

To circumvent some of the problems caused by permanent employment, many European companies insist on a six-month trial period as part of the employment contract. Although lower-level workers generally accept the trial period, many executives are reluctant to accept it. This can present a special problem in recruiting executives, who understandably want to be guaranteed a permanent position before leaving their current job.

### What Not to Do

Just as American companies should not expect Europeans to behave like Americans, they shouldn't expect Europeans to embrace some uniquely American management practices. For example, Europeans have a hard time understanding the egalitarian culture of U.S. business. Although European workers have more rights than do American workers, they operate in a unionized environment where workers and management view each other as different species, and they may find the very American notion of "team spirit" difficult to grasp.

Also, be aware that certain icons of American management, such as pay-for-performance and commission salaries, are not well received in Europe. Many Europeans—particularly in the south—value highly subjective factors like loyalty, process and perseverance, and can be insulted by "objective" measurement and reward systems.

Despite the single economy that is forming in Europe, each European country has its own management style, corporate structure, and employee rights' laws. It is crucial for U.S. executives to be familiar with them and how they affect their company's operations in the EC.

Simply being aware that there are differences in style between America and Europe that are more fundamental than handshakes, business cards and meal times is an essential first step; the final step is incorporating this knowledge into the strategic and tactical decisions that will spell success in Europe.

Listed below are some of the characteristics of corporate structure, management style, and employee rights discussed in the preceding article. Alongside each characteristic, indicate by means of a check mark the country in which the characteristic is most prevalent.

| Characteristic | Great Britain | France | Germany | Sweden |
|---|---|---|---|---|
| 1. Consensus management with workers' councils . . . . . . . . . . . . . . . . . . . . . . . . | | | | |
| 2. Companies most similar to American companies . . . . . . . . . . . . . . . . . . . . . . . | | | | |
| 3. Executives tending to have extensive technical training and often with advanced degrees . . . . . . . . . . . . . . . . . . . . . . . . | | | | |
| 4. Very participative style of management . | | | | |
| 5. Criminal behavior is only grounds for immediate dismissal . . . . . . . . . . . . . . . | | | | |
| 6. Tightly controlled management structure . | | | | |
| 7. Corporations are pretty much a one-person show . . . . . . . . . . . . . . . . . . . . . . . | | | | |
| 8. Management hierarchy that discourages informality . . . . . . . . . . . . . . . . . . . . | | | | |
| 9. High-level executives often out of touch with workers. . . . . . . . . . . . . . . . . . . | | | | |
| 10. Unions bypass employers and negotiate wage increases directly with government . | | | | |

# Project 1–6 • Computer Hands-On: Learning About Diversity

How diverse is the group with whom you are studying administrative office management? Would you venture the guess that your group is as culturally and ethnically diverse as most groups of office workers in your community? Well, let's see. However, before we do so, let's examine the word *diversity*, one of today's very popular buzzwords.

Many speak of *diversity* when referring to the different human qualities found in individuals and groups. The *primary* dimensions of diversity have been defined as "those immutable human differences that are inborn and/or that exert an important impact on our early socialization and an ongoing impact throughout our lives."[1] Age, ethnicity (ethnic traits, background, allegiance, or association), gender, and race are examples of this category. *Secondary* dimensions of diversity—those differences that we acquire, discard, or modify throughout our lives—include educational background, marital status, religious beliefs, and work experience.

**Directions:** With the use of a graphic software program:

1. Design a questionnaire that you will distribute to members of your class to determine their primary and secondary dimensions of diversity. When obtaining data about ethnicity and race diversity, you may wish to use headings such as European American, African American, Native American, Asian American, Hispanic, Cuban, Puerto Rican, and Pacific Islander.
2. Prepare a data chart for each kind of data you collected. Select a bar chart, pie chart, map, and so on that most effectively displays each different kind of data. Two different kinds of charts are described below.

## Pie Charts

A **pie chart,** so called because it is round and divided or "sliced" into pie-like pieces, allows the reader to quickly grasp the relationship of each group analyzed (each "slice") to the whole and to other parts. The entire pie always represents 100 percent of whatever the "whole" may be.

A simple concept, the pie chart works best when it is kept simple, that is, when it compares only a few elements. Too many elements will clutter a pie chart and defeat its purpose.

Some pointers to follow in designing a pie chart are:

1. Use no more than 6 pie slices. If necessary, combine slices into one group labeled "Other" or "Miscellaneous," or develop a second chart in which you separate all the groups within that "Other" category.
2. Arrange the pie slices beginning with the largest slice at the 12 o'clock position. Moving clockwise (as such data are read), create each other slice. (If the program default is counterclockwise, rearrange the slices accordingly when entering the data.)
3. Use bright, contrasting colors for emphasis. For added emphasis, some spreadsheets provide an option that allows you to pull one slice out of the circle, giving the chart a 3-dimensional look (but sometimes distorting the importance of the larger, pulled-out slices).
4. Place the identifying label inside the slice whenever possible—next to each slice when not possible. Along with the label, include the statistical data in whole numbers. Remember, the purpose is to show relationships, not exact, minute details.

## Bar Charts

**Bar charts** are used to show relationships of data over time periods. By positioning two or more sets of bars side by side, you make it easy for the reader to compare one data set with another set.

In preparing bar charts, keep these points in mind:

1. Use as few bars as necessary, and no more than 6 (unless you are comparing 12 months).
2. Divide each bar into sections, each section showing one part of the whole, as in pie charts.
3. To distinguish sections within each bar, use different colors or patterns.
4. Place the statistics on the outer frame, at the top of the bars or inside the bars in contrasting colors.
5. To add pizzazz to horizontal and vertical bar charts, use images, not bars. For example, use images such as small outline drawings of females and of males to highlight a breakdown of accountants by gender.

---

[1]Marilyn Loden and Judy B. Rosener, *Workforce America! Managing Employee Diversity as a Vital Resource* (Homewood, IL: Business One Irwin, 1991), p. 18.

2

# APPLYING BASIC MANAGEMENT PRINCIPLES

Administrative office managers rely heavily upon management principles that pertain to the objectives of the organization, the assignment of responsibility, unity of functions, use of specialization, delegation of authority and responsibility, unity of command, span of control, and centralization or decentralization of managerial authority.

In their organizing activities, office managers are concerned with the work, the workplace, and the workers. The function of organizing brings these three elements together to form a controllable (manageable) unit—the *organization*—to accomplish specific objectives. The workable features of the line and the functional organizations are often blended to form the line-and-staff organization. As an adjunct to the traditional line-and-staff organization, companies use committees, such as the task force, staff group, or labor-management committee. Also, today we find more and more companies experimenting with nontraditional types of organization, such as work teams, matrix structures, and broad banding.

For each form of organization, the office manager is aided by a valuable tool, the *organization chart*, that shows graphically the formal relationships, span of control, and lines of authority and responsibility. Regardless of the type of formal organization pattern, however, office workers group themselves into *informal* relationships that must be recognized, understood, and effectively used by the office manager.

When applying the management principles in their daily activities, office managers exhibit leadership styles that reflect their unique personalities, philosophies, and behavioral traits. Thus, we find some managers who are labeled autocratic, bureaucratic, or diplomatic. Others have a leadership style that is best described as participative or free-rein.

## SECTION A • REVIEW QUESTIONS

**Directions:** In the Answers column, write the letter of the item in Column 1 that is described by each statement in Column 2.

| Column 1 | Column 2 | Answers |
|---|---|---|
| **A** Accountability | 1. The number of employees who are directly supervised by one person | 1. ______ |
| **B** Authority | 2. A desired goal, sometimes considered a target or an aim ......... | 2. ______ |
| **C** Committee organization | 3. An informal oral communication network within an organization .. | 3. ______ |
| **D** Delegation | 4. A broad guideline for operating the organization ............... | 4. ______ |
| **E** Grapevine | 5. A graphic picture of the functional units in a firm showing the principal lines of authority ................................ | 5. ______ |
| **F** Objective | 6. The right to command and to give orders, and the power to make decisions ................................................ | 6. ______ |
| **G** Organization chart | 7. An organization structure where authority and responsibility are jointly held by a group of individuals rather than by a single manager | 7. ______ |
| **H** Policy | 8. A broad, general statement widely considered to be true and that accurately reflects real-world conditions in all walks of life ....... | 8. ______ |
| **I** Principle | 9. The obligation and accountability for properly performing work that is assigned ........................................ | 9. ______ |
| **J** Responsibility | 10. The process of entrusting work to employees who are qualified to accept responsibility for doing the work ...................... | 10. ______ |
| **K** Span of control | | |

**Directions:** Indicate your answer to each of the following questions by circling "Yes" or "No" in the Answers column.

| | | Answers | |
|---|---|---|---|
| 1. | Does the responsibility for organizing work exist with managers at all levels? | Yes | No |
| 2. | As we move down the levels of management in a company, do we find less authority and responsibility? | Yes | No |
| 3. | Does the unity-of-functions principle require the maintenance of a reasonable amount of stability in human resources? | Yes | No |
| 4. | Are managers and supervisors in most firms exceptionally skilled in delegating authority? | Yes | No |
| 5. | Should office employees receive orders from more than one supervisor? | Yes | No |
| 6. | When there is a narrow span of control, do we usually find close supervision? | Yes | No |
| 7. | With the advent of computerized information systems, has the span of control narrowed in most firms? | Yes | No |
| 8. | Does downsizing usually bring about a flatter organization structure? | Yes | No |
| 9. | In organizations with centralized authority, are most major decisions made at the operative level? | Yes | No |
| 10. | Can an office manager develop a sound office organization by closely adhering to Parkinson's Law? | Yes | No |
| 11. | Does the existence of a well-prepared organization chart assure good organization? | Yes | No |
| 12. | In a line organization, does authority flow in an unbroken line from the president to the individual office worker? | Yes | No |
| 13. | Is the "pure" functional organization often found in today's businesses? | Yes | No |
| 14. | In a line-and-staff organization, are the policies and practices at the top-management level carried out on a line plan? | Yes | No |
| 15. | Is the assistant-to a form of staff authority? | Yes | No |
| 16. | Is speed in reaching decisions one of the outstanding advantages of committee organization? | Yes | No |
| 17. | Is the matrix organization designed to obtain a higher degree of coordination than can be obtained in conventional organization structures? | Yes | No |
| 18. | Is broadbanding usually found in organizations having tall, pyramidal structure? | Yes | No |
| 19. | Do formal organization charts reflect the interpersonal relationships within a company? | Yes | No |
| 20. | When each department does its own hiring and firing, do we have an example of functional decentralization? | Yes | No |
| 21. | In a satellite administrative services center, are the information processing activities for several offices handled at one workstation? | Yes | No |
| 22. | Does Fiedler's contingency theory suggest that the situation confronting the leader and the workers determines successful leadership behavior? | Yes | No |
| 23. | Are those who work for an autocratic leader usually highly motivated to make their own decisions? | Yes | No |
| 24. | Does the bureaucratic leader openly invite workers to join in and take part in making decisions? | Yes | No |
| 25. | Is a diplomatic leader one who "sells" rather than "tells"? | Yes | No |
| 26. | Does the participative leader follow fixed rules and a rigid hierarchy of authority? | Yes | No |
| 27. | Do free-rein leaders delegate as much as they can in order to remove accountability for their actions? | Yes | No |

Name ______________________________ Date ____________________ 

## SECTION B • PROJECTS

### Project 2–1 • Analyzing the Span of Control

*Span of control* refers to the number of employees who are directly supervised by one person. A basic principle of management states that the span of control should be limited to a manageable number. Among other factors, the span of control is related to the type of direction and control exercised over the workers and the latitude extended them in decision making.

**Directions:** Two different spans of control are illustrated in Charts 2–1 and 2–2. As you see, a wide span of control creates a flat structure, while a narrow span of control creates a tall structure. After you have studied the charts, indicate below each one those office conditions under which the span of control would be an appropriate organization pattern.

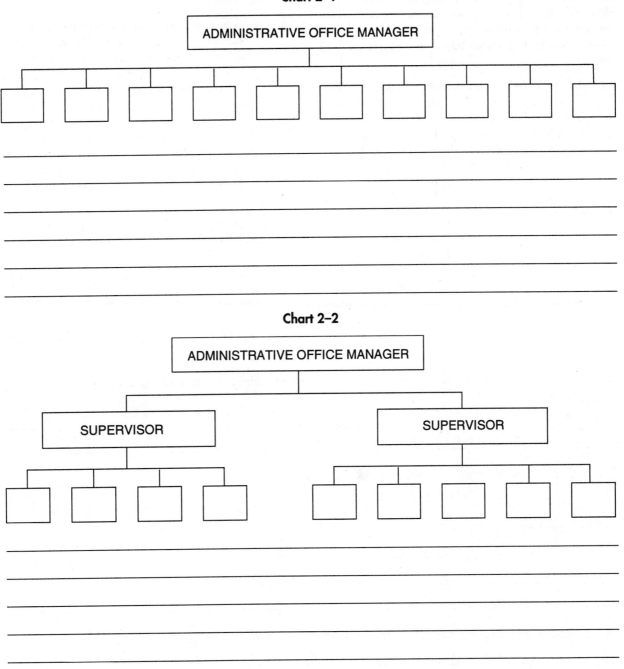

**Chart 2–1**

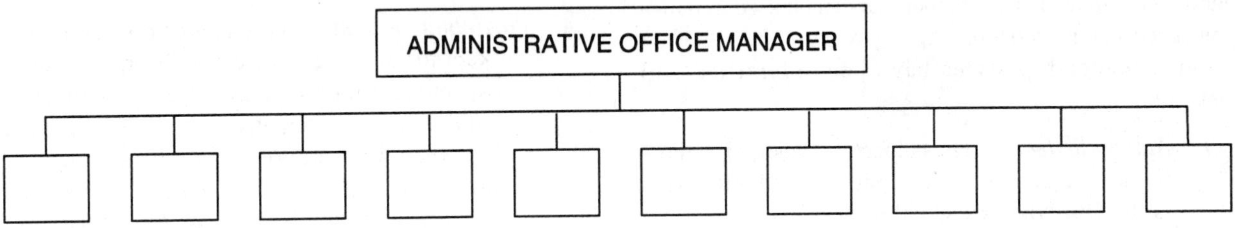


______________________________________________________________________

______________________________________________________________________

______________________________________________________________________

______________________________________________________________________

______________________________________________________________________

______________________________________________________________________

**Chart 2–2**

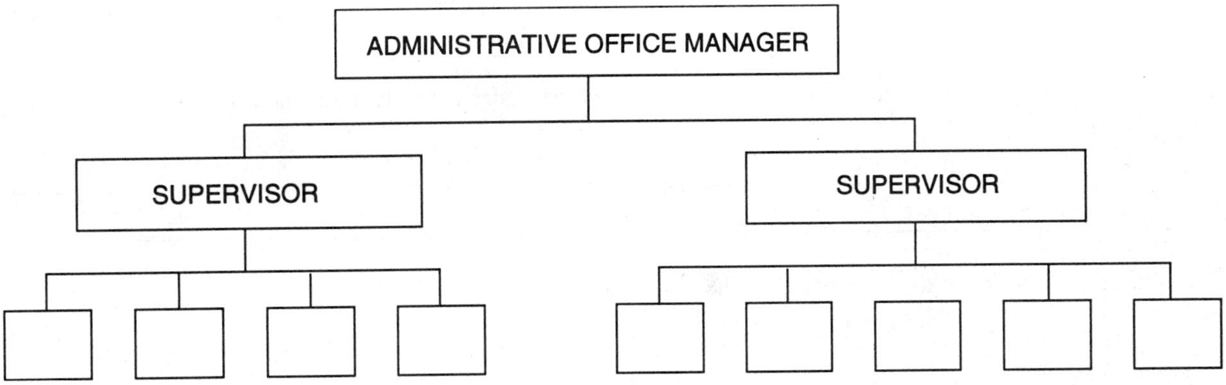


______________________________________________________________________

______________________________________________________________________

______________________________________________________________________

______________________________________________________________________

______________________________________________________________________

______________________________________________________________________

## Project 2–2 • A Philosophy of Office Management

For some, one of the objectives of studying administrative office management is to develop a philosophy of office management. For others, the study will aid in refining and more clearly delineating their philosophy. It will be rewarding from time to time during this course to sit back and reflect upon your own beliefs, concepts, and attitudes regarding the process of office management.

As a first step in your thinking about a philosophy of office management, we shall examine a classification of leadership styles offered by the behavioral school of management thought. These leadership styles will provide you with an analytical tool that can be used in building successful leadership.

Five leadership styles have been identified and defined:

1. *Autocratic leader.* The autocratic leader, or authoritarian leader, rules with unlimited authority. This is the OM who "tells" rather than "sells" or "consults." The autocratic OM keeps the bulk of the power and influence in the decision-making process to himself or herself. Thus, those who report to an autocrat are provided little, if any, motivation to engage in problem solving or in decision making at their levels.
2. *Bureaucratic leader.* This leader sets and follows fixed rules; a hierarchy of authority; and narrow, rigid, formal routines. The OM viewed as a bureaucrat "tells" the office workers what to do. The bases for the OM's orders are the policies, procedures, and rules of the organization.
3. *Diplomatic leader.* The diplomatic leader is skillful in helping people to solve their problems or to meet the needs of a particular situation. This manager is expert in employing tact and conciliation and rarely arouses hostility among workers. The diplomatic OM, who prefers "selling" rather than "telling" people, manages by persuasion and individual motivation. The office workers are usually provided some freedom to react, to question, to discuss, and even to present arguments that support their views.
4. *Participative leader.* This leader openly invites workers to join in and take part in making decisions, setting policies, and analyzing methods of operation. Some participative OMs are democratic and let their workers know in advance that the group's decision, usually arrived at by consensus or majority vote, will be binding. Other participative OMs are consultative, and although they invite involvement, discussion, and recommendations from the group, they make it clear that they alone are accountable and reserve the final decision.
5. *Free-rein leader.* The free-rein leader sets goals and develops clear guidelines for subordinates who then operate freely with no further direction unless they ask for help. However, the free-rein or "hands-off" OM does not abandon all control since the manager is ultimately accountable for the actions (or lack of actions) of the office employees. The free-rein OM delegates to the greatest extent in an effort to motivate the office workers to their fullest.

1. At this stage of your management development, which of the leadership styles best characterizes your total personality?

______________________________________________

______________________________________________

2. What are the strengths and weaknesses of the autocratic style? ______________________

______________________________________________

______________________________________________

3. What are the strengths and weaknesses of the participative style? ______________________

______________________________________________

______________________________________________

4. What do you look upon as the "best"—the ideal—leadership style? Why? ______________________

______________________________________________

______________________________________________

## Project 2–3 • Measuring Your Effectiveness as a Manager

**Directions:** To measure your effectiveness as a manager, circle the number on the 1–5 scale that best indicates how you really feel.[1] You may wish to make a copy of the chart and toward the end of this course, take a second measurement and compare your scores. Or, if you are presently employed, make several copies of the chart and ask your coworkers (including those who report to you) to rate you. How does your perception of yourself compare with their perception of you?

### HOW EFFECTIVE ARE YOU AS A MANAGER?

| | | | | | | | |
|---|---|---|---|---|---|---|---|
| 1. | I'll wait until things settle down. | 1 | 2 | 3 | 4 | 5 | I really like change. |
| 2. | Most of my staff meetings are about internal procedures and budgeting. | 1 | 2 | 3 | 4 | 5 | I spend much of my time talking to and about customers. |
| 3. | If there's a way, I'll find it. | 1 | 2 | 3 | 4 | 5 | Top management should make the first move. |
| 4. | I'll wait for orders from above. | 1 | 2 | 3 | 4 | 5 | Let's get it done right now. |
| 5. | I seek responsibilities beyond my job description. | 1 | 2 | 3 | 4 | 5 | I fulfill my job description. |
| 6. | How can I enhance revenue? Add value? | 1 | 2 | 3 | 4 | 5 | I'll stay within my budget plan. |
| 7. | My people should "challenge the system." | 1 | 2 | 3 | 4 | 5 | I carefully review my subordinates' work. |
| 8. | If I haven't been told *yes*, I can't do it. | 1 | 2 | 3 | 4 | 5 | If I haven't been told *no*, I can do it. |
| 9. | I'll take responsibility for my failures. | 1 | 2 | 3 | 4 | 5 | I usually make excuses for my failures. |
| 10. | I won't take risks because I may fail. | 1 | 2 | 3 | 4 | 5 | I'll take risks although I may fail. |
| 11. | We've got to do things faster. | 1 | 2 | 3 | 4 | 5 | We can't turn things around that fast. |
| 12. | I want to know what other departments are doing and what their needs are. | 1 | 2 | 3 | 4 | 5 | I protect my own department. |
| 13. | I talk mainly to those people who are formally linked to me. | 1 | 2 | 3 | 4 | 5 | I'll go beyond the organization chart to share information and resources. |
| 14. | Leave me and my people alone and let us get our job done. | 1 | 2 | 3 | 4 | 5 | I'll cross departmental lines to get the job done. |
| 15. | I truly trust only a few people within the firm. | 1 | 2 | 3 | 4 | 5 | I volunteer to share ideas and resources with people in other departments. |

*To measure your effectiveness as a manager: For questions numbered 1, 2, 4, 8, 10, 13, 14, and 15, simply add up the scores. For questions 3, 5, 6, 7, 9, 11, and 12, flip the scale so that a response of 1 becomes 5, 2 becomes 4, 4 becomes 2, and 5 becomes 1. Summing it all up, a score of 60 means you have the mindset of an effective manager. If you scored below 45, you have some work to do.*

[1] From "A New Decade Demands a New Breed of Manager" by Oren Harari and Linda Mukai. Reprinted, by permission of Mr. Harari, from *Management Review* (August, 1990), p. 23.

## Project 2–4 • Preparing an Organization Chart of the Administrative Office Management Function

You have just accepted the position of administrative office manager of the Gerardi Company, which has 120 office employees. The company is planning to centralize as many administrative services as possible and develop a staff department whose assignment will be to study and improve administrative systems. In addition, it is your plan to organize the work so that it will be properly supervised and controlled. As administrative office manager in charge of all administrative services, you report to the treasurer of the company, who in turn reports directly to the president.

The proposed plan of supervision includes the following personnel: (The estimated number of employees needed in each department, including the supervisor or the officer of that department, is given in parentheses.)

a. Mary Jo Carman, assistant administrative office manager, handles space management, office machines and equipment, and reports. (19)

b. Pamela H. Wong, chief accountant, is responsible for general accounting, budgeting, and data processing. (15)

c. Glenn T. Sinatra, assistant human resources manager, handles factory personnel problems. Sinatra reports to the director of human resources, Janice D. Mangine, who, in her staff position, reports directly to the president. (12)

d. Lucy Key Crespin, assistant to the president, handles all legal affairs. (4)

e. Frederick M. McKnight is responsible for administrative systems, a staff position. (4)

f. Carolyn Healey-Bacon is in charge of internal auditing, a staff position. She has the title of auditor. (5)

g. Cynthia R. Corturillo, supervisor, directs the word processing center. (15)

h. Patrick N. Shoemaker, supervisor, directs the records management department and the mailing center. (25)

i. Mark D. Cervini, supervisor of office communications, is responsible for telecommunications, reprographics, and micrographics. (20)

**Directions:**

1. On the basis of the preceding information, use the grid paper on page 19 to prepare a partial organization chart showing the line-and-staff organization of the Gerardi Company. On the chart below each person's title, place the name of the person responsible for the direction or supervision of the work. Under each supervisor's name, indicate some of the typical activities that would be directed by that person.

2. Give a brief explanation of the line-and-staff authority as outlined on your chart.

____________________________________________

____________________________________________

____________________________________________

____________________________________________

3. Estimate the weekly cost of office salaries of all employees, except the president, assistant to the president, and the treasurer. Assume an average salary of $385 a week for the 110 general office workers; for the 10 supervisors and officers, assume salaries commensurate with the responsibilities of their positions. Current salaries for office personnel may be obtained from such sources as "National Survey of Professional, Administrative, Technical, and Clerical Pay," prepared by the Bureau of Labor Statistics; and research studies and salary surveys undertaken by *Nation's Business, Personnel Journal, Training,* The Bureau of National Affairs, Inc., Robert Half International, Inc., Dartnell, Hay Group, American Payroll Association, Towers Perrin, American Management Association, Data Processing Management Association, National Association of Working Women, and Society for Human Resource Management.

   Total weekly cost of office salaries $ ________

4. Assume that office salaries represent 5 percent of gross sales. What is the approximate annual sales volume required to justify the cost of this office work? . . . . . . . . . . . . . . . . . . . . . $ ________

Name ______________________ Date ______________ 

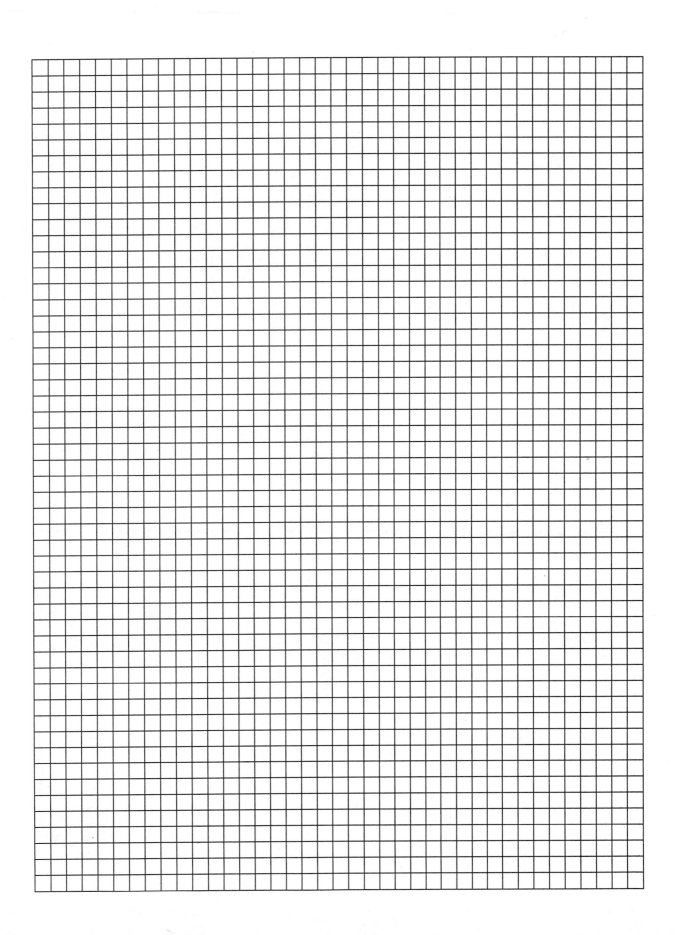

## Project 2–5 • Computer Hands-On: Preparing an Organization Chart and Estimating Weekly Salaries and Annual Sales

**Directions:**

**PART 1:** This past week you began a new position as administrative office manager of the Gerardi Company, which has 120 office employees. The company is now centralizing its administrative services into one new staff department, which you will organize, supervise, and control. You report to the treasurer of the company, who in turn reports directly to the president.

Using your word processing software, develop a chart showing the organization of the administrative office management function for Gerardi. First, refer to the background information for the Gerardi Company presented in Project 2-4 and review the line-and-staff organization information it provides. Next, list the name and the title of each supervisor, followed by typical activities he or she is responsible for. Finally, explain briefly the line-and-staff authority as outlined on your chart.

**PART 2:** Estimate the *weekly* cost of office salaries of all Gerardi employees (except the president, assistant-to the president, and the treasurer). For the 110 general office workers, the average salary is $385 a week. For the 10 supervisors and officers, check the average salary for each position in sources such as:

"National Survey of Professional, Administrative, Technical, and Clerical Pay" (U.S. Bureau of Labor Statistics)

*Administrative Management, Nation's Business, Payroll Exchange, Personnel Journal, Training*

International Office Management Association

The Bureau of National Affairs, Inc.

Robert Half Towers Perrin

American Management Association

National Association of Working Women

Society for Human Resource Management

Data Processing Management Association

If administrative salaries represent 5 percent of Gerardi's gross sales, what is the approximate annual sales volume required to justify this cost?

3

# DEVELOPING PROBLEM-SOLVING SKILLS

With experience, office managers learn to become skillful in applying a set of mental processes to all problem-solving situations—human problems, systems problems, or economic problems. Through a sequence of systematic questioning and analytic steps, office managers gather and use relevant information efficiently, regardless of the environment in which they find themselves. Using such a *rational* thought process, office managers become proficient in following a consistent approach to problem solving, extracting the relevant information from the superfluous, and communicating their decisions orally or in writing.

Other office managers solve problems by relying mainly upon their feelings rather than solely upon facts. Using their *intuition*, they solve problems by looking at the whole picture, sometimes with inadequate information or data at hand. Their decisions are reached through intuitive insights, flashes of awareness, or hunches. Management courses that are designed to develop intuition skills stress that managers must *believe* in intuition, *practice* the skill to the fullest, and *create* a personal and organizational environment in which intuitive skills are valued in daily decision making.

## SECTION A • REVIEW QUESTIONS

**Directions:** Indicate your answer to each of the following questions by circling "Yes" or "No" in the Answers column.

| | | **Answers** | |
|---|---|---|---|
| 1. | May a problem be defined as a question to be answered? | Yes | No |
| 2. | Does one type of office problem involve acquiring something that is not present but desired? | Yes | No |
| 3. | Is it relatively easy to measure the output of an office staff since much of the work is mental and intangible? | Yes | No |
| 4. | Do most surveys show that office workers are producing less while earning higher salaries? | Yes | No |
| 5. | Can an administrative office manager exercise control over *all* the resources used in an office? | Yes | No |
| 6. | Are the multicultural backgrounds of people relatively unimportant in solving problems involving people? | Yes | No |
| 7. | Are human attitudes usually easy to change? | Yes | No |
| 8. | Can a problem be viewed as a condition that requires improvement? | Yes | No |
| 9. | Is the desired state usually referred to as an objective toward which all work is directed? | Yes | No |
| 10. | In a brainstorming session, as each idea is presented, is it immediately evaluated as to its worth? | Yes | No |
| 11. | Can the nominal group technique (NGT) be effectively used in solving problems related to office productivity improvement? | Yes | No |
| 12. | Is the programming of a computer an example of how one's intuitive ability is used to solve a problem? | Yes | No |
| 13. | Does the informal approach to problem solving require that one follow each of the steps in the problem-solving process? | Yes | No |

14. Is the collection of relevant information restricted to Step 3 in the problem-solving cycle? . . . Yes No

15. Do human problems make up one of the least important sets of problems facing the office manager? . . . . . . . . . . . . . . . . . . . . . . . . . . . . . . . . . . . . . . . . . . . . . . . . . . . . . . . . . . Yes No

16. Are systems problems more objective and measurable than human problems? . . . . . . . . . . . . . Yes No

17. Is the misuse of money a common economic barrier to the solution of problems in the office? Yes No

**Directions:** In the Answers column, write the letter of the item in Column 1 that is described by each statement in Column 2.

| Column 1 | Column 2 | Answers |
|---|---|---|
| **A** Brainstorming | 1. The ratio between the resources used by a business firm and what the firm realizes from using those resources . . . . . . . . . . . . . . . . . . | 1. ______ |
| **B** Creativity | 2. A framework for solving problems that has general use in solving all types of problems . . . . . . . . . . . . . . . . . . . . . . . . . . . . . . . . . . . | 2. ______ |
| **C** General problem-solving model | 3. The signs or conditions that indicate the existence of a problem . . . | 3. ______ |
| **D** Hypotheses | 4. Alternate solutions to a problem . . . . . . . . . . . . . . . . . . . . . . . . . . | 4. ______ |
| **E** Idea quota | 5. A technique for stimulating the creation of ideas in which a fixed number of new ideas is required in a stated period of time . . . . . . . | 5. ______ |
| **F** Nominal group technique (NGT) | 6. The ability to apply imagination and ingenuity in developing a unique solution to a problem . . . . . . . . . . . . . . . . . . . . . . . . . . . . . . | 6. ______ |
| **G** Problem | 7. A group technique for creating a large quantity of ideas by free-wheeling contributions made without criticism . . . . . . . . . . . . . . . . | 7. ______ |
| **H** Productivity | 8. A technique for developing creativity in which participants work alone, silently, in small noninteraction groups . . . . . . . . . . . . . . . . | 8. ______ |
| **I** Symptoms | | |

---

**Directions:** Given below in mixed sequence are the eight steps involved in the problem-solving process. Arrange these steps in their logical ordering by numbering them 1, 2, 3, etc.

## STEPS IN THE PROBLEM-SOLVING PROCESS

________ Analyze relevant information.

________ Choose the best solution.

________ Collect relevant information.

________ Define the problem.

________ Develop alternate solutions to the problem.

________ Evaluate the results.

________ Implement the solution.

________ Recognize the problem.

## SECTION B • PROJECTS

### Project 3–1 • Brainstorming in the Classroom

Students and instructors often express the opinion that learning and teaching would be enhanced if the classroom presented an environment wherein both students and teacher were motivated to be more productive. Like a business office, a classroom has its own psychophysiological environmental needs. In this project, you will examine the several environments of your classroom as you take part in a brainstorming session.

The problem to be solved is this: *What can be done to improve the environmental factors in our classroom?*

**Directions:** Your instructor will divide the class into groups of four to seven and set a time limit of 15 to 25 minutes for the brainstorming session. During this time, each group will generate ideas for improvements in each of the following classroom environments:

1. *Surface* environment (colors and coverings of walls, ceilings, and floor).
2. *Seeing* environment (quantity and quality of light, glare, sources of light).
3. *Hearing* environment (sources of noise, noise control).
4. *Air* environment (temperature, humidity, circulation, cleanliness).
5. *Safe and secure* environment (slipping, tripping, falling; use of equipment; wiring).

The members of each group are to present ideas off the tops of their heads, with no concern about the quality of ideas presented. The objective is to generate a huge quantity of ideas by being very imaginative and possibly "hitching a ride" on the ideas presented by other classmates. Any idea is welcome as long as it may be useful for discussion purposes.

As you start to "freewheel," keep the following points in mind:

1. There is to be no criticism or evaluation of ideas.
2. No one is to be complimented on the idea presented.
3. There are to be no questions or discussion regarding the ideas.

One person should be selected by each group to serve as recorder. This person will record *all* ideas presented by the group members, regardless of whether or not the ideas appear valuable. Possibly the groups may have access to tape recorders for recording the discussions. Later, the tapes can be replayed and the ideas transcribed. The person serving as recorder is responsible for seeing that the rules above are followed and that the group stays on target during the time limit.

The instructor will set the due date for collecting the transcription of each group's ideas. The instructor, either acting alone or aided by other faculty members or students, can evaluate the economic feasibility of the ideas presented. At a later date, a report may be made to the class of those ideas that merit being passed along to the appropriate individuals on campus for evaluation.

### Project 3–2 • How Creative Are You?

In this project, you will be taking a "little test," the answers to which will enable an evaluator to determine just how creative you are and whether or not you have the knack for finding new solutions.

The sample test in this project was assembled for *Nation's Business* by psychologist Eugene Raudsepp, an expert in business creativity. Raudsepp cautions that while great progress has been made in testing for creative ability, certain tests may not measure the particular type of creativity businesses need. Premature conclusions could demoralize and even fail to single out potentially creative employees.

**Directions:** Complete the test given on pages 26 and 27. Your instructor has a copy of Raudsepp's interpretation of your test scores and will be able to pass along to you some idea about your imaginative ability as measured by this particular test.

## HOW CREATIVE ARE YOU?[1]

**1** *Word hints to creativity*

OBJECT: Find a fourth word that is related to *all* three words listed below.

For example, what word is related to these?
cookies sixteen heart ______________

The answer is "sweet." Cookies are sweet; sweet is part of the word "sweetheart" and part of the phrase "sweet sixteen."

What word is related to these words?
poke go molasses ______________

Answer: slow

Now try these words:

| | | | | |
|---|---|---|---|---|
| 1. | surprise | line | birthday | ________ |
| 2. | base | snow | dance | ________ |
| 3. | rat | blue | cottage | ________ |
| 4. | nap | rig | call | ________ |
| 5. | golf | foot | country | ________ |
| 6. | house | weary | ape | ________ |
| 7. | tiger | plate | news | ________ |
| 8. | painting | bowl | nail | ________ |
| 9. | proof | sea | priest | ________ |
| 10. | maple | beet | loaf | ________ |
| 11. | oak | show | plan | ________ |
| 12. | light | village | golf | ________ |
| 13. | merry | out | up | ________ |
| 14. | cheese | courage | oven | ________ |
| 15. | red | star | house | ________ |

**2** *Pictures test your creativity*

OBJECT: Tell whether you like or dislike each of the drawings shown at the top of the next column.

Answer by circling "L" (for like) or "D" (for dislike). If you can't decide, guess.

| | | | | | |
|---|---|---|---|---|---|
| 1. | L D | | 5. | L D | |
| 2. | L D | | 6. | L D | |
| 3. | L D | | 7. | L D | |
| 4. | L D | | 8. | L D | |

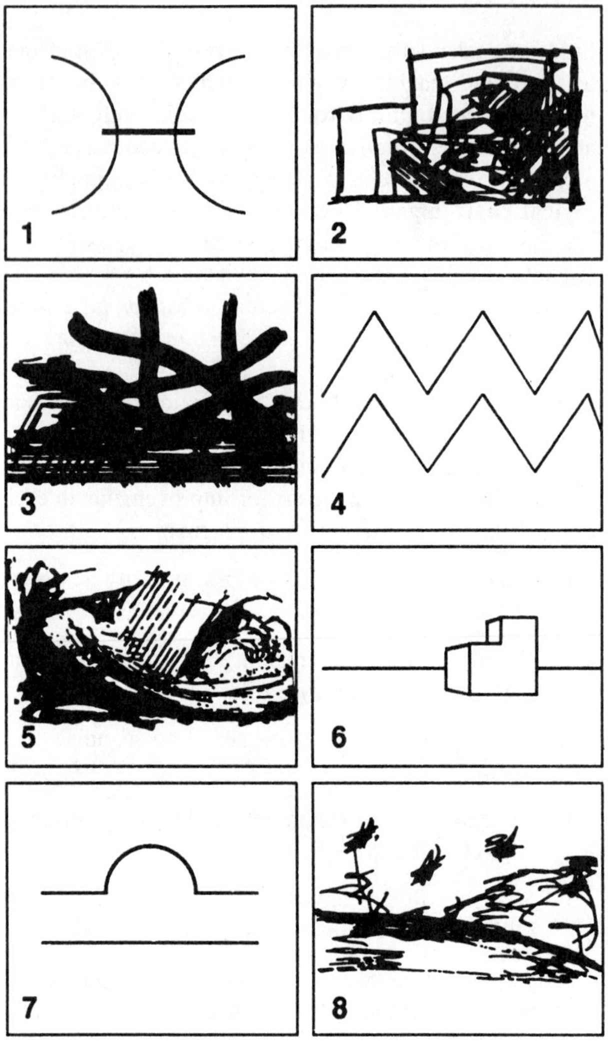

**3** *Which traits describe you?*

OBJECT: Check the adjectives that you believe really describe you. Your selections can clue to your creativity.

| | | |
|---|---|---|
| determined | life-of-party | stern |
| responsible | dynamic | sociable |
| tolerant | polite | sensitive |
| independent | informal | restless |
| inventive | impulsive | reflective |
| enthusiastic | excitable | rational |
| clear-thinking | popular | preoccupied |
| understanding | cheerful | practical |
| individualistic | obedient | peaceable |
| industrious | self-demanding | organized |
| dependable | unassuming | moody |
| absentminded | worrying | masculine |
| logical | polished | loyal |
| versatile | fashionable | good natured |

[1]Reprinted by permission, *Nation's Business* (June, 1965). Copyright, © 1965 U.S. Chamber of Commerce.

**4** *Your choice shows creativity*

OBJECT: Check the responses that you feel apply to you.

1. Would you rather be considered:
   a____a practical person?
   b____an ingenious person?

2. If you were a teacher, would you rather teach:
   a____fact courses?
   b____courses involving theory?

3. Does following a schedule:
   a____appeal to you?
   b____cramp you?

4. When there is a special job to be done, do you like to:
   a____organize it carefully before you start?
   b____find out what is necessary as you go along?

5. Do you often get behind in your work?
   a____yes
   b____no

6. Do you prefer specific instructions to those which leave many details optional?
   a____yes
   b____no

7. Do hunches come to you just before going to sleep?
   a____yes
   b____no

8. Do you often fret about daily chores?
   a____yes
   b____no

9. Do you like to introduce the speaker at a meeting?
   a____yes
   b____no

10. Do you get your best ideas when you are relaxed?
    a____yes
    b____no

11. Do you sometimes feel anxious about the success of your efforts?
    a____yes
    b____no

12. Do you like work in which you must influence others?
    a____yes
    b____no

13. Are you fundamentally contented?
    a____yes
    b____no

14. Do you like work that has regular hours?
    a____yes
    b____no

15. Do you spend many evenings with friends?
    a____yes
    b____no

16. As a child, were you inclined to take life seriously?
    a____yes
    b____no

17. Do you frequently daydream?
    a____yes
    b____no

18. Do you remember the names of people you meet?
    a____yes
    b____no

19. Do you like to keep regular hours and run your life according to established routine?
    a____yes
    b____no

20. Is it hard for you to sympathize with a person who is always doubting and unsure about things?
    a____yes
    b____no

# Project 3–3 • Integrating Two Cultures to Form a Decision-Making Process

**Directions:** The following article tells how National Semiconductor, Israel, integrated the strengths of the Israeli culture with those of its U.S. parent company to form a decision-making process that suited its needs best. After you have read the article, answer the questions that follow.

## Values Must Blend in Overseas Operations

National Semiconductor, Israel, is a subsidiary of Santa Clara, California–based National Semiconductor. The general set of values and goals is similar in both companies. The organizational culture and management style of the Israeli subsidiary, however, are different from the culture and style of its parent company in California.

As an American-owned company operating in Israel, three different factors influence the culture of National Semiconductor, Israel:

- The U.S. parent company
- Israeli society
- The individual characteristics of its gold-collar workers (highly skilled employees who set their own priorities and desire autonomy but don't aspire to be leaders of the organization).

For example, the American culture has its foundations in the Protestant ethos of Western societies. This ethos concentrates on private enterprise and places the individual in the center. The emphasis is on the individual, not on the group. The cultures of both Eastern Europe and Islam, on the other hand, influence the Israeli culture. In Israeli culture, the emphasis is on the group. The individual acts primarily within—and as part of—a group.

Management principles at National Semiconductor, Israel, therefore, must compensate for the weaknesses of the Israeli culture and take advantage of its strengths. These principles must capitalize on the high technical ability and personal integrity of the Israeli worker, and compensate for the low managerial ability that results from a tendency toward informality, openness, and indistinct lines of authority.

At the same time, management at the Israeli company must try to introduce the strengths of the U.S.-parent-company culture without introducing its weaknesses. Management must introduce the tendency to be systematic, which is characteristic of the American gold-collar worker, but exclude features that would be inappropriate for the Israeli culture.

This was the challenge faced by the company as it implemented a new decision-making process that impacted the organizational culture at its R&D Center. (The R&D Center includes 150 engineers, who develop and design such products as integrated circuits, software, fax machines, modems, answering machines, and other technologies.)

A survey conducted in April 1990 revealed how employees at the center felt about the company, and in particular, the organization's decision-making process. The survey revealed that:

1) Individual workers were dissatisfied with their ability to influence events in their own departments. They indicated that they were excluded from all stages of the decision-making process, including receiving information on the final decisions.

2) Because the team didn't participate in the decision-making process, the decisions didn't affect the accumulated knowledge of the team.

3) The procedure for making decisions was unclear, as it was for following up on final decisions to verify that they were being implemented properly.

Management set up a committee to investigate the problem. Its goal was to improve the decision-making process so that it would be appropriate to the existing organizational structure while accommodating the cultural characteristics of the Israeli gold-collar workers. The group included senior management members, the human resources manager of the design center, and two consultants from outside the organization.

The committee members talked with employees and managers throughout the design center about the issues. They came to the conclusion that how decisions were made was the central issue of everyone

---

Source: Eli Lazar, "Values Must Blend in Overseas Operations," *Personnel Journal* (February, 1993). 

concerned. They decided, therefore, to clarify this process in theory before developing techniques to improve it.

The committee first produced a set of management norms to describe how managers in the organization should make decisions. Then they identified methods that managers could use to implement these norms. The norms fell into the following three categories:

- Teamwork
- Authority and responsibility
- Decision making

The committee developed the teamwork norms first because teamwork drives the Israeli organization. These norms were:

- Decision makers must have the most current and complete information possible, including the degree of uncertainty that's inherent in the decision.
- Everyone who may have to implement a decision must know about it and agree with it.
- Everyone should be involved in making all decisions that affect them.
- Although decisions are a team effort, each individual is responsible.
- There should be a clear distinction between meetings held for the purpose of making decisions and meetings held for other purposes.

The committee then discussed who should have the authority and responsibility for decisions. It was decided:

- Decisions should be made at the lowest level possible—the level of the supervisors for the individuals affected by the decision.
- A decision must identify an implementing authority, an explanation of how the decision furthers organizational strategy, and a division of duties and detailed responsibility limits that ensure implementation of all parts of the decision.
- The objectives and assignments of each manager include responsibility for all the decisions that he or she must implement as well as for the decisions of those employees under his or her management.

Next, the committee agreed upon which factors impact decision making. These factors were:

- Clearly defined parameters, such as cost and personnel time, so that decisions could be classified by priority.
- Consideration of the practicality of a decision and how easy it was to implement. A decision that isn't practical to implement won't be approved.
- Ability to make changes in decisions.
- Evaluation of the decision for cost, time, and other quantitative and qualitative effects.
- A clearly defined procedure that all managers could follow when they implement decisions and evaluate their effects.

**Management doesn't make and implement all decisions.** It's a popular belief that management is responsible for forming and making the decisions, and implementing them on all levels, in any organization. Here's where the cultural values of the organization are most evident, however. National Semiconductor, Israel, decided to demonstrate its nature, both in word and in deed.

In principle, the management team only should recommend changes. All other levels in the organization should be free to react, comment, make suggestions or object to that recommendation before management reaches a decision officially and it becomes binding on all concerned.

The company agreed that the management team should submit its conclusions to a different, independent team, which would include representatives from all levels of the organization, from the most junior to the top. This second team then must review, evaluate, revise (if necessary) and develop an implementation program for the changes. This would provide continuous feedback to management on how the implementation process was progressing. As a result, management could detect and correct implementation problems immediately and suggest and apply remedies.

Management understands that a set of values can't be imposed on an organization but must come from all levels of the organization. Considering and respecting the values of individuals improves morale within the employee community. In this way, employees feel that they can make a real contribution and impact on making decisions.

At first glance, the decision-making process appears to be a technical one. It may seem possible to codify the process as a set of rules that usually lead to a wise decision. In reality, however, National Semiconductor, Israel, found the process was more complicated. Decisions are heavily influenced by cultural background. The ideal decision-making process must allow expression of different cultures.

A successful decision-making process allows the organization to adjust itself, as necessary, to the changing external reality. It doesn't interfere with the organization's ability to continue to perform all necessary tasks and to meet the demands of both the foreign subsidiary and the parent company.

**Directions:** Indicate your answer to each of the following questions by circling "Yes" or "No" in the Answers column.

| Question | Answers | |
|---|---|---|
| 1. Is the management style of the Israeli subsidiary pretty much the same as that of the parent company? | Yes | No |
| 2. Does the Israeli culture emphasize the individual rather than the group? | Yes | No |
| 3. Is the Israeli management style characterized by informality and openness? | Yes | No |
| 4. Did the April 1990 survey reveal that workers at the R&D Center actively participated in the decision-making process? | Yes | No |
| 5. Did the problem-solving committee come to the conclusion that most employees and managers were concerned with how decisions were being made? | Yes | No |
| 6. Of the three categories of norms, did the committee develop the teamwork norms first? | Yes | No |
| 7. Did the teamwork norms state that the team alone is responsible for all decisions made? | Yes | No |
| 8. Regarding the authority and responsibility for decision making, did the committee decide that decisions should be made at the lowest level possible? | Yes | No |
| 9. Does the Israeli management team recommend, make, and implement all decisions? | Yes | No |
| 10. Did the Israeli management team find the decision-making process to consist of a fairly simple set of rules? | Yes | No |

# 4

# ADMINISTERING OFFICE SYSTEMS

*Administrative office systems* are designed to plan, organize, operate, and control all phases of the information cycle in order to provide information for decision making. Small firms, even those wherein much information processing is completed manually, are as dependent upon administrative office systems as large firms. Managers and employees in *all* sizes of companies must have an understanding of basic systems concepts and be able to apply these in their respective jobs.

The study of administrative office systems embodies all of the processes required to define, analyze, and structure a business problem and to develop alternative solutions for management decision making. After the systems analyst has gotten a broad view of the exact nature of a business problem, he or she next breaks down the problem into its individual parts, expressed as a logical sequence of steps. Each step of the system is written down and often illustrated with charts, tables, and diagrams so that a clear picture is obtained of how information flows through the organization and who is responsible. The objective of such an analysis is to develop streamlined and efficient techniques of doing business so that the firm is able to maximize its use of human and material resources and thus increase the productivity of operations.

If office operations are to be effective, they must be improved continuously, not just when there is an economic downturn. The office manager has a responsibility to create that kind of environment in which workers are permitted to correct any personal weaknesses that affect their performance. This is the kind of environment in which the worker can freely ask the question, "What if?" as the basis for determining a better way of doing the job.

## SECTION A • REVIEW QUESTIONS

**Directions:** In the Answers column, write the letter of the item in Column 1 that is described by each statement in Column 2.

**Column 1**

**A** Administrative office systems
**B** Control
**C** Database
**D** Feedback
**E** Input
**F** Method
**G** Model
**H** Output
**I** Procedure
**J** Program
**K** Synergism
**L** Systems study
**M** Transformation process

| Column 2 | Answers |
|---|---|
| 1. The process of improving systems . . . . . . . . . . . . . . . . . . . . . . . . . . | 1. ______ |
| 2. A simplified, general explanation of the complex interrelationships and activities of an organization or its parts . . . . . . . . . . . . . . . . . . | 2. ______ |
| 3. The systems phase that compares the system's output with standards of performance . . . . . . . . . . . . . . . . . . . . . . . . . . . . . . . . . . . . . . . . | 3. ______ |
| 4. The first phase of any system in which data, energy, or information are received from another system . . . . . . . . . . . . . . . . . . . . . . . . . . | 4. ______ |
| 5. A planned sequence of operations for handling recurring transactions uniformly and consistently . . . . . . . . . . . . . . . . . . . . . . . . . . . . . . . | 5. ______ |
| 6. A set of instructions for processing data in a computer system . . . . | 6. ______ |
| 7. The manual, mechanical, or automated means by which each procedural step is performed . . . . . . . . . . . . . . . . . . . . . . . . . . . . . . | 7. ______ |
| 8. Specialized systems responsible for managing all phases of the information cycle . . . . . . . . . . . . . . . . . . . . . . . . . . . . . . . . . . . . . | 8. ______ |
| 9. The systems phase that dictates what can and cannot be done in each of the other phases . . . . . . . . . . . . . . . . . . . . . . . . . . . . . . . . . . . | 9. ______ |
| 10. A central master file containing company-wide information about a firm or department-wide information within a department . . . . . . . | 10. ______ |

**Directions:** Indicate your answer to each of the following questions by circling "Yes" or "No" in the Answers column.

| | Answers | |
|---|---|---|
| 1. Do all systems depend upon the proper coordination and operation of all their elements in order to achieve their assigned goals? . . . . . . . . | Yes | No |
| 2. In a major business system such as purchasing, are there various procedures set up to complete the work required in each of the subsystems? . . . . . . . . | Yes | No |
| 3. Are the manual, mechanical, or automated means by which procedural steps are performed known as *systems*? . . . . . . . . | Yes | No |
| 4. Is a feasibility study undertaken to find out if specific systems operations can be improved and if the addition of new resources is economically justified for making these improvements? | Yes | No |
| 5. Does a general systems model represent a broad explanation of the system to which more concrete details can be added as needed? . . . . . . . . | Yes | No |
| 6. Is a business organization a fairly good example of a *closed* system? . . . . . . . . | Yes | No |
| 7. Are incoming telephone calls from prospective customers an example of input in a sales system? . . . . . . . . | Yes | No |
| 8. Is the transformation process a systems phase in which the input is changed into a desired form? . . . . . . . . | Yes | No |
| 9. Is *feedback* the regulating force that compares the output of a system with the performance standards for the system? . . . . . . . . | Yes | No |
| 10. Is *output* that phase of a system which dictates what can and cannot be done in each of the other phases of the administrative office system? . . . . . . . . | Yes | No |
| 11. Is a *system* a distinct entity that is unrelated to other systems in an organization? . . . . . . . . | Yes | No |
| 12. In a management information system, are many of the activities in the information cycle performed by the computer? . . . . . . . . | Yes | No |
| 13. Is one of the disadvantages of establishing a database the necessity for storing information in many duplicate files? . . . . . . . . | Yes | No |
| 14. Are manual systems the least prevalent type of system? . . . . . . . . | Yes | No |
| 15. Does the computer system depend upon a code to represent data within the machine? . . . . . . | Yes | No |
| 16. Do people serve as the main control element in the computer system? . . . . . . . . | Yes | No |
| 17. Is problem solving the primary objective of systems analysis? . . . . . . . . | Yes | No |
| 18. Does *synergism* refer to the fact that interrelated parts produce a total effect less than the sum of each of the parts working independently? . . . . . . . . | Yes | No |
| 19. Is the systems study cycle a set of sequential, problem-solving steps that are followed to improve the systems function? . . . . . . . . | Yes | No |
| 20. Is a systems study typically initiated whenever a recurring problem of some importance is recognized by the information user? . . . . . . . . | Yes | No |
| 21. For most efficient operations, should the systems staff report directly to the manager of human resources? . . . . . . . . | Yes | No |
| 22. In small companies, may the responsibility for systems work be assigned the office manager? | Yes | No |

# SECTION B • PROJECTS

## Project 4–1 • Shopping for a New Payroll System

**Directions:** After you have read this article dealing with the process of evaluating a new in-house payroll system, answer the questions at the end. The author of this article, Ann Claridge, is Cross Industry Marketing Director for Lawson Software, a Minneapolis-based vendor of accounting, payroll, human resources, distribution, materials management, and retail business applications.

### Points to Ponder. . . When You're Shopping for a New Payroll System

While it isn't required that you be a computer expert to successfully implement and manage an in-house payroll system, you may feel that way when beginning the evaluation process.

Do you know what kind of hardware and operating system your company uses? Does your MIS department plan to continue using the same hardware, or are there plans to downsize to a smaller platform? Are there current payroll procedures that should be altered, at this point, to increase efficiency?

These questions may seem overwhelming. But take heart: When shopping for an in-house payroll system, your confusion can be greatly reduced just by knowing which questions to ask and getting a few simple answers.

#### It's Not Just About Software

When searching for software, remember that you are looking for more than just the programs. It's important to evaluate the company behind the software.

Eventually, you'll be relying on that company for support and future product enhancements. You may want to take advantage of emerging technologies in the years to come, so you need to know how the software vendor evaluates new technologies and how it enables its products to take advantage of these advances. Options like executive information systems, imaging, and telephony may not be crucial today, but they might be tomorrow's highest priority.

Communication between everyone who will be affected by the system gives your project a much better chance of being successful. So you must find out who is responsible for making decisions regarding hardware. And because data processing will always be impacted by the implementation of new software, it's important to include data processing personnel from the beginning of the selection process. Also, data processing may have ideas that will make their lives easier—as well as yours.

Representatives from payroll, human resources, MIS, and data processing should establish the hardware issues involved in the software purchase decision. You need to consider what type of system will be or is being used for payroll. In addition to hardware type, your hardware configuration requirements should include computer disk space, system memory, and the desired programming language. These decisions and requirements should whittle down the list of software vendors.

#### Features, Features, Features

After discussing hardware configuration, you must determine which features you want in a software application package. It is vital to determine your requirements before being faced with sales pitches and product demonstrations. It is sometimes helpful to split your wish list into "required" and "desired" features.

Analyze the current processes to determine how they could be streamlined, because now is the time to make changes. This is a good time to eliminate the "because that's the way we've always done it" processes.

Think about your future needs. Remember that you will be using this software package a long time. Consider what kind of growth and/or changes in organization might be in your company's future. Try to consider pending regulatory changes that may affect your software needs.

Keeping the following five areas in mind can help you avoid disappointment with your new payroll system.

**(1) Time record entry.** This is one of the most commonly overlooked areas when considering new software. Your company's method of time record entry and any current

---

Source: Ann Claridge, "Points to Ponder. . .When You're Shopping for a New Payroll System," *PaytecH* (May–June, 1993), pp. 24–26. Reprinted by permission of the American Payroll Institute, Inc.

procedures must be evaluated. The software you choose should have multiple methods of entering time records to accommodate your company's needs.

Some features you might want to consider:

- individual and/or multiple employee time record entry;
- user-defined time record entry screens;
- interface with a time clock system;
- the ability to maintain time records until the actual payroll run; and
- the ability to do exception entry via a time and attendance system.

In addition, there are reporting features to consider:

- multiple time record edit reports;
- balancing capabilities by division, department, or user defined groups; and
- missing time records report.

**(2) Tax reporting.** The software must have the ability to adhere to federal, state, and local government tax law changes within relatively short time frames. Tax changes are inevitable, so a method to verify newly implemented changes can be crucial and can save you from incorrect tax reporting. An evaluation of the state requirements that affect your company will help in your software search.

The software should be able to produce any reports required by law so that proper tax deposits can be made. Social Security Administration, state, and local standards must be met for annual wage reporting on magnetic media and W-2 forms.

Another necessity is proper quarterly reporting to federal, state, and local governments. The payroll system should also have the flexibility to provide reports for balancing pay periods monthly, quarterly, or yearly.

**(3) Payroll processing.** Because the results of the payroll process are visible, it should go without saying that a payroll system's accuracy and timeliness are crucial. The ability to troubleshoot potential payroll mishaps is an important feature. Through the use of multiple editing capabilities, such as deduction reports, problems can be solved right up until the time actual checks are cut.

Another consideration is your accounting department. When your payroll is complete, do you post manually to the general ledger? The software you choose should automatically post to your general ledger via an interface, or the payroll software should have its own general ledger system. This will ensure accurate and timely information is being given to the accounting department without additional manual labor.

Certain payroll systems offer greater flexibility than others. You may want software that has multiple check formats so you can choose the type of checks your company prefers. Does your company track vacation time, sick time, or other company-defined plans? A good payroll system should be able to work with other systems to calculate accrual and usage of time for multiple plans within your company.

**(4) Integration with human resources.** Consider whether you want to integrate the human resources system with the payroll system. Companies often want to integrate the two so that employee data need only be entered once and data can be shared. Even if integration isn't a concern now, it may be in the future.

Many systems offer report writers. This can be an important feature to human resources software simply because of the nature of human resources and payroll. Ad hoc reports are often more necessary than standard ones.

**(5) Benefits administration and reporting.** An evaluation of your current benefit plans should take place prior to viewing a demonstration of any software. Again, a look into your company's future plans can help in your search for software.

Does your company have 401(k) and/or profit-sharing plans? Does your company have a flexible benefits plan? Is there talk about implementing them in the future? The ability to administer benefits through the payroll system is a consideration.

For example, the ability to print certain benefits on the check stub may be especially important for your company. Make sure that all of the benefits added, dropped, or changed by employees can be easily updated by the software system.

Don't forget to consider your reporting needs. Your new system should have the ability to create user-defined reports as needed by management. The need for auditing reports, premium reports to insurance carriers, and defined contribution, as well as defined benefits information to third-party administrators, should not be overlooked.

## A World of Possibility

The list of possible features and requirements can be endless. It will help, though, to remember that your goal is to find full-featured products that can meet your changing needs and increase efficiency by giving you the capability to take advantage of the latest technologies. If you keep this in mind during your evaluation and selection process, you'll be one step ahead and will eliminate much unnecessary frustration.

1. When searching for software, why is it important to evaluate the company that produced the software?

2. In the process of evaluating software, what is the value of establishing good communications with the data processing personnel?

3. Explain the significance of "tax reporting" when designing a new payroll system.

4. What benefits may be gained by designing an in-house system that integrates the payroll system and the human resources system?

5. Why is it important to evaluate a company's current benefit plans before inspecting any vendor's software?

## Project 4–2 • Let's Debate

**Directions:** Given below are four rather widespread ideas that office workers have expressed about systems. With the help of your instructor, form groups to debate one or more of these observations.

1. If an administrative office system does not work well, it should be "put on the computer" so that it will be better.
2. If a company installs a system, costs will always be reduced.
3. With a good administrative office system in operation, a firm does not need as many office workers.
4. Office workers who are involved with administrative office systems should know all about computers. The best way for them to learn is to enroll in a course in programming.

## Project 4–3 • Calculating the Annual Depreciation Expense of a Computer System

The purchase price of a computer system, like other assets owned by a company, may be *depreciated* (written off as an operating expense) over the useful life of the machines and equipment. The Tax Reform Act of 1986 established a Modified Accelerated Cost Recovery System (MACRS) that generally applies to all assets placed in service after December 31, 1986. Under the Tax Reform Act, property classes were established for the various kinds of assets for the purpose of determining the depreciation method and the recovery period. The *recovery period* is the period of time over which the purchase price of the asset may be spread or "written off" as an expense. For example, the 5-year property class includes computers and peripheral equipment and office machinery (typewriters, calculators, copiers, etc.). The 7-year property class covers office furniture and fixtures, such as desks and files.

One method used to determine the amount of depreciation expense is called the *straight-line* method. Under MACRS, a new depreciation rate is determined for each tax year in the recovery period. For any tax year, the straight-line rate is determined by dividing the number 1 by the years remaining in the recovery period at the beginning of the tax year. The rate is applied to the *unrecovered* basis of the property. If the remaining recovery period at the beginning of any tax year is less than 1 year, the straight-line rate for that tax year is 100 percent.

Under MACRS, a half-year convention is used when calculating the depreciation for property such as office machines and equipment. The *half-year convention* treats all property placed in service (or disposed of) during a tax year as having been placed in service (or disposed of) on the *midpoint* of that tax year. *Thus, the cost of a 5-year asset is actually recovered in 6 years.*

As an example, assume a company purchased several office copiers on January 3, 1995, for a purchase price of $4,000. As we saw above, for purposes of calculating depreciation, the copiers are classified as 5-year property. To calculate the depreciation expense for each year, we proceed as follows:

1. Determine the straight-line rate for a full tax year by dividing 1 by 5. The straight-line rate is 20%.
2. Apply the half-year convention to obtain the depreciation rate for the first year (1/2 of 20% = 10%).
3. Calculate the depreciation expense for the first year:

   $$10\% \times \$4{,}000 = \$400$$

4. At the beginning of the second year, the remaining recovery period is 4.5 years as a result of the half-year convention. The straight-line rate for the second year is 22.22% (1 divided by 4.5).
5. To calculate the depreciation expense for the second year, apply the second-year rate, 22.22%, to the cost of the equipment reduced by the depreciation taken in the first year.

   $$(\$4{,}000 - \$400) \times 22.22\% = \$799.92$$

6. Using the same procedure, we can obtain the depreciation for years 3 through 6, as shown below. Keep in mind that the remaining recovery period at the beginning of the sixth year is less than one year; therefore, the straight-line rate for the sixth year is 100%.

| Year | Depreciation Rate (%) | Unrecovered Basis of the Asset (Cost Reduced by Accumulated Depreciation Taken in Prior Years) | Annual Depreciation Expense |
|---|---|---|---|
| 1 | 10.0 | $4,000.00 | $400.00 |
| 2 | 22.22 | $3,600.00 | $799.92 |
| 3 | 28.57 | $2,800.08 | $799.98 |
| 4 | 40.00 | $2,000.10 | $800.04 |
| 5 | 66.67 | $1,200.06 | $800.08 |
| 6 | 100.0 | $ 399.98 | $399.98 |
| | | Total Depreciation Expense. . . . . . . . . . . . . . . . . | $4,000.00 |

**Problem:** Following a feasibility study, the Harvey Company decided to install seven new computers and to use the straight-line method to calculate the depreciation on the machines, which are classed as 5-year property. The computers, which cost $3,500 each, were put into use on January 3, 1995.

**Directions:** On the form below, record the amount of annual depreciation expense on the seven computers.

| Year | Depreciation Rate (%) | Unrecovered Basis of the Asset (Cost Reduced by Accumulated Depreciation Taken in Prior Years) | Annual Depreciation Expense |
|---|---|---|---|
| 1 | ________ | ________________ | ________ |
| 2 | ________ | ________________ | ________ |
| 3 | ________ | ________________ | ________ |
| 4 | ________ | ________________ | ________ |
| 5 | ________ | ________________ | ________ |
| 6 | ________ | ________________ | ________ |
| | | Total . . . . . . . . . . . . . . . . . . . . . | ________ |

5

# COMMUNICATING IN THE OFFICE

In the communication process, the sender is especially important since very often breakdowns in communication are caused by the sender rather than by the channel selected or the form of message. The sender's objective is to transmit messages that are read or heard and understood by the receiver so that the desired action is taken. Whether the desired action (or inaction) is taken is revealed by feedback, where the receiver becomes a sender and the original source becomes the receiver.

In the office, successful communication flows in several directions—upward, downward, laterally, and diagonally. In each of these flows, the sender must be aware of communication barriers that may prevent the effective transmission of messages. Some of these barriers are caused by differences in perception, semantics, status, organizational climate, and reading skills. Also, the sender must be concerned with nonverbal communication, such as body language and the physical space used by people in their interactions with others.

Much communication in the office depends upon the development of written reports, which are very expensive to produce. Because of the element of cost and the fact that oral communication in many cases provides a more effective communication channel, office managers should be highly critical of reports and try to avoid overreporting, known as "information pollution."

## SECTION A • REVIEW QUESTIONS

**Directions:** In the Answers column, write the letter of the item in Column 1 that is described by each statement in Column 2.

| Column 1 | Column 2 | Answers |
|---|---|---|
| **A** Bias | 1. A way of interpreting situations based upon the individual's personal experiences . . . . . . . . . . | 1. ______ |
| **B** Body language | 2. The transmission of a message from one person (the sender) to another person (the receiver) . . . . . . . . . . | 2. ______ |
| **C** Communication audit | 3. The study of word meanings and their effect upon human behavior | 3. ______ |
| **D** Communication process | 4. Technical terms and idioms that are peculiar to a specific group or activity . . . . . . . . . . | 4. ______ |
| **E** Grapevine | 5. An informal communication network in which messages are rapidly transmitted, usually on a one-to-one basis . . . . . . . . . . | 5. ______ |
| **F** Jargon | 6. The study of how individuals use physical space in their interactions with others and how physical space influences behavior . . . . . . . . . | 6. ______ |
| **G** Kinesics | 7. The conscious manipulation of facts in order to distort events . . . . | 7. ______ |
| **H** Paralanguage | 8. A person's gestures, expressions, and body positions . . . . . . . . . . | 8. ______ |
| **I** Perception | 9. The study of the relationship between body motions and communication . . . . . . . . . . | 9. ______ |
| **J** Proxemics | 10. An evaluation of the communication system to determine how effectively and efficiently it is working . . . . . . . . . . | 10. ______ |
| **K** Semantics | | |
| **L** Slanting | | |

**Directions:** Indicate your answer to each of the following questions by circling "Yes" or "No" in the Answers column.

| | | **Answers** | |
|---|---|---|---|
| 1. | Does the communication process begin with the selection of the channel to be used in transmitting the message? | Yes | No |
| 2. | Is the formal communication network based upon the chain of command and its lines of authority? | Yes | No |
| 3. | Is the formal communication network used solely for the downward transmission of messages? | Yes | No |
| 4. | Is the grapevine a formal means of quickly spreading information? | Yes | No |
| 5. | Is the office supervisor the main formal channel for downward and upward communication? | Yes | No |
| 6. | Generally are informal discussions among office employees and their supervisor or manager the most effective channels for upward communication? | Yes | No |
| 7. | Are all the employees in an organization usually eligible to participate in the firm's employee suggestion system? | Yes | No |
| 8. | Is the grievance-handling procedure in a nonunion office an example of downward communication? | Yes | No |
| 9. | Does diagonal communication usually occur in the formal communication network shown on the firm's organization chart? | Yes | No |
| 10. | Do the differences in perception among office workers determine the manner in which they interpret the messages received? | Yes | No |
| 11. | Is it easier for a worker and a manager to share their feelings than for persons of equal rank? | Yes | No |
| 12. | Do workers often slant communication in order to appear competent in the eyes of their supervisor? | Yes | No |
| 13. | With the advent of computers, has there been a significant decline in information overload? | Yes | No |
| 14. | Does information overload often cause a barrier to effective communication among top-level managers? | Yes | No |
| 15. | Is bias a barrier in face-to-face communication rather than in written communication? | Yes | No |
| 16. | May nonverbal communication occur at the same times as spoken words? | Yes | No |
| 17. | When body language contradicts an oral message, do the spoken words always more accurately express the message? | Yes | No |
| 18. | When planning a meeting at which 30 workers will probably engage in heated arguments, should the office manager select a very small conference room? | Yes | No |
| 19. | Are the type and frequency of reports determined by the size and structure of the organization? | Yes | No |
| 20. | Does good report writing dictate that the recommendations and summary be located at the end of the report? | Yes | No |

## SECTION B • PROJECTS

### Project 5–1 • Selecting Media for Downward Communication

**Directions:** Listed on the form below are several different messages that are often communicated downward in business offices. For each message (1) identify the intended recipients of the messages, (2) select one or more media appropriate for use in transmitting the messages, and (3) state the provisions you would make for feedback to assure that the recipients received and clearly understood the messages.

**Selecting Media for Downward Communication**

| Message | (1) Recipients | (2) Media | (3) Provisions for Feedback |
|---|---|---|---|
| 1. Company downsizing of 250 workers (plant and office) because of increased foreign competition | | | |
| 2. Annual employee appraisal of office worker | | | |
| 3. Changes in top-level personnel—newly elected president and two vice presidents and retirement of chairperson of the board | | | |
| 4. Annual company bonus to be paid all workers in their next paychecks | | | |
| 5. Notice to office worker of payroll deduction for excessive absenteeism | | | |
| 6. Suggestion system award to worker who submitted a cost-reduction idea that will save the company $5,000 annually | | | |
| 7. Target date for starting the last phase of the firm's expansion program | | | |
| 8. Adoption of a new safety procedure for office workers in the reproduction center | | | |

## Project 5–2 • Removing Communication "Static" from a Business Report

Paul Licitra, supervisor of the word processing center of Stuart Electronics, Inc., has just been handed a report transcribed by Judy Geren, one of the correspondence secretaries. This report is reproduced on page 43. Geren transcribed the report exactly as it was dictated by Sally Grant, a newly hired sales correspondent. Geren brought the report to Licitra's attention since she is very concerned about the effect it will have upon the recipient, the assistant sales manager. As Licitra reads the report, he becomes very alarmed because of Grant's inability to compose her thoughts into an understandable communication.

One of Licitra's responsibilities is to conduct in-house training sessions for the sales correspondents. Looking ahead to next week's session, he plans to use Grant's report as an example of how the firm's communications must be improved. Using this report, Licitra plans to stress the need for organizing one's thoughts before dictating, expressing oneself clearly, and eliminating jargon and excess words that add nothing to the message.

Another of Licitra's responsibilities is to provide cross training for the correspondence secretaries. Thus, they will be able to step into other positions when vacancies occur and when peak workloads justify temporary reassignment. Licitra has been grooming Geren to assume more supervisory responsibilities and to develop greater insight into the role of leader in the center. With this thought in mind, he asks Geren to rewrite the report so that her version may be used for comparison with the original during the training session.

**Directions:** Assuming the role of Geren, rewrite the report, keeping in mind each of the following questions:

1. Is there a specific purpose in writing the report that will enable the recipient to take action?
2. Is the report well planned and well organized?
3. Has the report been kept as short as possible?
4. Has simple language been used so that the recipient will quickly and easily understand the contents and take action?

After you have completed the rewriting of the formal business report, do you feel that your reporting could have been handled more economically and effectively by means of oral reporting? Explain.

**TO:** Tim Adkins, Assistant Sales Manager

**FROM:** Sally Grant, Sales Correspondent

**DATE:** December 15, 19—

**SUBJECT:** James V. Gunn's Order of the Tenth of November, 19—

SUMMARY

In regard to your memo of the fourteenth of December which I received on my desk yesterday and which is now lying in front of me, I must confess to you that I, too, am utterly distressed that the goods ordered by James V. Gunn on the tenth of November under purchase order No. 6753 have not yet arrived in their warehouse nor have they received any word from us as to a late shipment or a back order. Do permit me to utilize a little time today to respond to your memo and to explain fully the innumerable difficulties that have transpired in our production facilities which have been instrumental in creating such an inordinate delay for Gunn.

PROBLEM AND SOLUTION

On our X-10 stamping machines which are used to fabricate the pieces ordered by Gunn, one of the tungsten-alloy springs (#3476-AO) malfunctioned as a result of oxidation. Upon sensing the difficulty being experienced in the stamping process, the plant manager notified by telephone the supplier of the stamping machine who, in turn, communicated to us that we would be hearing from one of his service representatives within the next day or two. It was a period of three long days of waiting, waiting, and waiting before the service representative made an appearance and replaced the spring. But, of course, it was mandatory that the machine be entirely dismantled in order to insert the new spring, all of which necessitated two days' labor by the representative and the complete shutdown of our stamping processes for a 36-hour period. I am sure that our other customers are upset with this malfunctioning, as Gunn is, and possibly we shall be hearing from them also.

CONCLUSION

Let me assure you that I today personally inspected Gunn's shipment and finalized the information on the outgoing sales invoice before it was picked up by Reo Trucking at our shipping docks. You can rest assured that the goods are on their way to Gunn and that they should be in their plant on or around the eighteenth of this month unless, of course, the severe winter storms in their part of the country impede the truck driver from proceeding as quickly as the trek is ordinarily made from here to their city.

# Project 5–3 • Computer Hands-On: Reporting on the Reduction of Communication Costs

You have been employed recently as office manager of the Orono Manufacturing Company, a retail mail-order firm. Often, there are complaints that require adjustment. The processing of outgoing written communications requires a staff of 20 full-time sales correspondents and 8 full-time correspondence secretaries. Because of the volume of correspondence, you feel that priority should be given to studying this phase of office work so that its cost may be reduced. You have studied a large sample of the outgoing letters and analyzed the stereotyped and redundant phrases used by the sales correspondents. As a result, you feel that many words could be eliminated to reduce the length of letters, improve the effectiveness of communication, and reduce costs.

The data you collected for March are:

| | |
|---|---|
| Number of letters written | 28,800 |
| Average length of each letter (not including letter address and complimentary close) | 12 lines |
| Salaries paid correspondents | $52,500 |
| Salaries paid correspondence secretaries | $22,700 |
| Nonproductive labor (absenteeism, employee benefits) | $18,500 |
| Fixed expenses (overhead, office maintenance, etc.) | $29,300 |
| Materials costs (stationery, envelopes, etc.) | $ 2,600 |
| Mailing costs (including rental of postage meter equipment) | $ 9,600 |
| Filing costs | $ 8,800 |

Among 8,000 letters that were sampled as part of your study, the frequency of the unneeded expressions was as follows:

| | |
|---|---|
| "Enclosed you will find" | 600 |
| "As per your letter" | 600 |
| "At the present writing" | 800 |
| "Regret to advise" | 1,200 |
| "Contents noted" | 800 |
| "Acknowledging your letter of March 10, we wish to state that" | 400 |
| "We trust that you will give this matter your earliest attention" | 300 |
| "The enclosed check for $00.00 is being sent along with this letter" | 250 |
| "I have your letter of" | 1,700 |
| "In re" | 600 |
| "Please be advised" | 1,400 |

Other trite, outmoded expressions covered more than 15,780 words.

**Directions:** As office manager, prepare a report for Bernard J. Little, vice president, administrative services, giving the facts of your study and your recommendations for cost reduction. Retrieve template file PO5-3.TEM for your report format. Present the data in tabular or graphic form and indicate your interpretation of the data compiled.

## Project 5–4 • Fighting the Fog in Written Communication

Each year businesses lose billions of dollars because of confused writing which is often called "fog." The unnecessary words and phrases that should never be put on paper waste tons of paper and ink and hours spent by executives, secretaries, and others who keyboard the messages. Because of carelessly prepared office manuals and handbooks and long, complex documents and reports, unreadable writing causes costly mistakes by persons who get the wrong meaning.

Several yardsticks are used to measure reading complexity. These measurement tools show how the length of sentences and the "mix" of long words can be used to predict how well recipients will understand written communication. One of these tools, called the *Fog Index,* is based on a count of the long words and the average sentence length in a sample passage from the communication. The *Fog Index formula*, described below, translates this count into the approximate number of years of education needed to understand the communication. The higher the Fog Index, the more difficult the writing is to understand.

To determine the Fog Index:[1]

1. Select a representative passage from the document. (Select several passages if a long document is being analyzed.)
2. Count out 100 words, ending with the sentence nearest to 100. Treat independent clauses as separate sentences, regardless of whether a comma or semicolon separates the clauses. For example: "We read. We learned. We improved." This would count as three sentences even if commas or semicolons were used in place of periods.
3. Determine the average number of words in a sentence by dividing the total number of words by the number of sentences.
4. Count the number of difficult words per 100 words. In counting, omit (a) capitalized words, (b) combinations of short words like "hardware" or "output," and (c) verbs made into three syllables by adding "-es" or "-ed," like trespasses or created.
5. Add the two factors—average number of words per sentence and the number of difficult words per 100 words.
6. Multiply the total by 0.4, ignoring in your answer the digit following the decimal point.

The result obtained in Step 6 is the approximate number of years of education needed by the recipient to understand the message. Because few readers have more than 17 years of schooling, any passage above 17 is given a Fog Index of "17-plus."

In Figure 5–1, the Fog Index is calculated for the opening paragraphs of this project. The Fog Index of 14 indicates, as shown in Figure 5–2, that the reading level of this sample passage is "college sophomore."

The use of a readability formula, such as the Fog Index, may result in a low reading level, such as "seventh grade." However, this is no guarantee that the writing is clear. For example, consider this very short sample of Iago's reply to Othello's question: *"What dost thou mean?"*

> Good name in man and woman, dear my lord,
> Is the immediate jewel of their souls.
> Who steals my purse steals trash; 'tis something, nothing;
> 'Twas mine, 'tis his, and has been slave to thousands;
> But he that filches from me my good name
> Robs me of that which not enriches him,
> And makes me poor indeed.[2]

Although the Fog Index for this passage is only 5, the meaning of Iago's words is not immediately clear; and we wonder how well he answered Othello's question.

To develop good writing habits, you should periodically audit your writing to determine the reading level. You will then be able to improve and strengthen the communication process and assure yourself that your messages are clearly stated. When samples of your writing have a reading level higher than 12, consider these points: (1) avoid needless words, (2) be courteous, but do not waste the reader's time with excess words that reveal false courtesy, (3) keep sentences short, (4) use short, simple words, and (5) use active verbs.

---

[1]Adapted from Robert Gunning, *The Technique of Clear Writing,* rev. ed. (New York: McGraw-Hill, 1968). Used with permission. "Fog Index" is a service mark of Gunning-Mueller Clear Writing Institute, Inc., Santa Barbara, CA 93110

[2]William Shakespeare, *Othello* (Act III, Scene III).

**DETERMINING THE FOG INDEX**

Each year businesses (3) lose billions of dollars because of confused writing, which is often called "fog." The unnecessary (18) words and phrases that should never be put on paper waste tons of paper and ink and hours spent by executives, (39) secretaries, (40) and others who keyboard the messages. (46) Because of carelessly (49) prepared office manuals (52) and handbooks and long, complex documents (58) and reports, unreadable (61) writing causes costly mistakes by persons who get the wrong meaning.

Several (73) yardsticks are used to measure reading complexity. (80) These measurement (82) tools show how the length of sentences (89) and the "mix" of long words can be used to predict (100) how well recipients (103) will understand (105) written communication (107) . . . .

1. The opening paragraphs of Project 5-4 are used as the sample.
2. The count of 100 words ends with "predict," which is in the middle of a sentence. The sentence ends with 107 words.
3. $\frac{107 \text{ words}}{5 \text{ sentences}} = 21$, average number of words in a sentence
4. The number of difficult words (underlined in the passage) is 16. A difficult word is defined as one with three or more syllables.
5. 21 (average number of words in a sentence)<br>+16 (number of difficult words)<br>37
6. 37 x 0.4 = 14, the Fog Index Level

**Figure 5–1 Determining the Fog Index**

**THE FOG INDEX READING LEVELS**

| Fog Index | By Grade | By Publication Studied |
|---|---|---|
| 17 | College graduate | |
| 16 | College senior | |
| 15 | College junior | No popular magazine this difficult |
| 14 | College sophomore | |
| 13 | College freshman | |
| | Danger Line* | |
| 12 | High school senior | *Harper's, The Atlantic* |
| 11 | High school junior | *The Wall Street Journal* |
| 10 | High school sophomore | *Time, Newsweek* |
| 9 | High school freshman | *Reader's Digest* |
| 8 | Eighth grade | *Ladies' Home Journal* |
| 7 | Seventh grade | *National Enquirer* |
| 6 | Sixth grade | *True Confessions, People, TV Guide* |

*This danger line of reading difficulty corresponds with the reading skill of a high school senior.

Source: Adapted from Robert Gunning, *The Technique of Clear Writing*, rev. ed. (New York: McGraw-Hill, 1968). Used with permission. "Fog Index" is a service mark of Gunning-Mueller Clear Writing Institute, Inc., Santa Barbara, CA 93110.

**Figure 5–2 The Fog Index Reading Levels**

**Directions:**

1. Calculate the Fog Index for Grant's report and your rewritten report in Project 5–2. How do the two reading levels compare? If the Fog Index of your written report is higher than 12, what steps can you take to make the report more readable?
2. Calculate the Fog Index for the report you prepared for Project 5–3. How does this index compare with that of the report you rewrote in Project 5–2? Which report has the higher Fog Index? Should this report be rewritten to lower the Fog Index? Explain.
3. Evaluate any reading difficulties you found in the 107-word sample of the author's writing at the beginning of Project 5–4. Since the Fog Index of this passage is 14 (college sophomore), do you recommend the writing be revised to lower the index? If so, what words would you simplify or eliminate? Which sentences would you shorten?

## Project 5–5 • Communicating Without Words

The oldest form of human communication—nonverbal—consists of any information not spoken or written that you perceive with your senses. Some examples of nonverbal communication are gestures, facial expressions, body positions, mannerisms, tone of voice, use of physical space, and touching. In this project, you will look for such nonverbal cues in a presentation arranged by your instructor and see how the cues affect the content of the message.

**Directions:** Although nonverbal communication cues may last only a second or two, list all the cues that you perceive during the classroom presentation. Following the presentation, evaluate each of the cues noted by the group to learn which ones contributed positively to the communication process and which ones negatively affected the content of the message.

# Project 5–6 • Computer Hands-On: Reporting the Costs of Written Communications

Mannino's Public Service Company has a word processing center in which all written communications except specialized or confidential messages are transcribed. Costs of producing correspondence have greatly exceeded budgeted amounts during the past three months. As a result, the office manager, Rosa Torres, has asked you, supervisor of the center, to make a study of all correspondence costs to find ways to reduce costs.

After studying the various measurement techniques, you decide to use a one-page, single-spaced letter as the yardstick for measuring correspondence costs. Costs are to be classified in the following categories: word origination (the dictation process), transcription, filing, and mailing and messenger service.

During the two-month period in which your study was undertaken, the production was 10,000 one-page letters; 1,000 two-page letters; and 500 three-page letters. The number of form letters sent out was 10,000; but these required only the insertion of a letter address and the preparation of an envelope for mailing, which requires about one-tenth of the time a transcriber uses in preparing a one-page letter. The costs compiled for the two months are shown in Table 5–1.

**Directions:** Retrieve template file PO5-6.TEM and prepare a report, addressed to your office manager, in which you:

1. Compute the cost of a one-page letter using the information given.
2. Suggest ways to reduce the per-page cost of letters.
3. Use graphs and tables as a means of further conveying your message and of impressing Torres with the cost of written communication.

**Table 5–1**
**COST COMPILATION**
**for November and December, 19—**

| Cost Item | Word Origination | Transcription | Filing | Mailing & Messenger |
|---|---|---|---|---|
| Salaries . . . . . . . . | $36,560 | $38,900 | $3,050 | $1,360 |
| Supplies . . . . . . . . | . . . | 1,825 | 225 | . . . |
| Postage . . . . . . . . | . . . | . . . | . . . | 6,235 |
| Depreciation: | | | | |
| Equipment . . . . | 1,075 | 3,215 | 180 | 110 |
| Furniture . . . . . . | 1,575 | 1,465 | 1,270 | 40 |
| Operating costs | | | | |
| (rent, utilities, etc.). | 1,240 | 1,730 | 1,410 | 880 |
| Totals. . . . . . | $40,450 | $47,135 | $6,135 | $8,625 |

# Project 5–7 • Making Yourself Understood Among Global Cultures

In this article, you will find some helpful hints on how to adjust to the cultural differences in countries with which your organization may transact business or in which you may be relocated as part of your job assignment. As you read, note especially the significant role played by body language.

## A World of Differences

The following is just a sampling of how different parts of the world view such factors as time, space, eating and drinking, the role of women, language, greetings, and gifts.

### Language

It is best to learn the language of the country you're visiting, but since there often isn't time for that, there are steps to take to make yourself understood:

- Learn at least a few key phrases in the language of your host country, for example, greetings, "please," and "thank you."
- When speaking English, speak slowly and distinctly, and avoid idioms. Speaking English loudly won't make it easier for your listener to understand you.
- When using an interpreter, make sure he or she can interpret the spirit of your message, not just the words. Pepsi Cola's slogan "Come alive with Pepsi" was translated in China as "come out of the grave with Pepsi," hardly the message the company intended.
- Your body language is important. Be careful; some common American gestures have an entirely different meaning to other nationalities. In the Middle East and Far East pointing with one finger is considered impolite. Making a circle with the thumb and index finger, a sign for "okay" in America, is a vulgar sign in Brazil, is considered impolite in Russia and Greece, means "money" in Japan, and "zero" or "worthless" in southern France. In the Arab world and the Middle East, avoid showing the sole of your shoe or pointing the sole of your shoe at someone.
- Whereas making eye contact in America is a sign of confidence and sincerity, in Japan, Korea, and India, looking away is a sign of respect. In France eye contact is even more intense than in the United States, and the French may take it as a sign of insincerity or weakness when Americans don't return their intense gaze. Long, direct eye contact among Arab men is important.
- Culture also determines how close you stand to someone when talking and the amount of physical contact you're comfortable with. Italians who are good friends, male or female, embrace upon meeting and parting, and men may walk arm in arm. Arabs, Middle Easterners, and Latin Americans stand very close to each other when conversing.
- Dean Allen Foster, in his book *Bargaining Across Borders,* tells about the Argentines who roped off a section of a low-railed balcony because so many Americans had inadvertently backed off of it while trying to protect their space when talking with their Argentine associates. At the other end of the spectrum are the British and Japanese, who value their space and don't like to be touched.

### Time

Schedules, deadlines, being on time, and accomplishing as much as possible in a short time is the American way. But in other countries time is not so important.

- The Arabs and Latin Americans begin their meetings with lots of social amenities. They serve many cups of tea or coffee and inquire about health and family before getting down to business.
- In Latin America meetings may or may not begin on time.
- In Spain there is a saying that the only thing that begins on time is Mass, but punctuality is a must in most of the rest of Europe.

### Greetings

Most people know that Americans shake hands when meeting and are not offended if we do not follow their custom. But it is wise to know what to expect—whether a handshake, a kiss, or a bow.

Reprinted from *Keying In* (March, 1993) by permission of the National Business Education Association, 1914 Association Drive, Reston, VA 22091.

- The Japanese bow when greeting each other, but there are rules as to who bows to whom, how many times, when, and how deeply.
- The Europeans shake hands, but their grip is not so strong as that of Americans.
- A kiss on both cheeks (and in some countries three kisses) is common in France and other French-speaking European countries, especially among friends.
- In the Gulf States the Arabs first shake hands, then put their right hand on your left shoulder and kiss you on both cheeks. Do not shake hands with Arab women.

### Names and Titles

Generally, other nationalities are more formal than Americans when it comes to names. Most do not address each other by given names unless they are family or old friends.

- When addressing a Japanese put Mr., Mrs., or Miss before the Japanese surname, or attach "san" (honorable) to the end of the surname. But don't add "san" to your name when introducing yourself. Some Asians are reversing their normal way of ordering the names so as not to confuse Americans. To be on the safe side, ask.
- The Spanish and Latin Americans will often add their mother's maiden name to their surname. Use the next to last name when addressing them. For example, Juan Chavez Blanco should be called Senor Chavez (Blanco is his mother's name).

### Business Cards

Whereas Americans exchange business cards only when they need to pass on information about addresses and telephone numbers, business persons in other countries use them to establish rank and status and exchange cards before doing any business. The cards themselves must be treated with respect, not scribbled on or stuffed into a back pocket and sat upon. Business cards should have the English translated into the language of the hosts, either on the back of the card or immediately below each line on the front. The cards should include company name, position, and any titles—and no abbreviations. In most of Southeast Asia, Africa, and the Middle East, it is not proper to present the card with your left hand. In Japan, one should present the card with both hands, making sure the type is facing the recipient and is right-side up.

### Gifts

The exchange of gifts is expected in many countries. Anyone doing business in another country would be well advised to do some research as to when gifts are expected, when is the proper time to present them, what and what not to give, and even what kind of wrapping to use.

- In most European countries, flowers are a proper gift for a hostess—with the exception of carnations, which are for cemeteries only.
- In the People's Republic of China clocks are not an appropriate gift: they convey bad luck.
- Liquor is forbidden in Moslem countries. Gifts for the wives or wife of an Arab are not appropriate but gifts for the children will be welcomed.
- A knife in Latin America is not a proper gift because it signifies cutting off a relationship. Neither are handkerchiefs; they're associated with tears.
- Avoid junk gifts in any country, or cheap items such as matchbooks, baseball caps, or bumper stickers imprinted with the company logo.
- Wrapping is important in Germany, but don't use black, brown or white wrapping paper or ribbon. Always wrap gifts for the Japanese, but avoid black, white, or bright red wrappings.

### Proper Dress

- In Europe, coats and ties are required for business. Coats stay on in offices and restaurants, even in the hottest months. Women do not wear pants to a dressy restaurant. A striped tie in England may be mistaken for a regimental tie, worn only by those who have been members of certain military regiments.
- Women visiting strict Moslem countries should wear dresses and skirts well below the knee, keep elbows covered, and necklines high.
- It is not advisable to wear the costume of the country you are visiting.

### Women in Business

Women can represent their companies almost anywhere in the world, but how they conduct themselves while doing business is important. In Asian countries men are often uncomfortable doing business with women, but are more accepting of women if they are not too aggressive, immediately establish their credentials, and dress conservatively. A woman doing business in Japan can have a distinct advantage, since she is not expected to stay out most of the night drinking with her hosts.

### Holy Days and Holidays

Before visting a country take time to find out what the major holidays are. Trying to do business on a foreign holiday is tantamount to being expected to do business on Christmas in the United States.

- Arabs observe Friday as their Sabbath; some businesses will close early on Thursdays as well. During Ramadan, the Moslem month-long fasting season, not much business is done.
- In Israel the Sabbath is observed on Saturday.
- Many Catholic countries have a carnival season just before Lent (like Mardi Gras in New Orleans). It is called *Fasching* in Germany and *Carnival* in South America.
- In China and elsewhere in Confucian Asia, the New Year celebration, also called the Spring Festival, is held sometime in the winter and lasts two weeks.
- The Japanese have many holidays, including the New Year holidays, which last for five to 10 days beginning December 28. Many firms also close from April 29 to May 5.
- In Europe many people go on vacation the entire month of August, closing their shops, restaurants, and business offices.

**Eating**

In some countries people eat with their hands, in others with chopsticks, and in others with knives and forks. Arabs eat using the right hand only. Europeans eat with knives and forks but don't switch them from hand to hand the way Americans do; they use the right hand for holding the knife and cutting and the left hand for holding the fork and eating.

- Meal times vary too. The main meal may be at midday and followed by a siesta. In Spain and Latin countries the evening meal is hardly ever eaten before 10 p.m., although it may be preceded by visits to bars for drinks and appetizers.
- Some dishes in foreign countries may seem strange to Americans, but it is polite to try just a little. When John Olivo, Bloomsburg University, Pennsylvania, traveled to China, he tried everything, even the duck's feet. "Meat is very expensive in China, so when I went to a house for a banquet and they served meat I knew they had spent a whole month's food allowance. I didn't want to hurt their feelings," Dr. Olivo explained.

By now you should have the idea that there are almost as many ways to do something as there are countries in the world. Those who travel to another country to transact business will have an advantage if they learn as much as possible about that country's communication and etiquette.

## CROSSWORD PUZZLE 1

### Across

1. Maslow's hierarchy of ______
3. Question to be answered
7. First phase of any system
10. Husband of one's aunt
12. Hard wood
13. Alabama
16. Lithium
17. Earliest and most prevalent system
18. Fathers
20. Quality management pioneer
21. Iridescent gem
24. Father of scientific management
25. Alternate solutions
28. Delivered
29. Earliest form of organization
30. Authored GENERAL AND INDUSTRIAL MANAGEMENT
31. Home office?
33. Elevated railroad
34. Technical terms and idioms
35. Relationship between body motions and communications
37. ______ "Principles of Effective Work"
38. Variation of brainstorming
39. Expectorate
41. Creating large quantity of ideas
47. Wee
48. Grate
49. ______ Marwick Mitchell & Co.
50. Form of group endeavor
52. A pig
54. Manipulating facts to distort
56. Informal communication network
58. The under jaw
59. Gram
62. Precious metal
64. Heart of an MIS
65. Developed motivation-hygiene theory
66. American Samoa
67. Administrative office manager
69. Prejudice
70. "in" with the boss
71. Certain rodents
73. Professional certification
74. Shrub with thick glossy leaves
75. Group of interrelated parts
79. Maker of clothing
85. Levy
86. Fishing poles
87. Associate of Arts degree
88. Discover

### Down

1. Tide
2. Froth on soapy water
3. Broad guideline for firm's operation
4. Drops of water
5. Approve
6. Business degree
8. Synthetic material
9. Laid aside
11. Number cruncher
14. Communication among personnel at same level
15. Chief executive officer
17. Ideal form of operation
19. Right to command
22. Venomous snake
23. Father of office management
26. Writing utensil
27. Kon ______
28. Entrusting work to qualified persons
30. Banquet
31. Reducing size of workforce
32. Printer's measure
36. Name (Fr.)
37. $5 bill
40. Greek letter
41. Model of formal organizational design
42. Subsides
43. Musical syllable
44. Three strikes
45. Runs batted in
46. System interacting with its environment
51. Desired goals
52. Mayo's ______ Experiments
53. Frank and Lillian
54. Wet spongy land
55. Prepares for a position
56. Snatches
57. Building additions
60. Ultimate goal of a system
61. Spoken or ______ communication
63. Fertile spot in a desert
68. To leave out
72. Turf
76. Year
77. Thus
78. Touchdown
80. Alabama
81. This is
82. Musical syllable
83. Oregon
84. Registered nurse

## CROSSWORD PUZZLE 1

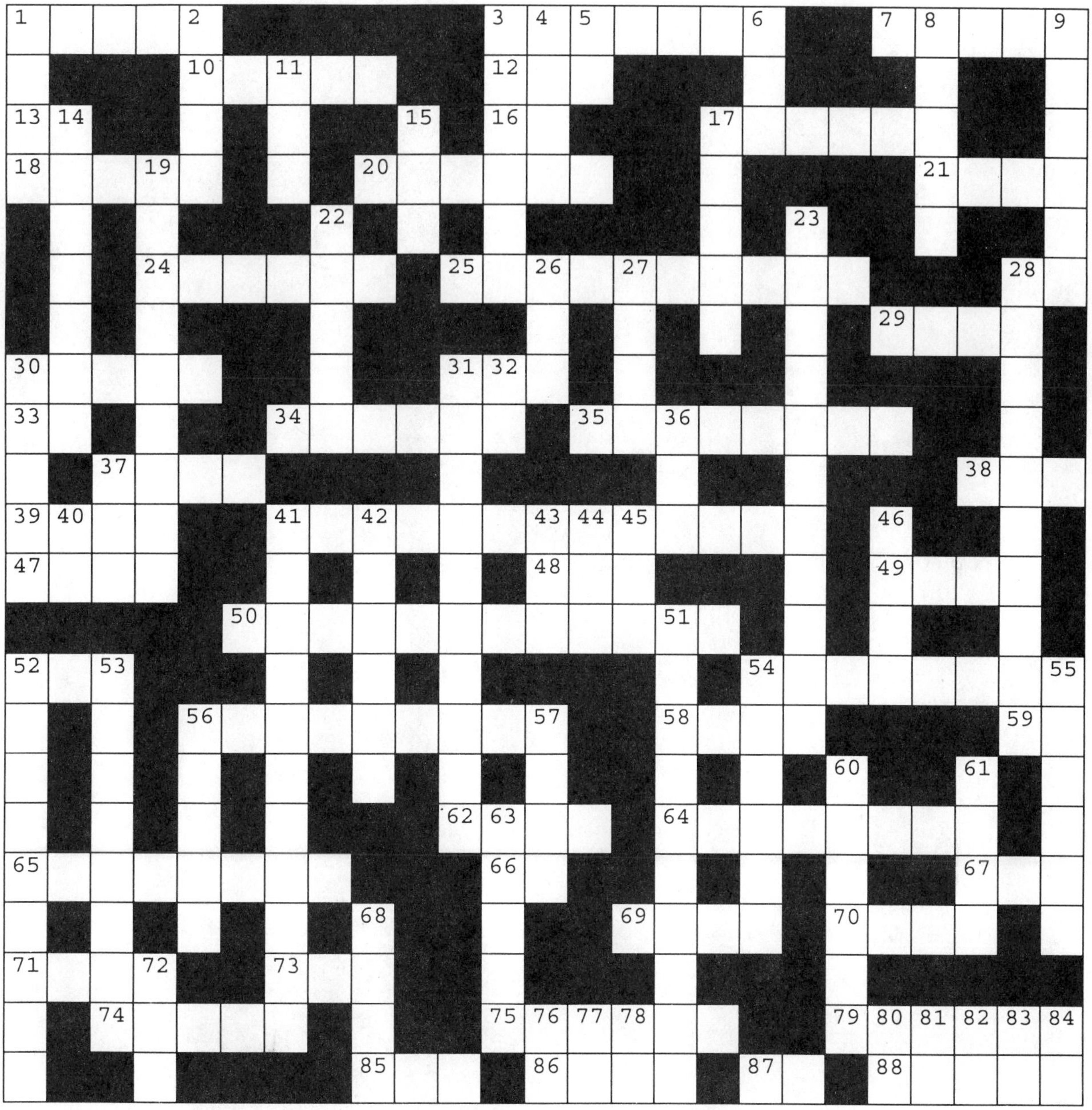

# 6

# RECRUITING AND ORIENTING THE WORKFORCE

Age-based discrimination . . . the Americans with Disabilities Act . . . testing and screening for drug abuse . . . verifying the employment of immigrants. . . high costs of hiring and training—to name several problem areas with which today's office managers and supervisors must cope as they assume responsibility for staffing the office. In many medium-size and large companies, the recruiting-hiring process may be a function of the human resources department. However, the process is really a team effort in which office supervisors play a pivotal role in advising and in participating during interviews.

In spite of all the rules and regulations affecting the staffing function, the office supervisor must still evaluate what job applicants have to offer immediately to the firm and determine what their potential will be after orientation and training. Like a coach, the supervisor must build the work unit into a cohesive team, working toward the goal of being winners in the quality and quantity of work output. The supervisor must understand that *Catholics, Jews, Protestants, African Americans, whites, Hispanics, males, females, straights, gays* do not work for him or her—only people work; and it is *through* and *with* these people that the office supervisor can effectively guide the team in making each daily touchdown.

## SECTION A • REVIEW QUESTIONS

**Directions:** Indicate your answer to each of the following questions by circling "Yes" or "No" in the Answers column.

| | | **Answers** | |
|---|---|---|---|
| 1. | Does Job Service charge a fee for the services it provides employers? | Yes | No |
| 2. | When using a temporary office help service, do employers usually pay the service a flat fee? | Yes | No |
| 3. | Does an employee leasing service typically assign its workers to short-term jobs, such as replacements for vacationing full-time workers? | Yes | No |
| 4. | Have federal, state, and local laws brought about a decrease in the need for keeping records of job applicants? | Yes | No |
| 5. | Does a department head complete a personnel requisition in order to specify the number of workers required and the kind of work to be done? | Yes | No |
| 6. | May job applicants be asked their religious faith if religion is a bona fide occupational qualification (BFOQ)? | Yes | No |
| 7. | In a direct interview, does the interviewer rely mainly upon the use of open-ended questions? | Yes | No |
| 8. | Do office managers find a job applicant's letters of reference the most effective background check? | Yes | No |
| 9. | In the *Griggs v Duke Power* ruling, did the U.S. Supreme Court prohibit the use of aptitude tests as part of the employee selection procedure? | Yes | No |
| 10. | Are aptitude tests designed to measure mental and reasoning ability? | Yes | No |
| 11. | When a test measures consistently the items it is designed to measure, is the test said to be reliable? | Yes | No |
| 12. | Does federal law prohibit private employers from refusing to hire a job applicant who is a drug abuser? | Yes | No |

| | | |
|---|---|---|
| 13. May employers legally ask job applicants if they have ever been convicted of a criminal offense? | Yes | No |
| 14. May an employer legally use the services of a credit agency to obtain information about a job applicant? | Yes | No |
| 15. Does the Employee Polygraph Protection Act bar public employers from requiring that job applicants be given a lie-detector test? | Yes | No |
| 16. Does an orientation checklist contain items that should be covered when new employees are introduced to their jobs? | Yes | No |
| 17. Under a sponsor system, is the new employee assigned to a worker who explains the duties of the new job? | Yes | No |
| 18. Do the employment discrimination provisions contained in the Civil Rights Act apply to a state government? | Yes | No |
| 19. If sex is a *BFOQ*, may an employer legally place a help-wanted advertisement that specifies the sex of job applicants? | Yes | No |
| 20. Is it lawful for an employer to refuse to hire a woman because she is pregnant? | Yes | No |
| 21. Does the Age Discrimination in Employment Act support an employment practice that requires employees to retire at age 65? | Yes | No |
| 22. Under the Americans with Disabilities Act, is it lawful for an employer to require disabled job applicants to undergo a preemployment medical test? | Yes | No |

**Directions:** In the Answers column, write the letter of the item in Column 1 that is described by each statement in Column 2.

**Column 1**

**A** Achievement test
**B** Americans with Disabilities Act
**C** Aptitude test
**D** Civil Rights Act, as amended
**E** Employee leasing service
**F** Executive orders
**G** Personality or psychological test
**H** Public employment service
**I** Reliability
**J** Validity

| Column 2 | Answers |
|---|---|
| 1. An employment test designed to measure the ability to perform a particular kind of task and to predict future performance on the job | 1. ______ |
| 2. An organization that assigns workers to client firms under contract to provide on-the-job services, usually on a permanent basis | 2. ______ |
| 3. A federal law that prohibits discrimination on the basis of race, color, religion, national origin, or sex | 3. ______ |
| 4. An employment test designed to measure abstract factors such as honesty | 4. ______ |
| 5. The extent to which a test serves the purpose for which it was intended | 5. ______ |
| 6. An employment test that measures the degree of proficiency in a given type of work | 6. ______ |
| 7. The presidential directives that strive to require equal employment opportunities in firms doing business with the government | 7. ______ |

## SECTION B • PROJECTS

### Project 6–1 • Computer Hands-On: Writing a Letter of Application

Assume that each of the following ads appears in today's edition of your local newspaper. As you read each ad, decide which one offers the greatest challenge to you and represents the job opening for which you are best qualified.

**Directions:** Retrieve template file PO6-1.TEM and key your resumé and application letter. Print out a letter of application, enclosing a resumé, in answer to one of the job openings described. In preparing your resumé, organize your biographical sketch under each of the following headings:

*Personal:* full name, address, telephone number

*Education:* high school from which you were graduated and post-high school education completed; dates of attendance; degrees or diplomas received

*Work Experience:* present and former places of employment; dates of employment; job titles; description of job duties; names of immediate supervisors

*References:* List three.

**_ADMINISTRATIVE ASSISTANT_**

Human services agency seeks assistant. Requires AA or BA in business administration, accounting, computer science, or related field. Must have solid background in accounting, payroll, and computers. Must type 50–55 WPM. Ideal candidate will have strong oral and written communication skills, be self-motivated, and enjoy working in a team environment. Send resumé with salary requirements to

Y2208 CITY BULLETIN

**_OFFICE MANAGER/ BOOKKEEPER_**

Part-timer needed to assist owner of film and video production company. Energetic, well-organized professional to handle A/R, A/P, payroll, and other administrative duties. Bookkeeping experience required. PC proficiency and good attitude are musts! Please send resumé with salary history to

X-73 CITY BULLETIN

**_ADMINISTRATIVE ASSISTANT/SECRETARY_**

Must have advanced Lotus and word processing skills. Microsoft, Word Perfect, and MAC skills, a plus. Strong typing and communication skills are necessary. Responsibilities will include handling a wide assortment of computer projects for president and management staff as coordinator of travel arrangements, seminars, and various training classes. Salary commensurate with experience. Competitive benefits package. Fax your resumé to (215)555–9993 or write

Box 210 CITY BULLETIN
We are an equal opportunity employer

### Project 6–2 • Completing the Application Form

In response to your letter of application and the resumé that you completed in Project 6–1, the Headley Company has called you and made an appointment for an interview. Upon arriving at the human resources office, you are first asked to complete the application form given on pages 58 to 61.

**Directions:** As you fill in the application, pay special attention to your handwriting, spelling, and accuracy of information provided. Remember that an initial impression of you will be gained by those reading your application and that the information you provide will enable the interviewer in the following project to raise specific questions about your qualifications for the job opening.

**Page 1**

## THE HEADLEY COMPANY
## (AN EQUAL OPPORTUNITY EMPLOYER)
## Application

**Date** ________________19___

**Name** ______________________________________ **Telephone No.** ________________
(Last) (First) (Initial)

**Street** ______________________ **City** __________________ **State** _____ **Zip** __________

| Please Leave Blank | Office Use Only |
|---|---|
| Dates Interviewed | Date Hired ________________ |
| ____________________ | Dept. Assigned to ______________ |
| ____________________ | Position Assigned to ____________ |

### Instructions to Applicants

The filing of an application is the preliminary step to employment with Headley and does not imply that the applicant is bound to accept employment or eventually will be hired.

This application should be filled out fully since the information given by you will be of assistance in determining whether your experience and training are suitable for the job opening and also in selecting a position for which you are well fitted.

All appointments to positions are on a trial basis and subject to satisfactory work. If it is found that you are not adapted to the job, the engagement may be terminated at any time at the discretion of the management.

---

Please write a brief statement in which you express the kind of work you desire, your career interests, and why you want to work at Headley.

______________________________________________________

______________________________________________________

______________________________________________________

______________________________________________________

______________________________________________________

______________________________________________________

Page 2

## PERSONAL HISTORY

This form should be completed in *pencil.* Either printing or longhand may be used. Items relating to school subjects, hobbies, activities, etc., require specific answers. If history was your favorite or your most disliked subject, it should be made clear whether American or Ancient history was the subject. Sports should be listed specifically, such as football, tennis, or swimming. The job history section of the form should be as complete as possible, including part-time jobs held during school years if space permits.

Date of birth ______________ Age ____ Sex ______ U.S. Citizen: Yes ____ No ____

Other names you have been known by ______________________________
(nicknames, maiden name, etc.)

**FAMILY:**

1. Home owned ________ Rented ________ Apartment ________ Room ________
2. Car(s) owned ______________ Description(s) ______________
3. Single _______ Engaged _______ Married _______ Date(s) of marriage(s) __________
   Separated _______ Date(s) of separation(s) ______________
   Divorced _______ Date(s) of divorce(s) ______________
   Widowed _______ Date of spouse's death _________ Cause of death __________
4. Number of dependent children __________ 5. Ages and names of children __________
   ______________________________
6. Number of other dependents _______ Relationship(s) ______________
   ______________________________
7. Spouse's name ______________ 8. Age _____ Education ______________
   ______________________________
9. Is spouse employed or regularly occupied with volunteer work? ______________
   Where? ______________ What capacity? ______________
10. In the event of an emergency, whom would you wish notified (other than spouse)?
    Name ______________________________
    Address ______________________ Telephone __________
11. Parents' address ______________________________
    (City and State)
12. Place of parents' birth ______________________________
    (father) (mother)
13. Father's occupation (or former occupation) ______________
14. Mother's occupation (or former occupation) ______________

**Page 3**

**PHYSICAL DATA:**

1. Condition of health: Good ___ Average ___ Fair___ Color of hair ______ Color of eyes ______
2. Weight________ Height _________ Build ______________ 3. Vision ________________
4. Do you have any physical disability that might interfere with, or be aggravated by, your work? If so, explain ________________________________________________
5. Do you have: Hay fever ________ Asthma ________ Allergies (list) ________________

   Stomach disorders _______ Colds _______ Headaches _______ Other ______________
6. Date of last blood test ______________ Reason ______________________________
7. List any serious illness, operations, accidents, or nervous disorders you have had in the last five years, with approximate dates of occurrence ________________________________
8. Do you drink alcoholic beverages? __________ How many drinks per week? ____________
9. Do you smoke? _______________ How many packs per day? ______________________
10. Do you take part in the recreational use of drugs or narcotics? ______ If yes, what kinds? _____ ________________________________________ How often? ______________

**EDUCATION:**

1. Indicate highest grade completed:
   High school 1 2 3 4; College 1 2 3 4 5 6 7 8 Grade average ______________
   (e.g.,2.5/4 or 3.6/5)
2. Number in high school graduating class _______________ Class standing ______________
   School ____________________________________________________________
3. Favorite high school subjects ________________________________________________
4. Least-liked high school subjects ____________________________________________
5. Extracurricular activities ____________________________________________________
6. Class offices held ________________________________________________________
7. College(s) attended ______________________________________________________
8. Major field(s) __________________________________________________________
9. Subjects least liked ______________________________________________________
10. Degree(s) awarded ______________________________________________________
11. Other education; specify __________________________________________________
12. If you type, indicate speed __________ 13. Other skills, specify ___________________

**Page 4**

## ACTIVITIES:

1. Membership in civic, professional, or social organizations ____________________
______________________________________________
2. Hobbies and interests ______________________________
3. In what additional activities would you like to engage? ____________________
______________________________________________
4. What type of vacation do you prefer? ____________________
______________________________________________

## U.S. SERVICE EXPERIENCE:

1. If in the service, indicate: Branch ______________________
   Date entered ____________________ Date discharged ____________________
2. Service overseas? ____________________ Highest rank or grade ____________________
3. Type of discharge ____________________ Terminal rank or grade ____________________
4. What did you gain from the service that was worthwhile? ____________________
______________________________________________

## BUSINESS EXPERIENCE:

(Please start with your present position; if not currently employed, give last date of employment)

____________________
Soc. Sec. Number

I. 1. Firm ____________________ Address ____________________
2. Title ____________________ Nature of work____________________ No. supervised __________
3. Kind of business ____________________ Date began ____________________
4. Immediate superior ____________________ 5. Salary ____________________
6. What do you most like about your job? ____________________
______________________________________________
7. What do you least enjoy? ____________________
8. Reasons for leaving ____________________

Other Positions Held:

| | Name of Company | Type of Work | Date Began | Date Left | Reasons for Leaving |
|---|---|---|---|---|---|
| II. | | | | | |
| III. | | | | | |
| IV. | | | | | |

I HEREBY AFFIRM that I have read the instructions and the foregoing questions and that my answers to them are true and correct, and that I have not knowingly withheld any fact or circumstance that would, if disclosed, affect my application unfavorably.

____________________
Signature

## Project 6–3 • "Please Be Seated . . ." The Interview

In Project 6–2 you completed the first bit of paperwork as part of applying for the job opening. In this project, you will be interviewed for the position, with your instructor or another faculty member assuming the role of interviewer.

The interview will be held on a day and at an hour set by your instructor. Since the interview will be held in the classroom and in front of the members of your group, the setting will not be realistic nor ideal. However, members of your group will be able to study the interview process and the roles of the applicant and the interviewer, and to critically evaluate the procedure. (Your instructor may decide to videotape the interview for viewing and critiquing at a later time.) More important, you will gain added experience in putting yourself at ease before the interviewer and the group as you assume the role of job applicant.

**Directions:**

(a) *For the student to be interviewed:*

1. Prepare to put your best foot forward during the mock interview, just the same as if you were "doing it for real."

2. Dress the part. Although beards, mustaches, jeans, sweaters, and gym shoes do not mean automatic rejection when applying for a job, the firm for which you may want to work will have its own dress standards. Play it safe and dress the part until you land the job and find out what the dress code is from the employee handbook or from other workers. For the interview, women should consider a skirt and blouse, a dress, or a suit. Men, when applying for an office position, wear a tie with a sports jacket or suit.

3. Make sure that your fingernails are clean and neatly trimmed and that your hair (long or short) is well groomed. Women, hold back on the make-up—you are applying for an office position, not for the starring role in a cabaret!

4. An initial flurry of butterflies is to be expected, but try to appear at ease. When you sit down, use the entire chair seat—not just the front edge. Let your body language speak, at times, by slightly bending forward. Remember that you are an invited guest in the interviewer's office and that while you are seeking a job, the interviewer is seeking an employee.

5. Look directly at your interviewer—not out the window, down at the floor, or at a painting on the wall.

6. Speak slowly and distinctly, carefully weighing your words.

7. Sell yourself—your skills, abilities, and your ideas. Don't undersell or oversell yourself! You have prepared yourself for this position, and you are now in the marketplace competing with others. You stand ready to accept as much money for your services as you can for what you bring to the prospective employer. The value that you place upon yourself will very likely be the value that others put on you.

(b) *For the students evaluating the interview process:* Use the checklist on pages 63 and 64 to aid you in recording your impressions of the interview and the overall ability of the job applicant to put his or her best foot forward and land that job.

## STUDENT REPORT OF INTERVIEW

Name of job applicant ______________________________ Date ____________________

Candidate for ______________________________
(Job Title)

Interviewer ______________________________

*Instructions:* Record your impression of the interview by checking the appropriate statement under each of the factors to be evaluated.

1. **APPEARANCE**

____ Very well groomed; neat; outstanding taste in dress.

____ Good taste in dress; above average appearance.

____ Satisfactory personal appearance.

____ A little careless about personal appearance; somewhat untidy.

2. **FRIENDLINESS**

____ Distant and aloof.

____ Warm; friendly; sociable.

____ Very sociable and outgoing.

____ Extremely friendly and sociable.

3. **POISE**

____ Exceptionally well composed; seems to thrive under pressure.

____ About as poised as an average applicant.

____ Somewhat tense; seems easily irritated.

____ Very ill at ease; "jumpy" and appears nervous.

4. **ABILITY TO CONVERSE**

____ Average fluency and expression.

____ Talks well and "to the point."

____ Excellent expression; exceptionally fluent; forceful.

____ Talks very little; poor expression.

5. **INFORMATION ABOUT FIELD OF WORK**

____ Excellent knowledge of field.

____ Fairly well informed; knows more than average applicant.

____ Fair knowledge of field.

____ Poor knowledge of field.

6. **EXPERIENCE**

____ Little, if any, relationship between applicant's background and requirements of job.

____ Average amount of background and experience.

____ A very good background; considerable experience.

____ Excellent background and experience.

7. **DRIVE**

____ Seems to set high goals and strives to achieve these.

____ Has poorly defined goals; seems to act without purpose.

____ Appears to have average goals and puts forth average effort to attain them.

____ Seems to strive hard and has high desire to achieve.

8. **OVERALL IMPRESSION**

____ Outstanding.

____ Definitely above average.

____ Average.

____ Substandard; definitely unsatisfactory.

Would you hire the applicant? Yes _______________ No _________________

What recommendations can you offer to the applicant to improve his or her "interviewability?"

## Project 6–4 • Back to That Application

Congratulations to you! You landed the position with the Headley Company. As the weeks pass by, you think back to the application you completed in Project 6–2.

**Directions:** Take another look at the application on pages 58 to 61, inspecting line by line each bit of information that the company has asked you. List below each of the inquiries that you believe constitutes an unlawful inquiry as determined by the courts, the EEOC, and your state or local fair employment practices agency.

## Project 6–5 • Computer Hands-On: Writing a Help-Wanted Ad

As a result of the growth in sales for the Headley Company, you find it necessary to employ an assistant who will aid you by shouldering some of the office responsibility—reprographics, micrographics, word processing, and records management. As you reflect on the kind of person you seek, these thoughts run through your mind:

"I want a young person, aged 25 through 30, someone 'who is with it' and 'has his or her head on straight.' I don't want an old-timer who is too set in his or her ways. But, of course, I do want experience—at least two years of supervisory work in office services.

"I can probably best work with someone of my own sex, but I won't get uptight about that point—I'm looking for a qualified assistant, not for a male or a female. Someone told me—I don't recall who—to steer away from divorced persons, for they are not dependable or stable.

"Looking around our offices, I see that we have few workers from any of the minority groups—guess I had better make a big push to bring in a minority worker. Let's see, my budget for next year will allow me to offer $20,500 to the right person."

**Directions:** Use your word processing software to compose and print out a help-wanted ad that will excite the interest and spark the imagination of the very person you are searching for! Make sure that your completed ad complies with the law and in no way will bring forth a complaint from the local EEOC.

## Project 6–6 • Which Fork Do I Use?

Ever think that your interview for that new job might take place over luncheon in a chic restaurant? Or on a new job, you are faced with "wining and dining" your first client? The following article is offered as a change in pace—no questions for you to answer—and to pass along a few etiquette pointers.

Barbara Regina surveyed the forks and knives and spoons at her place setting. Shiny and silvery, perfectly aligned, they reflected the low, romantic light of the dining room.

There were eight pieces, and as she looked around the room, which held 24 identical settings at three tables, she thought back to the last time she saw so much silverware.

"In a dishwasher," she said.

Obviously, Regina does not often find herself all dressed up in an elegant place like the Regency Room of the Radnor Hotel, in St. Davids.

But that's just where she and 18 other seniors from Cabrini College were last night, taking part in a unique business class—unique, that is, to every student who has never taken notes while eating cornbread oysters, mixed wild greens, pecan crusted catfish, and, for dessert, creme caramel.

The sumptuous meal, explained professor John Heiberger, was to give students a taste, so to speak, of what it's like to dine in a fancy place with an employer, or a client. The dinner included speakers who discussed everything from where a woman should put her pocketbook to what wines go with what foods.

"The thrust is to make them comfortable so they're not threatened or worried about 'Am I using the right fork?' and can't get to the business they're there for," said Heiberger, who was presiding over his fourth formal dinner.

"We want them comfortable with the dining experience so they can concentrate on getting the job, or selling the product, or explaining to a client the services they need."

The idea for the meal grew out of conversations Heiberger had with graduating seniors a few years ago. Heiberger posed this question: What do you wish you knew that you didn't get in class?

"One of the fellows who had an internship said he was uncomfortable entertaining clients in a dining situation," Heiberger said. "Other students said they had the same experience during job interviews."

Students this year had the same concerns.

"I'm not uncomfortable in this setting now," said Stacey Conesky, who, at one point last night, found it necessary to admonish table mate Joyce Talotta for taking the wrong roll. "But I don't know how I'd feel in a corporate atmosphere."

Students learned how to properly eat their rolls ("Never slice it, but tear small pieces off"); when to put their napkins on their laps ("As soon as you sit down"); and what foods to stay away from.

"Unless you're really good with spaghetti," said Heiberger, "don't order it. And men, if you have beards or mustaches, don't get ribs, because you'll have barbecue sauce hanging down from your fuzzy stuff. Order food that's easy to handle."

Heiberger emphasized that the meal was not solely a quickie course in etiquette or gourmet dining.

Equally important, he said, was helping students who are about to enter the real world avoid some potentially sticky situations.

Suppose, for instance, that during a job interview, the waiter asks if you would like a drink. Without knowing if the company has a policy against drinking during business hours, what do you do?

"You turn to the host and say, 'What are you going to have?'" said Heiberger. "If he says iced tea, you should have something similar. On the other hand, if the host has six martinis, don't do that. But it's OK to have one."

Likewise, said Heiberger, there are times when a host has to tactfully get the message to a client that he or she has had too much to drink. Blurting out "you miserable lush" is considered bad business practice in most professional circles.

"It's kind of insulting to say, 'You've had too much to drink,'" said Heiberger. "But you're also concerned about the client being intoxicated. So when the waiter comes over and asks if you want more to drink, you quickly say, 'No thanks, we've had enough. We'd like coffee.'"

Menu interpretation was also offered last night. If, for instance, you like chicken but don't know the difference between cordon bleu and Pepe Le Pew, simply ask the waiter, "How is it prepared?" Usually the answer will give a pretty good clue to the ingredients.

"The whole business of certain decorum during meals is becoming more important," said Heiberger, "particularly with international business."

If that's the case, though, Christopher Cirino probably deserved to flunk. After studying his menu, he had just one question.

"Where," he asked, "are the nachos?"

## Project 6–7 • Field Research: Determining the Access to Your Office by Applicants and Employees with Disabilities

In this project, you will evaluate your own office or one selected by your instructor to determine its accessibility by a job applicant or an employee who has a disability. The article includes a checklist that may be used by companies to determine how well they meet the requirements of the Americans with Disabilities Act (ADA) by providing barrier-free environments.

**Directions:** After you read the article, determine to what extent the office environment is barrier-free by completing the checklist provided. Your instructor may ask you to bring your findings together as part of an oral or written report.

Countless areas must be considered to make a building's design as functional as possible. As ADA takes effect, businesses will be including barrier-free access among those considerations because employers must make reasonable accommodations for applicants and employees with disabilities.

Companies should not view ADA as a measure that applies only to a small group of people, but rather as an inclusive measure that seeks to provide comfortable and responsive spaces for the entire workforce population. The spirit of the law is that equal opportunity and access should be available to everyone and become the rule, not the exception. This is the idea behind universal design.

Criteria used to determine office layout and design, furniture purchases and emergency evacuation procedures will have to be redesigned in terms of equal access. Effective this month [July, 1992], companies with 25 or more employees cannot discriminate against any qualified individual with a disability. In 1994, the provisions of the law will broaden to include companies with 15 or more employees. Anyone who works in government offices is familiar with barrier-free design because the Rehabilitation

Act of 1973 has required total accessibility.

Companies can derive a number of benefits from barrier-free design. As the skilled U.S. workforce shrinks, competition for skilled workers will be fierce. One way to attract and retain a competitive workforce is to eliminate physical barriers that unnecessarily narrow the pool of prospective employees.

According to the Census Bureau, 16.7 percent of the U.S. population has a physical or mental impairment. Because of the 1975 Education for All Handicapped Children Act, which mandated that all children receive a free, appropriate public education regardless of the severity of a disability, thousands of students with disabilities were educated and trained.

A poll conducted by Louis Harris and Associates, however, revealed that 70 percent of working-age people with disabilities are unemployed. Of those, 66 percent said they want to work but are prevented from doing so. Offices with barrier-free design not only provide an environment where these people can work, but also increase the number of skilled workers from which an employer can choose.

Another skilled group that barrier-free design supports is the elderly. An increasing number of Americans are 65 years of age or older. As people get older, they often acquire some physical limitations. Barrier-free office design will help keep this knowledgeable and experienced group of people in the available workforce.

Barrier-free design also can have a positive impact on your company's current employees. For instance, providing highly adjustable furniture that meets the needs of employees with disabilities, such as articulating chairs and flexible keyboard trays for computer users, can benefit all workers by allowing them to adjust the components of the workstation to suit their individual dimensions. The result will be more comfortable and productive employees.

Consider the number of people who suffer from temporary disabilities—a broken arm, a twisted ankle, a viral infection that causes loss of hearing. These typical situations can cause productivity to falter or even come to a halt if that employee cannot function in the work environment. Barrier-free design will help cut down on absences or slowdowns in work caused by temporary physical impairments.

Companies that have not considered equal access will need to take steps to ensure compliance with the law. To help companies conform to the provisions of the ADA, the International Facility Management Association suggests taking an audit of your company's facilities and has developed a checklist that companies can use as a preliminary audit to determine accessibility (see box).

Cost is a typical concern generated by these considerations. According to a study done for the U.S. Department of Labor, however, half of the accommodations needed to make offices more accessible cost little or no money at all, and another 30 percent can be accomplished for $100 to $500. In fact, many companies already have these accommodations in place to comply with local fire and safety codes.

In addition, the Internal Revenue Service currently is offering businesses tax incentives of up to $15,000 toward the expenses incurred in removing architectural, transportation, or communication barriers in facilities owned or leased for use in trade or business. A new provision allows eligible small businesses to take a credit for 50 percent of the modification costs, up to $5,000, for removing barriers. In the long run, the benefits of a barrier-free environment far outweigh the costs involved.

## IS YOUR OFFICE BARRIER-FREE?

[ ] Do the restrooms have at least one stall that is wheelchair accessible?

[ ] Are restroom sinks and towel dispensers accessible?

[ ] In addition to stairs, is there a ramp or alternative access to the building lobby?

[ ] Does your company have telecommunications equipment for visually impaired or hearing-impaired personnel?

[ ] Is the majority of the building accessible via wheelchair?

[ ] Are the door entrances wide enough to accommodate wheelchairs?

[ ] Are light switches, power outlets, work surfaces, copy machines, drinking fountains, etc. within reach from a wheelchair?

[ ] Is the cafeteria accessible to workers with disabilities?

[ ] Do emergency evacuation procedures take into consideration employees with disabilities?

Source: *International Facility Management Association.*

# 7

# SUPERVISING THE OFFICE STAFF

Even though they are very diverse, all office workers share pretty much the same needs—for affection, acceptance, recognition, a sense of belonging, and a sense of achievement. An office supervisor must be sensitive to their needs, since an insight into their needs and abilities earns big dividends—the right to be known as and to be perceived as a *leader*.

As a coach, the office supervisor directs the team toward its goal and keeps the members working together as a cohesive unit. In other words, the office supervisor must be both *goal* oriented and *team* oriented if he or she is to pass the ultimate test of leadership: *effectiveness in getting the job done.*

In working with and through the office force to reach mutually established goals, the office supervisor keeps people informed about what is going on in the office, delegates commensurate responsibilities and authorities to qualified subordinates so that they may become empowered in their jobs, sets an example with a display of enthusiasm and energy, recognizes and rewards good work, sees that all workers are treated as fairly and objectively as possible, maintains ethical standards that he or she wants to see reflected in subordinates, and, above all, possesses a sense of humor.

## SECTION A • REVIEW QUESTIONS

**Directions:** In the Answers column, write the letter of the item in Column 1 that is described by each statement in Column 2.

**Column 1**

**A** Attitude survey
**B** Climate survey
**C** Discipline
**D** Diverse workforce
**E** Empowerment
**F** Ethics
**G** Job Enrichment
**H** Morale
**I** Theory X
**J** Theory Y
**K** Theory Z
**L** Value system

| **Column 2** | **Answers** |
|---|---|
| 1. The view of worker behavior in which workers are seen as willing to work and accept responsibility, capable of self-direction and self-control, and able to use their imagination and originality .... | 1. ______ |
| 2. The mental and emotional attitudes of persons toward the tasks expected of them by their group and their loyalty to that group ... | 2. ______ |
| 3. The teaching or molding of employees in a constructive and consistent manner so that they may learn to change their behavior and performance in the future .......................... | 3. ______ |
| 4. A technique of increasing employee participation by delegating to them the authority to act and to make decisions on their own ..... | 4. ______ |
| 5. The systematic study of that part of science and philosophy dealing with moral conduct, duty, and judgment .............. | 5. ______ |
| 6. A two-way feedback process in which superiors and subordinates provide for interpersonal exchange of opinions ............... | 6. ______ |
| 7. The sum of one's moral and social perception of those things that are intrinsically desirable or valuable ...................... | 7. ______ |
| 8. The redesigning of a job by building in higher-order responsibilities and authorities and more challenging content ............ | 8. ______ |
| 9. Employees who differ in gender, age, race, culture, religion, education, lifestyle, sexual orientation, etc. .................... | 9. ______ |
| 10. A polling of workers to determine their moods and feelings toward supervisory treatment, salaries and employee benefits, their jobs, and the firm ................................ | 10. ______ |

**Directions:** Indicate your answer to each of the following questions by circling "Yes" or "No" in the Answers column.

| Question | Answers | |
|---|---|---|
| 1. Is it projected that by the year 2005, the number of women in the labor force will have increased more than the number of men? | Yes | No |
| 2. Does true discipline *correct* at the same time it *teaches*? | Yes | No |
| 3. In a system of progressive disciplinary action, is a written reprimand usually the first action taken? | Yes | No |
| 4. Does an employee assistance program (EAP) provide specially trained persons who diagnose and offer help in solving employees' personal problems? | Yes | No |
| 5. Once the primary needs of a worker have been satisfied, do they continue to motivate that worker? | Yes | No |
| 6. In his hierarchy of needs, did Maslow classify *the desire for affection* as a primary need? | Yes | No |
| 7. Does Herzberg look upon an office worker's salary as a motivator factor? | Yes | No |
| 8. Does Herzberg's motivation-maintenance theory state that the factors which cause employee dissatisfaction are the same as those which cause employee satisfaction? | Yes | No |
| 9. Do some supervisors fail to delegate because of their basic psychological feelings of fear and insecurity? | Yes | No |
| 10. Are supervisors operating under Theory X usually found in authoritarian organizations? | Yes | No |
| 11. According to McGregor's Theory Y view of worker behavior, does the average person prefer to be directed and thus avoid responsibility? | Yes | No |
| 12. Is participative management put into practice when subordinates accept responsibility for the work delegated to them? | Yes | No |
| 13. Is the structure of American society sufficiently similar to that of the Japanese so that Japanese management practices may be easily adopted by American firms? | Yes | No |
| 14. Are the ethics of employees related to their religious convictions and personal philosophies? | Yes | No |
| 15. Should inspiration for ethical behavior originate at the top level of management? | Yes | No |
| 16. Do attitude surveys and climate surveys aid supervisors in learning what employees expect from their jobs? | Yes | No |

## SECTION B • PROJECTS

### Project 7–1 • Computer Hands-On: An In-Basket Problem

This in-basket problem is a variation of the traditional case problem. Here, you are placed in a realistic, stressful position where you simulate the role of an office manager (Ann Hope) in solving office problems that arise during your absence from the office and at the time of your superior's death. The problem consists of letters, memos, and notes sent you and your superior while you have been out of the office. You will analyze each letter or memo and then decide the appropriate action to take. Finally, you will present to your class, as a printout, the specific actions you have taken.

Your instructor may assign the in-basket problem to you individually or to teams in your class. The challenge is to do a top-notch job of decision making in the time allotted. If a team approach is used, another goal is to compete with the other teams in relation to the quality of decisions made under the pressure of time. Your instructor will serve as judge and announce the winning team.

**Directions:**

1. Read the following company background and become familiar with the company's organization chart shown on page 72.
2. At this point, your instructor will give you the procedures to follow and inform you of the time allotted for completing the problem.
3. Now that it has been decided whether you will tackle the in-basket problem individually or in teams, closely read the following instructions:

   a. It is Saturday evening, June 15, and you (Ann Hope) have just flown back to your city from an unexpected trip to one of the branch offices. At the airport, you are met by the company president, Lori Franck, who tells you that Todd Nelson, the vice president of administrative operations, underwent open-heart surgery that morning and died in the operating room.

   b. While driving you to your apartment, Franck remarks that she wants you to step in and take over Nelson's post, but she is aware that you are booked on an overseas flight at 8 a.m. Monday for a well-earned *three weeks' vacation.* Your first thought is: "There go Vienna, Paris, and Amsterdam." But Franck insists that you go ahead with your vacation plans. She does ask, however, that you come into the office tomorrow morning and go over several pressing items of business lying on Nelson's desk.

   c. The following morning—Sunday—you arrive at the office, sit down behind Nelson's desk, and stare into space—thinking about his jovial personality, family, and love for life. Then you are jolted back into reality as you begin to sift through the stack of letters and memos in Nelson's in-basket—items that require your immediate attention—*today*—so that you can leave with a "clear conscience" tomorrow morning. Nelson's secretary, Michael Fox, has also placed on the desk some memos addressed to you.

   d. *No one but you is in the office. The switchboard is closed over the weekend. Fox has locked all of Nelson's confidential office files.*

4. You may want to print out a copy of the letters and memos on template file PO7-1.TEM before proceeding. Take whatever action you deem appropriate for each item. *Every action* that you or your team wishes to take should be written down, or keyed in, including memos to Fox and to yourself (Hope), using your word processing software. When appropriate, draft letters and memos, agendas for meetings or conferences, etc., that you plan. If you are solving the problem as part of a team, each of you will be joining forces and using your combined experiences in assuming the role of Hope.

## Company Background

Franck's, a manufacturer of cosmetics, has its home offices in your city. In the home offices, there are 150 office employees and 840 workers in the manufacturing, assembly, and shipping departments. Each of the branch offices in Albany, Chicago, and Houston has a staff of five to six office employees and 15 to 20 workers in the shipping department. In charge of each branch office is a branch sales manager, who has jurisdiction over 8 to 10 sales representatives who call on wholesalers and retail outlets. Shipments are made from each of the branch offices and the home office. Each branch office handles its own processing of orders. The information contained on all shipping orders is transmitted daily to the home office, which handles all billing. All requests for credit approval from the branch offices are handled in the home office by the credit manager, Ricardo Fuentes.

In addition to about 200 orders that are processed daily in the home office, data contained on 600 to 750 shipping orders are received from the branch offices. Thus, an average of 800 shipping orders are verified for stock numbers, description, and unit price daily in the home office. Presently, all invoices are completed on printers attached to microcomputers, which are operated by 10 data-entry personnel. On some occasions, such as during the rush season, the lag between shipping date and invoice preparation may exceed one workweek.

The order processing and billing is under the supervision of Susan Renz, a conscientious, faithful employee who has been with the company 30 years. Renz is often looked upon by the data-entry operators as a tough supervisor, but one whom they all respect and admire for her loyalty and drive. She prides herself on the meticulous care with which each order is processed and each invoice is printed out. She has often told the operators, "We may not get all the orders out today, but we know they'll be 100 percent correct!"

The word processing center answers all correspondence from customers in the several states serviced by the home office. The center also follows up on all correspondence and salespersons' contacts, forwarded from the branch offices.

Franck's has a small business computer, which was bought five years ago. Magnetic disks, a by-product of the computer operations, are used primarily for stock control and inventory purposes. For each item listed on a sales invoice, the disks contain the customer's account number, date of sale, stock number, units sold, and amount of sale. After the information on the disks has been processed by the computer, sales reports are analyzed by branch office, by stock number, and by sales representative. Disks are also prepared as part of processing the biweekly paychecks for employees in the home office and the branch offices and weekly paychecks for employees in the plant. After the paychecks are printed out on the computer and signed, they are hand-distributed to employees in the home office and mailed by overnight express to employees in the branch offices.

All sales promotion literature—brochures, flyers, catalogs, price lists, broadsides—is mailed from the home office. Direct-mail pieces may amount to as many as 20,000 each month. The database for all past, present, and prospective customers is stored on a magnetic disk that serves as input to the small business computer for

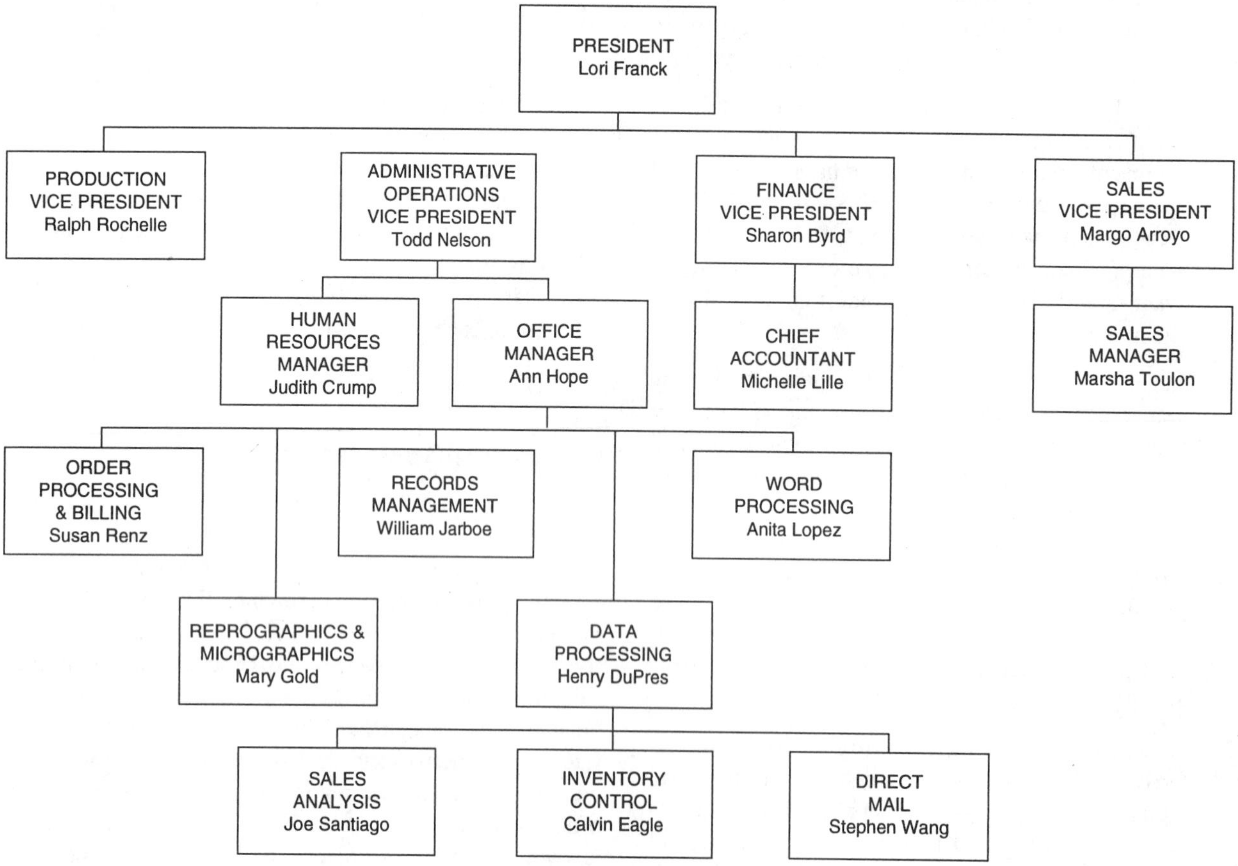


**Figure 7–1 Partial Organization Chart for Franck's**

preparing address labels. Customer information is coded numerically by each branch office and the home office territory so that, as needed, specialized geographic mailings may be made.

At the present time, five persons work in the mail room keeping the customers' address file up to date, attaching the address labels, and sorting the bulk mailings by ZIP Code numbers. The department is supervised by Stephen Wang, age 60, who has established a warm relationship with his subordinates. Due to his failing eyesight, many errors creep past Wang; but management is reluctant to dismiss him because of his long and faithful service to the company. He is one of the few workers who has been with the firm since its establishment. The mailings are characterized by numerous errors such as wrong street addresses and box numbers, incorrect spellings, and incorrect ZIP Code numbers. Speaking of the ZIP + 4 Codes, Wang has been heard to say, "What is this world coming to? Pretty soon I'll have to apply six months in advance for a number on my casket. Why all these numbers, I don't know . . . ."

## Project 7–2 • What Is Your Leadership Style? Your Followership Style?

The questionnaire on pages 77 and 78 has proven to be a very valuable training and learning device for supervisors in helping them think about the various dimensions of their management styles. It has been used within the context of consulting practice, classroom training, and throughout a series of management training seminars. The questionnaire is easily self-administered, self-scored, and self-interpreted within a 15- to 20-minute time period. As you will see in the Scoring and Interpretation section of the form on page 78, your score will enable you to identify your leadership and followership styles on the range *Very Autocratic to Very Democratic.*

## Project 7–3 • How Safe Is My Job?

Within the following article written in 1990, you will find a quiz that provides an idea about your job security. Although the quiz is several years old and claims no scientific basis, you will gain an opportunity to examine your job in the way your employer does.

How safe is my job?

For many people, that's *the* issue of the 1990s. It's becoming clear that corporate cutbacks weren't an '80s oddity, but rather are likely to persist through the new decade. So far this year, by one estimate, U.S. employers have been trimming 30,000 people from their payrolls—*a month.*

Today's edgy employees can get some clue about how secure their jobs are by taking the quiz offered here. It was developed by exploring both those factors that have determined just who has been laid off in the past and the outlook for specific jobs, career paths and industries with a number of academics, consultants, and corporate executives.

A high tally on this unscientific quiz (on which possible scores range from 24 to zero) shouldn't prompt people to start cleaning out their desks. Paul Hirsch, a professor at Northwestern University's Kellogg School of Management, notes that in any cutback, "more people are scared than wind up getting hurt. Whenever 10% get cut, 90% worry that it will happen to them."

Further, a company's particular style of treating employees—whether paternalistic, coldblooded or in between—will be a factor. "You might come up with all the right answers," says Robert Tomasko, a consultant with Arthur D. Little Inc. and author of a book on corporate cutbacks. "But you can't assume your company is acting rationally."

Still, the answers provide clues to help people look at their jobs the way their bosses do.

### Test Yourself

1. **What industry is your company in?**
2. **How big is your company, in annual sales?**
   Large: over $500 million
   Medium: $50 million to $500 million
   Small: under $50 million
3. **Has your company's market share or revenue declined recently?**
4. **What region do you work in?**
   Northeast
   South/Southwest
   Midwest
   West
5. **Has your company pared staff before?**
6. **What kind of job do you have?**
   Senior management
   Middle management
   Supervisory
7. **If a supervisor or manager, how many people report to you?**
   Zero to two
   Three to seven
   Eight or more
8. **Can your job be done more cheaply by outsiders?**
9. **Do you have contact with customers?**
10. **How old are you?**
    Under 30
    30 to 39
    40 to 49
    50 or older
11. **How have your performance reviews rated in recent years?**
    Excellent
    Good
    Satisfactory
    Poor
12. **Are your skills flexible?**

### Scoring the Results

1. **Industry:** *Score a point for financial-services industries such as banking, brokerage, and insurance companies.*

These, says Mr. Tomasko of Arthur D. Little, are the industries most prone to cutbacks in the early 1990s, along with utilities, local telephone companies, consumer goods makers (still takeover candidates), defense contractors (hurt by spending cutbacks) and retailers. Score a point for all of these fields.

Give yourself a zero if you are in an industry less likely to cut back, including heavy manufacturers such as machine-tool companies, which already cut heavily in the '80s.

2. **Size:** *Score two points if your employer is a large company, one if medium-sized, and zero if small.*

"In general, the bigger the company, the more likely it is to be cutting," says Dan Lacey of Lacey & Co., consultants. An American Management Association survey of personnel managers at more than 1,200 companies with annual sales exceeding $500 million showed that these companies plan staff cuts; fewer than 10% of companies with under $10 million in sales reported such plans.

3. **Market share:** *Count three points for a recent big drop in market share.*

"Market share was probably the most prevalent reason" for staff cuts in the '80s, says Aneil Mishra, a research associate working on a continuing University of Michigan study of 30 automotive suppliers. Even within individual companies, units with poorer market-share performance were "much more aggressive" in cutting staff, he says.

4. **Location:** *Score two points if your job is in the Northeast, one for the Midwest, and zero for the South or West.*

In the past three years, "the big unemployment increases have been largely in the Northeast; the big employment increases have been largely in the West," says Samuel Ehrenhalt, Northeast regional commissioner for the Bureau of Labor Statistics. He notes that New York dropped to No. 45 among states in job growth last year from No. 27 in 1987. In the past three years, the bottom 10 states for job growth have included New Jersey, Pennsylvania, Massachusetts, and Connecticut. Over the same time, Idaho, Washington, Oregon, and Utah all climbed into the top 10.

5. **History:** *Give yourself two points if your company has already had early retirement or layoff programs, zero if it hasn't.*

If you think you're safe because your company has made cuts, think again. The recent American Management Association study concluded that "the best predictor of future work-force cuts was past work-force cuts," says Eric Greenberg, editor of the study. Of companies that had cut staff in the past, he says, 29% planned to do so again; of companies that had never cut staff, only 7% planned future cuts.

6. **Type of job:** *Point scores depend on individual factors.*

If your company recently has faced, or faces, a leveraged buy-out or merger, give yourself a point if you're a senior manager or supervisor. "The highest executives are vulnerable in a company that is being bought out," says James Buttimer, director of organizational planning at Arthur D. Little. And, he advises, don't be reassured by a friendly takeover team: "Watch what they do, not what they say."

But where staff cuts reflect the need to cut costs, Mr. Buttimer says, middle managers are more vulnerable. Give yourself a point there.

In any case, holders of staff jobs should give themselves two points. When outplacement firm Drake Beam Morin Co. studied displaced managers over the last three years, they found that nearly 30% were from general management or administration; an additional 16% had finance or accounting backgrounds.

7. **Number of subordinates:** *Tally two points if you have fewer than three people reporting directly to you; one point for three to seven subordinates; and zero for more than eight, because cost-cutting companies try to squeeze more managing from fewer managers.*

Today, an average manager supervises 3.5 workers, down from about 10 in the '60s, says Jewell Westerman, a vice president with consultants Temple, Barker & Sloane Inc. But today, he says, companies are trying to increase that number. Phillips Petroleum Co., for example, cut its management costs to 28 cents a payroll dollar from 30 cents by moving to one manager per 7.3 people from one per 5.8 in 1983, says Jerry D. Fultz, manager of employee relations.

8. **Dispensability:** *If outside contractors can do your job better than you, give yourself three points; if not, score a zero.*

Employers are making tough make-or-buy decisions about nearly everything they do. Mr. Tomasko suggests asking yourself: "If they had to go outside and buy what I do, would they do it—and would they pay enough for it to cover my salary?"

9. **Customer contact:** *Give yourself two points if you*

*never deal with the outside world, zero if you do.*

Many companies, such as International Business Machines Corp., are shifting their focus from managing to meeting customers. At American Telephone & Telegraph Co., "the Maalox moments are if you have little to do with sales or with the public," says Burke Stinson, a spokesman. AT&T is cutting 6,000 positions at its long-distance unit. "There's quite often a battalion of people who . . . do little else than meet with other in-house people in a series of meetings, essentially writing memos to themselves," Mr. Stinson says. "If you are in one of those jobs, you may be able to duck attention for a while, but you may not be able to do it forever."

10. **Age:** *Give yourself a point if you're a man over 40 or a woman over 30; otherwise, score a zero.*

The Drake Beam Morin survey found that in the three years ended June 11, the bulk of men displaced—47%—were 40 to 49 years old. For women, the largest age group—44%—was 30 to 39. Low seniority also mattered: More than 60% had been with their companies for less than 20 years, three-quarters for less than 15 years.

11. **Performance reviews:** *Everyone gets a zero on this one.*

"Performance reviews are more irrelevant than relevant," says Mr. Tomasko of Arthur D. Little. One reason is their unreliability. "They are too lenient," says Craig Schneier, a managing director of consultants Sibson & Co. "Everyone is rated too high."

Companies in the University of Michigan study found that as a result, the number of marginal performers identified was small, while "the sheer numbers of people they needed to get rid of was so great" says Mr. Mishra. So, they had to abandon using performance reviews as a criterion.

12. **Flexibility:** *Give yourself a zero if you're confident of your ability to take new jobs, or willing to move to new places. Add one point if you can't relocate, two points if you consider yourself unlikely to be able to change jobs, or four points if your approach to work is inflexible.*

"The No. 1 skill in the American economy is the ability to adapt to change," says Mr. Ehrenhalt of the Bureau of Labor Statistics.

Companies increasingly cut back in one area while adding employees in others. Moreover, when working with a leaner staff, companies are likely to value switch-hitters more. "When you still have 100% of the work, but only 80% of the workers, you have to appraise who is going to be a helpful survivor," says Norman Abazoris, a partner with Hewitt Associates.

## LEADERSHIP AND FOLLOWERSHIP STYLE TEST

### Structural Leadership Profile

The following twenty statements relate to your ideal image of leadership. We ask that as you respond to them, you imagine yourself to be a leader and then answer the questions in a way that would reflect your particular style of leadership. It makes no difference what kind of leadership experience, if any, you have had or are currently involved in. The purpose here is to establish your ideal preference for relating with subordinates.

The format includes a five point scale ranging from strongly agree to strongly disagree for each statement. Please select one point on each scale and mark it as you read the twenty statements relating to leadership. You may omit answers to questions which are confusing or to questions that you feel you cannot answer.

| | Strongly Agree | Agree | Mixed Feelings | Disagree | Strongly Disagree |
|---|---|---|---|---|---|
| 1. When I tell a subordinate to do something, I expect him/her to do it with no questions asked. After all, I am responsible for what he/she will do, not the subordinate. | (1) | (2) | (3) | (4) | (5) |
| 2. Tight control by a leader usually does more harm than good. People will generally do the best job when they are allowed to exercise self-control. | (5) | (4) | (3) | (2) | (1) |
| 3. Although discipline is important in an organization, the effective leader should mediate the use of disciplinary procedures with his/her knowledge of the people and the situation. | (1) | (2) | (3) | (4) | (5) |
| 4. A leader must make every effort to subdivide the tasks of the people to the greatest possible extent. | (1) | (2) | (3) | (4) | (5) |
| 5. Shared leadership or truly democratic process in a group can only work when there is a recognized leader who assists the process. | (1) | (2) | (3) | (4) | (5) |
| 6. As a leader, I am ultimately responsible for all of the actions of my group. If our activities result in benefits for the organization I should be rewarded accordingly. | (1) | (2) | (3) | (4) | (5) |
| 7. Most persons require only minimum direction on the part of their leader in order to do a good job. | (5) | (4) | (3) | (2) | (1) |
| 8. One's subordinates usually require the control of a strict leader. | (1) | (2) | (3) | (4) | (5) |
| 9. Leadership might be shared among participants of a group so that at any one time there could be two or more leaders. | (5) | (4) | (3) | (2) | (1) |
| 10. Leadership should generally come from the top, but there are some logical exceptions to this rule. | (5) | (4) | (3) | (2) | (1) |
| 11. The disciplinary function of the leader is simply to seek democratic opinions regarding problems as they arise. | (5) | (4) | (3) | (2) | (1) |
| 12. The engineering problems, the management time, and the worker frustration caused by the division of labor are hardly ever worth the savings. In most cases, workers could do the best job of determining their own job content. | (5) | (4) | (3) | (2) | (1) |
| 13. The leader ought to be the group member who the other members elect to coordinate their activities and to represent the group to the rest of the organization. | (5) | (4) | (3) | (2) | (1) |
| 14. A leader needs to exercise some control over his/her people. | (1) | (2) | (3) | (4) | (5) |
| 15. There must be one and only one recognized leader in a group. | (1) | (2) | (3) | (4) | (5) |
| 16. A good leader must establish and strictly enforce an impersonal system of discipline. | (1) | (2) | (3) | (4) | (5) |
| 17. Discipline codes should be flexible, and they should allow for individual decisions by the leader given each particular situation. | (5) | (4) | (3) | (2) | (1) |
| 18. Basically, people are responsible for themselves and no one else. Thus a leader cannot be blamed for or take credit for the work of subordinates. | (5) | (4) | (3) | (2) | (1) |
| 19. The job of the leader is to relate to subordinates the task to be done, to ask them for the ways in which it can best be accomplished, and then to help arrive at a consensus plan of attack. | (5) | (4) | (3) | (2) | (1) |
| 20. A position of leadership implies the general superiority of its incumbent over his/her workers. | (1) | (2) | (3) | (4) | (5) |

## Structural Followership Profile

This section of the questionnaire includes statements about the type of boss which you prefer. Imagine yourself to be in a subordinate position of some kind and use your responses to indicate your preference for the way in which a leader might relate with you. The format will be identical to that within the previous section.

| | Strongly Agree | Agree | Mixed Feelings | Disagree | Strongly Disagree |
|---|---|---|---|---|---|
| 1. I expect my job to be very explicitly outlined for me. | (1) | (2) | (3) | (4) | (5) |
| 2. When the boss says to do something, I do it. After all, he/she is the boss. | (1) | (2) | (3) | (4) | (5) |
| 3. Rigid rules and regulations usually cause me to become frustrated and inefficient. | (5) | (4) | (3) | (2) | (1) |
| 4. I am ultimately responsible for and capable of self-discipline based upon my contacts with the people around me. | (5) | (4) | (3) | (2) | (1) |
| 5. My jobs should be made as short in duration as possible so that I can achieve efficiency through repetition. | (1) | (2) | (3) | (4) | (5) |
| 6. Within reasonable limits, I will try to accommodate requests from persons who are not my boss since these requests are typically in the best interest of the company anyhow. | (5) | (4) | (3) | (2) | (1) |
| 7. When the boss tells me to do something which is the wrong thing to do, it is his/her fault, not mine, when I do it. | (1) | (2) | (3) | (4) | (5) |
| 8. It is up to my leader to provide a set of rules by which I can measure my performance. | (1) | (2) | (3) | (4) | (5) |
| 9. The boss is the boss. And the fact of that promotion suggests that he/she has something on the ball. | (1) | (2) | (3) | (4) | (5) |
| 10. I only accept orders from my boss. | (1) | (2) | (3) | (4) | (5) |
| 11. I would prefer my boss to give me general objectives and guidelines and then allow me to do the job my way. | (5) | (4) | (3) | (2) | (1) |
| 12. If I do something which is not right it is my own fault, even if my supervisor told me to do it. | (5) | (4) | (3) | (2) | (1) |
| 13. I prefer jobs which are not repetitious, the kind of task which is new and different each time. | (5) | (4) | (3) | (2) | (1) |
| 14. My supervisor is in no way superior to me by virtue of position. He/she simply does a different kind of job, one which includes a lot of managing and coordinating. | (5) | (4) | (3) | (2) | (1) |
| 15. I expect my leader to give me disciplinary guidelines. | (1) | (2) | (3) | (4) | (5) |
| 16. I prefer to tell my supervisor what I will or at least should be doing. It is I who am ultimately responsible for my own work. | (5) | (4) | (3) | (2) | (1) |

## Scoring and Interpretation

You may score your own leadership and followership styles by simply averaging the numbers which are included in parentheses below your answers to the individual items. For example, if you scored item number one strongly, you will find the point value of "1" below that answer (Leadership Profile). To obtain your overall leadership style, add the numerical values which are associated with the twenty leadership items and divide by twenty. The resulting average is your leadership style. Followership is measured the same way, using the sixteen items contained within Part II of the instrument.

### INTERPRETATIONS

| Score | Description | Leadership Style | Followership Style |
|---|---|---|---|
| Less than 1.9 | Very Autocratic | Boss decides and announces decisions, rules, orientation | Can't function well without programs and procedures. Needs feedback |
| 2.0–2.4 | Moderately Autocratic | Announces decisions but asks for questions, makes exceptions to rules | Needs solid structure and feedback but can also carry on independently |
| 2.5–3.4 | Mixed | Boss suggests ideas and consults group, many exceptions to regulations | Mixture of above and below |
| 3.5–4.0 | Moderately Participative | Group decides on basis of bosses' suggestions, rules are few, group proceeds as they see fit | Independent worker, doesn't need close supervision, just a bit of feedback |
| 4.1 & up | Very Democratic | Group is in charge of decisions: boss is coordinator, group makes any rules | Self-starter, likes to challenge new things by him/herself |

*It should be noted that scores on this instrument will vary depending upon mood and circumstances. Your leadership or followership style is best described by the range of scores from several different test times.

8

# TRAINING, APPRAISING, AND PROMOTING OFFICE PERSONNEL

Many businesses are faced with the problem of recruiting entry-level workers capable of doing the job for which they are interviewed. To alleviate this problem, many firms form partnerships with educational institutions and the community to provide resources to schools so that the students' performances may be improved and economic literacy strengthened. In turn, business expects a trained workforce prepared to adapt to changes in the workplace.

Training, when viewed as the firm's investment in human resources, concerns itself not only with the skills and knowledge to be gained for the immediate situation but also with the attitudes, concepts, and ideas being fostered, which will exert a significant impact upon the employees' working lives in years ahead. Basic to the design and implementation of any training and development program are the principles and findings from learning theory and research. Armed with such concepts, the trainer is able to diagnose, design, and implement the learning strategy, and evaluate and possibly redesign the program.

After the entry-level training has been completed, an ongoing learning and developmental program follows, during which office employees are appraised as to their job performance and promotional potential. An assessment of on-the-job performance and growth should be welcomed by office workers so that if they move up in the firm, they realize they are well prepared for and warrant the promotion.

When appraisal indicates that the office worker is not qualified for the position or is not performing satisfactorily, the person charged with firing the employee should have a well-planned termination procedure to follow. Such a procedure provides a fair hearing during which documentation shows that just cause (job-related, valid reasons) exists for the termination.

## SECTION A • REVIEW QUESTIONS

**Directions:** In the Answers column, write the letter of the item in Column 1 that is described by each statement in Column 2.

**Column 1**

**A** Cross-training
**B** Employee performance appraisal
**C** Entry-level training
**D** Learning
**E** Mentoring
**F** Multimedia
**G** Plateau
**H** Remedial training
**I** Videoconferencing
**J** Virtual reality
**K** Multimedia

| Column 2 | Answers |
|---|---|
| 1. The changes that occur in trainees' behavioral patterns and attitudes as a result of training . . . . . . . . . . | 1. ______ |
| 2. A communication method that uses a combination of audio and video equipment to join two or more distant groups . . . . . . . . . . | 2. ______ |
| 3. Training designed to qualify employees for entry-job assignments . | 3. ______ |
| 4. The study of an employee's traits, personal qualifications, attitudes, and behavior . . . . . . . . . . | 4. ______ |
| 5. Training to remedy or correct deficiencies in work habits, attitudes, knowledge, skills, or job performance . . . . . . . . . . | 5. ______ |
| 6. Training to develop multiskilled workers who can adapt to changes in job requirements and advancing technology and thus become ready to assume more responsible or more demanding positions . . . | 6. ______ |
| 7. A training arrangement whereby senior managers impart their expertise to younger managers and supervisors in the company . . . | 7. ______ |
| 8. A period of time or a level of learning where no observable improvement occurs or where the rate of increase in learning levels off . . . | 8. ______ |
| 9. The combining of audio, video, text, graphics, still images, and animation to present learning materials in a computer-based setting . . | 9. ______ |

**Directions:** Each of the following statements is either true or false. Indicate your choice in the Answers column by circling "T" or "F."

| | Answers |
|---|---|
| 1. The quality of a firm's office training program is greatly influenced by the policies established by top management | T F |
| 2. In large organizations, the responsibility for organizing an effective office training program usually rests solely with a staff assistant | T F |
| 3. It is more difficult to evaluate the effectiveness of a skills training program than a training program designed to improve human relations | T F |
| 4. A trainee may reach a plateau as the result of reduced motivation | T F |
| 5. Reinforcement of learning is ineffective if it occurs too soon after a correct response has been made | T F |
| 6. In many small firms, the responsibility for conducting the training program rests with a first-line supervisor | T F |
| 7. The most common method of training entry-level office employees is job rotation | T F |
| 8. The lecture method is a nonparticipative, one-way communication technique | T F |
| 9. Vestibule training, when contrasted to on-the-job training, is an especially economical method of training office personnel | T F |
| 10. Videoconferencing combines audio and video equipment for communications among two or more distant groups | T F |
| 11. In order for mentoring to operate successfully, the mentor must be carefully matched to the protégé | T F |
| 12. Assessment centers are used to identify managerial talent among workers | T F |
| 13. Employee performance appraisal is a study of the services provided by an employee and an analysis of the job held by that employee | T F |
| 14. Because of its subjective elements, the rating scale is seldom used to evaluate employee performance | T F |
| 15. The simple ranking method of appraising employee performance is most effectively used in offices having at least 50 workers | T F |
| 16. In most companies, the performance of office workers is evaluated once each quarter | T F |
| 17. An office worker's loyalty to the organization and its management is the most important factor to be considered at the time of promotion | T F |
| 18. In a horizontal promotion, a capable worker is transferred to another department where promotional opportunities are greater | T F |
| 19. Employee performance appraisals should provide a tangible basis for terminating unqualified office workers | T F |
| 20. The just-cause standard requires that a job-related, valid reason must exist for a discharge | T F |
| 21. Civil Service rulings and court decisions have strengthened the absolute right of employers to discharge workers without any reason whatsoever | T F |

## SECTION B • PROJECTS

### Project 8–1 • Field Research: The Office Manager's Education and Training

This research project takes you into an office to talk with an officer manager or office supervisor about the kind of formal education and training completed prior to assuming the present position and the extent of additional training provided by the company since the time of employment. Your objective will be to determine where the managerial skills were acquired, the value of on-the-job training for office managers, and the kinds of management courses that have proven beneficial to the worker.

**Directions:** Arrange for an interview with the office manager or an office supervisor in one of the firms in your community. (Or you may wish to talk with the business manager, human resources officer, academic dean, etc., of your college.) After you have fully informed the interviewee about the nature of your visit and the information you are seeking, complete as fully as you can the questionnaire on pages 83 and 84. If several others in your class are assigned this project, combine your findings to see what "patterns" of response, if any, emerge.

### Project 8–2 • On-the Job Training–Role Playing

This project provides an opportunity for you and one of your classmates to take an active part in *role playing*, where you will assume the role of trainer. You will be conducting the first on-the-job training session with one of your office workers—your classmate—on how to operate office equipment.

With the help of your instructor, determine what equipment can be made available for classroom demonstration—typewriter, computer terminal, FAX machine, copier, film projector, overhead projector, dictating equipment, videocassette recorder, and so on. Of course, before you take part in this training session, be sure you are thoroughly acquainted with the equipment and its proper operation.

Select a classmate who will role play with you by assuming the part of a newly employed office worker. The simulation will be more meaningful and realistic if the person selected knows little or nothing about operating the equipment selected. On a day mutually agreeable to you, your "employee," and your instructor, take a few minutes to arrange the classroom furniture and position the equipment to simulate as well as possible an office layout. Have the employee sit at a desk, introduce the employee and yourself, and commence your presentation of how to operate the equipment selected. For the purposes of this simulation, budget your time to allow about 20 to 25 minutes for the training session.

Following your presentation, allow time for your classmates, your employee, and your instructor to "critique" the training session. You may wish to engage in some self-evaluation, too. Here are some questions that might be considered during this critique session:

1. Did the trainer put the office worker at ease and establish rapport before instruction began?
2. Were the overall function and the operation of the equipment explained to the worker before any detailed operating instructions were given?
3. Was use made of the operating manual supplied by the equipment manufacturer?
4. Did the trainer present the task as a whole unit or was the task broken down into steps, with each step clearly presented to the worker?
5. Was the office worker complimented at any time on his or her mastery of a particular operation? Was there any other reinforcement of learning?
6. Were all the necessary training materials made available for use by the worker?
7. Was time allowed for the worker to practice any machine operations that were proving to be especially difficult to learn?
8. What evidence is there that learning took place?

## EDUCATION AND TRAINING QUESTIONNAIRE

Title of Person Interviewed ______________________________

Name of Company ____________________ Years with Company ____________

I. Describe the formal education, training, and career experience completed *before the employee assumed the present position*. Was the career experience as important as, or less important than, the formal management education?

______________________________

______________________________

______________________________

______________________________

II. What formal training was provided by the worker's employer *at the time of assuming the new job?* What was the nature of the training—college or university, mentoring, on-the-job training, etc.? What was the length of the training period?

______________________________

______________________________

______________________________

______________________________

III. Describe the kind of management development program completed by the worker *following the initial job training*. Where was the training offered? What was the length of the management development program? Indicate the specific skills emphasized in the program.

______________________________

______________________________

______________________________

______________________________

IV. Does the worker believe there is a need for the company to provide short courses in managerial skills so that the employee may improve job effectiveness? If so, in what areas—*personal activities* (skills) or *interpersonal activities* (skills)—should the courses be offered?

______________________________

______________________________

______________________________

______________________________

V. To what extent, if any, was the employee exposed to the following motivation theories as part of the management development program?

A. McGregor's Theory X and Theory Y ____________________

B. Maslow's Needs Hierarchy ____________________

C. Herzberg's Satisfiers-Motivators ____________________

D. Other ____________________

VI. Indicate whether or not the worker believes that the company's on-the-job training *alone* is sufficient for each of the following aspects of promotional training:

A. When the person is promoted to a supervisory position . . . . . . . . . . . . . . . . . Yes No
B. When the person is promoted to a senior management position . . . . . . . . . . . Yes No
C. When the person is promoted to a top-management position . . . . . . . . . . . . . Yes No

VII. To what extent were the following training techniques and methods used as part of the management development program? How useful was the kind of training in preparing the employee for daily managerial practice?

A. Role playing________________________________________
B. In-basket training ____________________________________
C. Case studies________________________________________
D. Assessment center ____________________________________
E. Other ______________________________________________

VIII. Indicate for each of the following courses whether or not it was completed by the employee and whether it was "Very Useful" or "Of Little Use" in preparation for daily management practice:

| Course | Completed Yes | Completed No | Very Useful | Of Little Use |
|---|---|---|---|---|
| A. Accounting: | | | | |
| 1. Principles . . . . . . . . . . . . . . . . . . . . . . . . | | | | |
| 2. Intermediate . . . . . . . . . . . . . . . . . . . . . | | | | |
| 3. Cost . . . . . . . . . . . . . . . . . . . . . . . . . . . | | | | |
| 4. Auditing . . . . . . . . . . . . . . . . . . . . . . . | | | | |
| 5. Other ____________________ | | | | |
| B. Management: | | | | |
| 1. Office . . . . . . . . . . . . . . . . . . . . . . . . . | | | | |
| 2. Human Resources or Personnel . . . . . . . . | | | | |
| 3. Principles . . . . . . . . . . . . . . . . . . . . . . . . | | | | |
| 4. Industrial . . . . . . . . . . . . . . . . . . . . . . . | | | | |
| 5. Human Relations . . . . . . . . . . . . . . . . . | | | | |
| 6. Other . . . . . . . . . . . . . . . . . . . . . . . . . | | | | |
| C. Behavioral Sciences . . . . . . . . . . . . . . . . . . | | | | |
| D. Computer Science . . . . . . . . . . . . . . . . . . . . | | | | |
| E. Economics . . . . . . . . . . . . . . . . . . . . . . . . . | | | | |
| F. Finance . . . . . . . . . . . . . . . . . . . . . . . . . . . | | | | |
| G. Insurance . . . . . . . . . . . . . . . . . . . . . . . . . | | | | |
| H. Law . . . . . . . . . . . . . . . . . . . . . . . . . . . . . | | | | |
| I. Marketing . . . . . . . . . . . . . . . . . . . . . . . . . | | | | |
| J. Mathematics and Quantitative Analysis . . . . . | | | | |

IX. Describe the types of self-development and self-study programs in which the employee has participated during the past three years:

A. Seminars, conferences, workshops attended:______________________________
______________________________________________________________

B. Periodicals, journals, etc., currently read:______________________________
______________________________________________________________

C. Correspondence courses completed:______________________________
______________________________________________________________

# Project 8–3 • Computer Hands-On: Design an Employee Appraisal Form

In the computer center of the Jepsen Company, there are 16 office workers whom you, as supervisor, plan to evaluate once a year on each employee's anniversary date. The employees are to be appraised on the basis of their job performance (75 percent) and their personality (25 percent). After you have sat down and discussed with each employee his or her evaluation, the appraisal forms are to be reviewed by your office manager and then placed in the personnel file of each employee.

**Directions:** Design an Employee Appraisal Form on template file PO8-3.TEM. List five appropriate factors in the Job Performance section and weigh each factor 15 percent. List five factors in the Personality section and weigh each factor 5 percent. Print out enough copies to use in evaluating the three employees described below.

## Nancy Malmos

Volume of production is above average.
Dresses carelessly; careless about cleanliness to a point of offending.
Comes in several minutes late about twice a week.
Averages two absences each month, usually on Friday.
Makes quite a few errors and has to do her work over.
Satisfied to stay in present job—not ambitious.
Often bothers others to help her find her errors.
Does not understand why she made the errors.
Is in no hurry to go home at 4:30. Usually last one out of the office.
Frequently borrows items from others and forgets to return them.
Likes to gossip about other people, including those in the office.
Most of her coworkers do not like her; others tolerate her but regard her as "different."

## Mark Yun

Dresses casually, but in good taste.
Very punctual in attendance; rarely absent.
Volume of work below average, but exceptionally accurate.
Readily accepts constructive criticism.
Reluctant to try new ideas and suggestions.
Quits promptly at 4:30 p.m.
Considers his job monotonous and boring but readily admits that it is a good source of income.
Does not help anyone in the center except when asked to do so by the supervisor.
Not very popular with his coworkers. Does not seem to "mix" well.
Minds his own business and gives little information about himself.
Information about his outside activities or interests is not known.

## Elizabeth Eller

Consistently produces an average volume of work.
Always willing to help others in the center, even if it slows down her output.
Is well groomed, but wears a little too much cologne.
Averages one absence each month.
Tries to find out why she or others have made errors.
Always seeks to improve methods of doing work.
Attends college at night, studying toward her degree in data processing management.
Comes to work on time or a few minutes early and quits promptly.
Commences to work as soon as she arrives, even though the official starting time is not until 8:30 a.m.
Very popular with most of her coworkers.
Expresses much interest in promotional opportunity with company.

## Project 8–4 • Preparing for a Three Months' Assignment in Madrid

For the past six years you have been employed as manager of office services in the New York office of Rojas of Madrid. Last month you completed your work as a member of the feasibility study team that decided to install a telecommunication system linking Madrid with all European and New York offices. You have been asked by the company president, Pablo Medina, to spend three months in the Madrid home office to train workers in operating the new system. Prior to your departure, you decide to improve your understanding of and feeling for Spain's culture. Although most workers in the Madrid office speak English very well, you want to brush up on your "high school Spanish" so you can better communicate with them and others in their own native tongue.

**Directions:** To enable you to learn more about the languages, culture, customs, etc. of Spain, prepare a report covering topics such as the following:

- Languages spoken in Spain
- Currency (exchange rate, examples of United States–Spain currency conversions)
- Culture and courtesies (anticipated differences between United States and Spain, greetings, gift giving, visiting, eating, tipping, gestures)
- People (population, religion, attitudes)
- Lifestyles (the family, socializing, recreation)
- The nation (land and climate, history and government, economy, education, health, traveler information)
- Time zone differences
- International telecommunications (telephone, FAX, country and city codes)
- International mail (postage rates, letter format and style)
- Major public holidays

# Project 8–5 • Training About Foreign Cultures

The following article tells how several organizations train their expatriate employees to learn more about the cultures of different people throughout the world. After you have read the article, prepare the report as instructed.

## Trainers Help Expatriate Employees Build Bridges to Different Cultures

La Hulpe, Belgium—At a training center here, Bob Waisfisz is introducing young managers from **International Business Machines Corp.** to the mysteries of foreign cultures.

To stir discussion, he asks them to explain the British ideal of keeping a stiff upper lip.

"What is 'stiff upper lip'?" asks Daan Kooman, an IBM manager from the Netherlands. Walter Sum, a German colleague, suggests that it means "I can absorb pain without showing emotion." Mr. Waisfisz then expounds on scientific data showing that Britons tend to put a high value on "masculine" traits.

Dave Wilkin, a Canadian, puts up his hand and raises a tougher question: "Why do French women always dress in such a sexy way?" Mr. Waisfisz, a Dutchman fizzing with energy and wisecracks, dances around the question by noting that the French and Italians generally consider it important to project a certain image of themselves by dressing smartly.

Some of the chatter may sound trivial, but Mr. Waisfisz, who heads a training firm based in The Hague, and a growing band of other trainers are persuading big companies that their managers ought to attend such seminars in "multicultural" management.

### Don't Pat That Child

These seminars, which began to pop up in Europe in the 1980s, go beyond the traditional short course on how an expatriate executive can cope with the folkways of a particular country. The goal is to help executives come to terms with a wide range of people with different values and ways of solving problems. The trainers try to change attitudes and challenge biases—rather than merely parroting a list of admonitions against, say, patting a Thai child on the head or arriving late for a meeting in Frankfurt.

Multicultural management is "a question of attitude, an openness to human variety, not a question of knowledge," says Fons Trompenaars, another Dutchman who is one of Mr. Waisfisz's rivals on the seminar circuit. These culture gurus have a new sales pitch for their courses and consulting work: Many companies that rushed into cross-border mergers and acquisitions in the late '80s now realize that such projects are more complicated than they appeared. "The missing element is the human factor," says Rudi Plettinx, a training official at the Management Centre Europe in Brussels.

The gurus also tell potential clients that Anglo-Saxon business theories and practices—dominant in many multinationals—are ill-suited for much of the world outside of the U.S. and Britain. David Howell, a culture trainer based in Ashley, England, says that Americans and Britons tend to be impatient to get down to business when they meet foreigners. "Americans say, 'If there is a buck in it, we'll do business with them,'" Mr. Howell says, "but people in other parts of the world say, 'Unless we like you, we won't do business together.'"

Not all companies feel compelled to call in outsiders to explain cultural mysteries. Some use in-house experts or figure that their executives learn by doing. Tony Preedy, vice president, personnel, at London-based PolyGram NV, says that many of the music company's executives travel frequently and get used to working with colleagues all over the world. If multicultural management is the wave of the future, PolyGram figures it has an advantage: It already has 15 different nationalities among its 33 top managers.

"No one nationality dominates," says Mr. Preedy. "I think it's the way multinationals will have to go. You can't believe the head office knows best."

Others are eager to smooth over cultural differences, rather than cultivate them. "We try to build a common corporate culture," says Peter M. Dessau, the head of human resources at the European division of **Colgate-Palmolive** Co. "We want them all to be Colgaters."

Then there are the true believers in multicultural training. Among them is Knud Christensen, a Danish personnel manager at BP Oil Europe, a Brussels-based unit of **British Petroleum** Co. "No culture is better or worse than another," Mr. Christensen says. "They're just different. We have to understand that."

Toward that end, the company has put about 250 of its managers through 2 1/2-day courses led by

Mr. Waisfisz over the past three years. The cost per manager is around $1,500, Mr. Christensen says. Among other benefits, he says, the courses have helped BP oil managers adapt policies to fit varying national needs.

For example, the company promotes "upward feedback" under which managers comment on their bosses' performance. That works well in Scandinavia, Britain, and the Netherlands, where managers tend not to be overly intimidated by their superiors, Mr. Christensen says. But it is more difficult in France, Turkey, and Greece, where tradition calls for showing more deference toward authorities. Managers in such countries "might be less direct" in providing their feedback, Mr. Christensen says.

**Motorola** Inc. has gone so far as to open a special center for cultural training at its headquarters in Schaumburg, Illinois. The electronics company is putting hundreds of its managers through short courses there, using programs partly developed by Mr. Trompenaars. "It is imperative that we understand all national cultures and respect all cultures—and use it as a competitive advantage," says Rs Moorthy, a Malaysian who runs the training center. Mr. Moorthy's goal? To make Motorola managers "transculturally competent."

On the other side of the Atlantic, Philippe Alloing is nearly as enthusiastic. A Frenchman who has spent most of his career outside France, Mr. Alloing became convinced of the need for cultural training a few years ago when he was head of human resources at BP Nutrition, another British Petroleum unit, and found himself dealing with " a melting pot in which things didn't melt very well."

Mr. Alloing still uses cultural training now that he is human resources chief at CarnaudMetalbox SA, a huge Paris-based maker of packaging, formed by the 1989 merger of rivals from France and Britain. At the moment, he is using Mr. Trompenaars's services to try to resolve cultural clashes between British and German managers whose business units are merging. "In Germany, you are a beginner until you are 38," Mr. Alloing says. "In England, at 38 you are a has-been and looking at early retirement."

This kind of contrast is a culture guru's bread and butter. During his seminars, Mr. Trompenaars reports a correlation between the number of lawyers in a society and spending on pet food. "This has nothing to do with what lawyers eat," he quips. Rather, he explains, people in the U.S. and other largely Protestant cultures often are so suspicious of humanity that they turn to lawyers and dogs.

Mr. Waisfisz explains all kinds of cultural differences by reference to the writings of Geert Hofstede, a Dutch academic who devised a way to rank nations according to such criteria as their degree of individualism, respect for authority, and aversion to uncertainty. Within an hour or two, Mr. Waisfisz has his students batting around such terms as "power distance" and "uncertainty avoidance." Lest the jargon and data send students to sleep, Mr. Waisfisz keeps jabbing them with humor.

A sample: "In Germany, everything is forbidden unless it's allowed. In Britain, everything is allowed unless it's forbidden. And in France, everything is allowed even if it's forbidden."

**Directions:** Throw yourself into the role of a trainer in an American firm, where you will be working with expatriate employees from Germany, France, and Italy. Prepare a written or oral report in which you list the 10 most important cultural values, attitudes, customs, etc. that will form the basis of your initial training and orientation session. Explain why these items make up your "top ten."

___

___

___

___

___

___

___

___

# 9

# ANALYZING OFFICE JOBS

*Job analysis* involves gathering information about the duties and responsibilities of specific jobs and their ergonomic conditions. Following the analysis of jobs, *job descriptions* and *job specifications* are prepared. Potentially one of the office manager's most powerful tools, job descriptions and job specifications are instrumental in planning human resources requirements, diagnosing training needs and designing training programs, and developing performance standards. With today's emphasis upon compliance with federal and state legislation affecting management-employee relations, the maintenance of up-to-date, accurately prepared job descriptions is more important than ever before.

A program of office job analysis includes the *job evaluation*, which sets an equitable monetary value for each job. To accomplish this goal, office jobs are compared as to their degree of *skill, effort, responsibility,* and *working conditions.* As a means of exercising control over an equitable salary compensation program, job evaluation (1) guards against the growth of salary inequities, (2) aids in identifying and gradually eliminating out-of-line or "red-circle" salary rates, (3) assures that salary rates in multioffice operations will be comparable, and (4) very importantly, provides the office supervisor with a means of explaining the relation between a job and its salary in a way that is understandable to the employee.

## SECTION A • REVIEW QUESTIONS

**Directions:** Each of the following statements is either true or false. Indicate your choice in the Answers column by circling "T" or "F."

| | Answers | |
|---|---|---|
| 1. Job analysis is fundamental to the preparation of job descriptions and job specifications ..... | T | F |
| 2. The simplification and improvement of jobs are a by-product of job analysis ............ | T | F |
| 3. An advantage in using the questionnaire method of gathering job information is the ease of designing a questionnaire that obtains all the data required by the analyst ............... | T | F |
| 4. To obtain reliable and valid results, the jobholders' completed questionnaires must be carefully analyzed and edited ............................................... | T | F |
| 5. The interview method of gathering job information is generally much less expensive than the questionnaire method ............................................... | T | F |
| 6. The observation method of gathering job information is ineffective when analyzing repetitive jobs such as statistical keyboarding ............................................... | T | F |
| 7. Job descriptions should be reviewed and revised every five years ...................... | T | F |
| 8. To be reliable, a job description should rest upon the supervisor's interpretation of what the job should be rather than upon the job as it is actually performed ...................... | T | F |
| 9. Employee specifications are the minimum qualifications a person must possess to be considered for employment ............................................... | T | F |
| 10. Job evaluation aims at developing an equitable payroll policy based on the estimated worth of each job in relation to other jobs ............................................... | T | F |
| 11. The ranking method is an example of a quantitative job evaluation plan ................ | T | F |
| 12. The simplest and oldest method of job evaluation is the point-factor method ............. | T | F |

13. The ranking method is most effectively used in offices having at least 40 different jobs ..... T F

14. Under the job classification method, a number of predetermined classes is selected, and then the jobs are analyzed and grouped into these classes ................................ T F

15. The General Schedule is based upon use of the point-factor method .................... T F

16. One of the main advantages of the job classification method is its objective grading and rating of jobs by their total content .................................................... T F

17. Under the factor-comparison method, jobs are compared with benchmark jobs, which have been rated in terms of money ................................................ T F

18. The point-factor method is more objective in its approach and provides more consistency of results than any other job evaluation method .............................. T F

19. A company searching for a job evaluation method should adopt in its entirety a method that has proven effective in another firm ........................................ T F

20. A company should use only one job evaluation method to evaluate all the jobs in that organization ............................................................ T F

**Directions:** In the Answers column, write the letter of the item in Column 1 that is described by each statement in Column 2.

**Column 1**

**A** Employee specification

**B** Factor-comparison method

**C** General Schedule

**D** Job description

**E** Job evaluation

**F** Job specification

**G** Point-factor method

**H** Work measurement and setting work standards

| Column 2 | Answers |
|---|---|
| 1. A method of evaluating jobs in which the factors of skill, effort, responsibility, and job conditions are divided into subfactors and degrees ........................................ | 1. ______ |
| 2. The process of appraising the value of each job in relation to other jobs in order to set a monetary value for each specific job ........ | 2. ______ |
| 3. The minimum qualifications a person must possess to be considered for employment ........................................ | 3. ______ |
| 4. The procedure for determining the time required to accomplish each job or task and for setting up criteria by which the degree of performance may be measured ........................... | 4. ______ |
| 5. A detailed record of the minimum job requirements explained in relation to the job factors ............................... | 5. ______ |
| 6. An outline of the information compiled from the job analysis, which describes the content and essential requirements of a specific job .. | 6. ______ |

## SECTION B • PROJECTS

### Project 9–1 • Computer Hands-On: Editing a Questionnaire and Preparing a Job Description

**Directions:** As a job analyst, you have been contacted by Smith-Barr, Inc., to prepare job descriptions for its office personnel. One of the questionnaires completed by a clerk and reviewed by his supervisor is illustrated below and on page 92. After you have edited this questionnaire, prepare a job description using template file PO9-1.TEM. If any further information is needed, assume that you have met with the supervisor, who provided all the data you require.

**Page 1**

**QUESTIONNAIRE**

**Employee's Name** *Bob Martens* **Date** *5/10/--*
**Job Title** *Accounts Payable Clerk* **Department** *Accounting*
**Supervisor's Name and Title** *Bette Hankish, Senior Accountant*

**Instructions**

**Employee: Complete Section I. Describe in detail the primary or most important duties you perform. List the duties in clear, concise sentences. Indicate the frequency (daily, weekly, monthly) and amount of time spent performing the duties. Be certain you provide sufficient information about each duty to enable persons unfamiliar with your work to understand what the duty entails. Questions should be directed to your supervisor.**

**Supervisor: Complete Section II.**

**SECTION I**

1. Duty (what) *I prepare checks in payment of all amounts due creditors when OK'd by my boss, Bette.*
   Procedure (how) *I confirm that all invoices, memos authorizing payment, etc. are properly approved for payment. I check all calculations and make sure that invoices are timely paid in order to take advantage of all cash discounts. I prepare checks and route them to the V-P, Finance, for signature and mailing.*
   Reason for duty (why) *I pay creditors on time to earn cash discounts and maintain our very fine credit rating.*
   Frequency *Daily* and Percentage *60* of time spent performing above duty.

2. Duty (what) *I maintain a ledger for all raw materials used in production.*
   Procedure (how) *I post the quantity of all raw materials received and used and initiate purchase requisitions when reorder points are reached.*
   Reason for duty (why) *Sufficient materials must be on hand at all times so that production is not interrupted.*
   Frequency *Daily* and Percentage *30* of time spent performing above duty.

3. Duty (what) *I keep a record of all plant assets bought.*
   Procedure (how) *I record purchase date, assign asset numbers, determine useful life, and periodically calculate depreciation. I record the cost of all maintenance and repair for each plant asset.*
   Reason for duty (why) *All plant assets are identified by ID decals to safeguard and account for each one. Accumulating all expenses for repairs aids in determining date and amount of trade-in.*
   Frequency *Varies, at least monthly* and Percentage *10* of time spent performing above duty.

What machines/equipment are you required to use proficiently on your job? How much time per day or week is spent using each machine/equipment listed?

**Page 2**

| Machine/Equipment | Time in Use |
|---|---|
| PC | 5-6 hours daily |
| Electronic calculator | 2-3 hours daily |
| Typewriter | 1/2 - 1 hour daily |

What are the most difficult decisions you make? What do you consider the most important task(s) you perform?

When our cash position is low, I must rank creditors according to priority in paying them to make sure that the greatest dollar volume of discounts is taken. It is very important that I record daily all raw materials received and used to make sure we do not run out of anything, especially when we work overtime in second and third shifts.

Describe the working conditions that may cause a feeling of pressure or discomfort. Consider environment, distractions, and interference that might make completion of task(s) difficult.

It is very noisy and dirty when I must walk through the plant to talk with the receiving department to check on incoming materials. Sometimes there are too many people milling around in the accounting department and it gets so noisy I lose my train of thought.

Describe the personal contacts you are required to make to perform your job.

Who (Title?) Bette Hankish, Senior Accountant
Reason Confer regarding payment of creditors, get approval of depreciation rates for new items purchased.

Who (Title?) Henry Dalton, Purchasing Agent
Reason Check on reordering of materials and follow-up on delivery dates.

Who (Title?) Mario DeVita, Supervisor, Receiving Department
Reason Follow up on missing shipment receipts.

Signature Rob Martens
(Employee)

**SECTION II**

Section I reviewed and approved by Bette Hankish
(Immediate Supervisor)

Comments: Bob needs more time for processing incoming invoices for raw materials and keeping the raw materials ledger up to date. Therefore, in the next three months I am thinking about assigning all of his work on the plant asset ledger to another person in the department.

Errors that may occur in performance of this job are: (Check one)

✓ easily detected in normal routine of checking results.
___ detected in subsequent steps.
___ not detected until they have caused other departments considerable inconvenience.
___ not detected until they have caused considerable inconvenience to another company.

Describe responsibility of this jobholder for work of other employees. (Check one)

___ No responsibility for work of others. May show other employees how to perform a task or assist in orientation of new employees.
✓ Guides and instructs other employees, assigning, checking, and maintaining the flow of work.

## Project 9–2 • Job Evaluation: The Ranking Method

This project and the three that follow will provide experience in evaluating several office and clerical jobs found on the campus of a college or university. The four projects provide for the use of four methods of job evaluation in order to give you a better understanding of each method.

In a job analysis completed at Trimble Junior College, 12 distinct office and clerical jobs were described. The job descriptions, labeled A through L, appear on pages 97 and 99 and may be separated at the perforation marks for ease in analysis and grouping. Your instructor may call upon you to evaluate the jobs individually, or the evaluation may be assigned to several job evaluation teams from your class.

**Directions:** Using the set of 12 office and clerical job descriptions on pages 97 and 99, evaluate the jobs, using the ranking method. Rank the jobs in the order of their contribution to the two main objectives of the college:

1. To offer residents of the county a comprehensive selection of career courses and programs based upon identifiable community interests and needs.
2. To offer residents of the county a comprehensive selection of programs and courses which will transfer to baccalaureate degree-granting institutions.

Place the rank of the job, starting with No. 1 for the most important job, on the job description in the upper left corner.

## Project 9–3 • Job Evaluation: The Job Classification Method

**Directions**: Using the set of 12 office and clerical job descriptions on pages 97 and 99, evaluate the jobs using the U.S. government job classification method. Classify each job according to one of the 18 General Schedule (GS) job classes given in Table 9–1. Place the number of the job classification in the upper right corner of the job description.

**Table 9–1**
**KEY PHRASES FROM UNITED STATES GOVERNMENT JOB CLASSIFICATION METHOD THAT DIFFERENTIATE ONE JOB CLASS FROM ANOTHER**

| General Schedule Job Classification No. | JOB FACTORS AND THEIR VARYING REQUIREMENTS | | |
|---|---|---|---|
| | Difficulty | Responsibility | Qualifications |
| 1. | simplest routine work | | |
| 2. | routine work | | some training or experience |
| 3. | somewhat difficult | somewhat responsible | working knowledge |
| 4. | moderately difficult work | moderately responsible work | moderate training, good working knowledge |
| 5. | difficult work | responsible work | considerable training, broad working knowledge, college graduate |
| 6. | difficult work | responsible work | broad working knowledge, special and complex subject |
| 7. | considerable difficulty | considerable responsibility | comprehensive and thorough working knowledge |
| 8. | very difficult | very responsible | comprehensive and thorough working knowledge |
| 9. | very difficult | very responsible | administrative experience, sound capacity for independent work |
| 10. | highly difficult | highly responsible | somewhat extended administrative experience |
| 11. | marked difficulty | marked responsibility | marked capacity for independent work |
| 12. | very high order of difficulty | very high order of responsibility | leadership and attainments of a high order |
| 13. | work of unusual difficulty | work of unusual responsibility | leadership and marked attainments |
| 14. | exceptional difficulty | exceptional responsibility | leadership and unusual attainments |
| 15. | outstanding difficulty | outstanding responsibility | leadership and exceptional attainments |
| 16. | unusual difficulty and national significance | unusual responsibility and national significance | leadership and exceptional attainments involving national significance |
| 17. | exceptional difficulty | exceptional responsibility | exceptional leadership and attainments |
| 18. | outstanding difficulty | outstanding responsibility | outstanding leadership |

## Project 9–4 • Job Evaluation: The Factor-Comparison Method

**Directions:** Using the set of 12 office and clerical job descriptions on pages 97 and 99, evaluate the jobs using the factor-comparison method. The job titles, descriptions, and weekly salary rates which have been selected as benchmark jobs to represent a cross section of all 12 jobs to be evaluated are given in Table 9–2 shown below. Place the dollar value of each of the 12 jobs on the job description in the lower left corner.

**Table 9–2**
**BENCHMARK JOBS AND AVERAGE WEEKLY SALARY RATES**

| Benchmark Job and Description | Average Weekly Salary Rate | Benchmark Job and Description | Average Weekly Salary Rate |
|---|---|---|---|
| **Switchboard Operator/Receptionist** Operates a single or multiple position PBX telephone switchboard. May keep records of calls and toll charges and may operate a paging system and perform duties of receptionist. | $340 | **Word Processing Operator** Use word processing equipment to input, edit, customize, and deliver documents of medium-to-complex difficulty with established quality and time standards. Proofreads and edits own work. Is familiar with department terminology and company practices. Equipment includes the use of a standalone word processing system utilizing a CRT screen. May also perform general secretary duties. | $360 |
| **Clerk—Typist** Keys letters, reports, tabulations, and other material in which setups and terms are generally clear and follow a standard pattern. May prepare offset masters. Performs clerical duties of moderate difficulty. | $315 | **Secretary A** Performs secretarial duties for a top-level executive or a person responsible for a major function or geographic location. Does work of a confidential nature and relieves principal of designated administrative details. Requires initiative, judgment, knowledge of company practices, policy, and organization. | $410 |
| **Mail Clerk—File Clerk** Circulates office mail, delivers messages and supplies. May process incoming or outgoing mail and operate related machines and perform other routine duties. Performs routine filing and sorting operations according to an established system. Locates and removes material upon request and keeps records of its disposition. May perform related clerical duties. | $295 | **Accounting Clerk A** Performs complex and responsible clerical duties requiring independent analysis, exercise of judgment, and a detailed knowledge of department or company policies and procedures. Minimum supervision required. | $425 |

# Project 9–5 • Job Evaluation: The Point Factor Method

**Directions:** Using the set of 12 office and clerical job descriptions on pages 97 and 99, evaluate the jobs using the point-factor method described below. Place the number of points that each job is worth on the job description in the lower right corner.

## POINT-FACTOR METHOD

This point-factor method provides for the use of factors and subfactors, which are grouped under the headings that follow. You will see that 25 percent of the maximum credits allowed are allocated to the factor "Elemental," 50 percent to "Skill," 20 percent to "Responsibility," and 5 percent to "Effort." Complete details of factor definitions, and point values applicable thereto, will be found below and on pages 101 and 102.

| | Maximum Point Values | | Percentage of Total | |
|---|---|---|---|---|
| 1. ELEMENTAL | | 250 | | 25% |
| 2. SKILL | | | | |
| (a) General or special education | 160 | | 16 | |
| (b) Training time on job | 40 | | 4 | |
| (c) Memory | 40 | | 4 | |
| (d) Analytical | 95 | | 9.5 | |
| (e) Personal contact | 35 | | 3.5 | |
| (f) Dexterity | 80 | | 8 | |
| (g) Accuracy | 50 | | 5 | |
| Total | | 500 | | 50% |
| 3. RESPONSIBILITY | | | | |
| (a) For company property | 25 | | 2.5 | |
| (b) For procedure | 125 | | 12.5 | |
| (c) Supervision | 50 | | 5 | |
| Total | | 200 | | 20% |
| 4. EFFORT | | | | |
| (a) Place of work | 5 | | .5 | |
| (b) Cleanliness of work | 5 | | .5 | |
| (c) Position | 10 | | 1 | |
| (d) Continuity of work | 15 | | 1.5 | |
| (e) Physical or mental strain | 15 | | 1.5 | |
| Total | | 50 | | 5% |
| Grand Total | | 1,000 | | 100% |

## DEFINITIONS OF EVALUATION FACTORS, SUBFACTORS, AND POINT VALUES

1. ELEMENTAL—250 POINTS
This element is credited to each job to be evaluated and covers the normal characteristics required of any employee hired, such as honesty, appearance, deportment, physical fitness, etc.

2. SKILL—500 POINTS

a. *General or special education—160 Points*
This factor covers the minimum basic knowledge that an employee must have in order to dispose of the duties of a job properly. The education may be acquired either within or without school and may represent the experience that an employee must have had on previous jobs either within or without the company before qualified to fill the job being evaluated.

| | | |
|---|---|---|
| (1) | Elementary school or equivalent | 4×10 = 40 |
| (2) | High school or equivalent | 4×13 = 52 |
| (3) | College or equivalent | 4×17 = 68 |
| | | 160 |

b. *Training time on job—40 Points*
This factor represents the experience an employee must have on the job being evaluated before he or she can be considered fully competent to handle it.

| | | |
|---|---|---|
| (1) | 1 to 6 days | = 0 |
| (2) | 2 to 4 weeks | = 1 – 8 |
| (3) | 2 to 6 months | = 9–20 |
| (4) | 6 months to maximum | = 21–40 |

c. *Memory—40 Points*
This factor represents the demand that is made on an employee for memorizing certain functions of his or her work. It may range from repetitive, unimportant factors to nonrepetitive, complicated factors.

| | | |
|---|---|---|
| (1) | Routine job—minimum memory required | = 0 |
| (2) | Memory would be desirable | = 1 – 4 |
| (3) | Requires memory of certain items | = 5 – 8 |
| (4) | Requires memory of many items | = 9–20 |
| (5) | Requires memory of complex items occasionally | = 21–40 |

*(continued on page 101)*

### A. BOOKSTORE CLERK

Rank ______ Class ______

Under the direct supervision of the Bookstore Manager, performs specifically assigned duties such as selling textbooks, supplementary supplies, and other items offered for sale in the bookstore; sorting and distributing incoming mail and preparing outgoing mail for delivery to post office; assisting in the taking of physical inventory; and preparing reports and forms such as purchase orders and inventory records.

May be delegated responsibility for exercising control over the receipt and issuance of stock and the handling of cash funds.

May operate a variety of business machines and equipment such as a cash register, mailing machine, computer, calculator, FAX machine, and copier.

May act as receptionist for students, faculty, visitors, and vendors in either personal or telephone contacts, which require full knowledge of bookstore operations.

Operates in an atmosphere that requires a moderate degree of tact and trust.

F-C $ Value ______ # Points ______

### B. WORD PROCESSING OPERATOR

Rank ______ Class ______

Under direction of a department secretary or other supervisor, operates word processing equipment for inputting, editing, and delivering typed documents such as examinations, routine correspondence, reports, and news releases; proofreads and edits own work.

May perform some secretarial duties under supervision of a department secretary or member of the administrative staff; may be assigned specific responsibilities such as gathering internal data and information, and assisting in the registration process.

May assist in orienting and training full-time and/or part-time office workers and student clerical aides. May be called upon to assume the duties of the department secretary when that person is absent.

Operates in an atmosphere that requires tact and diplomacy and a moderate degree of confidentiality.

F-C $ Value ______ # Points ______

### C. ACCOUNTING CLERK B

Rank ______ Class ______

Under the direct supervision of the Chief Accountant, assists Accounting Clerk A in the handling of various phases of accounting operations and preparation of accounting records and reports. Responsibilities are:

1. Receiving, depositing, and accounting for incoming monies and assisting in accounting for expenses.
2. Processing invoices and bills for payment; filing; and writing, recording, and mailing checks.
3. Assisting in preparation of payroll data for computer input.
4. Keying statements and bills.
5. Opening and sorting incoming mail.
6. Assisting in registration process during school year.
7. Acting as receptionist for and working with students, faculty, administrative staff, bank representatives, auditors, and the Internal Revenue Service in either personal or telephone contact.

May operate office machines and equipment such as calculator and computer.

Works in an atmosphere that requires a high degree of accuracy, tact, and diplomacy with a high degree of confidentiality.

F-C $ Value ______ # Points ______

### D. DEPARTMENT SECRETARY

Rank ______ Class ______

Performs the duties of secretary and aide and reports directly to a department chairperson; gathers internal data and information and prepares reports, forms, and correspondence under guidance; often acts as liaison between chairperson and professional staff, operating personnel, and the community.

May act as receptionist for students, faculty, and visitors in either personal or telephone contacts, which require full knowledge of department organization and operations, schedule of events, etc.

May supervise, orient, and train one or more full-time and/or part-time office workers and student clerical aides. Clerical work may include tasks such as processing and keying reports and letters; preparing transparencies; and operating calculating, reproduction, and transcription machines and equipment.

Operates in an atmosphere that requires accuracy, tact, and diplomacy and a moderate degree of confidentiality.

F-C $ Value ______ # Points ______

### E. SWITCHBOARD OPERATOR/RECEPTIONIST

Rank ______ Class ______

Operates a multiple-position PBX telephone switchboard, keeps records of calls and toll charges, and operates the base mobile radio.

Other duties include the maintenance of a current directory of all personnel authorized to use the telephone, orients and trains part-time relief operators, and keeps records of hours worked by relief operators.

Works in an atmosphere that requires a high degree of tact and diplomacy and a moderate degree of trust.

F-C $ Value ______ # Points ______

### F. ADMINISTRATIVE SECRETARY

Rank ______ Class ______

Performs the duties of executive secretary and aide and reports directly to an administrative staff member (other than department chairperson); gathers internal data and information and prepares reports, forms, and correspondence under guidance; in administrative matters, often acts as liaison between administrator and professional staff, operating personnel, and the community.

May act as receptionist for students, faculty, and visitors in either personal or telephone contacts, which require full knowledge of administrative organization of the college, schedule of events, etc.

May supervise, orient, and train one or more full-time and/or part-time office workers and student clerical aides. Clerical work may include tasks such as processing and keying reports and letters; preparing transparencies; and operating calculating, reproduction, and transcription machines and equipment.

Operates in an atmosphere that requires an exceptionally high degree of accuracy, tact, and diplomacy, and a high degree of confidentiality.

F-C $ Value ______ # Points ______

## G. ACCOUNTING CLERK A

Rank Class

Under the direct supervision of the Chief Accountant, handles various phases of accounting operations, prepares accounting reports; performs secretarial duties for the Chief Accountant; may train, orient, and supervise the work of junior accounting clerks; acts as receptionist for and works with students, faculty, administrative staff, bank representatives, auditors, and the Internal Revenue Service in either personal or telephone contacts.

Specific responsibilities and duties include:

1. Accounting for, safeguarding, and disbursing monies received from various groups such as Financial Aid, Student Government, and Student Activity.
2. Preparing various accounting reports such as monthly pension and monthly encumbrances and expenses.

Operates office machines and equipment such as calculator and computer.

Works in an atmosphere that requires an exceptionally high degree of accuracy, tact, and diplomacy with a high degree of confidentiality.

F-C $ Value # Points

## H. RECEPTIONIST, EVENING PROGRAM

Rank Class

Under the supervision of the Director of Business Affairs, performs the duties of receptionist, such as greeting the public personally and on the telephone, answering questions regarding course offerings, admissions procedures, community services programs, sporting events, plays, and concerts, etc.; recording and transmitting telephone messages for faculty and staff personnel; assisting students with the completion of various forms; and directing students to classrooms and visitors to appropriate offices on the campus.

Additional duties may include the sale of parking stickers, the proctoring of make-up examinations, and the distribution of mail to Evening Program faculty members.

Operates in an atmosphere that requires tact, diplomacy, and patience, and a moderate degree of confidentiality.

F-C $ Value # Points

## I. ADMINISTRATIVE ASSISTANT TO THE PRESIDENT

Rank Class

Performs the duties of administrative secretary, serves as aide to the President of the college, and renders secretarial service to the Board of Trustees; gathers statistical data and information and prepares reports, under direction; acts as liaison between the President's office and the college community.

With little or no supervision, completes duties specifically delegated by the President of the college. Serves as receptionist for students, faculty, administrative staff, and visitors.

Operates in an atmosphere that requires an exceptionally high degree of tact and diplomacy and a high degree of confidentiality.

F-C $ Value # Points

## J. ADMINISTRATIVE ASSISTANT TO THE DIRECTOR OF BUSINESS AFFAIRS

Rank Class

Performs the duties of administrative secretary and serves as aide to Director of Business Affairs; gathers statistical data and information and prepares reports, under direction; acts as liaison between the office of the Director of Business Affairs and the college community.

With little or no supervision, completes specifically delegated duties such as administering the insurance program of the college, including the processing of claims; reviewing and preparing invoices for final approval by the Director; compiling timekeeping records for clerical personnel; registering keys and parking stickers; and coordinating vacation schedules.

Operates in an atmosphere that requires a high degree of tact and diplomacy and a high degree of confidentiality.

F-C $ Value # Points

## K. MAIL CLERK

Rank Class

Under the direction of the Bookstore Manager, picks up all classes of mail at the post office and sorts and delivers the mail on campus; picks up, sorts, and delivers the interoffice campus mail; prepares packages, films, and tapes for mailing and transports all classes of mail to the post office.

Additional assigned duties may include the recording of mailing machine meter readings, purchasing postage for the mailing machine, accounting for the postal petty cash fund, and performing general housekeeping tasks.

Operates a motor vehicle and works in an atmosphere that requires a moderate degree of trust.

F-C $ Value # Points

## L. CLERK-TYPIST

Rank Class

Under the direction of an administrative secretary or other supervisor, keys letters, examinations, reports, and other forms and written materials. May be assigned clerical tasks such as assisting in preparation of class schedules and transcripts; filing correspondence, records, and reports; sorting and distributing incoming mail; and assisting in the registration process.

May prepare transparencies and operate a wide variety of office machines and equipment such as copier, collator, binder, folding and inserting machine, paper shredder, calculator, addressing machine, fax machine, and microfilm camera, reader-cutter, and reader-printer.

May act as receptionist in directing faculty, students, and visitors to locations on campus.

F-C $ Value # Points

d. *Analytical—95 Points*
This factor represents the complexity of the job to be evaluated and is a measure of the demands made on an employee's judgment and ingenuity to do properly the assigned work. Included therein should be the credit allowed for the number and importance of decisions an employee must make of his or her own accord without recourse to supervision.
(1) Routine job = 0
(2) Requires some judgment, ingenuity, and initiative = 1–20
(3) Requires considerable judgment, ingenuity, and initiative = 21–45
(4) Job entirely analytical. No routine, jobs varied = 46–95

e. *Personal contact—35 Points*
*Personal contact with public*—as well as *contact with other employees*—should be consolidated, inasmuch as they represent varying degrees of contact. This factor should recognize personality and sense of cooperation necessary to meet requirements of the job.
(1) Normal employee relationship = 0
(2) Within own department = 1 – 5
(3) Elsewhere within the company = 1–10
(4) Contacts with the public = 1–20

f. *Dexterity—80 Points*
This factor represents the credit allowed for the demands of a natural or acquired physical ability that is necessary to perform all manual duties of the job.
(1) None = 0
(2) Low = 1–20
(3) Medium = 21–50
(4) High = 51–80

g. *Accuracy—50 Points*
This factor gives credit for the degree of accuracy required, which will vary because in one job, while the chances of error may be small, the importance of error may be great; in another job, where the chances of error may be numerous, relatively little importance would attach to any one error.
(1) Work verified—not serious in case of error = 0–10
(2) Work not verified—not serious in case of error = 11–20
(3) Work verified—serious in case of error = 21–30
(4) Work not verified—serious in case of error = 31–50

3. RESPONSIBILITY—200 POINTS

a. *For company property—25 Points*
(1) Not responsible for more than desks and related equipment = 0
(2) Responsible for typewriters, adding machines and/or similar equipment = 1–10
(3) Responsible for cash funds or valuable papers = 11–25

b. *For procedure—125 Points*
This factor gives credit for the degree of responsibility placed on a position for performance of duties in accordance with policies or procedures set up by the company. The responsibility may pertain to the drafting of contracts, orders, etc.; handling items of a confidential nature, or passing out information where divergence from set procedures may result in a loss of money or time or would adversely affect operations in own department, operations in other departments, or relations with customers or the public.

| | Confidential | Loss of Money or Time | Operations in Department | Operations in Other Departments | Relations with Public |
|---|---|---|---|---|---|
| None | 0 | 0 | 0 | 0 | 0 |
| Low | 1 – 5 | 1 – 5 | 1 – 5 | 1 – 5 | 1 – 5 |
| Medium | 6–10 | 6–10 | 6–10 | 6–10 | 6–10 |
| High | 11–20 | 11–20 | 11–20 | 11–20 | 11–20 |

Compensating factor values applicable to any unusual condition in any bracket 1—25 points

Maximum applicable to any combination 125 points

c. *Supervision—50 Points*
This factor is used to evaluate supervision exercised over others, such as that of a group leader, who, in addition to doing essentially the same type of work, is responsible for the flow of work within the group and, in some degree, for the correctness of the work performed by the group. The number of persons supervised should be considered.
(1) None = 0
(2) Low = 1–10
(3) Medium = 11–25
(4) High = 26–50

4. EFFORT—50 Points

a. *Place of work—5 Points*
This factor should allow for the credit due the job because of physical surroundings and environment, such as noise, heat, light, atmosphere, hazards, etc.

| | | | |
|---|---|---|---|
| (1) | Good | = | 0 |
| (2) | Fair | = | 1 – 2 |
| (3) | Poor | = | 3 – 5 |

b. *Cleanliness of work—5 Points*
This factor gives credit for working conditions relative to the immediate position. The immediate surroundings may be ideal, but the nature of the job may be messy.

| | | | |
|---|---|---|---|
| (1) | Clean | = | 0 |
| (2) | Moderately dirty | = | 1 – 2 |
| (3) | Very dirty | = | 3 – 5 |

c. *Position—10 Points*
This factor covers the demands made upon a person to dispose the task properly. It should be borne in mind that it is normal to have positions such as sitting for a while, then walking, then stooping. If these are not distributed in a normal manner, credit should be allowed. If a job requires an excessive amount of any one, or combination of them, credit should be given accordingly.

| | | | |
|---|---|---|---|
| (1) | Normal | = | 0 |
| (2) | Tiring | = | 1 – 4 |
| (3) | Very tiring | = | 5–10 |

d. *Continuity of work—15 Points*
This factor refers to the continuous performance on the job. It may vary from duties that may be normal in nature, where an employee may momentarily change or stop work, to a type of job that requires continued concentration and attention for a definite period of time.

| | | | |
|---|---|---|---|
| (1) | Intermittent | = | 0 |
| (2) | Fairly continuous | = | 1 – 4 |
| (3) | Constant | = | 5 – 9 |
| (4) | Monotonous | = | 10–15 |

e. *Physical or mental strain—15 Points*
This factor varies from "c" and "d" in that it refers to mental, eye, or nervous strain. The factor would be enhanced by constant interruptions, close concentration or figure work.

| | | | |
|---|---|---|---|
| (1) | Normal | = | 0 |
| (2) | Low | = | 1 – 4 |
| (3) | Medium | = | 5 – 9 |
| (4) | High | = | 10–15 |

10

# ADMINISTERING OFFICE SALARIES

Administrative office managers and supervisors are often involved in wage and salary considerations. For example, they may be asked to answer office workers' questions and explain company policy on setting salaries, awarding increases, and providing employee benefits. Thus, office managers need to understand the bases for salary decisions. An office manager may not be able to change the company policy on salary administration or alter an employee's salary. However, the manager does need to know what the firm's philosophy is toward wages and salaries, whether salaries are competitive with those paid outside the company, and which nonsalary payments are considered part of the compensation package.

To make recommendations and influence those who have the authority to change company policy, the office manager must be well informed about the complex subject of administering salaries, which often represent the firm's largest operating expense. The office manager must work toward keeping the salary program up to date, especially in view of the growing technology inherent in many office positions. Office positions change—they grow, they shrink, they are eliminated, and new positions are created. Other factors that contribute to the complex nature of the salary program include the role played by employee benefits, incentives, and indirect compensation; government regulations; collective bargaining; inflationary pressures; and the drive toward equal pay for jobs of comparable worth.

With an intelligently administered salary program for its office workers, the company moves toward its goals of promoting and attaining salary equity, thus minimizing dissatisfaction and grievances among workers; attracting and retaining qualified, competent workers; stimulating and rewarding high-level performance; and maintaining a competitive position with other companies in the same geographic labor market.

## SECTION A • REVIEW QUESTIONS

**Directions:** Each of the following statements is either true or false. Indicate your choice in the Answers column by circling "T" or "F."

| | | **Answers** | |
|---|---|---|---|
| 1. | A firm should build its salary program upon a foundation of job analysis | T | F |
| 2. | In his theory of motivation, Herzberg concluded that money is the strongest motivator that can be used to satisfy an employee's needs | T | F |
| 3. | The key elements in Vroom's expectancy theory are needs, performance, and rewards | T | F |
| 4. | A reliable salary survey states the amount of salaries that office managers should pay their firms' workers | T | F |
| 5. | The most representative figure in an array of salaries, arranged from high to low, is the average salary | T | F |
| 6. | The dollar spread between salaries at the first quartile and the third quartile is sometimes referred to as the effective salary range | T | F |
| 7. | Office employees covered by the Fair Labor Standards Act must be paid the minimum wage, *unless* they are working under a piece-rate incentive plan | T | F |
| 8. | The Equal Pay Act prohibits employers from setting different wages that are based solely on the *sex* of the workers | T | F |
| 9. | If office employees qualify for overtime pay, they must be paid at a rate that is at least one and one-half times their regular pay rate | T | F |

| | | | |
|---|---|---|---|
| 10. | The COLA clause in a labor contract is designed to keep the employees' salaries more or less in step with inflation . . . . . | T | F |
| 11. | When salary ranges are accurately developed and kept current, the midpoint of each range is used as the beginning salary for new employees . . . . . | T | F |
| 12. | Workers' salary rates that fall below the minimum salary line are called *red-circle rates* . . . . | T | F |
| 13. | To motivate office employees, the spread of a pay grade should be at least 60 percent . . . . . . | T | F |
| 14. | Broadbanding enables a firm to provide more mobility and flexibility in transferring workers | T | F |
| 15. | Under a pay for performance plan, the employee's seniority is the basis for granting salary increases . . . . . | T | F |
| 16. | In a skill-based pay system, salary increases are awarded as employees acquire additional knowledge and skills . . . . . | T | F |
| 17. | Incentive systems enable workers to increase their earnings by maintaining or exceeding established standards of work performance . . . . . | T | F |
| 18. | Under the piece-rate system, the employee receives a fixed price for each unit produced . . . . | T | F |
| 19. | In a gainsharing plan, office workers share with their coworkers and employer the savings realized from improvements in productivity . . . . . | T | F |
| 20. | The Scanlon plan is the most frequently used individual incentive system . . . . . | T | F |

**Directions:** In the Answers column, write the letter of the item in Column 1 that is described by each statement in Column 2.

**Column 1**

A Arbitration
B Check-off
C Collective bargaining
D Effective salary range
E Gainsharing plan
F Median
G Mediation
H Piece-rate system
I Quartile
J Right-to-work law
K Skill-based system
L Third quartile
M Union shop agreement
N Variable pay

| Column 2 | Answers |
|---|---|
| 1. The middle position in a distribution of values . . . . . | 1. ______ |
| 2. The requirement that after workers are hired, they must join the union or pay their dues within a specified time period or be fired . | 2. ______ |
| 3. A compensation plan in which workers receive a fixed price for each unit produced . . . . . | 3. ______ |
| 4. A measure of position that divides an array into four equal parts . | 4. ______ |
| 5. Any form of direct compensation not included in the employee's base pay . . . . . | 5. ______ |
| 6. The process in which an impartial third party tries to bring labor and management to a point of common agreement . . . . . | 6. ______ |
| 7. The process of deducting union dues from paychecks by the employer and remitting the collections to the union . . . . . | 7. ______ |
| 8. A negotiation process between an employer and labor union representatives on work-related issues such as wages, hours of work, and working conditions . . . . . | 8. ______ |
| 9. A group incentive plan in which the savings realized from improvements in productivity are divided among workers and their employer . . . . . | 9. ______ |
| 10. The spread between the salaries found at the first and the third quartiles of a distribution . . . . . | 10. ______ |

## SECTION B • PROJECTS

### Project 10–1 • Investigating the Wage Gap Between Salaries Paid Women and Men

It is estimated that nearly two-thirds of the people having entered the workforce between 1985 and 2000 will be women; of all women of working age, 61 percent are expected to have jobs by 2000.[1]

Most women will continue to be found in positions that pay them less than men. However, there will be an increasing number of women entering higher-paying professional and technical fields. When we make executive comparisons, we find that female executives earn twice as much as they did a decade ago; however, in 1992, their average compensation was less than two-thirds of male executives' salaries and bonuses.[2]

**Directions:** The data given below compare the median earnings of women and men by expressing the women's earnings as a percentage of the men's earnings and showing the earnings gap in constant 1990 dollars. After you have studied the data, answer the questions that follow.

**RATIO OF WOMEN'S TO MEN'S EARNINGS**
**Selected Years, 1960–90**

| Year | Median Earnings: Women | Median Earnings: Men | Women's Earnings as a Percent of Men's | Earnings Gap (Constant 1990 Dollars) |
|---|---|---|---|---|
| 1960 | $3,257 | $5,368 | 60.7 | $8,569 |
| 1970 | 5,323 | 8,966 | 59.4 | 11,529 |
| 1980 | 11,197 | 18,612 | 60.2 | 11,776 |
| 1985 | 15,624 | 24,195 | 64.7 | 10,411 |
| 1990 | 19,822 | 27,678 | 71.6 | 7,856 |

Source: Department of Commerce, Bureau of the Census, 1990.

1. How do you explain the wage gap between the earnings of women and men?

_______________________________________________

_______________________________________________

_______________________________________________

2. To narrow the wage gap, what action do you recommend be taken by the government, public and private employers, unions, and organized women's groups?

_______________________________________________

_______________________________________________

_______________________________________________

[1] *Workforce 2000: Work and Workers for the Twenty-first Century* (Indianapolis, IN: Hudson Institute, June, 1987), p. xx.
[2] Chris Swingle, "Study: Women Attribute Part of Success to Luck," *USA Today* (June 30, 1993), p. 4B.

# Project 10–2 • Field Research: Management Reaction to Salary and Benefits Programs

Different salary and benefits programs—some variations on an old familiar theme—come and go. Some are looked upon as "passing fads." Others are implemented, and, after modification, take their place as effective salary administration plans. However, many companies, bound to traditional compensation practices, are reluctant "to try something new." Possibly these same firms are not obtaining the maximum return possible on the money they spend for salary and employee benefits.

In this project, you will talk with a manager in your firm, in some other company in your community, or on your college campus to determine what appeal, if any, several salary and benefits programs have to offer. At the same time, you will try to learn to what extent the manager is satisfied with his or her present salary, benefits program, and working conditions. The salary practices that you will discuss with the interviewee are briefly described below.

## Broadbanding

By means of broadbanding, a company reduces the number of its salary grades to provide fewer grades but with more pay potential in each grade. For example, a company that once had 25 or more rungs on its compensation ladder may now place its managers in four or five much wider bands. Thus, a manager might remain in one pay category ranging from, say, $60,000 to $130,000 through an entire career. With the broader bands, workers can move into more challenging and better-paying jobs faster. The company, in turn, is provided added mobility and flexibility in transferring workers.

## Skill-Based Pay Plan

Under this plan, the employee's compensation is based upon the knowledge or skills that the person brings to the job. The employee is encouraged to learn new job-related skills and to acquire additional knowledge, and the compensation increases as the employee does so. Supporters of skill-based pay plans claim that workers become more competent because they are provided financial incentives for learning and performing. When employees have many skills, they increase a firm's flexibility because they can cross over into other jobs and fill vacancies when and where they are needed. Further, as employees acquire more knowledge and skills, they become capable of handling higher-level decision making and problem solving.

## Lump-Sum Salary Increases

Employees are provided flexibility with respect to when they will receive their salary increases. Thus, to receive the full amount of their annual increase they need not wait a full year during which they are receiving a part of the annual increase in each paycheck. Employees are given the opportunity to say when they wish to receive their annual increase under several options. For example, an employee can ask for his or her annual increase in one lump sum at the beginning of the year, since the selection of a different option is offered each year.

The company treats the lump-sum salary increase as a loan; if employees should leave the firm before the end of the year, they must pay the company back for that part of the increase not yet earned.

## Flexible Benefits (Cafeteria-Style) Plan

Flexible benefits plans provide a "menu" or choice of benefits from which employees select those benefits they want or need. In many instances, employees must take some coverage in a company-selected core offering of benefits, such as medical insurance, life insurance and disability coverage. After coverage in the core benefits program is provided, the company determines the amount of remaining money available for the employees' benefits packages. The remaining money is "given" to the employees to be "spent" as they wish. Employees select such benefits as deferred compensation, additional retirement income, tuition assistance, financial counseling, and increased vacation days. In some plans, if the employees do not use all of the benefit allowances for the options available, any balance is paid to the employees in cash.

**Directions:** Plan an interview with your chosen manager and obtain as complete answers as possible to the questions listed on the form on page 107. Explain as well as you can each of the salary practices before you ask for the manager's reaction. Be a good listener and do not let your own bias show as you discuss each of the salary plans. Bring together your findings in either a written or an oral report, as directed by your instructor.

## QUESTIONNAIRE ON SALARY AND BENEFITS PROGRAMS

1. Position held by manager interviewed ______________________________
2. Age: ☐ under 26 ☐ 26–35 yrs. ☐ 36–45 yrs. ☐ 46–55 yrs. ☐ 56 yrs. and over
3. Sex: ☐ male ☐ female
4. Years of service: ☐ under 1 year ☐ 1–4 yrs. ☐ 5–9 yrs.
   ☐ 10–14 yrs. ☐ 15–24 yrs. ☐ 25 yrs. and more
5. Number of persons directly supervised by manager ______________________________
6. Describe the salary plan under which the manager is now compensated. Indicate any incentives such as profit sharing, gainsharing, bonuses, and stock options that are provided by the company.
7. What is the extent of the manager's satisfaction with the present salary plan?
8. What improvements would the manager like to see in the present salary plan?
9. What is the reaction of the manager to the company's present benefits package? Which benefits are most important? See if the manager can rank the benefits in the order of their importance.
10. What improvements would the manager like to see in the present benefits package? What benefits should be increased or possibly eliminated?
11. What is the manager's reaction to each of the salary practices:
    (A) Broadbanding: ______________________________
    (B) Skill-based pay: ______________________________
    (C) Lump-sum salary increases: ______________________________
    (D) Flexible benefits (cafeteria-style) plan: ______________________________
12. Some companies make public their salary information, such as salary ranges and median salaries for various positions, thus no longer being completely secret about management salary rates. Firms may decide to give out information on the size of salary increases and who is receiving the raises. If the manager's firm were to adopt such a practice, what does he or she see as the effects of the move?
13. To what extent does the manager participate in the decision made about his or her salary? If the manager were to participate directly in designing and implementing his or her salary program, what effect is anticipated upon the quality of the pay decision? What would be the effect upon the manager's level of satisfaction and his or her motivation?

# Project 10–3 • Computer Hands-On: Using the Least Squares Method to Compare Salaries Paid with Community Wage Curve

In this project, you will learn how the *least squares method* may be used to compare actual salaries paid with those obtained from a community salary survey. You will find that the method effectively shows the average relationship between internal job differentials (as defined by a company's job evaluation plan) and external job differentials (as defined by the rates paid for similar work in other firms).

The following example illustrates the steps that are followed in using the least squares method. After you have studied this example closely, solve the problem given on page 110.

## Example

### Compiling the Data

As the first step in comparing salaries paid with the community wage curve, bring together all necessary data as follows:

1. From the salary survey, select those data that relate to *benchmark jobs*—jobs whose duties tend to be similar from company to company and for which the job content does not change rapidly.
2. List each benchmark job title, the points assigned each job as determined by your job evaluation method, and the survey dollar value. Salary surveys usually provide several statistical measures, such as the arithmetic mean (average), median, and effective salary range. In Table 10–1, the survey dollar values are the weekly mean salaries paid the benchmark jobholders.

### Preparing the Scattergram

Prepare a *scattergram,* or *scatter chart,* as shown in Chart 10–1. This chart shows the relationship between the job evaluation points for each benchmark job and the surveyed weekly salary paid for that job. For each job, plot a dot on the chart that represents the number of job evaluation points (given at the bottom of the chart along the horizontal *X* axis) and the surveyed weekly salary (given along the vertical *Y* axis).

**Table 10–1**
**BENCHMARK JOB DATA AND SURVEYED WEEKLY SALARIES**

| Benchmark Job Title | Job Evaluation Points | Surveyed Weekly Salaries |
|---|---|---|
| File Clerk | 115 | $255 |
| Mail Clerk | 125 | 260 |
| Clerk-Typist | 140 | 300 |
| Senior Clerk | 225 | 325 |
| Secretary | 230 | 370 |
| Administrative Assistant | 295 | 425 |
| Junior Accounting Clerk | 150 | 300 |
| Data-Entry Operator | 230 | 350 |
| Word Processing Operator | 200 | 325 |
| Computer Operator | 225 | 390 |

**Chart 10–1**
**Scattergram Showing Job Evaluation Points and Surveyed Weekly Salary for Each Benchmark Job**

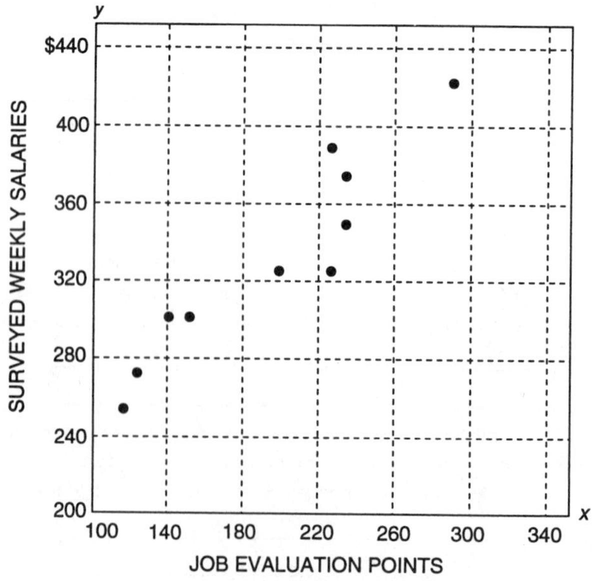

Name ________________________________ Date ________________ 

## Calculating the Line of Best Fit

Chart 10–1 shows that as the number of job evaluation points rises, the surveyed weekly salary values also increase. Such a relationship would be expected. By inspection, we could draw a straight line that would "fit," or represent, most of the plotted dots. However, we want to locate a single straight line that, when drawn through the dots, will be the *average* of all the data. The least squares method enables us to draw this line, which is referred to as the *line of best fit.* Some dots will lie above the line and some below it; the sum of the squares of the distances to the line from all the dots above the line will approximate the sum of the squares of the distances to the line of the dots below the line.

To obtain a precise location of the line of best fit, we make the following calculations to obtain a formula for the line:

1. Prepare Table 10–2, in which you record:
   a. The titles of all benchmark jobs.
   b. The job evaluation points for each job in Column *X*.
   c. The surveyed weekly salary for each job in Column *Y*.
   d. The square of each *X* value in Column $X^2$. For example, for File Clerk, enter 115 × 115, or 13,225.
   e. The product of each *X* value and each *Y* value in Column *XY*. For File Clerk, 115 × 255 = 29,325.
2. Add each column to obtain the values shown in Table 10–2. *N* is the number of benchmark jobs.
3. Substitute the Sum values from Table 10–2 into the following formulas:

$$a = \frac{\text{Sum } X^2\,(\text{Sum } Y) - \text{Sum } X\,(\text{Sum } XY)}{N\,(\text{Sum } X^2) - (\text{Sum } X)^2}$$

$$b = \frac{N\,(\text{Sum } XY) - \text{Sum } X\,(\text{Sum } Y)}{N\,(\text{Sum } X^2) - (\text{Sum } X)^2}$$

By making the substitutions from Table 10–2, we arrive at:

$$a = \frac{405{,}025(3{,}300) - 1{,}935(665{,}675)}{10\,(405{,}025) - (1{,}935)^2}$$

$$= 158.49$$

$$b = \frac{10(665{,}675) - 1{,}935(3{,}300)}{10(405{,}025) - (1{,}935)^2}$$

$$= .8864$$

4. Substitute these values for *a* and *b* into the formula:

$$Y = a + b(x)$$

The result is:

$$Y = 158.49 + .8864(x)$$

This formula represents the best average linear relationship between the internal job hierarchy as defined by the job evaluation system and the external job hierarchy as defined by the salaries paid in the community for similar work.

## Drawing the Line of Best Fit

Since two points are required to draw the line of best fit, we need to solve the formula twice. Proceed as follows to locate these two points:

**Table 10–2**
**CALCULATING THE LINE OF BEST FIT**

| Benchmark Job Title | X | Y | $X^2$ | XY |
|---|---|---|---|---|
| File Clerk | 115 | 255 | 13,225 | 29,325 |
| Mail Clerk | 125 | 260 | 15,625 | 32,500 |
| Clerk-Typist | 140 | 300 | 19,600 | 42,000 |
| Senior Clerk | 225 | 325 | 50,625 | 73,125 |
| Secretary | 230 | 370 | 52,900 | 85,100 |
| Admin. Assistant | 295 | 425 | 87,025 | 125,375 |
| Jr. Account. Clerk | 150 | 300 | 22,500 | 45,000 |
| Data-Entry Operator | 230 | 350 | 52,900 | 80,500 |
| Word Process. Operator | 200 | 325 | 40,000 | 65,000 |
| Computer Operator | 225 | 390 | 50,625 | 87,750 |

| | | | | | |
|---|---|---|---|---|---|
| N = 10 | | | | | |
| Sum X | = | 1,935 | | | |
| Sum Y | = | | 3,300 | | |
| Sum $X^2$ | = | | | 405,025 | |
| Sum XY | = | | | | 665,675 |

**Chart 10–2**
**SCATTERGRAM SHOWING THE LINE OF BEST FIT**

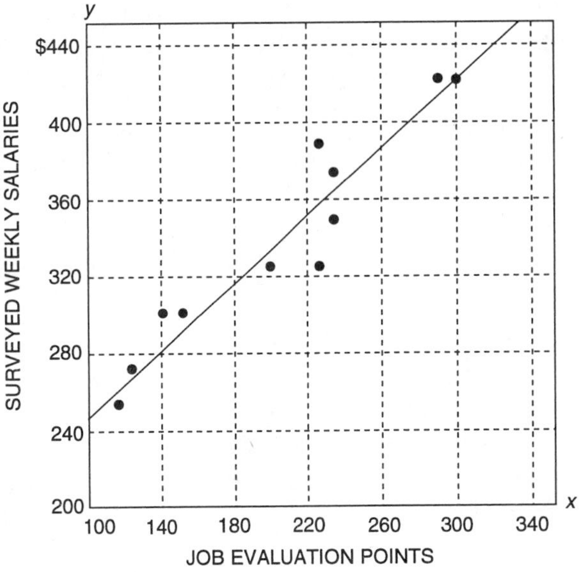

1. Substitute any two job evaluation point scores, one from the left side of the scattergram and one from the right side, for "$x$" in the formula above. In our example, we shall use 100 and 300 job evaluation points. Then solve each time for "$Y$":

$$Y = 158.49 + .8864(100) = \$247.13$$

$$Y = 158.49 + .8864(300) = \$424.41$$

2. On Chart 10–1, locate 100 job evaluation points on the $X$ axis. Read up to $247.13 on the $Y$ axis and place a new dot on the scattergram; do the same for 300 points and $424.41. Then connect the dots as shown in Chart 10–2.

The line of best fit, which you just drew, represents the average relationship between *internal* job evaluation points and *external* rates of pay. This line is often called the *community wage curve.*

To provide additional data needed for salary administration purposes, in this project you will compare the *salaries actually paid* with the *community wage curve* by preparing a second line of best fit. In these calculations, as indicated below, you will use the actual weekly salaries paid and the job evaluation points for each job.

**Directions:** Prior to developing a community wage curve, Betz, Inc., has identified the 11 benchmark job titles listed in Table 10–3. This table also shows the job evaluation points for each job, which have been determined as a result of a recent job evaluation study in which the point method was used. From a salary survey conducted two months ago, the company obtained dollar values for each benchmark job title. Also listed in Table 10–3 are the actual average salaries paid the holders of the 11 benchmark jobs.

1. Use your word processing software with graphing capabilities to construct a scattergram showing the job evaluation points for the 11 benchmark jobs and the survey weekly dollar values. Use the grid on page 111.

2. Calculate the line of best fit, using the top work sheet on page 112. Draw the line of best fit on the scattergram prepared in step 1.

3. On the scattergram prepared in step 1, plot the job evaluation points for the 11 benchmark jobs and the weekly salaries actually paid. Use a different color of pen or pencil for plotting these dots. Or a sheet of onionskin paper may be used to prepare an overlay.

4. Using the bottom work sheet on page 112, calculate another line of best fit for the weekly salaries actually paid and the job evaluation points assigned each job. This line should be drawn in the same color that was used for plotting the dots in step 3.

**Table 10–3**
**BENCHMARK JOBS, JOB EVALUATION POINTS, SURVEY SALARY VALUES, AND ACTUAL PAID SALARIES**

| Benchmark Job Titles | Job Evaluation Points | Survey Dollar Value (weekly | Actual Paid Salaries (weekly) |
|---|---|---|---|
| Mail Clerk-File Clerk . . | 235 | $250 | $230 |
| Clerk-Typist . . . . . . . . . | 300 | 260 | 245 |
| Data-Entry Operator B . | 340 | 270 | 275 |
| Switchboard Operator/ Receptionist . . . . . . | 365 | 285 | 320 |
| Word Processing Operator . . . . . . . . | 390 | 330 | 310 |
| Data-Entry Operator A | 405 | 295 | 310 |
| Photocopy Machine Operator . . . . . . . . | 420 | 280 | 330 |
| Computer Operator B . | 490 | 315 | 300 |
| Secretary A . . . . . . . . | 505 | 370 | 410 |
| Computer Operator A . | 570 | 355 | 345 |
| Programmer . . . . . . . | 620 | 450 | 500 |

5. How does the second line of best fit (actual paid salaries) compare with the community wage curve? Identify the actual paid salaries that are significantly out of line with the community wage curve.

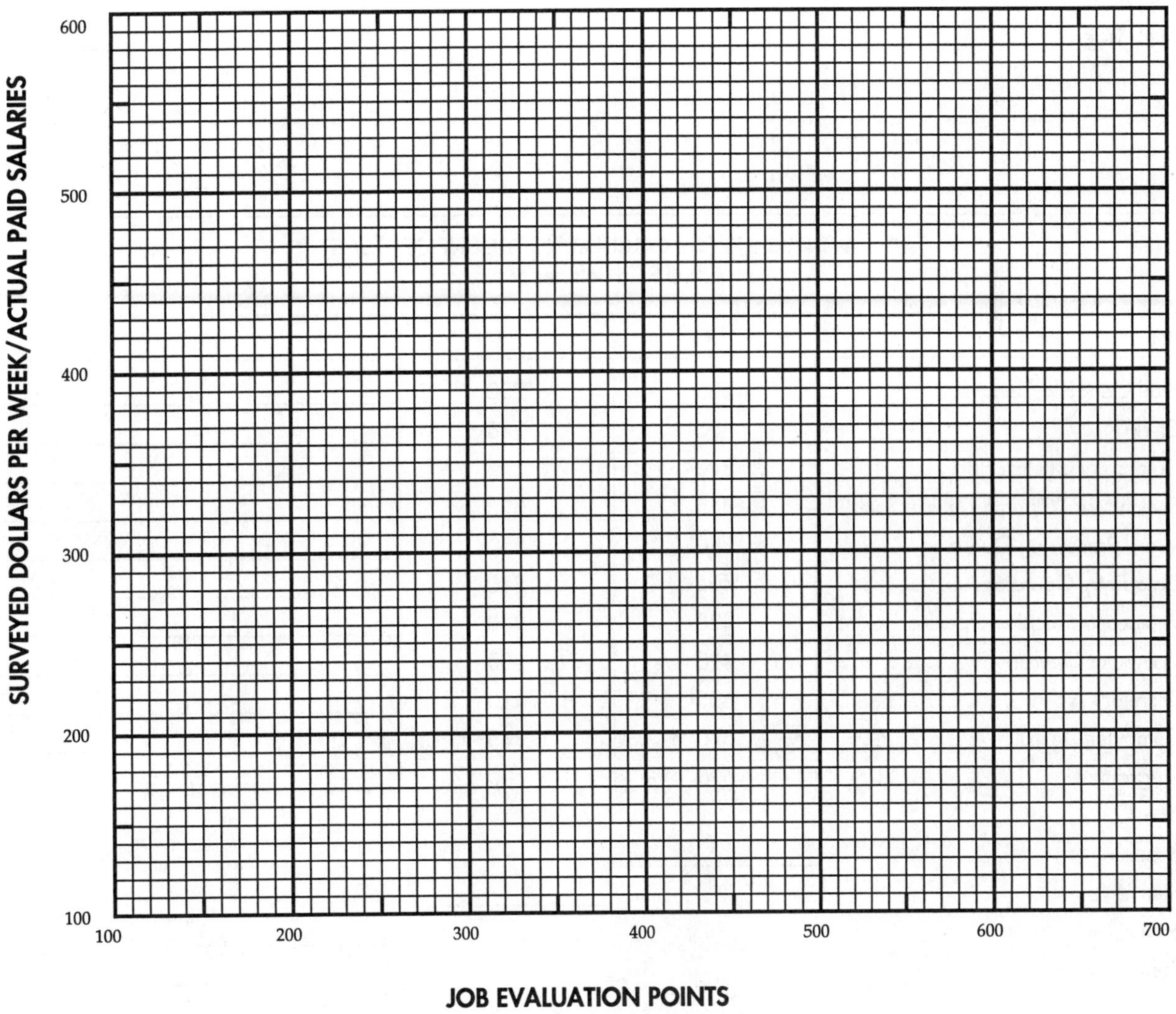

**WORK SHEET FOR CALCULATING THE LINE OF BEST FIT**
**Survey Dollar Values (weekly)**

| Benchmark Job Titles | X | Y | $X^2$ | XY |
|---|---|---|---|---|
| Mail Clerk-File Clerk | 235 | 250 | | |
| Clerk-Typist | 300 | 260 | | |
| Data-Entry Operator B | 340 | 270 | | |
| Switchboard Operator/Receptionist | 365 | 285 | | |
| Word Processing Operator | 390 | 330 | | |
| Data-Entry Operator A | 405 | 295 | | |
| Photocopy Machine Operator | 420 | 280 | | |
| Computer Operator B | 490 | 315 | | |
| Secretary A | 505 | 370 | | |
| Computer Operator A | 570 | 355 | | |
| Programmer | 620 | 450 | | |

$N = 11$

Sum $X$ = ______

Sum $Y$ = ______

Sum $X^2$ = ______

Sum $XY$ = ______

**WORK SHEET FOR CALCULATING THE LINE OF BEST FIT**
**Actual Paid Salaries (weekly)**

| Benchmark Job Titles | X | Y | $X^2$ | XY |
|---|---|---|---|---|
| Mail Clerk-File Clerk | 235 | 230 | | |
| Clerk-Typist | 300 | 245 | | |
| Data-Entry Operator B | 340 | 275 | | |
| Switchboard Operator/Receptionist | 365 | 320 | | |
| Word Processing Operator | 390 | 310 | | |
| Data-Entry Operator A | 405 | 310 | | |
| Photocopy Machine Operator | 420 | 330 | | |
| Computer Operator B | 490 | 300 | | |
| Secretary A | 505 | 410 | | |
| Computer Operator A | 570 | 345 | | |
| Programmer | 620 | 500 | | |

$N = 11$

Sum $X$ = ______

Sum $Y$ = ______

Sum $X^2$ = ______

Sum $XY$ = ______

# Project 10–4 • Field Research: Studying a Union Contract

In this field research project, you will become familiar with the specific provisions of a union contract that covers white-collar workers. If it is not possible to obtain a copy of the collective bargaining contract from a firm in your community, check with the librarian on your campus or at the public library to locate an up-to-date contract. If none of these sources are able to provide a contract, you may write the offices of a labor union to obtain a sample copy.

**Directions:** Examine the collective bargaining agreement and indicate the specific provisions contained in the contract with reference to each of the items listed below. To see how the contents of this contract compare with those commonly found in other contract agreements, consult the latest edition of *Basic Patterns in Union Contracts,* published by The Bureau of National Affairs, 1231 25th Street, NW, Washington, DC 20037. (The Bureau maintains a file of over 5,000 agreements reflecting the latest renewals or amendments. As a result of having computerized the contents of these agreements, the Bureau periodically provides an updated edition of the *Basic Patterns* booklet.) Your findings will be presented in either an oral or written report, as requested by your instructor.

## PROVISIONS CONTAINED IN UNION CONTRACT

1. *Length of contract term* (number of years)
2. a. *Contract reopener* (reopening of contract for amendment prior to its scheduled expiration)

   b. *For what reasons contract may be reopened* (wages, fringes, occurrences beyond control of the parties, etc.)
3. *Contract renewal* (automatic renewal, for what time period)
4. *Discharge* (grounds for discharge, procedure for discharging, appeals procedure for discharged worker)
5. *Discipline,* short of discharge (disciplinary measures to be taken)
6. *Grievance procedure* (steps to be taken in the processing of complaints)
7. *Arbitration* (procedure to be followed)
8. *Holidays* (number provided: specify days observed as holidays, provision for holiday pay)
9. *Hours and overtime* (daily work schedule, weekly work schedule, requirements for overtime premiums, regulations for the distribution of overtime work, length of lunch and rest periods, rules governing pay for time lost on a day of injury, rules governing pay for time spent traveling to and from work)
10. *Income maintenance* (description of type: work or pay guarantee, severance pay, supplemental unemployment benefits)
11. *Insurance benefits* (kinds of coverage)
12. *Layoff* (factors considered in selecting employees for layoff), bumping, recall, work sharing
13. *Leave of absence* (duration of each kind)
14. *Seniority* (employment service credit), provision for accrual of seniority, loss of seniority, seniority lists, promotion, transfer, etc.
15. *Strikes and lockouts*
16. *Union security* (union shop, modified union shop, agency shop, check-off, etc.)
17. *Vacations*
18. *Wages* (provisions for general wage increases during life of contract, cost-of-living escalator, deferred wage increases, supplementary pay, establishment of pay rates, hiring rates, job progression rates, etc.)
19. *Working conditions—safety and health; discrimination* (occupational safety and health, antidiscrimination, company rules that may conflict with contract, etc.)

## Project 10–5 • Administering Salary Programs in Japan

**Directions:** After you read the following article dealing with Japanese compensation policies and practices, answer the questions at the end.

**Japanese pay plan is based on loyalty.** One of those areas in which Japanese companies differ from their U.S. counterparts is in their compensation policies. "Japanese employees are paid on the basis of their loyalty to the company, whereas if someone is hired at a U.S. company to be a manager of real estate, the employee is paid for that job, whether he or she has had 10 years of experience or 25," explains Susan Schenkel-Savitt, a partner in the New York City office of Epstein, Becker & Green, a law firm specializing in human resources cases.

In Japanese companies, the gap between the lowest and highest salaries is far narrower than in the U.S., and managers typically don't receive such benefits as company cars, stock options or even their own offices. Pay scales are more rigid and offer little reward for individual initiative. In many Japanese companies, a bonus simply is a portion of the salary that's withheld and later paid out in a large installment.

Others may pay 75% of the base salary in regular wages and require the employee to bill the remaining salary in overtime hours. Given their long work hours, Japanese managers' overtime billings frequently raise their actual earnings to as much as 150% of the original salary.

Lifetime employment traditionally has been a major incentive for Japanese employees. U.S. nationals, by contrast, are highly mobile, carving out individualized career paths. The promise of long-term employment isn't a sufficient incentive for U.S. nationals, who are accustomed to pay based on merit.

To attract top managerial talent in the U.S. marketplace, some Japanese companies have started to offer compensation packages that are more generous, even if it means paying above the company's salary scale. At Fujisawa USA Inc., a pharmaceutical company based in Deerfield, Illinois, executives are offered a company car, an allowance for personal investment planning, a health club membership, and year-end bonuses that are tied to company profits. "We decided that to attract and retain the best U.S. managers, we needed to be competitive [in salaries and benefits]," says John Fowler, assistant to the chairman at Fujisawa.

Japanese companies don't like making individuals into star players, but they're realizing that in certain areas, they have to attract the best U.S. talent, according to Michiko Ito, a partner in the New York City office of the law firm Morrison & Foerster, which has represented several Japanese corporations in labor matters.

Recently, for example, a major Japanese company had to sweeten a benefits package to lure a senior U.S. executive. Persuaded by SpencerStuart, the executive search firm it hired to negotiate the deal, the Japanese company raised its vacation package from its standard one week to four weeks. "We thought their vacation offer would break the deal," recalls SpencerStuart director Davis Hawkins.

**The Japanese broaden employee skills.** Japanese manufacturers have drawn praise for their training programs. "We spend a great amount of time and resources training our employees—much more than any company I've ever been associated with," says Bucky Kahl, director of human resources at Nissan Motor Manufacturing Corporation U.S.A., located in Smyrna, Tennessee.

At the Nissan plant, for example, prospective employees begin training before they're hired. They undergo a 48-hour nonpaid, pretraining program to ensure that they can handle industrial work. Completion of that training, says Kahl, also demonstrates an employee's commitment to his or her prospective employer.

Companies tend to rotate employees through several different areas of operation, which not only builds worker expertise but also alleviates burnout. And rather than lay off workers during slow times, Japanese manufacturers put them through additional training to continue building their skills.

"After a Japanese company hires employees, it usually trains them to be generalists. Even though a person may have been hired as an accountant, three or four years later, the company may retrain him or her for a transfer into the sales department," Segiura explains.

Source: Elizabeth Klein, "The U.S./Japanese HR Culture Clash," *Personnel Journal* (November, 1992), pp. 36–38. 

On the other hand, in the service sector and in managerial positions, Japanese companies frequently offer less training than their U.S. competitors do. "The Japanese feel training happens largely on the job, whereas U.S. workers require classroom training," says Stehlik. She says that, at Nippon Credit Bank, the entry-level training program is only two weeks long, compared with six months for U.S. banks.

According to Pilnick, Matsushita Electric Company of America spent only about one-fiftieth as much on training compared with top U.S. manufacturers. "There's probably less spent on formal training, but they tend to use a lot of cross-training on the job," he says.

U.S. employee reaction to employment at Japanese companies tends to differ sharply between hourly workers and management-level staff. Many managers who were born and raised in the U.S. say that they feel constrained by the Japanese decision-making process, which rewards consensus rather than individual initiative.

By contrast, U.S. factory workers often praise the Japanese management style because it gives them greater input in the manufacturing process. Nissan Motor Manufacturing Corporation USA, for example, uses a participatory management style, which brings its line workers into all decisions that concern production.

In addition, at many U.S.-based Japanese plants, autoworkers are allowed to shut down the entire assembly line if they see a defect. Hourly workers "really are the winners in a Japanese environment," says Pilnick.

Compared with hourly workers, U.S. managers have less authority in Japanese companies than they would in U.S.-based firms, because decisions are reached only through extensive consultation with colleagues and even subordinates. In some cases, say human resources executives, U.S. managers may become frustrated because they're hired at a high salary and a senior position, but lack the authority they would have had in a U.S.-based company.

**The Japanese value seniority.** The promotions and raises in Japanese companies traditionally are based on such characteristics as seniority, age, gender, and marital status. The rationale for the system is that workers are rewarded for their loyalty.

Japanese workers are promoted along with others of their age and rank. Japanese managers, on the other hand, have found that such a strategy doesn't work as an incentive to U.S. workers, who are driven by salary and career advancement, not by lifetime employment. "In Japan, many of the older employees who aren't working as hard as the younger generation earn more money. That's accepted in the Japanese environment, but it doesn't work here," says Yoneda.

Annual performance reviews are superfluous for managers in Japanese companies. "In a Japanese organization, people work such long hours together that everyone knows where they stand. They don't feel the need to sit down for a performance review once a year," explains Hawkins.

U.S. human resources managers, however, are encouraging Japanese organizations to conduct more thorough evaluations, develop standard evaluation forms, and document evaluations. At Nissan Motor Manufacturing Corporation USA, for example, employees who are being considered for promotion are evaluated not only by their supervisors but also by their peers.

Because of the expectation of loyalty between the company and the employee, terminating employees is difficult for Japanese companies. The task becomes even more difficult in the U.S. because the companies fear that fired employees might sue the company.

At one company, for example, it took almost five months just to authorize the firing of a receptionist. "Ninety percent of Japanese companies here say they're afraid to terminate employees," says Ito.

Although Japanese managers continue to express frustration in what they perceive to be disloyalty and opportunism on the part of U.S. employees, who change jobs far more often than the Japanese, they're changing their practices so they can retain talented U.S. nationals. Some Japanese companies are starting to promote their local U.S. employees, instead of simply bringing in Japanese expatriates.

At the Nippon Credit Bank, for example, 70% of local employees have been promoted. And at Nissan Motor Manufacturing USA, line managers are encouraged to apply for manager positions. Clearly, savvy human resources management is a critical factor in the globalization of Japanese companies. Their success in building an international business depends on their ability to effectively manage and develop a truly global workforce. Says Kahl, "Fair treatment, teamwork, and development of our people—those are our global personnel management principles. But tailoring them to the local situation is the job of the human resources department."

1. List the factors that would motivate you to seek employment in a Japanese owned and managed organization located in the United States.

2. Would a work assignment in an office located in Japan appeal to you? Explain.

11

# PROVIDING EMPLOYEE BENEFITS

Representing more than 39 percent of the payroll dollar, employee benefits include legally required payments, paid holidays, sick leave, insurance, pensions, and numerous programs and services provided workers. On the average, employers spend more than $13,000 each year for the benefits provided each worker.

In comparing the cost of benefits not required by law with the return received by the company, the office manager is concerned with meeting the workers' needs. At the same time, the manager must maintain a well-balanced, cost-contained benefits program. As a result of its investment in employee benefits, a firm tries to meet the following objectives: to attract and retain qualified workers, to reduce out-of-pocket labor costs and the attendant payroll taxes and income taxes, to increase productivity through greater employee loyalty and dedication, to decrease absenteeism and turnover, to ward off unionization, and to meet the workers' needs for job satisfaction and job security.

Today's office manager must appraise the cost effectiveness of the newer kinds of benefits in relation to meeting the workers' needs and still permitting the firm to remain in a competitive position. Among these benefits are: vision care, prescription drug plans, physical wellness programs, outplacement and preretirement counseling, eldercare and childcare services, adoption benefit plans, domestic partner benefits, and personal services benefits.

Many firms provide a flexible benefits program, often known as a *cafeteria plan.* This plan enables employees to "pick and choose" those benefits, including cash, that will meet their particular needs in relation to their age, lifestyle, family situation, spending needs, and so forth.

## SECTION A • REVIEW QUESTIONS

**Directions:** In the Answers column, write the letter of the item in Column 1 that is described by each statement in Column 2.

| Column 1 | Column 2 | Answers |
|---|---|---|
| **A** Disability income insurance | 1. A plan in which employers make contributions to the individual retirement accounts on behalf of their employees .............. | 1. ______ |
| **B** Flexible benefits program | 2. A state insurance program designed to protect employees and their dependents against losses due to injury or death during the worker's employment ............................................. | 2. ______ |
| **C** Group life insurance | 3. Privileges, gains, or profits provided executives in addition to their regular salaries ......................................... | 3. ______ |
| **D** Hospital insurance | 4. An insurance plan that provides continuing income for workers unable to return to their jobs after they have exhausted their sickness and accident benefits ..................................... | 4. ______ |
| **E** Major medical insurance | 5. The process of conveying to employees the right to share in a retirement fund in the event they are terminated before the normal retirement age ........................................ | 5. ______ |
| **F** OASDHI benefits | 6. An employer-sponsored benefits package that provides employees a choice between selecting cash and certain qualified benefits ...... | 6. ______ |
| **G** Perquisites | 7. An insurance plan that protects employees and their dependents from huge medical bills resulting from serious accidents or prolonged illness | 7. ______ |
| **H** Simplified employee pension (SEP) plan | 8. The protection that covers all employees of a firm and is designed to provide benefits should a worker die or become totally disabled ... | 8. ______ |
| **I** Vesting | | |
| **J** Workers' compensation insurance | | |

**Directions:** Each of the following statements is either true or false. Indicate your choice in the Answers column by circling "T" or "F."

| | | Answers | |
|---|---|---|---|
| 1. | All employer-provided benefits are positive motivators that stimulate workers to become more productive | T | F |
| 2. | The Federal Insurance Contributions Act (FICA) imposes a social security tax on both the employer and the employee | T | F |
| 3. | A health maintenance organization (HMO) provides prepaid medical services to its participants | T | F |
| 4. | Employees are eligible to make tax-deductible contributions to their individual retirement accounts (IRAs) provided they participate in their company-funded retirement plan | T | F |
| 5. | Once an office worker is vested under the firm's retirement plan, the worker must wait until time of retirement to receive any benefits | T | F |
| 6. | A 401(k) retirement plan enables employees to shelter from federal income taxes a portion of their salaries and the earnings thereon | T | F |
| 7. | Office workers usually receive group life insurance coverage that provides a benefit equal to at least three times their annual salary | T | F |
| 8. | Most office employees receive two weeks' vacation with pay after one year of employment | T | F |
| 9. | The Pregnancy Discrimination Act of 1978 requires employers to place pregnant women on sick leave before the end of their fifth month of pregnancy | T | F |
| 10. | All 50 states require employers to grant employees time off from work to vote | T | F |
| 11. | For motor-task skills, such as data entry, work breaks should be scheduled within the first two hours of work in the morning | T | F |
| 12. | The Family and Medical Leave Act of 1993 (FMLA) requires employers with 50 or more employees to provide up to 12 weeks of paid leave for family emergencies, childbirth, or adoption | T | F |
| 13. | In their educational assistance programs, many firms require that the courses taken by employees be job related | T | F |
| 14. | Companies undertake outplacement counseling to help their workers who are approaching retirement | T | F |
| 15. | Childcare services are provided by about one-fourth of all American companies | T | F |
| 16. | In a small company, the office manager may be assigned responsibility for administering the employee benefits program | T | F |
| 17. | An outstanding feature of the flexible benefits program is that employees take an active role in developing their own benefits packages | T | F |
| 18. | Case management is a technique used by companies to contain their health insurance costs | T | F |
| 19. | To control the cost of their employee benefits, most large firms have abandoned their self-insurance plans | T | F |
| 20. | To reduce its record-keeping costs and provide better service to its employees, a company may "farm out" the administration of its benefits to a benefits consulting firm | T | F |

## SECTION B • PROJECTS

# Project 11–1 • Planning a Broader Offering of Employee Benefits

In the offices of the County Bank, where you are employed as manager of office services, there are 100 workers. As part of your year-end reporting, you have assembled the following data that show the average weekly cost of employee benefits for the bank:

| Salaries Paid for Time Not Worked | Cost per Employee per Week |
|---|---|
| Vacations (an average of 13 days each year) | $ 26.12 |
| Rest periods, lunch breaks, work breaks | 13.80 |
| Holidays (8 each year) | 20.48 |
| Sick leave | 5.56 |
| Free meals in the cafeteria | .60 |
| Short-term disability and salary continuation or long-term disability | 2.68 |
| Christmas bonuses, suggestion awards, etc. | 1.75 |
| Free checking accounts, free checks, etc. | .48 |
| **Nonsalary Payments** | |
| Pensions | $ 23.88 |
| Old-age, survivors, disability, and health insurance | 42.08 |
| Insurance premiums (life, hospital, surgical, medical, and major medical) | 34.44 |
| Profit-sharing payments | 5.04 |
| Unemployment compensation taxes | 4.04 |
| Workers' compensation insurance | 1.52 |
| Total cost of average weekly employee benefits | $ 182.47 |

In recent months, along with other officers of the bank, you have been discussing the possibility of providing a broader offering of benefits. It has been decided to budget the cost of benefits at $200 per employee per week. Thus, for the next year you have additional weekly funds of about $17.53 per worker.

**Directions:**

1. With the help of your instructor, form several teams of five to six persons each and reach a consensus of how you, as a management team, recommend that the $17.53 be distributed. You will want to consider increasing the size of the present benefits offered as well as adding new ones. The average cost of several benefits not presently provided by the County Bank have been estimated as follows:

| New Benefits for Consideration | Estimated Weekly Cost per Employee |
|---|---|
| Educational assistance | $1.68 |
| Prepaid legal service | 1.76 |
| Career apparel | 4.70 |
| Dental insurance for employees and dependents | 2.08 |
| Prescription drug plan | 4.30 |
| Vision care insurance | 2.95 |
| Annual physical examinations | .70 |
| Parental leave (maternity and paternity) | .65 |

2. Combine the findings of all teams into one set of recommendations to be offered to the bank officers. In the combined report, be sure to assign a priority ranking to each of the benefits recommended.

3. Develop a set of procedures for the County Bank to follow in communicating the changes in the employee benefits package. Indicate which communication media will be used to relay the information (a) to all employees as a whole and (b) to each individual employee. Lay out in rough form the format of those media you recommend be used to convey the average weekly cost of each benefit.

## Project 11–2 • Establishing an Educational Assistance Program

To meet the needs of its growing workforce and to develop further the skills and knowledge of its workers, LeBlanc, Inc., has decided to establish an educational assistance program, effective in the fall this year. You, as office manager of the firm, four supervisors, two office workers, and two plant workers have been selected as a task force to plan the establishment and administration of such a program.

**Directions:** By answering each of the questions given below and on pages 121 and 122, you will be aided in making a contribution as a member of the task force.

1. Present a workable definition of THE EDUCATIONAL ASSISTANCE PLAN AT LEBLANC, INC.—a definition that will be easily and clearly understood by all workers.

2. Should the plan be uniformly applied throughout all departments and divisions of the company? Explain.

3. Who will be responsible for administering the educational assistance program?

4. Who will be eligible to participate in the program? Should eligibility be restricted? In what respect?

5. Should the program provide that an employee may register as a full-time student and carry a full course load? Explain.

6. What kinds of schools should employees be allowed to attend?

7. Should employees be permitted to take any course they want, or must the courses be job related, or at least applicable to a degree that will help employees in their jobs?

8. Should any limit be placed on the number of, or the dollar value of, courses that a worker may take during a school year? If so, what are your recommendations?

9. What costs should the educational assistance plan pay for?— registration? tuition? books? test fees? laboratory fees? application fees? transportation? graduation fees?

10. How can the educational assistance program be maintained so that it is used correctly and achieves the objectives for which it was designed?

11. Should the amount of reimbursement depend upon the grade received by the employee? If so, spell out your recommended reimbursement plan.

12. What will be your "sales promotion pitch" to your employees to explain why the company is offering this new employee benefit? Incidentally, the program will cost your firm about $1.95 per week per employee who participates. How will you encourage employees to participate in the program?

13. How will LeBlanc, Inc., be able to determine if the educational assistance plan is benefiting the company? Develop a set of criteria to be used in evaluating the effectiveness of the plan.

## Project 11–3 • Viewing the Organization from the Bottom

In this article you will read how Michael Fitzgerald, the chairman and chief executive officer of a greeting-card company, structured his organization in a diamond-like shape, with the customers at the top and him at the bottom. Firmly committed to the philosophy that employees are the main reason a company succeeds or fails, the company provides its workers 40 paid days off each year. Other benefits about which you will read include the company's education-loan program and a four-day weekend every month.

There are no questions or exercises following this reading. It has been selected to show how, as a small organization grew, it created a highly motivated workforce that accepts the challenge of change. Enjoy!

I know what it's like to be low man on the organizational flowchart. As chairman and chief executive officer of Sunrise Publications, Inc., that's where I am now.

That may sound like a gimmick, but it's actually a key to treating employees in a way that keeps creativity and morale at peak levels.

Sunrise Publications is the Bloomington, Ind., greeting-card company I started with two friends in 1974. In the past five years, the company has more than doubled its workforce—to about 260—and has built revenues to about $20 million annually. Sunrise sells more than 33 million greeting cards a year.

But it's not the numbers that I'm proud of; it's our philosophy for dealing with people. With the company creating 1,000 new cards and other products each year, this business demands hard workers who maintain their individuality. In our management structure, the customer is on top, followed by the sales staff, support people, down to executive management, and, last, me. It's kind of a diamond shape rather than the traditional pyramid.

Skeptics might say that the customers aren't a part of our organization, but we think they are; if we do not have the involvement of customers as part of our organization—getting satisfaction from what they want and need from us—then we won't stay in business for long.

As with any other company, workers are dedicated to making the people at the top of the organizational chart happy; but in our case, that's not the chairman.

In order to build that please-the-customer-first philosophy, and to get workers to look at the customer first rather than at how they can get ahead themselves, we've tried to provide a creative atmosphere that challenges employees personally and professionally.

For example, we have an education-loan program that allows any worker to take employment-related seminars or classes. We lend the worker money to pay for the schooling, with the loan to be paid back with years of service. If the worker continues with the company for three years after an education loan is made, the loan is completely paid off.

By providing this type of job-related educational assistance, we allow workers to develop the credentials needed to advance. And as the worker gains expertise and training, the company—particularly the customer—benefits. About two-thirds of our managers and supervisors use this program, and, companywide, it is one of our most popular initiatives.

Unlike other organizations, we give the entire company a four-day weekend every month. When there is a holiday, we plan the two days off from work around it; otherwise, we just shut the place down for two days each month, either before or after a weekend, leaving only a skeleton crew to handle the phone calls and satisfy customers while the rest of us get away.

When those 24 days a year are added to vacation and personal days, a Sunrise employee gets 40 paid days off a year.

And, no, our initiatives are not excessive. We expect our people to work very hard, but we see no reason to burn them out—not when it would affect our productivity, creativity, morale, and our relationship with the customer.

Although there is a cost to every employee-benefit program, that cost is more than made up in terms of employee retention.

When Sunrise started, we didn't have the wherewithal to do the four-day weekends or to provide educational training. But as the company has grown, our philosophy for treating individuals with dignity and respect—giving worker and customer a say in the company's future—has paid off.

Every growing, competitive business undergoes significant and

---

Source: Michael Fitzgerald, "The View from the Bottom," *Nation's Business* (February, 1993), p. 6. Reprinted by permission. 

sometimes traumatic change, whether in installing new systems or procedures or demanding more from the workforce. Change, particularly as it affects workers, is the one constant of an entrepreneurial environment.

By creating a highly motivated, trained workforce and thereby reducing turnover, the effects of change on customers, employees, and company performance are dramatically reduced.

The view from the bottom of this organization is pretty good; customers appear pleased with the way things look from the top. Hopefully, that means we've done the right thing in training and motivating the people in the middle.

# 12

# EXAMINING WORKPLACE ISSUES

When faced with many of the issues and problems affecting the workers' physical and mental well-being, the office manager reaches a quick and easy decision by referring to the firm's policy manual or employee handbook. For other kinds of problems that emerge, however, the company may not have established a policy. In this case, the office manager must make a decision that will be equitable to both the worker and the company. To do so, the office manager profits by learning how other office administrators solved their personnel problems and by examining their firms' policies and practices.

The office manager tries to create a workplace environment in which potential issues pertaining to job attendance and work scheduling are anticipated. Today's office workers are better educated than their predecessors, and they expect to spend their working lives in an environment that recognizes their knowledge, skills, expectations, and diversity. Too much turnover in the office can often be traced to friction between managers and their workers. Such an economic waste can be lessened by developing an environment in which *effective human relations* and *communications* become the key words. This environment is characterized by mutual respect, mutual approval, and relatively stress-free relationships.

Despite a continuing decline in membership, unions still actively recruit new members, especially women and minorities. Thus, the office manager should understand why office workers join unions and what role the office manager plays in office unionism—before, during, and after a union recruitment drive.

## SECTION A • REVIEW QUESTIONS

**Directions:** Indicate your answer to each of the following questions by circling "Yes" or "No" in the Answers column.

| | | Answers | |
|---|---|---|---|
| 1. | Does the responsibility for detecting an alcoholic office worker lie with that person's coworkers? | Yes | No |
| 2. | Do all states give employers the right to test for drug and alcohol abuse? | Yes | No |
| 3. | Has the federal government ruled that AIDS is a handicap entitled to protection against discrimination? | Yes | No |
| 4. | When office workers become overly anxious about their work problems, may the situation become so stressful that they experience burnout? | Yes | No |
| 5. | Have all states enacted legislation that restricts smoking in private sector workplaces? | Yes | No |
| 6. | Does the federal government provide that victims of sexual harassment are entitled to a jury trial? | Yes | No |
| 7. | May a company legally bar a husband and wife from working together in the same department? | Yes | No |
| 8. | Is it legal for a company to have a policy against employing married women? | Yes | No |
| 9. | Have all states passed legislation whereby it is illegal for employers to deny employment to gays and lesbians? | Yes | No |
| 10. | May a company legally adopt a policy that bans moonlighting? | Yes | No |

11. Do research studies universally show that workaholics are emotionally disturbed? ......... Yes No

12. Are the perceptions that office workers have about their companies related to whether they might steal from their firms? ....... Yes No

13. Does the Electronic Communications Privacy Act ensure the privacy of personal information that office workers enter into their computers? ....... Yes No

14. Is tardiness in the office traceable more often to laxness in discipline than to any other cause? Yes No

15. Are the most chronic absentees found among newly hired employees? ....... Yes No

16. Is dismissal from the job the major reason for most terminations? ....... Yes No

17. Is the compressed workweek the most popular work schedule for office employees? ....... Yes No

18. Is flextime equally effective in insurance companies and in assembly-line manufacturing plants? ....... Yes No

19. In job sharing, is one full-time job shared by two people who split their working hours, responsibilities, and employee benefits? ....... Yes No

20. Does a telecommuter work at a site away from the traditional office setting? ....... Yes No

21. Have all states adopted legislation that permits work sharing as an alternative to layoffs? .... Yes No

22. A union organizer obtains authorization cards from 32 percent of the office workers in a company. Can the union demand that the employer recognize that union as the bargaining agent? ....... Yes No

23. Are employers required by federal law to bargain collectively with an organized group of office workers? ....... Yes No

24. After the first election whereby a union is certified, can management request another election any time 12 months later in order to decertify the union? ....... Yes No

25. Is an ombudsman hired by a union to investigate possible wrongdoings by management? .... Yes No

## SECTION B • PROJECTS

## Project 12–1 • "Hey, How Would You Handle This One?"

At this month's chapter meeting of the Metro Management Society, you are seated with a group of office administrators and supervisors who are discussing some of the personnel problems that faced them during the past week. Unfortunately, you learn that none of the companies represented have a formal policy to which the office administrators could turn for help in solving their problems. A digest of the conversations follows.

**Directions:** Either in small groups or individually, discuss how you would solve each of the personnel problems described. Then prepare a written policy statement to cover each problem.

### A. Debits and Credits Take the Vow

The head of our accounting department announced this week that she and a clerk in her department will be getting married in three months. We've never had a married couple working in one department—in fact, we've never had a married couple working in any of our offices or in the plant. I don't see how we can let the couple work together in the same department, especially since he would be reporting to her each workday. We will have to let one of them go, or possibly arrange a transfer. What do you think we should do?

Policy Statement: ______________________________

### B. AIDS in the Workplace

This morning Jim, one of our mail clerks, came into the office and told me he has AIDS (acquired immune deficiency syndrome). After overcoming my initial shock—this is our first case—I offered him my full support by telling him that I surely had no objections to his continuing to work. But, you know, I fear the repercussions—the discrimination, stigma, homophobia—when others in the office get wind of his dilemma; and you know they'll hear about it. What steps should my company take now?

Policy Statement: ______________________________

### C. Wheeling-Dealing Wendell

What can we do about Wendell? I would say that at least once each week he goes from desk to desk selling—homemade jewelry, greeting cards, and even fudge that he whipped up the night before! Not only is he wasting his own time during working hours, but he is also creating a big stir among his coworkers, some of whom buy anything from him just to get him off their backs. Have you people ever had a similar problem? What did you do?

Policy Statement: ______________________________

## D. Berta Bunny Goes Hippety-Hop

I've got a good one for all of you. What would you do if one night when you are "hitting the bars," you find Berta, your Number 1 computer technician, moonlighting as a barmaid in a bunny costume? Never had any problems with her on the job though—outstanding worker, good attendance record, and continues to grow in skill and responsibilities shouldered. But I wonder what my boss, the company president, will say when he finds out about her after-hours escapades! Tell me if you can top this one!

Policy Statement: ______________________________

______________________________________________

______________________________________________

______________________________________________

______________________________________________

______________________________________________

______________________________________________

## E. Sticky-Fingers Stewart

I can! We all know that one of our oldest and "most loyal" file clerks—Stewart—is a first-class thief! Everyone suspects that he has been stealing money, rings, and other personal items from the men's lockers in the lounge. But nobody is able to nab him in the act. Tomorrow morning we are going to "plant" a role of marked bills in one of the lockers and set a trap for him. Then bingo, out he goes . . . . What do you mean I can't do that?

Policy Statement: ______________________________

______________________________________________

______________________________________________

______________________________________________

______________________________________________

______________________________________________

______________________________________________

## F. "Hello, Lily . . . I Know Who You Are and What You Like to Do . . ."

I can do you one better than that! For the past four weeks, one of our word processors has been interrupted every Wednesday promptly at 2 p.m. by a telephone call from outside. And get this—it's one of those obscene calls that we all read about. Always the same husky panting and breathing—and the kinky things that he says to Lily! Well, I can't repeat all of them to you, but here is one . . . . Lily has become a nervous wreck. We have worked with the telephone company each time the call comes in, but they have not been able to trace it. Any ideas on how we can tackle this one?

Policy Statement: ______________________________

______________________________________________

______________________________________________

______________________________________________

______________________________________________

______________________________________________

## G. Transparent Terri

Speaking of obscene, let me tell you about our new receptionist, Terri, because her dresses are exactly that—obscene—for all to be seen! We had no difficulties with her during her first several weeks of employment—good telephone personality, warm, cordial, and greets visitors well. Then, there was a big commotion last Monday when Terri appeared wearing a low-cut sheer dress and no bra! Well, we can't have our women dress like that, especially when they are greeting our clients. After all, we are running a business office—not a stylish New York glamour salon! Since we have no dress code, I don't know how to approach this problem with Terri. What suggestions do you have?

Policy Statement: ______________________________

______________________________________________

______________________________________________

______________________________________________

______________________________________________

______________________________________________

## H. Gamblin' Gina

Last week one of our data-entry clerks, Gina, came into my office, complaining that she had lost $25 in the office baseball pool. She had also griped to a coworker who told her, "Serves you right—you know that gambling on the premises is a no-no." Gina is very upset about her loss and blames me for not having gotten the no-gambling point across to the workers. And she's unable to find any policy statement regarding gambling in the office. Well, she's right—we never included a statement on gambling. How do you people handle office pools?

Policy Statement: ______________________

______________________

______________________

______________________

______________________

______________________

## I. Monitoring Martin

I am sure that one of my service rep's, Martin, has been spending a great deal of time making personal telephone calls instead of dialing prospective customers. Last week, I began to listen in on all my telemarketers' calls. And I just read about a computer hook-up that will let me monitor all outgoing calls automatically on a random basis. But the cat is out of the bag—Martin caught me in the act and yelled at me: "You can't do that. You'll make me feel like I'm wired to a machine. Just wait until the union hears about this!" Have you people had any experience with monitoring your office workers' calls?

Policy Statement: ______________________

______________________

______________________

______________________

______________________

______________________

## Project 12–2 • Field Research: Investigating Office Practices That May "Get Out of Hand"

In your firm or another company in your community, plan an interview with the person responsible for office policies and practices. The purpose of this interview is to determine (a) to what extent each of the office practices described on pages 131 and 132 has been or is currently creating a problem for the firm, and (b) what action, if any, has been taken or is being studied in order to control the practice.

The questionnaire on pages 131 and 132 will aid you in presenting a short written or oral report summarizing your conversation with the office administrator. Combining the findings of all students will indicate to what extent the office practices have become exceptionally costly and may contribute greatly to decreased productivity in the firms.

## Project 12–3 • Hiring a Vice President's Daughter

The Dalton Company is considering hiring the daughter of one of the vice presidents for the position of administrative office manager. The daughter, Joyce McGregor, is as well qualified for the position as any other person who has been interviewed. The position involves responsibility for planning and controlling areas where services and technology are undergoing great change.

The company wants a manager who can "grow with the job," for the position is expected to grow rapidly in scope and status. Although the company has employed relatives of executives for other managerial posts in the company, there is no consensus that employing a relative for the administrative management job will work equally well.

The four executives who have the responsibility for making the final decision have evaluated the situation as follows:

1. Alex McGregor, Joyce's father, feels that since his daughter is well qualified for the position, she should be hired.
2. Joan Flores, vice president, human resources, also feels that Joyce should be hired. But Flores is aware that the position is subject to much stress and change. Therefore, she feels that special measures must be taken to see that Joyce's performance is evaluated objectively and impartially. Flores firmly believes that if Joyce should fail to measure up to the job, she should be replaced immediately.
3. Donna Renz, vice president, finance, feels that nepotism in a situation such as this is too much of a gamble. She sees that McGregor's daughter may not measure up, and, as a result, the company will be faced with a messy and extremely unpleasant decision.
4. You, as president of Dalton Company, are trying to reconcile the different points of view and reach a decision.

You hold a great deal of admiration and respect for the ability of Alex McGregor, but you know that this is no guarantee that his daughter will perform equally well. Still, as you realize, there is a family tie here. And if you vote against Joyce, what will be the effect upon her father?

You appreciate Flores' point of view and agree wholeheartedly that if Joyce is employed, her performance must be evaluated objectively, and her rating must not be influenced by the position of her father. But, you ask yourself, how can a *relative's* performance be evaluated *objectively?*

Renz has made a good point, too, for you recall that 10 years ago the former president's son-in-law was hired and turned out to be a misfit. It was a sticky situation, and the company had no alternative but to let the son-in-law "gracefully resign." After that, things were never the same with the former president up to the day he retired.

After listening to Alex McGregor, Flores, and Renz evaluate Joyce's capabilities and express their viewpoints on nepotism, you realize the next step is up to you.

**Directions:** Cast your vote and defend your stand by answering each of the following questions.

1. What is your vote? ______________________________

2. How would you justify your position to each of the three vice presidents if you were asked to do so? __________

______________________________

______________________________

3. How would you proceed to evaluate objectively the performance of an executive's relative such as Joyce McGregor? ______________________________

______________________________

______________________________

______________________________

______________________________

Name ______________________________ Date ____________________

## QUESTIONNAIRE

### Office Practices That May "Get out of Hand"

Name of firm ______________________________

Title of office administrator's position ______________________________

1. **Receiving personal mail at the office.** In small offices, a fair degree of freedom is usually allowed in receiving personal mail at the office. In larger offices, however, it is necessary to impose rules because the volume of personal mail may interfere seriously with the efficiency of work in the mail center.

   A. Extent to which the practice creates a problem for the firm: ______________________________

   B. Action taken or planned to control the practice: ______________________________

2. **Personal use of the telephone.** Personal telephone calls prevent a firm from receiving its business calls and can obstruct its business operations. Of course, no firm objects to receiving urgent or emergency telephone calls for an employee. It is the other incoming and outgoing calls that pose the problem.

   A. Extent to which the practice creates a problem for the firm: ______________________________

   B. Action taken or planned to control the practice: ______________________________

3. **Collections in the office.** In many offices, a common practice is to collect money to provide gifts for office employees or members of their families. Many firms feel that this is not a problem of management. Others feel that such collections interfere with the morale and efficiency of office workers because collections are made too often and disrupt the workflow.

   A. Extent to which the practice creates a problem for the firm: ______________________________

B. Action taken or planned to control the practice: ______________________________

______________________________

______________________________

______________________________

4. **Giving and receiving gifts.** On many occasions, such as Christmas, firms are faced with the problem of giving and receiving gifts. Some firms establish a policy of accepting no gifts that are likely to obligate the employees or the company and to give only nominal or token presents not likely to embarrass the recipient. Other firms donate to charities the money that would have been spent on Christmas gifts and cards for their customers, clients, and employees.

   A. Extent to which the practice creates a problem for the firm: ______________________________

   ______________________________

   ______________________________

   ______________________________

   B. Action taken or planned to control the practice: ______________________________

   ______________________________

   ______________________________

   ______________________________

5. **Office parties and picnics.** Many firms sponsor parties, such as at Christmas, off the company premises. Other companies plan their holiday celebrations, such as informal employee parties preceding Christmas or New Year's Day, in the offices. Alcoholic beverages may or may not be permitted at these informal parties. Annual company picnics are still fairly popular as a means of bringing the "company family" together in a full day's program of planned activities—ball games, swimming, horseshoes, racing, amateur hour, food and drink, etc.

   A. Extent to which the practice creates a problem for the firm: ______________________________

   ______________________________

   ______________________________

   ______________________________

   B. Action taken or planned to control the practice: ______________________________

   ______________________________

   ______________________________

   ______________________________

## Project 12–4 • Field Research: Evaluating a New Work Schedule

In undertaking this field research project, you will talk with an office manager or supervisor and one or more office workers who are employed by a firm that has converted from the traditional 5-day, 40-hour workweek to a different work schedule. It will also be interesting to learn if any employees are sharing a job, telecommuting, or working on a permanent part-time schedule. When interviewing the employees, your objective will to gain a sincere, frank appraisal of the overall effectiveness of the new work schedule.

**Directions:** Using as a guide the questions contained in the form on pages 135 and 136, arrange for an interview with the office workers in a firm now operating under a new work schedule. Be sure to take complete notes on all impressions—good or bad—conveyed by the workers. When you make your written or oral report, you will want to present a comprehensive picture of how the office workers' lifestyle, productivity, and morale have been affected as a result of the company's conversion to a different work schedule.

## Project 12–5 • Snooping Electronically

As an office worker, what are your rights to privacy? Are your telephone calls "bugged?" Is someone reading your computer files over your shoulder? Can you safely lock "personal" articles in your desk or locker? Is your employer guilty of snooping electronically? Do you need "Federal Big Daddy" to step in and pass more laws to protect your privacy? Take a look at this short article and then think about your answers to these questions.

### Whose Office Is This Anyhow?

What rights do you, as an employee, have to make a totally private phone call or to type a completely confidential message into your computer? Virtually none. The Fourth Amendment bars the government from unreasonable search and seizure of your scribblings at home. It does not prohibit the boss from rifling the office he's letting you use.

Consider Bonita Bourke and Rhonda Hall, who traveled the U.S. training car dealers, sales staff, and mechanics on how to use Nissan's electronic mail system. They also logged on for racy conversations with students and some disparaging remarks about a supervisor.

Suspicious, the supervisor overrode the women's passwords to read their E-mail and, among other things, found himself called "numbnuts." He rebuked them. A few weeks later, Bourke and Hall filed a grievance with Nissan headquarters in Los Angeles, arguing they had a reasonable expectation of privacy while using E-mail. Within days Nissan fired them, and the women sued for reinstatement. Nissan says they were dismissed for generally poor performance, but that in any case they had no right to privacy on the E-mail network. So far the California courts have upheld Nissan.

In 1991 two male employees of the Boston Sheraton Hotel were secretly videotaped while changing clothes in the locker room during a hunt for a drug dealer. They were not suspects, simply bystanders. Indignant, they sued. But don't bet on them winning in court.

Legislation that would protect employees in such situations might curtail legitimate surveillance. Companies often have good reason to monitor telephone calls of service operators and of employees who handle customer complaints.

Sometimes, though, monitoring can be excessive or pure harassment. Since 1990, Senator Paul Simon has unsuccessfully tried to pass the Privacy for Consumers and Workers Act. Under that act, an employer could eavesdrop on operators with fewer than 60 days on the job. Over time, employer rights would diminish, so operators with five or more years of service could be monitored only if suspected of a crime. That may sound reasonable, but how do supervisors evaluate veteran operators who might get sloppy?

The key to dealing with employee anxiety about surveillance is to inform workers in writing about policy and the reasons for it. Also,

Source: Lee Smith, "What the Boss Knows About You," *Fortune* (August 9, 1993), p. 93. 

top management ought to keep a close watch on line supervisors who may abuse surveillance privileges.

Electronic snooping is so remote that it doesn't seem harmful at all—examining the patient with a CAT scan rather than cutting him open with a knife. But the practice is nonetheless invasive and sometimes addictive. Al Simon, who designs company security systems in New York, points out that you can acquire a voice stress analyzer or "truth phone" ($2,000 and up) to catch a thief but wind up cross-examining your wife. Supervisors who may hesitate to unlock employee desk drawers are less squeamish about invading electronic mailboxes. *Macworld*, a magazine for computer users, recently surveyed 301 companies from various industries and found that supervisors in 21% have examined employee computer files, E-mail, or telephone voice mail for the stated reasons of investigating larceny or measuring performance.

Reasonable ethics for employer spying seems simple. Says William Moroney, director of the Electronic Mail Association, a trade organization for those who create and use such systems: "Employees have the right to expect that naked pictures of them will not be passed around the office. If, however, you're running an illegal football pool, management has the right to know about it." But the line gets blurry between the poles of voyeurism and police work. Is it all right, for example, to monitor employee whereabouts constantly? Olivetti has recently developed "smart badge," an electronic ID card. Sensors around the building track the bearer as he moves and direct his phone calls to the nearest receiver. Very convenient. Unless you don't want the boss to know you're in a different division inquiring about a transfer. Before installing such devices, employers would do well to think about the ramifications.

Name ______________________ Date ______________ 

## EVALUATING THE NEW WORK SCHEDULE AT ______________________
(Name of Company)

1. Kind of business organization, product line, service rendered: ______________________

______________________

2. Describe the type of new work schedule and the old work schedule from which the conversion was made.

______________________

______________________

______________________

3. Number of office employees working under new work schedule: ______________________

4. Length of time employees have worked under new schedule: ______________________

5. Number of and nature of office employees not covered by new work schedule: ______________________

______________________

Reasons for excluding these workers: ______________________

______________________

6. If any employees are telecommuting, explain the nature of their work assignments and indicate the reactions of the workers and management to this kind of work scheduling. ______________________

______________________

______________________

______________________

7. Indicate the effect of the new work schedule on each of the following factors:

| Factor | Effect |
|---|---|
| a. Productivity of workers . . . . . . . . . . . . . . . . . . . | ______________ |
| b. Tardiness . . . . . . . . . . . . . . . . . . . . . . . . . . . | ______________ |
| c. Absenteeism . . . . . . . . . . . . . . . . . . . . . . . . . | ______________ |
| d. Number of personal leave days taken . . . . . . . . . . | ______________ |
| e. Turnover . . . . . . . . . . . . . . . . . . . . . . . . . . . | ______________ |
| f. Worker tensions (commuting to and from work, fatigue) . . . . . . . . . . . . . . . . . . . . . . . . . . . | ______________ |
| g. Personal telephone calls . . . . . . . . . . . . . . . . . . | ______________ |
| h. Morale level . . . . . . . . . . . . . . . . . . . . . . . . . | ______________ |

**EVALUATING THE NEW WORK SCHEDULE AT** ______________________
**(CONTINUED)**

(Name of Company)

| Factor | Effect |
|---|---|
| i. Cooperation among workers | ______ |
| j. Services provided customers | ______ |
| k. Customer communications | ______ |
| l. Record keeping | ______ |
| m. Special timekeeping equipment | ______ |
| n. Indirect labor costs | ______ |
| o. Overtime (premium pay) | ______ |
| p. Supervision | ______ |
| q. Scheduling of working hours | ______ |
| r. Security staff | ______ |
| s. Safety | ______ |
| t. Recruitment of new office workers | ______ |
| u. Use of office facilities and equipment | ______ |

8. Summary of my reactions to workers' overall impression of the new work schedule:

______________________________________________

______________________________________________

______________________________________________

______________________________________________

______________________________________________

______________________________________________

______________________________________________

______________________________________________

______________________________________________

______________________________________________

______________________________________________

## CROSSWORD PUZZLE 2

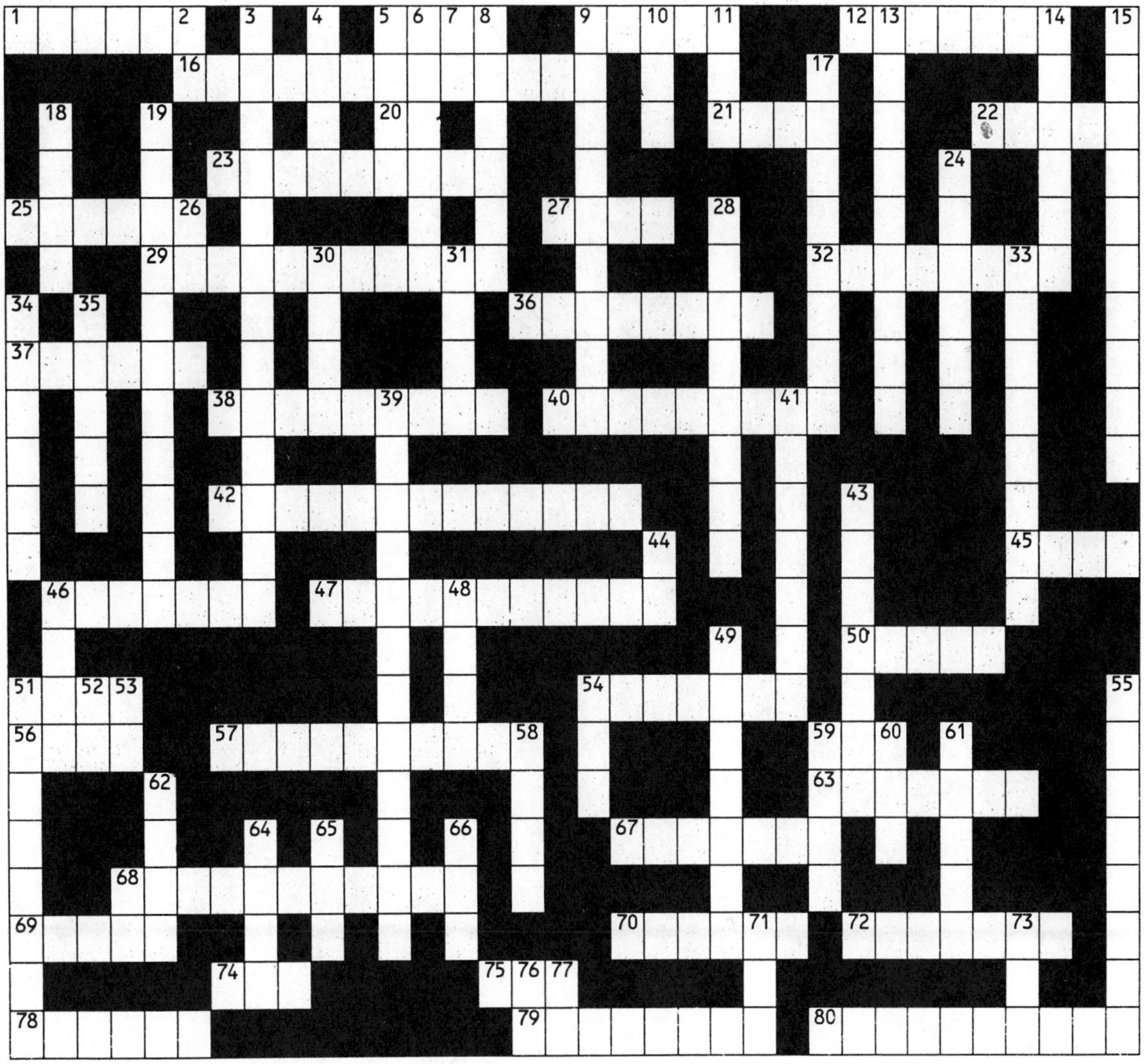

Name ______________________________ Date ______________________

# CROSSWORD PUZZLE 2

## Across

1. AOM's "home"
5. _______ ball
9. Temporary helpers
12. Oral reprimand
16. Information-gathering tool
20. Overdose
21. Griggs v _______ Power
22. _______ Defense
23. Increased production reward
25. 37
27. Discharge
29. Authority to act on one's own
32. Physiological need
36. Changes in behavior and attitude
37. Interest in business ownership
38. Key or _______ job
40. Training away from workstation
42. Working outside office setting
45. Scottish Isle
46. Depletion of physical and mental resources
47. Measure of consistency
50. Top-management privileges
51. _______ fide
54. Mentor's trainee
56. Greenish blue
57. Emotionally dependent on work
59. Lobster catcher
63. Polished
67. Arithmetic mean
68. _______ appraisal
69. Assumed name
70. _______'s Hierarchy of Needs
72. _______ reality
74. Employee assistance program
75. Fish eggs
78. _______ de corps
79. Flexible work schedule
80. _______ bargaining

## Down

2. Equation
3. Condition following a response
4. Eyelid swelling
5. Debatable
6. Salad plant
7. Article
8. Ability
9. Discharge
10. Management by objectives
11. Grass surface
13. Powerless to stop drinking
14. Donating
15. Lie detectors
17. Health insurance for aged
18. Compressed workweek
19. New worker's job introduction
24. Moral conduct and duty
26. Intramural
28. Communication medium
30. Regulatory body
31. Close by
33. Employment of relatives
34. Second quartile
35. Theory Z management
39. Working a second job
41. One-way communication technique
43. Transportation program
44. McGregor's Theories __ and __
46. Job-related requirement
48. Absent without leave
49. _______ Schedule
51. A whole new _______
52. Name unknown
53. Associate in arts
54. Hygienic factor
55. Measure of position
58. Retirement plan
59. Supervisor of equal rank
60. Beverage
61. Product of learning
62. United States Employment Service
64. Cost-of-living adjustment
65. Health maintenance organization
66. Title VII of Civil Rights Act
68. Pennsylvania
71. In debt
73. Drama division
76. Outfield
77. Overhead train

13

# MANAGING OFFICE SPACE

The wise, economic management of office space is essential to the successful operation of any organization. To develop the best possible office design plan, the person in charge of space management must carefully consider factors such as: (1) organizational and functional needs of the firm, (2) flexible arrangements that provide for expansion or contraction of workstations to meet the firm's needs, (3) efficiency and economy of workflows, (4) human space needs, (5) interpersonal communication needs of the workers, and (6) ergonomic factors.

To aid space planners, guidelines have been developed that provide space allocations for workflows, for human space needs, and for furniture and equipment. In traditional design plans, as well as in open plans, adherence to these guidelines enables space planners to bring together an effective "mix" of functional, behavioral, and technical factors to determine the most efficient layout of individual workcenters, work groups, and departments.

If the organization is considering the relocation of its offices, a decision must be made on whether to purchase or lease the space. Some of the factors to be evaluated in making such a decision are: (l) future space requirements, (2) availability of capital, (3) contents of the lease, and (4) resale value of the property.

## SECTION A • REVIEW QUESTIONS

**Directions:** In the Answers column, write the letter of the item in Column 1 that is described by each statement in Column 2.

| Column 1 | Column 2 | Answers |
|---|---|---|
| **A** Administrative services | 1. A designing technique in which the computer automates the drafting function . . . . . . . . . . | 1. ______ |
| **B** American plan | 2. A personal space ranging from about 4′ to 12′, which is generally maintained in business situations where people work together . . . . | 2. ______ |
| **C** Computer-aided design (CAD) | 3. The basic unit of office space where each employee performs the bulk of assigned responsibilities . . . . . . . . . . | 3. ______ |
| **D** Group workcenter | 4. Support functions responsible for meeting all the information needs of the organization . . . . . . . . . . | 4. ______ |
| **E** Individual workcenter | 5. The movement of information vertically between superiors and subordinates or horizontally among workers on the same level . . . . | 5. ______ |
| **F** Lease | 6. A long-range planning technique that is used to determine the time required to complete major projects after realistic time estimates have been made of the various activities associated with each project | 6. ______ |
| **G** Open plan | 7. An agreement between the landlord and the tenant that transfers possession of property for a period of time . . . . . . . . . . | 7. ______ |
| **H** Personal zone | 8. An office layout design characterized by open space, free of conventional walls and corridors, which brings together all the functional, behavioral, and technical factors needed to design individual workstations, work groups, and departments . . . . . . . . . | 8. ______ |
| **I** PERT (Program Evaluation and Review Technique | | |
| **J** Social zone | | |
| **K** Workflow | | |
| **L** Work letter | | |

**Directions:** Each of the following statements is either true or false. Indicate your choice in the Answers column by circling "T" or "F."

| | Answers | |
|---|---|---|
| 1. In large firms, the facility manager may be responsible for space planning . . . . . . . . . . . . . . . | T | F |
| 2. On a Gantt chart, the work planned and the work done are shown side by side in relation to each other and to time. . . . . . . . . . . . . . . . . . . . . . . . . . . . . . . . . . . . . . . . . | T | F |
| 3. A departmental plan of layout, arranged according to the organization's functions, is commonly found in small and medium-size offices . . . . . . . . . . . . . . . . . . . . . . . . . . . . . | T | F |
| 4. Effective space plans are determined mainly by the esthetic preferences of personnel . . . . . . . | T | F |
| 5. The most efficient office workflow is continuous, with intermittent storage stops having been eliminated . . . . . . . . . . . . . . . . . . . . . . . . . . . . . . . . . . . . . . . . . . . . . . . . . | T | F |
| 6. *Territoriality* refers to the physical area under the control of workers and designed specifically for their use . . . . . . . . . . . . . . . . . . . . . . . . . . . . . . . . . . . . . . . . . . . | T | F |
| 7. A personal zone, ranging from about 4′ to 7′, is usually maintained when two office employees work together on their daily assignments . . . . . . . . . . . . . . . . . . . . . . . . . . . . . . | T | F |
| 8. The conventional plan is characterized by open space, free of permanent walls and corridors . | T | F |
| 9. In the conventional plan, departments should be arranged so that the workflow proceeds in an uninterrupted manner and passes through as few hands as possible . . . . . . . . . . . . . . . . . . . . | T | F |
| 10. In theory, the office landscape is an open-plan model with no private offices . . . . . . . . . . . . | T | F |
| 11. Often the open plan is combined with the conventional plan so that high-level executives can keep their private offices for isolation and confidentiality . . . . . . . . . . . . . . . . . . . . . . . . . . | T | F |
| 12. There is a greater amount of usable space in the conventional plan than in the open plan . . . . | T | F |
| 13. One advantage gained through use of the "pure" open plan is the elimination of excessive noise . . . . . . . . . . . . . . . . . . . . . . . . . . . . . . . . . . . . . . . . . . . . . . . . . . . . . . . . | T | F |
| 14. Private offices are especially cost effective since they efficiently use about 75 percent of the space allocated to them . . . . . . . . . . . . . . . . . . . . . . . . . . . . . . . . . . . . . . . . . . . . . | T | F |
| 15. Office supervisors can more easily maintain control when their employees work in a large, open space rather than in several small room spaces cut out of one area . . . . . . . . . . . . . . . . . | T | F |
| 16. Generally an automated workstation requires 25 to 30 percent less space than a conventional workstation . . . . . . . . . . . . . . . . . . . . . . . . . . . . . . . . . . . . . . . . . . . . . . . . . . . . | T | F |
| 17. Unless office employees are clustered together in automated workcenters, their desks should generally face the same direction . . . . . . . . . . . . . . . . . . . . . . . . . . . . . . . . . . . . . . | T | F |
| 18. The CAD concept may be used to simulate an office layout on a VDT screen . . . . . . . . . . . . | T | F |
| 19. If the space requirements of an organization are expected to change rapidly over the next few years, the firm would be well advised to lease rather than purchase its office space . . . . . . . . . | T | F |
| 20. For a firm faced with a short supply of capital, it is strongly recommended that it purchase rather than lease its needed office space . . . . . . . . . . . . . . . . . . . . . . . . . . . . . . . . . . . | T | F |
| 21. The *work letter* is that portion of a lease which spells out the lessor's and the lessee's obligations for any work to be done to the building and who will pay for it . . . . . . . . . . . . . . . | T | F |

Name ______________________________ Date ______________________

## SECTION B • PROJECTS

### Project 13–1 • Field Research: Determining the Availability and Cost of Office Space

**Directions:** In this field research project, you will investigate the market for office space in your hometown, or the city in which your school is located, or in another area specified by your instructor. Some of the factors to be considered in your research are offered in the list of questions below, but you may want to include others depending upon local conditions and the kind of oral or written report you are asked to prepare. Consider the following sources of information when you plan your research activities: real estate agents, real estate consultants, banks, brokerage firms, office building developers, the chamber of commerce, and your local library.

1. Average annual rent per square foot of office space: ______________________

2. Availability of office space today: ______________________

3. Typical vacancy rates in office buildings: ______________________

4. Dollar volume (or square feet amount) of office building construction undertaken in last five years: ______________________

5. Outlook for office space construction by 2005: ______________________

6. Relocation of offices from center of city to less costly sites: ______________________

7. Approximate average cost to house each office worker in a new building in the center of your community. (Allow 200 square feet per employee.)

______________________

# Project 13–2 • Planning a Layout for the Business Department Offices

The second phase of the building program at Ness Community College will soon be completed. The chairperson of the business department, who also teaches office management, has asked you to aid her in planning space allocations and arranging furniture and equipment in the department offices.

Private offices will be provided for the chairperson, Julia Sontag, and her department assistant, Linda Vera. The large, open office will house a secretary, Beth White; a clerk-typist, Nancy McGrath, who also serves as receptionist; and two student workers, who spend about 20 hours each week keyboarding tests and handouts for the instructors.

On a typical workday, 30 instructors come and go in the office, picking up their mail, preparing coffee and tea, and socializing. Added to this volume of traffic are students, administrators, faculty members, and sales representatives from publishing companies and equipment manufacturers, who drop in to see the chairperson or her assistant. The receiving and screening of callers are important aspects of the clerk-typist's job, and it has been decided that her workstation must be positioned near the one entrance to the department office.

As shown on the grid paper on page 145, the dimensions of the open office are 5.5 m × 8 m, with each private office measuring 2.7 m × 4 m. Within these three office areas, the following furniture and equipment will be housed:

*Chairperson's private office:*

| (Centimeters) | |
|---|---|
| 1 desk | 152.4 × 76.2 × 76.2 |
| 1 swivel chair | 48.9 × 45.1 |
| 1 4-drawer file cabinet | 38.1 × 68.6 × 144.8 |
| 1 2-drawer file cabinet | 38.1 × 68.6 × 76.2 |
| 1 3-shelf bookcase | 91.4 × 38.1 × 106.7 |
| 1 worktable | 101.6 × 50.8 × 73.7 |
| 1 wardrobe, 76.2 × 182.9, extending 30.5 into the room | |
| 1 corkboard | 182.9 × 121.9 |
| 1 4-shelf wall bookcase (suspended) | 91.4 × 38.1 × 142.2 |
| 2 visitor's chairs | 55.9 × 48.3 |

*Assistant's private office:*

| | |
|---|---|
| 1 desk | 152.4 × 76.2 × 76.2 |
| 1 desk return (modular unit) | 81.3 × 50.8 × 66.0 |
| 1 swivel chair | 48.9 × 45.1 |
| 1 4-drawer file cabinet | 38.1 × 68.6 × 144.8 |
| 1 3-shelf bookcase | 91.4 × 38.1 × 106.7 |
| 1 4-shelf wall bookcase (suspended) | 91.4 × 38.1 × 142.2 |
| 1 visitor's chair | 55.9 × 48.3 |
| 1 wardrobe, 76.2 × 182.9, extending 30.5 into the room | |

*Open office:*

| | |
|---|---|
| 2 desks | 152.4 × 76.2 × 76.2 |
| 2 worktables | 101.6 × 50.8 × 73.7 |
| 4 posture chairs | 48.3 × 45.7 |
| 4 visitor's chairs | 55.9 × 48.3 |
| 1 typewriter utility table | 76.2 × 45.7 × 66.0 |
| 1 table, serving as base for faculty mailboxes and coffee maker | 152.4 × 50.8 × 73.7 |
| 1 4-drawer roll-out file | 106.7 × 39.4 × 152.4 |

**Directions**: Based upon the information given above, Sontag has asked you to prepare a "rough" layout for the three office areas, taking into consideration the typical workflow found in a college department office. Your layout is to be prepared on the grid paper provided on page 145.

For use with project 13–2.

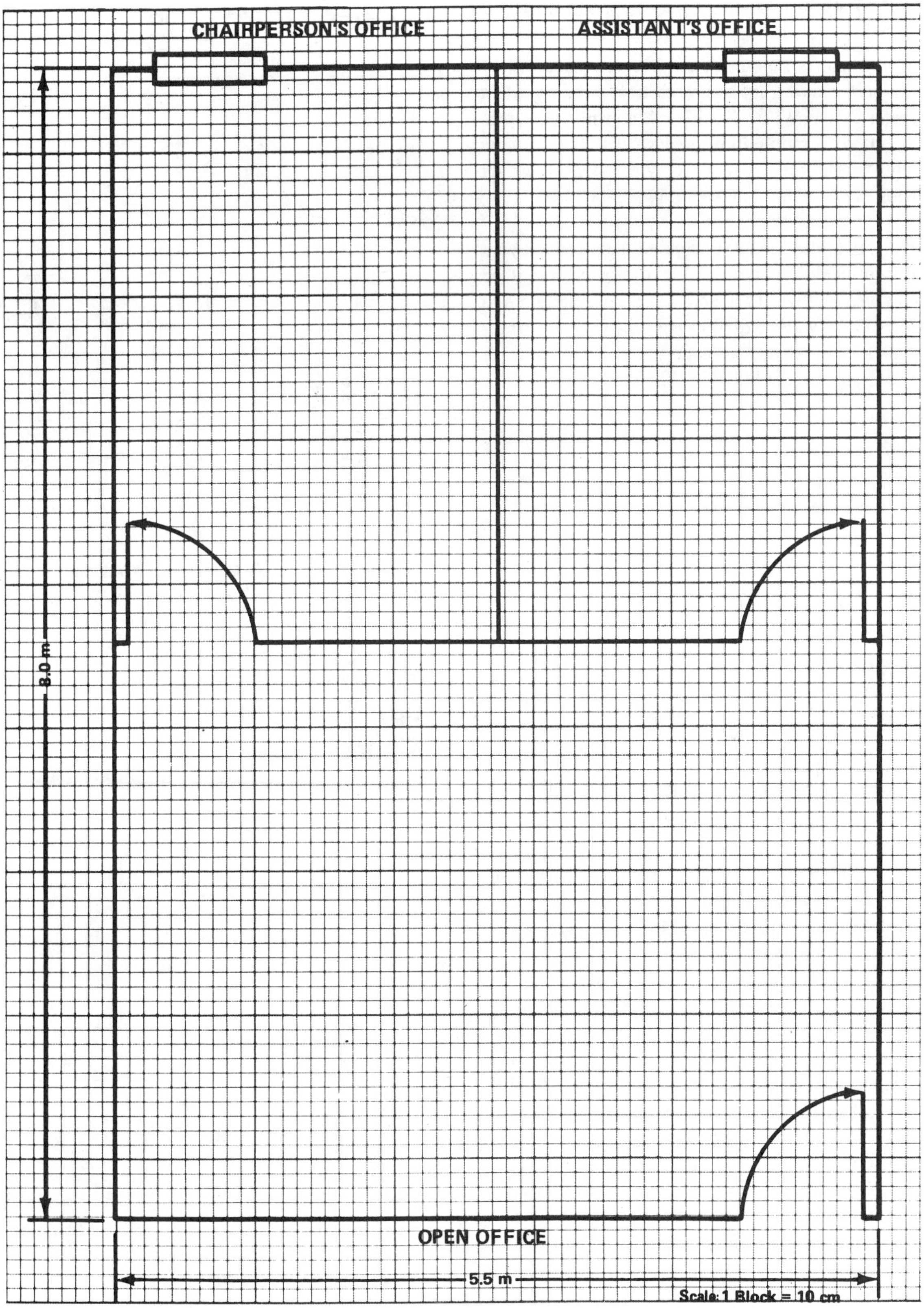

## Project 13–3 • Computer Hands-On: Revising the Layout for an Open Office Area

Figure 13–1 shows the open area presently occupied by the nine persons who make up the traffic management workcenter of the Willis Trucking Company. The company needs to provide additional workstations for its expanding workforce and asks for your suggestions for increasing the number of and rearranging the desks.

**Directions:** After you have studied the present layout carefully, print out your revised layout or present it on the grid given on page 147. Your major objectives are to provide as many workstations as possible without changing the size of desks and to retain one major circulating aisle. (See template file PO13-3.TEM.)

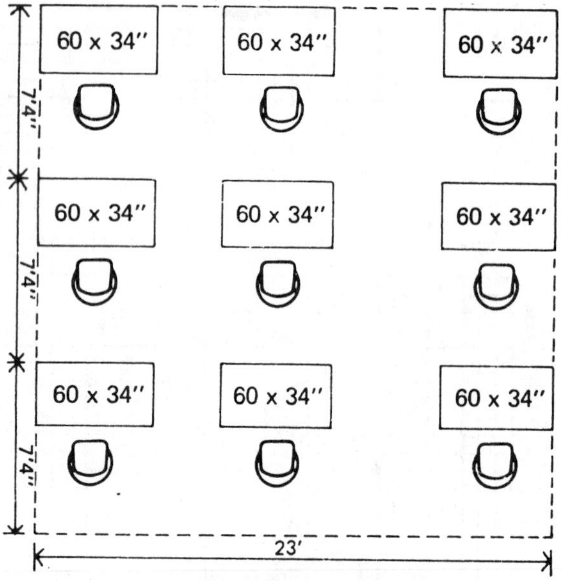


**Figure 13–1** Traffic Management Workcenter of the Willis Trucking Company

## Project 13–4 • Computer Hands-On: Expanding the Storage Capacity of a Records Center

In the records center shown in Figure 13–2, the north, east, and west walls are solid (without windows). Along the southern dimension, open space permits entrance to and exit from the records center. At the present time, the records center houses 52 four-drawer file cabinets, which the records manager plans to trade in on the purchase of new five-drawer cabinets.

**Directions:** On your template file PO13-4.TEM or on the grid on page 147, show how the new five-drawer cabinets can be arranged, with additional five-drawer units being purchased, to provide the maximum number of cabinets. The outside dimensions of each five-drawer unit are 57 1/2″ high, 15″ wide, and 27″ deep. No provision should be made for desks and chairs since these are located in a department adjacent to the records center.

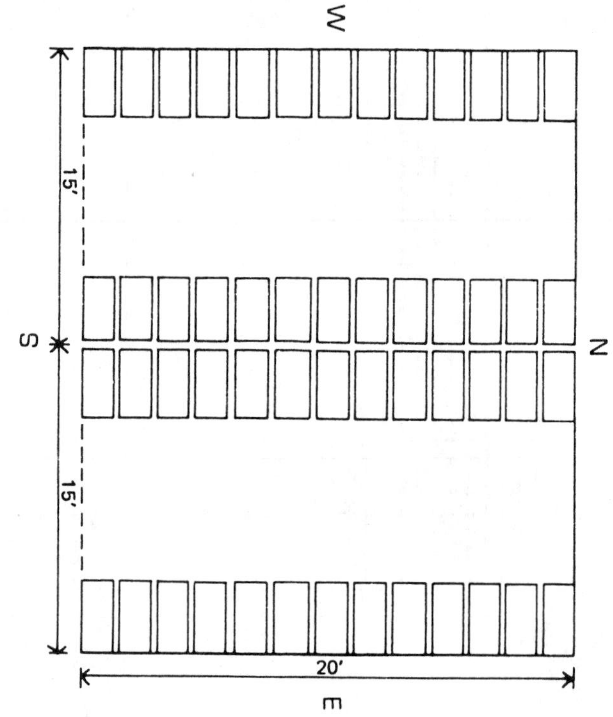


**Figure 13–2** A Records Center

For use with Project 13-3.

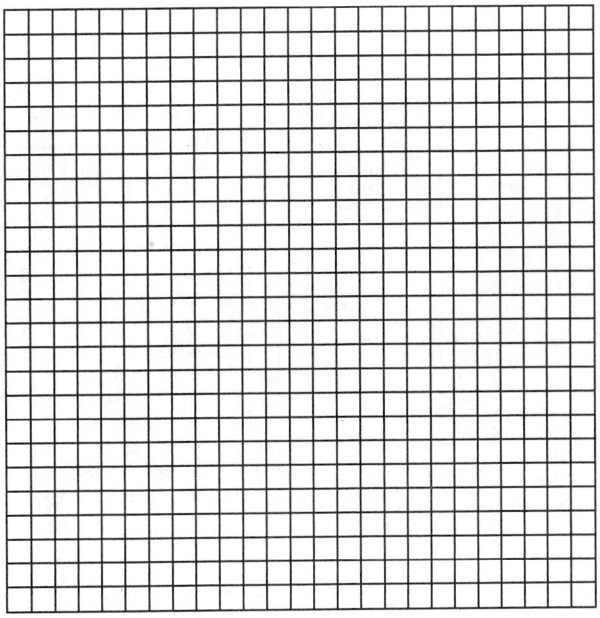

Scale: 1 block = 1 foot

For use with Project 13-4.

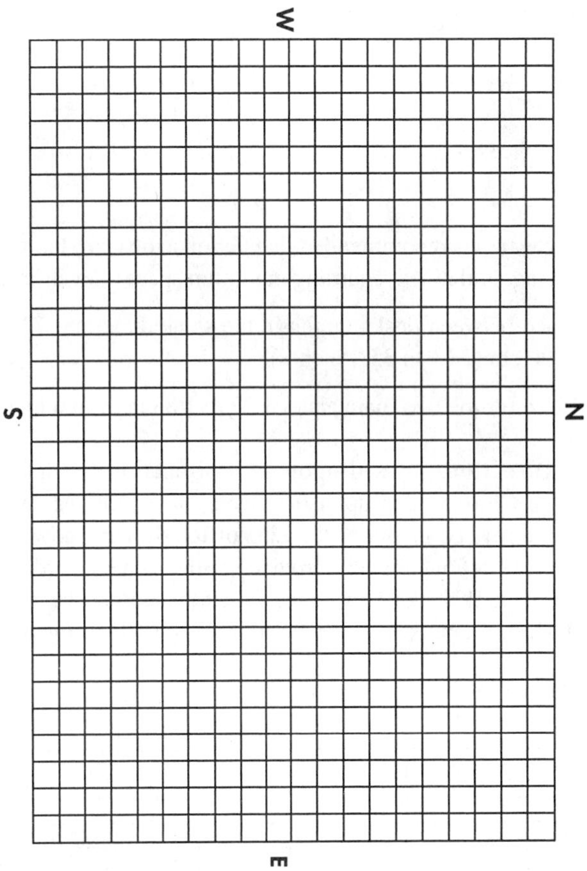


Scale: 1 block = 1 foot

## Project 13–5 • Revising a Proposed Layout for an Overseas Office

Schulte, Inc., a multinational corporation engaged in processing petrochemicals, has its manufacturing plant and headquarters office in New Orleans. Overseas plants and sales offices are located in Rotterdam, Lyons, Munich, and Zurich. A new plant and sales office are now being constructed in the suburbs of Linz, Austria.

Mitchell Swan, manager of administrative services, has responsibility for coordinating all phases of space management, forms design and control, and administrative systems in the home office and all overseas offices. The company has announced its plan for conversion to the metric system, and Swan is now faced with the problem of dual dimensioning of layouts and measurements of forms and office supplies. An example of the kind of dual dimensioning problem faced by Swan has arrived in this morning's mail.

Mignon Garonne, the newly selected manager of the sales office in Linz, has airmailed a layout of the new office to Swan. This layout, illustrated in Figure 13–3 on page 148, has been designed by Garonne for a staff of 12 persons. The office expects, however, to employ 14 workers when the plant opens and to provide workstations for three more persons three months later. In her accompanying letter, she has asked Swan for his ideas on rearranging the present 12 workstations to provide for the additional five. Garonne does not want the 17 workers to be overcrowded.

In earlier correspondence with Garonne, Swan had indicated that she should purchase office furniture with dimensions similar to the following:

| Furniture | Size in Centimeters (and inches) |
|---|---|
| L-shaped modular units consisting of a return measuring | 152.4 × 76.2 × 76.2 (60 × 30 × 30) |
| and | |
| a desk measuring | 152.4 × 76.2 × 76.2 (60 × 30 × 30) |

1 round table . . . . . . . . . . . . . . . . . . 106.7 × 76.2 (42 × 30)
3 cabinets, 2-door . . . . . . . . . . . . . 91.4 × 45.7 × 182.9 (36 × 18 × 72)
2 file cabinets . . . . . . . . . . . . . . . . 38.1 × 68.6 × 144.8 (15 × 27 × 57)
5 bookcases . . . . . . . . . . . . . . . . . . 91.4 × 38.1 × 106.7 (36 × 15 × 42)

Swan has recommended that Garonne observe the following guidelines regarding minimum space allocations:

Space between desks facing in the same direction: 72 to 90 cm (28.4 to 35.4 inches)

Space for the two main aisles: 1.22 to 1.83 m (4 to 6 feet)

**Directions:** Based upon the information Swan has given Garonne and upon the layout she submitted, prepare a revised layout of the Linz office showing how the 17 workstations may be provided without overcrowding. Additional desks and returns do not need to be purchased. Because of the permanent partitioning that encloses the conference room and the reference room, the arrangements of these two rooms must remain as shown in Figure 13–3. Use the grid below for preparing your layout.

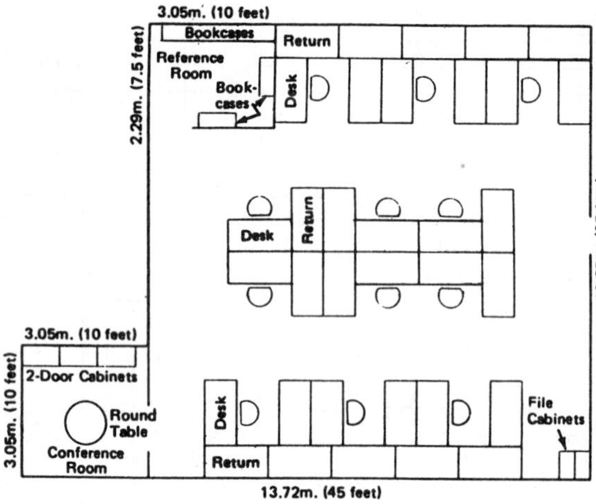


Figure 13–3 Proposed Layout of the Linz Sales Office

For use with Project 13–5.

# Project 13–6 • Taking Inventory of *Your* Office

A little on the lighter side now—an article solely for your enjoyment—no questions to answer or problems to solve! At the end of the article, *Management Review* stated that the author, Paul Hellman, either needs a little space in his office or a little office in space!

## Office Matters

Let's talk about your office. Not *the* office, but *your* office in the office, which is not really *your* office; otherwise, you could sublet it. What's the purpose of an office? You go to *the* office to work with other people. You go to *your* office to get away from these other people.

Plus, you need somewhere to put your stuff. An office is like a large gym locker—that you have to get into.

And out of. Management gurus have been telling us for a while now to get out of the office and practice "management by walking around," even if it's just walking around the outside of the building.

Where is your office? Often the higher up in the organization you are, the more out of sight. It's like the military. If you're an officer of the company, you're likely to be positioned behind the lines, unlike, say, the receptionist, who's at the front and completely exposed should there be an invasion. The receptionist can't hide anywhere—there's not even a trench.

Then there are the employees camped out in cubicles. They seem protected, until you get a close look at their barricade. Where's the door?

But even if you have a door, you need to be careful about closing it. Makes people nervous. I once had an office across from my boss. Whenever he closed his door, I got jittery. Was he talking about me? I was never sure—even when he was completely alone. When he met with his boss, they usually closed the door. I thought about trying to eavesdrop, but I figured I wouldn't be able to hear much. They probably weren't talking about me anyway. They were probably whispering about me.

Not everyone needs private space. Japanese executives often work in the same office as their employees. But that's Japan, where the focus is on the group, and where space is tight. Japan has a population about half the United States, but squeezed into a land mass the size of Montana. It's hard to imagine squeezing half the United States into Montana, and then expecting everyone to share an office, or even a ranch.

In North America, offices have a lot of meaning. I have an office; therefore, I'm an official. I'm an office holder, someone who can hold an office, or at least hold part of an office such as a stapler or some rubber bands. I identify with my office. And I'm not alone. One CEO spent more than $300,000 to renovate his office. The only problem: the company at the time was losing money and downsizing. He was installing a Jacuzzi while the company was taking a bath.

I prefer more conventional office equipment, like the desk. Desks intrigue me; not the desk itself, but what's on it. I look for clutter. When I'm in someone's office and see a nice pile of clutter, I feel reassured. Sure there's a better place for it; the clutter can't stay on this desk forever. Eventually, by some mysterious process, it will find its way to its true destination—*my* desk. I'm just grateful it hasn't arrived yet.

Then there's the chair. I bought my chair after reading an article on back problems. The article warned against a plush, cushy chair. These chairs are only good if you want to do something crazy, like get comfortable. But that's bad. That's why you need a no-nonsense, masochistic type chair that forces you to fidget, shift positions and occasionally writhe in agony. I have a straight-backed chair that fits the bill perfectly. I can't wait to get rid of it.

Every office invariably has pictures. Usually these are pictures of family or friends. Sometimes there are outdoor scenes—sailing, skiing, that sort of thing. But how come no one decorates their *homes* with pictures of the office; "This is me and the boss . . . And here's a picture of our new copier."

I never see diplomas on the wall, unless it's a doctor's office. Then I always see them. Is this some sort of medical regulation? I think it's the doctor's way of reassuring us that "yes, I really am a doctor. I know you may not believe it—sometimes even I don't believe it." When the doctor's out of the room, I usually study the diplomas carefully, and pray they're real.

I don't have any plants. But I admire those who do. One friend's company has a plant service. Periodically, the plant service replaces all the plants in the office with identical ones. This makes my friend nervous. He worries that one day they're going to come and uproot him. "Nobody's safe anymore," he says. "Not even if you're a plant."

I told him the best thing to do was stay out of his office. As an encouragement, I offered him my chair.

# 14

# PLANNING AN ERGONOMICALLY SOUND OFFICE ENVIRONMENT

To design environments that are satisfying to office employees and that meet the objectives of organizations, a scientific approach may be used. The applied science, *ergonomics*, brings together the following elements to meet the psychological needs of workers:(1) space, furniture, and equipment and (2) other physiological factors such as light, color, sound, and temperature. By closely studying these elements at the outset of planning, the office manager is assured of better offices—layouts planned for efficient information handling and flow; office areas that easily, quickly, and economically adapt to the changing needs of the organization and its workers; surroundings that are comfortable, satisfying, safe, and secure for the workers; workstations designed for maximum worker productivity; and an office image that imparts the success and personality of the organization.

Along with other managers in the organization, the administrative office manager is responsible for planning an energy conservation program. Working with the energy manager, the administrative office manager helps conduct energy audits and set energy conservation goals.

## SECTION A • REVIEW QUESTIONS

**Directions:** In the Answers column, write the letter of the item in Column 1 that is described by each statement in Column 2.

**Column 1**

**A** Ambient lighting
**B** Decibel (db)
**C** Effective
**D** Ergonomics
**E** Footcandle (FC)
**F** Noise-reduction coefficient (NRC)
**G** Reflection ratio
**H** Relative humidity
**I** Task lighting
**J** Visual comfort probability (VCP)

| Column 2 | Answers |
|---|---|
| 1. The unit of measure that determines the relative loudness of sounds, equal approximately to the smallest degree of difference of loudness detectable by the human ear . . . . . . . . . . . . . . . . . . . . . . . . . . . . . . | 1. ______ |
| 2. The temperature combined with proper humidity . . . . . . . . . . . . . . | 2. ______ |
| 3. A measure of the amount of light produced by a candle at a distance of one foot from the source of the light . . . . . . . . . . . . . . . . . . . . . . | 3. ______ |
| 4. The use of indirect fixtures or uplifts that direct light upward to be reflected off the ceiling onto other surfaces that surround the workstation . . . . . . . . . . . . . . . . . . . . . . . . . . . . . . . . . . . . . . . . . | 4. ______ |
| 5. The percentage of moisture in the air . . . . . . . . . . . . . . . . . . . . . . . | 5. ______ |
| 6. A science that explains how the performance and morale of workers on the job are dependent upon the physiological and psychological factors in the workers' environment . . . . . . . . . . . . . . . . . . . . . . . . | 6. ______ |
| 7. A measure of the amount of noise absorbed or removed from an area | 7. ______ |
| 8. A measure of the amount of light reflected from a surface as a percentage of the total amount of light striking that surface . . . . . . | 8. ______ |
| 9. A type of lighting system in which the light fixtures are built into open-plan office furniture to light specific work areas . . . . . . . . . . . | 9. ______ |

**Directions**: Indicate your answer to each of the following questions by circling "Yes" or "No" in the Answers column.

| | | Answers | |
|---|---|---|---|
| 1. | Is telephoning an example of an office activity that is mainly cognitive? | Yes | No |
| 2. | Are the ambient factors in the office both physical and psychological? | Yes | No |
| 3. | Is the color blue used to create a cool and calming effect upon people? | Yes | No |
| 4. | For offices with a southern or western exposure, is it recommended that the walls be painted with warm colors such as yellow, peach, and brown? | Yes | No |
| 5. | When painting office ceilings and walls, is it recommended that light gray be used because of its very high reflection ratio? | Yes | No |
| 6. | Should flat paint be used for ceilings and side walls in order to reduce glare? | Yes | No |
| 7. | For ease of reading the characters on a VDT screen, should equipment displaying dark characters on a light background be selected rather than light characters on a dark background? | Yes | No |
| 8. | For office areas where employees walk a great deal, does solid vinyl tile provide the most comfortable floor covering? | Yes | No |
| 9. | Should VDT operations be carried out in areas that have lower quantities of light than in the general office? | Yes | No |
| 10. | Is the *footlambert* used to determine the amount of brightness? | Yes | No |
| 11. | Is a lower visual comfort probability (VCP) recommended for VDT tasks than for paper tasks? | Yes | No |
| 12. | When emitting an equal amount of light, do incandescent bulbs give off more heat and consume more wattage than fluorescent lamps? | Yes | No |
| 13. | Do the chief advantages of using incandescent lighting include low operating cost and an even distribution of lighting? | Yes | No |
| 14. | Should the lighting plans for open offices provide for lighting the workstations by means of ceiling fixtures that emit uniform footcandles? | Yes | No |
| 15. | Does task/ambient lighting bring about increased costs as a result of the need for more ceiling fixtures and thus more energy consumption? | Yes | No |
| 16. | Is 60 db the recommended maximum noise level for general office operations? | Yes | No |
| 17. | Do hard surfaces, such as floors and walls, reflect sounds? | Yes | No |
| 18. | Is vocal music with a loud brass accompaniment appropriate music for offices? | Yes | No |
| 19. | For the most comfortable and healthful temperature for office work, is it recommended that the level range from 72 to 74°F? | Yes | No |
| 20. | Generally, do people over 40 require a higher effective temperature than young people? | Yes | No |
| 21. | On a cold day, does a high relative humidity make workers feel warmer? | Yes | No |
| 22. | For most office workers, is 60 to 75 percent the most comfortable range of humidity? | Yes | No |
| 23. | Does the sick building syndrome (SBS) reflect health problems associated with air pollution? | Yes | No |
| 24. | Do smart office buildings equipped with an integrated security system (ISS) rely upon a computer to control their burglar systems? | Yes | No |
| 25. | To conserve energy in the office, should the less expensive incandescent lamps be used rather than costlier fluorescent and high-intensity discharge lamps? | Yes | No |

## SECTION B • PROJECTS

### Project 14–1 • Field Research: Evaluating the Office Environment

In completing this project, you will evaluate the ergonomic factors in an office at your place of employment or on your campus—possibly your instructor's office. You will have an opportunity to study several phases of the office environment, appraise each one on the rating scale provided, and offer your recommendations for improvement. Following your investigation of the office environment, you may be asked to present your research findings in a written report or oral presentation.

**Directions:** Examine the office of your choice in relation to each of the environments described below and on page 154. On the scale below, evaluate the ergonomic effectiveness of the environment; in the space provided give your suggestions for improving the environment.

| ENVIRONMENTS | SCALE Poor 0 | 1 | 2 | 3 | 4 | Excellent 5 |
|---|---|---|---|---|---|---|
| **Surface** (walls, ceilings, floors, windows, pillars, furniture, equipment, and plants) | | | | | | |
| a. Functional use of color—color that "works" for the office in relation to the employees' job assignments | ___ | ___ | ___ | ___ | ___ | ___ |
| b. Walls and ceilings that are of a color light enough to reflect rather than absorb light but still produce no annoying glare | ___ | ___ | ___ | ___ | ___ | ___ |
| c. Suitable surface for furniture and equipment so that excess reflection and glare are avoided | ___ | ___ | ___ | ___ | ___ | ___ |
| d. Floor covering that provides a quiet, relaxed, static-free atmosphere in which to work | ___ | ___ | ___ | ___ | ___ | ___ |
| e. Plants located to provide privacy, brighten and warm areas, and add attractive coloring | ___ | ___ | ___ | ___ | ___ | ___ |

*Recommendations:* ______________________________

______________________________

______________________________

______________________________

| ENVIRONMENTS | 0 | 1 | 2 | 3 | 4 | 5 |
|---|---|---|---|---|---|---|
| **Seeing** | | | | | | |
| a. Use and control over natural light entering the office | ___ | ___ | ___ | ___ | ___ | ___ |
| b. Quantity of lighting—sufficient FC for tasks performed | ___ | ___ | ___ | ___ | ___ | ___ |
| c. Quality of lighting—satisfactory brightness ratio, properly shaded luminaires, glare-free and nonflickering screens on video display terminals | ___ | ___ | ___ | ___ | ___ | ___ |
| d. Use of task/ambient lighting | ___ | ___ | ___ | ___ | ___ | ___ |

*Recommendations:* ______________________________

______________________________

______________________________

______________________________

| ENVIRONMENTS | Poor 0 | 1 | 2 | 3 | 4 | Excellent 5 |
|---|---|---|---|---|---|---|
| **Hearing** | | | | | | |
| a. Noise levels—number of db, pitch or frequency of sounds | ___ | ___ | ___ | ___ | ___ | ___ |
| b. Noise-control program (sound-absorbing materials, acoustical cabinets and screens, isolation of noisy equipment, use of carpeting, wall and ceiling coverings) | ___ | ___ | ___ | ___ | ___ | ___ |
| c. Music (programmed, FM, quality, duration, effect upon workers) | ___ | ___ | ___ | ___ | ___ | ___ |

*Recommendations:* ______________________________

______________________________

______________________________

______________________________

| ENVIRONMENTS | Poor 0 | 1 | 2 | 3 | 4 | Excellent 5 |
|---|---|---|---|---|---|---|
| **Air** | | | | | | |
| a. Air conditioning (comfortable temperature and humidity levels) | ___ | ___ | ___ | ___ | ___ | ___ |
| b. Control over air pollution (dirt, dust, odors, smoke, and contaminants such as carbon monoxide, carbon dioxide, asbestos, ozone, formaldehyde, and radon) | ___ | ___ | ___ | ___ | ___ | ___ |

*Recommendations:* ______________________________

______________________________

______________________________

______________________________

| ENVIRONMENTS | Poor 0 | 1 | 2 | 3 | 4 | Excellent 5 |
|---|---|---|---|---|---|---|
| **Safe and Secure** | | | | | | |
| a. Measures taken to prevent slipping, tripping, or falling | ___ | ___ | ___ | ___ | ___ | ___ |
| b. Proper use of equipment | ___ | ___ | ___ | ___ | ___ | ___ |
| c. Equipment in working condition (three-wire grounding systems, no frayed wiring or exposed wires) | ___ | ___ | ___ | ___ | ___ | ___ |
| d. Control over placement of filing cabinets to prevent tipping | ___ | ___ | ___ | ___ | ___ | ___ |
| e. Precautions taken in use of combustible materials (adequate fire extinguishers and their locations) | ___ | ___ | ___ | ___ | ___ | ___ |
| f. Well-lighted exits, aisles, halls, and stairways | ___ | ___ | ___ | ___ | ___ | ___ |
| g. Periodic fire drills | ___ | ___ | ___ | ___ | ___ | ___ |
| h. Measures taken to aid disabled workers | ___ | ___ | ___ | ___ | ___ | ___ |

*Recommendations:* ______________________________

______________________________

______________________________

______________________________

Is there evidence of an energy management program? ______________________________

If so, what are the specific approaches followed in the office to reduce energy consumption? ______________

______________________________

# Project 14–2 • Using Three-Dimensional Drawings in Planning an Office Layout

"What will my space look like?"

"Can you give me a drawing showing the new workstations?"

You have planned the space. Now you need to communicate the answers to these questions to other people. The following pages will introduce you to an easy way to do this by constructing a three-dimensional drawing which can easily be colored and used on a presentation board. Remember that you will be working on a 45° angle—literally with parallelograms rather than rectangles.

You will find the first one strange to do; but after the first one, it is easy.

You have already prepared the floor plan of your open office area as shown in the traditional plan view illustrated at the bottom of page 162. As you will see, this plan has been drawn to 1/8″ scale. The small numbers (5, 7, 17, and 22) shown alongside each workstation refer to the three-dimensional drawings of those workstations at the top of page 162 and on page 167. Each of the workstations has been executed in 45° three-dimensional drawings, a method that will allow you to experience the workstation. All of these drawings are in 1/4″ scale.

**Directions:**

1. Remove the blank grid on pages 157 and 159. On a copying machine, make as many copies as you will need. The grid has a heavy rule every 10 units. It, too, is executed in 1/4″ scale.
2. On a copying machine, make sufficient copies of the four workstations (numbered 5, 7, 17, and 22) illustrated on pages 156 and 161.

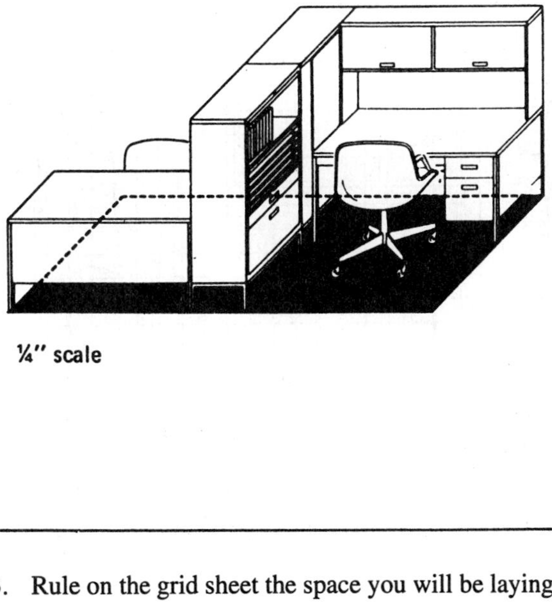

¼″ scale

3. Rule on the grid sheet the space you will be laying out.

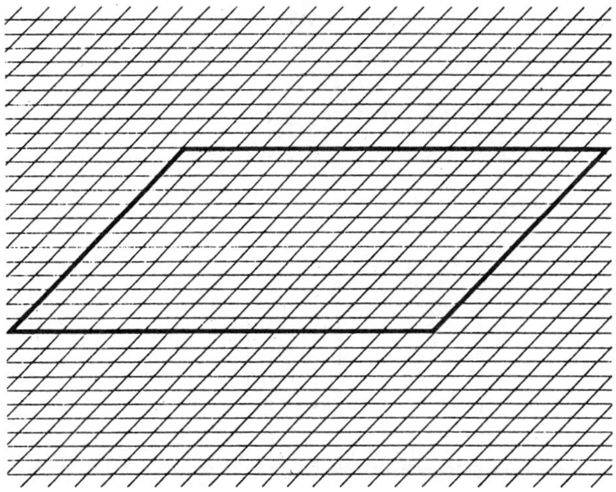

4. Begin with the top of the space and work downward. Tape or rubber cement each drawing into its proper position. Photocopy the finished product and color the workstations to provide a color-coordinated decor that will aid in improving morale and productivity.

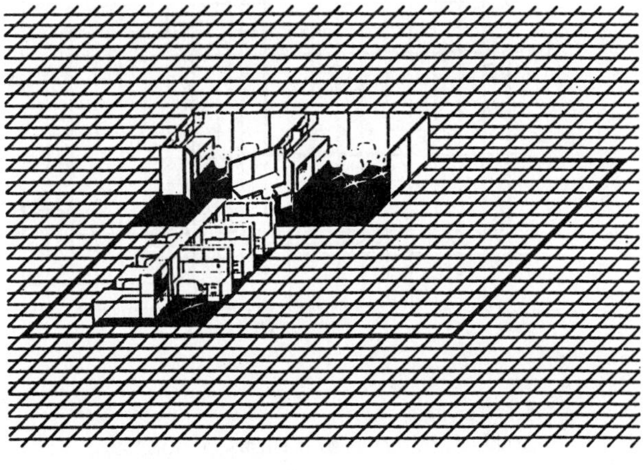

Source: "Using Three-Dimensional Drawings in Planning Office Layouts." Reproduced by permission of Steelcase Inc., Grand Rapids, MI.

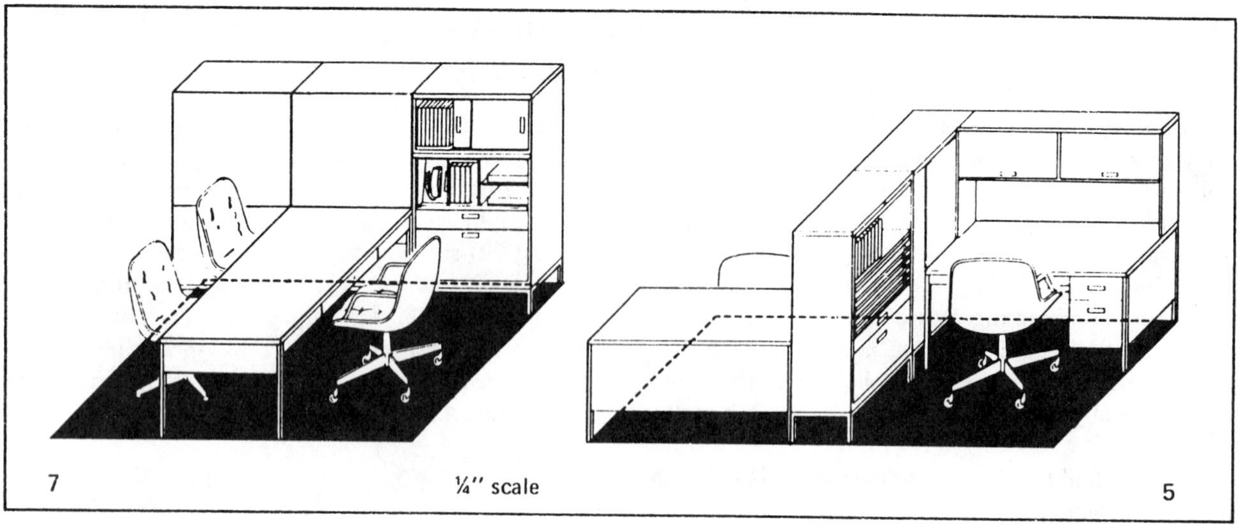


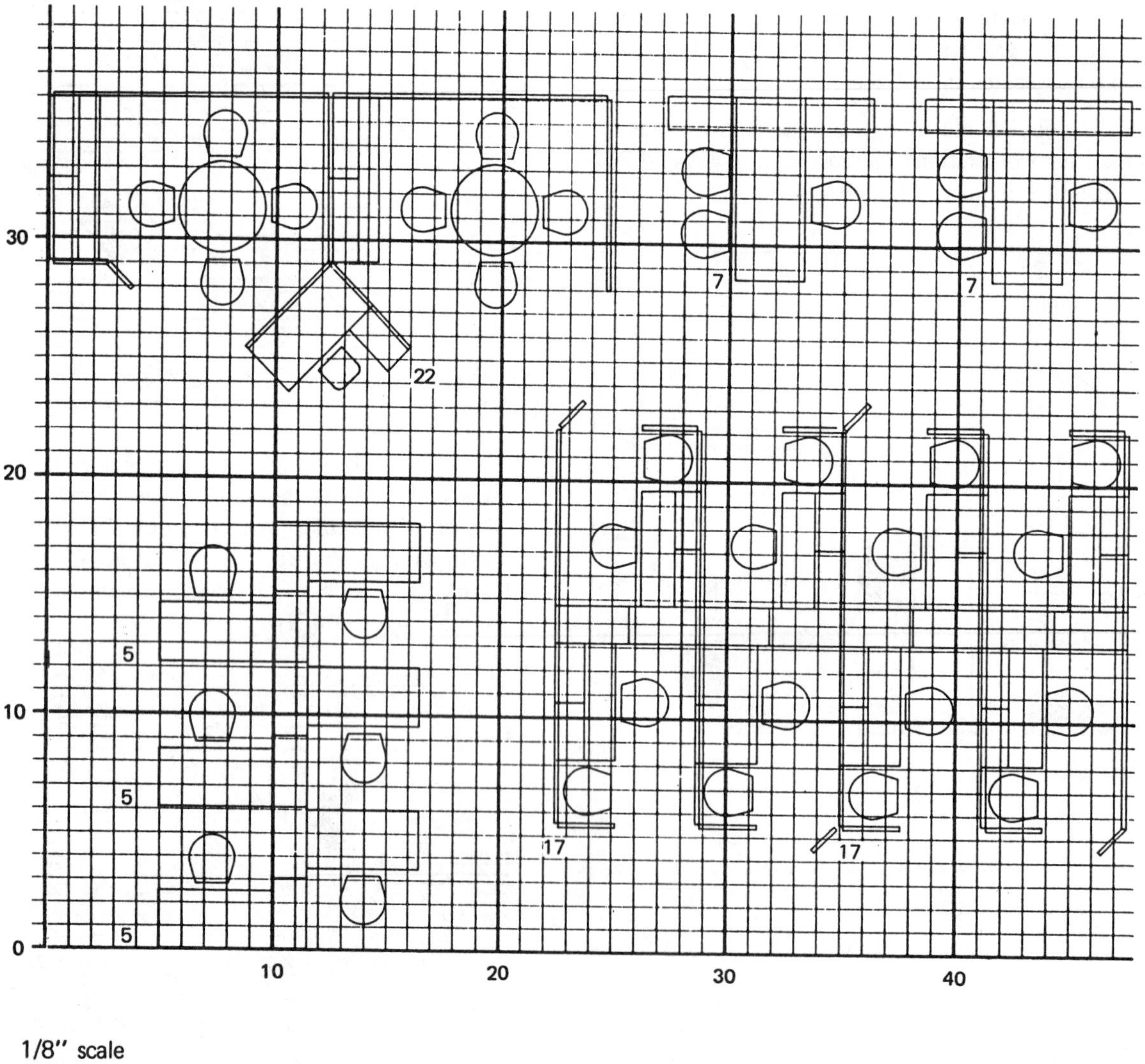


1/8" scale
Small numbers are illustration numbers.

80

70

60

50

40

30

20

10

0

10 20 30

40 50 60

Name ______________________ Date ______________________ 

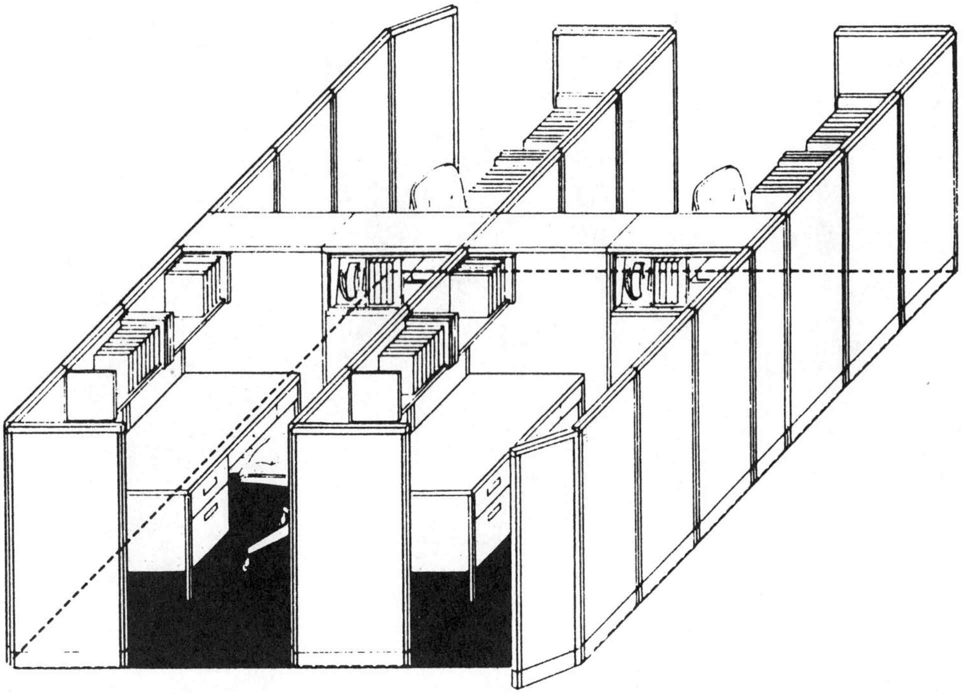

17

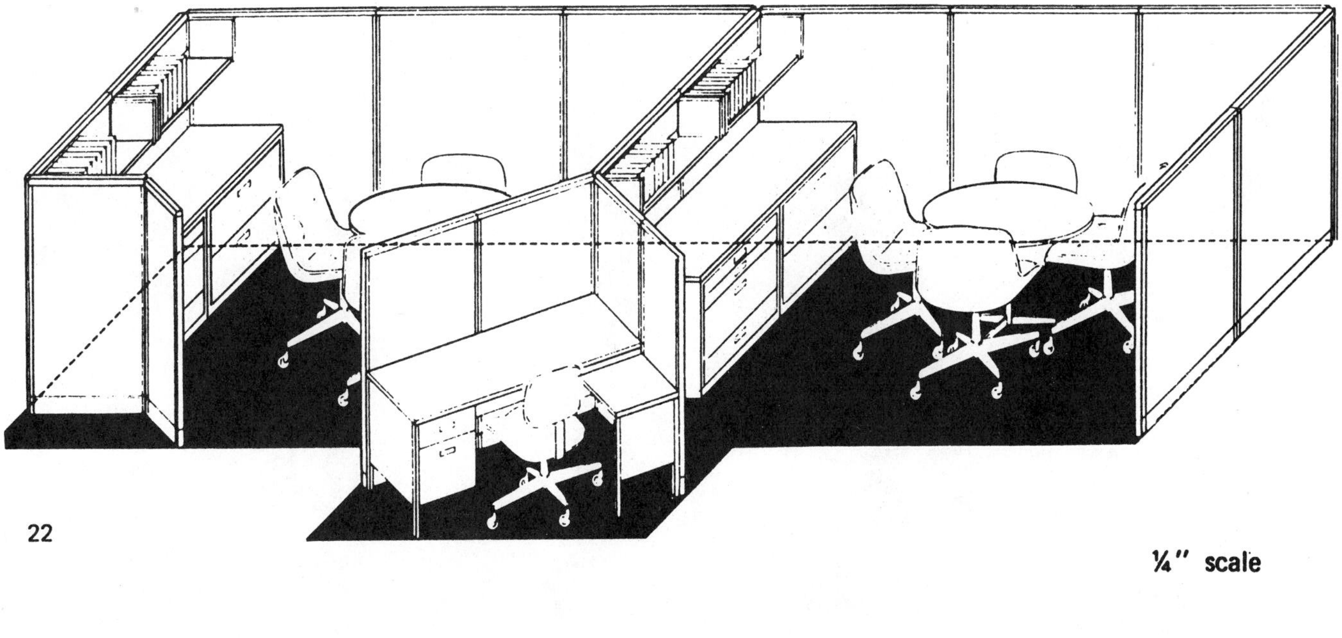

22

¼″ scale

# Project 14–3 • Avoiding the Sick Building Syndrome

In the following article, the writer shows how employees have come to expect clean indoor air as part of a productive and healthy work environment. After you have read the article, answer the questions at the end.

## Avoid Sick Building Syndrome with Clean Air

Providing a pleasant, up-to-date working environment is one way a company can compete for quality employees. Lavish furnishings, top-of-the-line furniture, correct lighting, and a facility with a pristine appearance all contribute to this goal.

However, judging from recent health studies, a top-notch environment may not be enough to keep quality employees working at a high level, particularly if the indoor air environment is unhealthy.

According to the U.S. Environmental Protection Agency, "Indoor air pollution is one of the top five environmental issues." It estimates that indoor air pollution costs Americans billions of dollars each year in medical expenses and lost productivity.

In fact, the EPA asserts that the average American—spending roughly 90% of their time indoors—can be breathing air more seriously polluted than outdoor air in even the largest and most industrialized cities. Also, medical research has linked indoor air pollution to various allergies, asthma, emphysema, bronchitis, heart disease, and cancer. Asthma and other allergies from indoor air, continues the agency, is the cause for over 130 million lost school days and 13.5 million lost work days each year.

And the news gets even worse if you are an employer. According to industry experts, more and more lawsuits concerning poor workplace air quality are being brought by employees. Also on the increase are Workers Compensation suits against employers. Making matters even more complex is OSHA, Occupational Safety and Hazard [*sic*] Act, which can take action against companies that fail to comply with the act's indoor air regulations. It could bring fines starting at $1,000 or, perhaps, force a business to shut down.

Fortunately, an organization can correct indoor air problems by paying the same attention it does to creating a topnotch corporate image.

The first task is to recognize the problem which, according to the EPA, is divided into two categories: those associated with sick building syndrome and those with building-related illness. The first one refers to situations in which occupants experience acute health and comfort effects that appear to be linked to time spent in a building, but with no specific illness or cause identified. Building-related illness, meanwhile, involves symptoms of diagnosable illness attributed to airborne building contaminants, such as Legionnaire's Disease.

Ailments connected with sick building syndrome are headaches; eye, nose, or throat irritation; dry cough; dry or itchy skin; dizziness; nausea and fatigue. Building-related sickness includes coughing, chest tightness, fever, chills, and muscle aches.

The primary sources of indoor air pollution are furnishings (pressed wood and carpet), copiers (which release ozone, a lung irritant), as well as human beings who release carbon dioxide. Solvents and tobacco smoke are other sources of indoor air pollution. Also, a poorly designed indoor ventilation system can bring in pollutants from outdoors.

The EPA says there are several ways to clean up indoor air. The most basic strategy is proper ventilation. Here, the more outdoor air supplied to a facility, the less indoor air is a problem. According to the building codes, the minimum amount of air that should be supplied to a building is 15 cubic feet per minute per person.

Indeed, the problem with indoor air increases with modern office buildings, which are airtight and energy efficient. Without adequate ventilation, these facilities provide a great source of poor indoor air. And, unfortunately, the oldest, cheapest remedy for the problem—opening a window—does not apply to many of these buildings because their windows are not made to open. The alternative? Construct more air ducts.

In addition, there are precautions one can take to prevent indoor air quality problems. First, says the EPA, maintain the HVAC (heating, ventilation and air-conditioning) system by cleaning filters, preventing stagnant water from collecting in cooling towers, and performing regular inspections. Different HVAC systems bring in different amounts of outdoor air. To calculate the amount of air needed in your building, consult an HVAC professional. Other cautions include replacement of water-stained ceiling tile and carpeting, which can become a breeding ground for bacteria, viruses, and mold which make up biological contaminants.

Also, be sure to provide separate exhaust systems in areas where copiers or solvents are used. Paints, adhesives, solvents, and pesticides should be stored in well-ventilated areas. In addition, make sure air-intake vents are not blocked by furniture or equipment. This obstructs admittance of outdoor air into the building.

As mentioned, placement of air intake vents or air ducts is also important. They should not be too close to exhaust vents, garages, traffic areas, loading docks, etc.

On HVAC systems, the EPA warns that their operation only during weekdays, and not weekends and nights when the building is unoccupied, may increase building-generated pollution to an unhealthy level. This may also occur if the HVAC system operates intermittently or at reduced rates during the day, or if it starts up after workers arrive. The EPA suggests turning on the system several hours before workers arrive and shutting it down after the last workers have left.

Also, the EPA continues to recommend restricted areas for smokers, an important suggestion when one considers that second-hand tobacco smoke causes 300,000 cases of respiratory illness and 3,000 cases of lung cancer each year.

One way companies believe they can maintain clean air is through the use of air cleaners. But, according to a report from Buyers Laboratory, Inc., a research and office equipment testing company in Hackensack, NJ, a company "should not expect too much from them." The comment is based on the EPA's position that while air cleaners can be helpful in some cases, they cannot remove all of the pollutants found in indoor air. They should only be considered an accessory, not a substitute, for controlling contaminants at the source.

Air cleaners are not able to effectively remove carbon dioxide. Also, the EPA says, electronic air cleaners and ion generators may produce ozone, an indoor air pollutant. Just as important, no air cleaner can adequately remove all the gaseous pollutants typically present in indoor air, or prevent gases and odors from particles collected by air cleaners from being redispersed into the air. Another drawback: air cleaner maintenance, especially routine replacement of filters, can be expensive.

Nonetheless, air cleaners do have a place in the office as they remove some of the particles that could be inhaled.

While the obvious means of correcting an indoor air problem is to increase the ventilation rate, there is a chance this won't cure the problem. If so, you may have to hire a consultant to investigate your building, find the problem, and solve it. The EPA recommends regular building investigations, which involve touring the facility and gathering information about the symptoms, activities of the occupants, the HVAC system, possible pollution pathways, and possible contamination sources. After collecting the information, a consultant will form a hypothesis and test it, repeating the process until a solution is achieved.

In so doing, the consultant can ensure that your building is full of clean air, providing a healthy, productive environment for your company's top asset—its workers.

**Directions:** Indicate your answer to each of the following questions by circling "Yes" or "No" in the Answers column.

| | **Answers** | |
|---|---|---|
| 1. Is OSHA the federal agency that enforces indoor air regulations? | Yes | No |
| 2. Are headaches, eye irritations, and nausea connected with the sick building syndrome? | Yes | No |
| 3. Do building codes specify that the minimum amount of air supplied to a building should be 5 cubic feet per minute per person? | Yes | No |
| 4. Does the construction of airtight and energy-efficient office buildings solve most problems associated with poor indoor air? | Yes | No |
| 5. Does the EPA recommend turning on and shutting down the HVAC intermittently during the workday? | Yes | No |
| 6. With today's HVAC systems, is there a need to restrict smoking to certain areas within the office building? | Yes | No |
| 7. Do air cleaners effectively remove the carbon dioxide found in indoor air? | Yes | No |
| 8. Can the indoor air problem be solved by increasing the ventilation rate? | Yes | No |

# 15

# SELECTING OFFICE FURNITURE AND EQUIPMENT

Today's manufacturers of office furniture sell *systems furniture*, which includes not only desks and chairs but also movable partitions, acoustical screens and panels, storage components, and service modules. Although manufacturers admit that systems furniture (used primarily in open offices) may cost more than conventional items, they report that the savings in an open office more than offset the additional cost. There are savings resulting from putting more workers in the same space, integrating storage into each workstation, and reducing the costs of energy (heating, ventilating, and lighting). Those who are planning an office building and its facilities, or renovating an older building, should work from the "inside out" and consider the use of systems furniture, which in the long run may mean that the firm is tying up less capital.

In obtaining office furniture and equipment (primarily the latter), the administrative office manager carefully studies the advantages and disadvantages of leasing arrangements. By financing the acquisition of office equipment through a leasing arrangement, (1) funds can be provided that otherwise might not be obtainable from more conventional financial sources, (2) working capital can be stretched, and (3) some of the risks of business expansion may be minimized. On the other hand, by purchasing its office equipment, the firm has assets that it can later sell. Further, the annual depreciation of the office equipment, an operating expense, reduces the amount of federal income taxes to be paid.

## SECTION A • REVIEW QUESTIONS

**Directions:** Complete each of the following sentences by writing in the Answers column the letter of the word or words that correctly completes each statement.

**Answers**

1. Of the following characteristics of modular office furniture, the most important to the office manager is: (A) integrated, interdependent modules, (B) rich appearance, (C) wide array of colors, (D) streamlined appearance, (E) none of these . . . . . . . . . . 1. ______

2. In selecting office furniture that is long lasting and rich in appearance, imparts a warm tone, and provides prestige to enhance the office worker's attitude toward the job, the office manager probably would choose furniture made of: (A) steel, (B) aluminum, (C) plastic, (D) wood, (E) none of these . . . . . . . . . . 2. ______

3. Which of the following does *not* represent an advantage to be gained from leasing office equipment? (A) Working capital is freed for daily cash flow; (B) Budgetary control is facilitated since the amount of the periodic lease payments is easily determined; (C) The lessee is obligated to provide maintenance service; (D) The lessor may offer a deferred-payment lease that ties the lease payments into the seasonal pattern of cash flow; (E) An additional source of financing is provided a new small company that does not have access to the usual sources of credit . . . . . . . . 3. ______

4. If office equipment is to be used for more than one eight-hour shift each day, (A) it is more economical for the firm to lease rather than purchase its equipment, (B) it is more economical for the firm to purchase rather than lease its equipment, (C) the firm should rely upon short-term rental of the equipment, (D) a capital budget study should be undertaken to determine the relative net costs of purchasing and leasing, (E) none of these . . . . . . . . . . 4. ______

5. An example of a fixed cost is: (A) real estate taxes, (B) direct labor costs, (C) office supplies, (D) all of these, (E) none of these . . . . . . . . . . 5. ______

6. The cost of a proposed capital expenditure is $20,000. The annual cash savings resulting from the purchase are estimated to be $3,000. The annual depreciation expense is $2,000. The payback period is calculated as: (A) two years, (B) three years, (C) four years, (D) six years, (E) none of these . . . . . . . . . . 6. ______

**Directions:** Indicate your answer to each of the following questions by circling "Yes" or "No" in the Answers column.

| | | **Answers** | |
|---|---|---|---|
| 1. | Generally, is office furniture leased rather than purchased? . . . . . . . . | Yes | No |
| 2. | Does a modular workstation typically occupy less space than that required for a conventional layout? . . . . . . . . | Yes | No |
| 3. | If office workers have to bring their work to their eyes, should they have armrests on their chairs? . . . . . . . . | Yes | No |
| 4. | Should the workstation for a full-time VDT operator feature a detachable keyboard? . . . . . . . | Yes | No |
| 5. | Is a feasibility study undertaken at the time of interviewing representatives of equipment manufacturers to examine their offerings? . . . . . . . . | Yes | No |
| 6. | Should an office equipment feasibility study answer the question of whether the equipment is cost effective as well as ergonomically sound? . . . . . . . . | Yes | No |
| 7. | May the depreciation that occurs during the estimated useful life of office equipment be claimed by the firm as an operating expense? . . . . . . . . | Yes | No |
| 8. | Does an equipment lease enable the lessee to obtain ownership of a tangible asset by making periodic payments to the lessor over a specified time period? . . . . . . . . | Yes | No |
| 9. | Is a short-term lease very much like a rental contract? . . . . . . . . | Yes | No |
| 10. | In a long-term lease with purchase option, does the lessee build up equity in the equipment leased? . . . . . . . . | Yes | No |
| 11. | When a company leases highly specialized equipment, is there an increase in the risk of working with obsolete equipment? . . . . . . . . | Yes | No |
| 12. | Is a short payback period usually desired so that a company is exposed to less risk of recovering its capital? . . . . . . . . | Yes | No |
| 13. | As a source of funds, does cash inflow consist *only* of the amount of cash remaining after income taxes have been paid? . . . . . . . . | Yes | No |
| 14. | Is the break-even point that level of operations at which revenues and costs are equal? . . . . . . | Yes | No |
| 15. | Are direct materials, such as office supplies, an example of fixed costs? . . . . . . . . | Yes | No |
| 16. | Do variable costs change in response to changes in the volume of work activity? . . . . . . . . | Yes | No |
| 17. | May break-even analysis be used to evaluate a proposed capital expenditure, such as the purchase of new office space? . . . . . . . . | Yes | No |
| 18. | To determine the average rate of return on a proposed capital expenditure, is the average amount of the investment divided by the average savings to be obtained from that investment? | Yes | No |
| 19. | When companies are faced with possible overnight obsolescence of their high-tech equipment, is it recommended that they purchase rather than lease the equipment? . . . . . . . . | Yes | No |
| 20. | When office equipment is purchased, is there generally a warranty period during which equipment repairs will be made by the manufacturer free of charge? . . . . . . . . | Yes | No |
| 21. | If a company plans to replace its office equipment before the end of the estimated useful life, is there need for a replacement program? . . . . . . . . | Yes | No |
| 22. | In large organizations having great sums invested in office machines, is there less need for centralized control of the equipment function than in smaller companies with little investment? | Yes | No |

## SECTION B • PROJECTS

# Project 15–1 • Calculating the Purchase Price of Office Furniture and the Annual Depreciation Expense

**Directions:** Refer to Project 13–2 on page 144 and refresh your memory about the furniture needs of the business department offices of Ness Community College.

1. Determine (a) the estimated cost of the office furniture to be housed in each of the three offices and (b) the total cost of all assets to be purchased. (Your library or the office of your school's business manager should be able to provide you with up-to-date catalogs of office furniture supplies.)

(a) *Chairperson's private office (desk is double pedestal):*

______________________________

______________________________

______________________________

______________________________

______________________________

______________________________

______________________________

______________________________

______________________________

*Assistant's private office (desk is single pedestal):*

______________________________

______________________________

______________________________

______________________________

______________________________

______________________________

______________________________

______________________________

*Open office (desks are double pedestal):*

______________________________

______________________________

______________________________

______________________________

______________________________

______________________________

______________________________

______________________________

______________________________

______________________________

(b) *Total cost of all assets to be purchased* .................. $________

2. Ness Community College uses the MACRS straight-line method of calculating depreciation, which is explained in Project 4–3 on page 37. All of the office furniture, which was purchased on March 4, 1995, is classified as 7-year property. On the form below, record the amount of annual depreciation expense on the office furniture.

| Year | Depreciation Rate (%) | Unrecovered Basis of the Asset (Cost Reduced by Accumulated Depreciation Taken in Prior Years) | Annual Depreciation Expense |
|---|---|---|---|
| 1 | ______ | ______ | ______ |
| 2 | ______ | ______ | ______ |
| 3 | ______ | ______ | ______ |
| 4 | ______ | ______ | ______ |
| 5 | ______ | ______ | ______ |
| 6 | ______ | ______ | ______ |
| 7 | ______ | ______ | ______ |
| 8 | ______ | ______ | ______ |
| | | Total Depreciation Expense | ______ |

# Project 15–2 • Selecting New Filing Equipment

The filing department of the Herring Company measures 46 2/3′ × 16 1/4′, as shown in Figure 15–1. The 100 four-drawer file cabinets are fully depreciated and are scheduled to be replaced. The records manager, Sue Temple, has narrowed down her sources of supply to two local vendors.

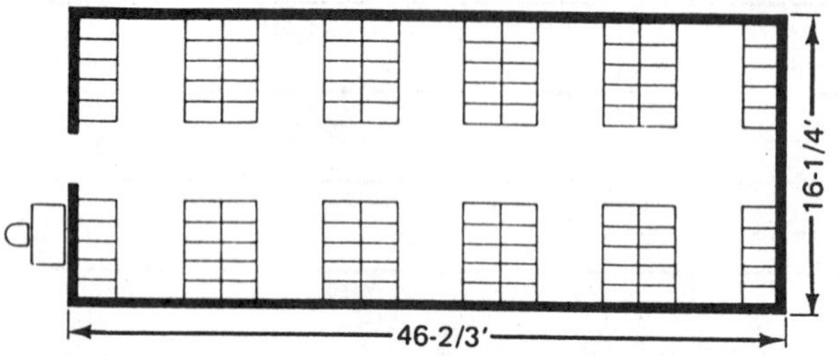


**Figure 15-1 Filing Department of the Herring Company**

Vendor A proposes to replace the present file units with 100 four-drawer steel file cabinets, each measuring 15″ wide, 29″ deep, and 52″ high. The vendor has quoted a price of $194.95 per unit. The major selling features of this vendor's line include the following: sides and back formed from a single sheet of steel, thus presenting a smoothly finished appearance from any angle; attractive, wraparound shell concealing a rugged interior built for years of quiet, easy operation and trouble-free service; choice of contemporary colors; and recessed handles, to the left of the label holder, which are fingertip controlled.

Vendor B proposes to replace the present units with 44 open-shelf files, each having five shelves. Each five-shelf unit measures 36″ wide, 18″ deep, and 68″ high. The purchase price of each unit has been quoted at $471.

Vendor B points out the following benefits to be realized from installing open-shelf filing: a savings of up to 60 percent in floor space, since one open-shelf unit holds more than eight conventional file drawers and the distance between the open-shelf files need be only 30″. (Presently the distance between the four-drawer units, which face each other, is 54″.) The vendor also points out that file clerks will find their work easier and that the overall appearance of the files will be neater. Finally, the vendor stresses that with the space saved, Temple will be able to move her workstation and those of her five assistants from the noisy accounting department where they are now located to the filing department. This point especially impresses Temple, for she would like to free the space that she and her assistants are now occupying in the accounting department. She is aware of the savings that would result since currently her budget includes the accounting office space (309 square feet) at $9.25 per square foot per year.

**Directions:** After you have studied each of the two vendors' proposals:

1. Determine which proposal will be the more economical pursuit for Temple to recommend. In your calculations, show the total costs involved under each proposal and the net savings resulting from your selection.

2. On the grid below, prepare a layout that reflects the suggestions made by Vendor B. Do you agree with the vendor's claim about the amount of floor space that can be saved by installing open-shelf filing? Are you able to relocate Temple and her five assistants in the filing department and provide a sufficient amount of space for their work?

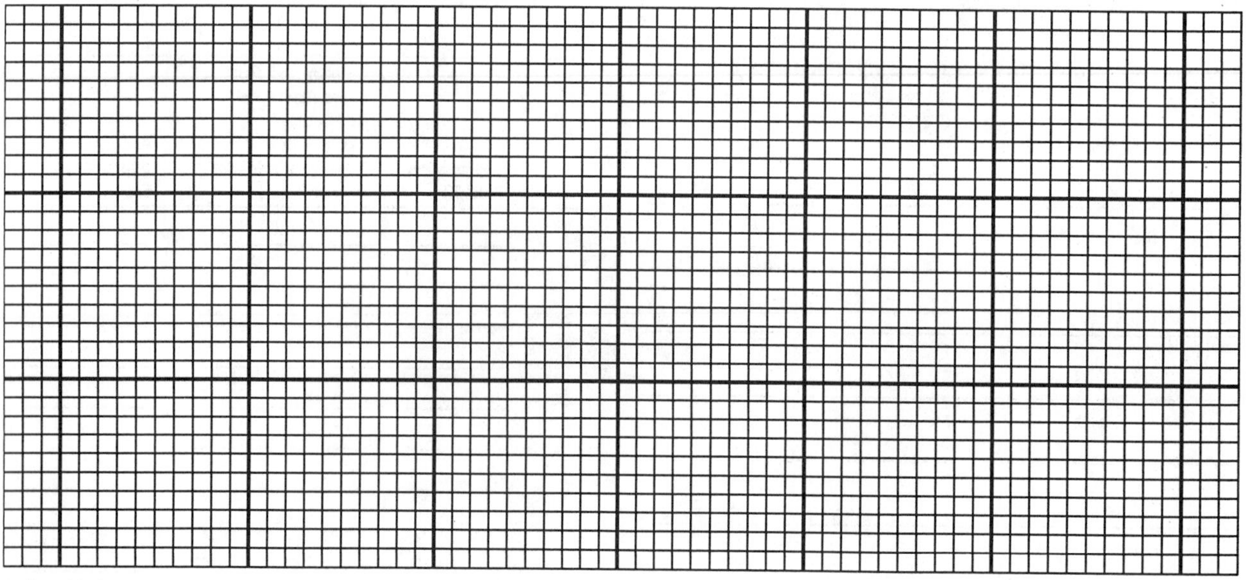

Scale: 1 block = ______

# Project 15–3 • Field Research: Surveying Users of Office Furniture

In this field research project, you will contact a company of your choice and arrange an interview with the person responsible for purchasing office furniture. In your meeting, your goal will be to determine the users' level of satisfaction with the present office furniture, to learn if the furniture is doing the job it was designed to do, and to uncover any problems that faced the company when purchasing the furniture. By obtaining answers to questions such as the following, you will be able to prepare an oral or written report, as requested by your instructor.

Company ______________________

Product or Service ______________________

Person Interviewed ______________________

Person's Title ______________________

No. of top-level executives? ____________ No. of senior managers and professionals? ____________

No. of secretarial and clerical staff? ______________________

1. What are the most important factors you consider when selecting office furniture? Rank each of the following eight factors on a scale of 1 to 8, with 8 being the most important factor:
   - _____ Price
   - _____ Manufacturer's reputation
   - _____ Features and functions of furniture
   - _____ Aesthetics and design
   - _____ Space requirements
   - _____ Quality
   - _____ Modularity—ability to add interlocking and interchangeable components
   - _____ Compatibility with existing furniture
2. What is the average age of the furniture used in the firm?

   ___ 1–3 years ___ 4–6 years ___ 7–10 years ___ over 10 years
3. How often does the firm replace its office furniture?

   ___ 1–2 years ___ 3–4 years ___ 7–10 years ___ over 10 years
4. What factors are considered when the firm decides to replace the office furniture? ______________________
5. From what source(s) does the firm purchase its office furniture? ______________________
6. Are the users of the furniture satisfied with its function, comfort, and safety? Explain any negative responses.
7. What are the major problems found when selecting and purchasing office furniture? ______________________
8. Is any office furniture leased? If so, which kinds? ______________________

# Project 15–4 • Capital Budgeting—A Tool of Planning (Payback Period)

This project is the first of several wherein *capital budgeting* is described as one of several tools of planning that may be used by the administrative office manager. In analyzing capital expenditures, the office manager is concerned with the evaluation of several proposals for the allocation of relatively large financial expenditures. To aid the company in obtaining the best use of its capital, the office manager, along with other managers, may participate in ranking the firm's capital expenditures in order of their relative desirability so that projects with higher returns are given priority over less profitable undertakings.

Like other managers, the office manager competes for a share of the company funds in order to have his or her proposals win priority. For example, as the cost of office furniture and equipment continues to rise, the office manager may be called upon to provide a more detailed, factual justification for the purchase of such assets. Capital budgeting provides the office manager with one tool that helps to justify such acquisitions.

Assume that an office manager is proposing the purchase of additional data processing equipment for which the following data have been gathered:

### Cash Outlay

| | |
|---|---|
| Total cost of equipment (including transportation and installation costs) | $25,000 |

### Estimated Cash Inflow

| | |
|---|---|
| Cash gain before cost recovery (depreciation) and federal income taxes: (These estimated cash savings result from the release of one part-time office worker, whose salary and benefits equal $18,000 a year) | $18,000 |
| Depreciation | $ 2,500 |
| Income before taxes | $15,500 |
| Federal income taxes, assuming a 34% rate | $ 5,270 |
| Net income after taxes | $10,230 |
| Net annual cash inflow (net income after taxes plus depreciation) | $12,730 |

The concept of cash inflow treats depreciation as a source of funds because depreciation represents an expense for which no cash is spent by the firm. Thus, the firm has available an amount of cash that consists of the net income after taxes plus depreciation.

The data given above are used to determine the payback period. As a financial test, the payback period enables the office manager to estimate the period of time in which the proposal will generate cash equal to the cost of the proposal. Thus, the office manager estimates how long the firm will have to wait in order to recover sufficient cash *from* the proposal that will equal the cash invested *in* the proposal.

Assuming that the annual cash inflow from the proposal is in equal amounts, the following formula is used to determine the payback period:

$$\text{Payback Period} = \frac{\text{Cost of Proposal}}{\text{Net Income after Taxes + Depreciation}}$$

$$= \frac{25{,}000}{12{,}730} = 1.96 \text{ years}$$

This payback period may now be compared with that of any other proposals that the office manager is considering so that from among all of the planned projects, the most desirable project may be recommended to those having responsibility for assigning priorities to capital expenditures. In this firm, the capital budgeting policy stipulates that any proposal must pay for itself within three years—the cutoff point. Generally a short payback period is desirable, since under a relatively short period of time the company is exposed to less risk—it will recover its capital in a short time period. Further, for the firm that is short of cash, a short payback period will improve the solvency position by generating additional cash inflow.

Although the payback test is a very commonly used method of analyzing capital expenditures, the method is criticized because the time element is ignored (dollars received today in cash flow are treated in the same way as those received at a later date) and any additional savings realized in succeeding years are not taken into account.

**Directions:** The office manager has two more proposals under consideration for which the following data are available:

| | Proposal A | Proposal B |
|---|---|---|
| Total cost | $16,000 | $6,000 |
| Depreciation | 1,600 | 600 |
| Cash gain | 3,000 | 3,400 |
| Federal income taxes | 34% | 34% |

1. What is the payback period for:

   Proposal A? ________

   Proposal B? ________

2. Rank the three proposals (A, B, and the one for the data processing equipment) in the order that you, as office manager, would present them to the person in charge of allocating capital funds:

________________________________

________________________________

________________________________

________________________________

# Project 15–5 • Break-Even Analysis

This project describes how break-even analysis may be used in planning future business activities such as an expansion or curtailment of office operations. Since such an analysis is concerned with future prospects and operations and relies upon estimates, the reliability of the analysis is influenced greatly by the accuracy of the estimates.

The *break-even point* is that level of operations at which the firm neither realizes income nor incurs loss, a point at which revenues and costs are exactly equal. As a result of charting the break-even point, the office manager is able to see graphically the relationship between sales volume, costs, and profits. A careful and accurate break-even analysis cannot be undertaken without the knowledge of costs and their behavior as the volume of business activity changes. Therefore, it is highly desirable that the office manager be familiar with the fixed and variable costs that are involved in company operations.

## Costs and Their Behavior

*Fixed costs* are those that tend to remain relatively stable over a stipulated time period, even when the volume of activity changes. Examples of fixed costs are rent of office space and equipment, real estate taxes, property insurance, and administrative and supervisory salaries. Over a period of time such as one year, the office manager has little or no control over fixed costs. The assumption that such costs are rigid is fairly realistic and aids in short-run planning.

*Variable costs* change in response to changes in the volume of activity. Examples of variable office costs include direct labor such as wages and salaries paid office workers, direct materials such as stationery and supplies, equipment repair and maintenance expenses, and mailing expenses. Variable costs represent the more important and more controllable costs, and office managers continually try to implement new methods and procedures designed to reduce such costs.

Whether or not a cost is classified as fixed or variable depends upon company policy and upon management's intent to control the element of cost as being fixed or variable. Thus, if company policy is to lay off certain office workers when work is slack, the cost of these workers' salaries is variable. If, on the other hand, the company feels that laid-off workers will seek jobs with competing firms, the company may decide to keep the workers on the payroll regardless of whether there is work for them to do. In such a case, the salaries of these office workers become a fixed cost.

## Constructing a Break-Even Chart

To illustrate the construction of a break-even chart, the following data have been taken from the projected income statement of the Hope Company for the year ended December 31, 1995:

| | Fixed | Variable | |
|---|---|---|---|
| Net sales (50,000 units @ $40 each) .... | | | $2,000,000 |
| Less costs and expenses: | | | |
| Direct materials .. | | $ 320,000 | |
| Direct labor ..... | | 360,000 | |
| Manufacturing expenses ..... | $300,000 | 160,000 | |
| Selling expenses .. | 220,000 | 80,000 | |
| General and administrative expenses ..... | 80,000 | 280,000 | |
| Total ....... | $600,000 | $1,200,000 | $1,800,000 |
| Net profit before federal income taxes | | | $ 200,000 |

In constructing a break-even chart such as that shown in Figure 15–2, proceed as follows:

1. Plot the sales volume activity on the horizontal axis and the expense items on the vertical axis.
2. Locate the amount of fixed costs ($600,000) on the vertical axis and draw a straight line parallel to the horizontal axis. This straight line indicates that the fixed costs do not vary as a result of the number of units produced up to and including 50,000 units

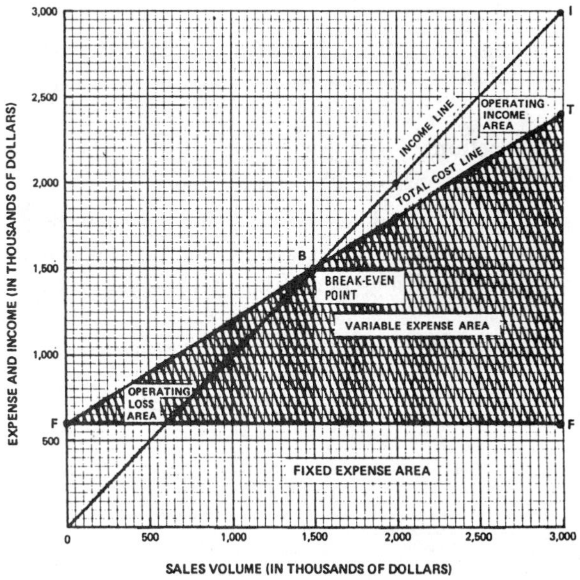


Figure 15–2 A Break-Even Chart

($2 million sales). The area below the fixed cost line is called the *fixed expense area.*

3. Plot the variable costs by starting on the vertical axis at zero sales, where there are no additional costs attributable to materials or direct labor. Since variable costs are added to fixed costs to obtain total costs, locate that point where total costs equal $1,800,000 ($600,000 fixed costs and $1,200,000 variable costs) for sales of $2 million.

   Next, draw a straight line from the point representing zero sales through $1,800,000 and continuing to the right edge of the chart. This line is labeled the Total Cost Line, since any point on this line represents a summation of the variable and fixed costs for that corresponding level of sales. The area lying between line F–F and line F–T is called the *variable expense area,* since it represents that portion of the total cost that is variable.

4. Plot the Income Line by locating that point where the current net sales, $2,000,000, lie directly over the $2 million mark on the horizontal sales axis. Since this point also represents total income for the company, the point is located directly across from the $2 million mark on the vertical expense and income axis. The vertical axis is labeled Expense and Income to show that expenses are paid out of income and that the difference remaining is profit.

   Draw a line from point 0 (zero sales and zero income) through the $2 million point and continue through the upper right corner. The Income Line crosses at the break-even point, B. At this point, the total sales volume, $1,500,000, equals the total expenses.

   The area enclosed by the triangle *FBO* represents the *operating loss area,* while the area enclosed by the triangle *IBT* represents the *operating income area.*

**Directions:** After you have studied the break-even chart in Figure 15–2, answer these questions.

1. What reasons can you advance to show that the break-even chart is not an exact tool of planning, but one that gives only approximate results?

______________________________

______________________________

______________________________

______________________________

______________________________

______________________________

2. (a) What is the effect as income from sales surpasses $1,500,000?

______________________________

______________________________

   (b) What is the effect as income from sales falls below $1,500,000?

______________________________

______________________________

3. If sales were to be increased from $2,000,000 to $2,500,000 (a 25 percent increase), what would be the impact of this change upon profits? What factors account for this favorable situation?

______________________________

______________________________

______________________________

______________________________

______________________________

______________________________

4. How would you proceed visually in reading from the chart the amount of sales needed to earn a profit of $300,000?

______________________________

______________________________

______________________________

______________________________

______________________________

______________________________

5. What would be the effect upon the "profit wedge" (operating income area) if during 1995:

   (a) The monthly rental charges for office equipment were increased?

______________________________

______________________________

______________________________

(b) The number of overtime hours worked by personnel in the billing department were reduced?

6. As another application of the break-even concept, an office manager has constructed the following chart to show the relative advantages and disadvantages of installing new automated retrieval equipment instead of continuing use of the present manual retrieval system.

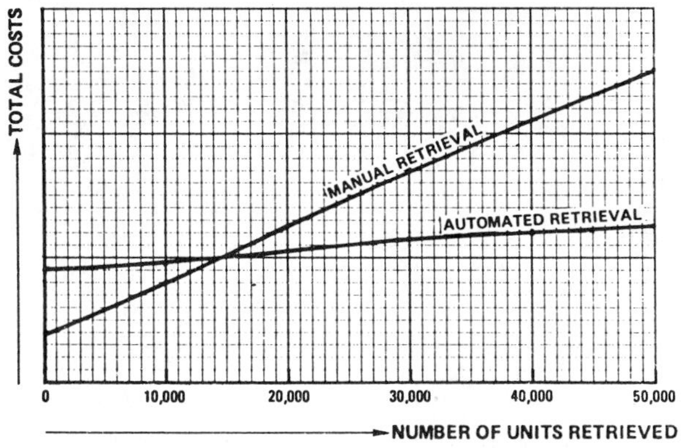


**Figure 15-3 The Characteristics of Two Retrieval Systems**

(a) Which system is characterized by high setup costs but low running costs?

(b) Which system is characterized by high running costs but a low setup cost?

(c) At what level does the automated retrieval system commence "to pay off"—to make a contribution to the profit wedge?

(d) During the forthcoming time period, it is projected that the number of units retrieved will be 12,000. With only this one bit of information available, would you recommend converting to the automated system? Explain.

7. The following data have been taken from the budget of the records center and the company's master budget for the six-month period ending June 30, 1995:

| | |
|---|---|
| Number of units | 600,000 |
| Sales income | $6,000,000 |
| Fixed costs | $1,400,000 |
| Materials cost | $1,000,000 |
| Labor cost | $800,000 |
| Other manufacturing expenses | $800,000 |
| General and administrative expenses | $1,200,000 |

Determine the break-even point by constructing a break-even chart on the grid on page 175.

Name ______________________________ Date ____________________

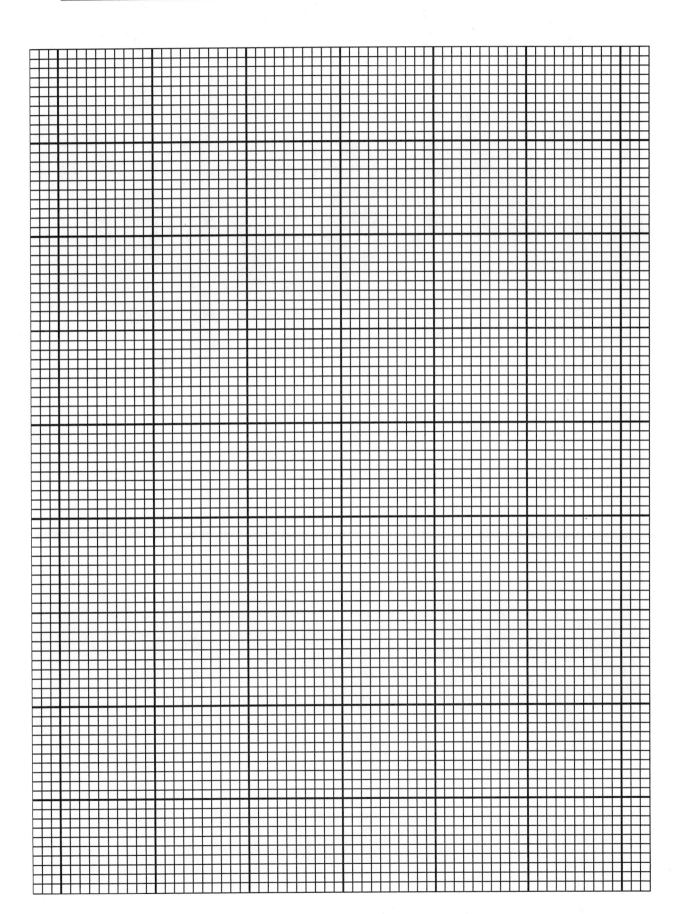

16

# AUTOMATING THE OFFICE

*Office automation* integrates the computer, communication, and related information technologies to support administrative services and to improve the productivity of office personnel. What is termed "office automation" is a very individual matter to an organization. For example, a small firm may pride itself on how it has implemented office automation—its several personal computers and one or two desktop minicomputers. A large multinational organization, on the other hand, may have two host computers—mainframes—tied in via a local-area network to minicomputers and microcomputers and expensive peripherals. However, the goals of both organizations are alike—to improve the accuracy of their information-processing services, to increase the speed of information flow, to save time for managers and supervisors, and to reduce the costs of administrative office services.

The computer system—the heart of office automation—relies on a computer to process data that have been converted to a machine code consisting of electrical impulses. A computer system combines (a) *hardware* (machines and equipment), (b) *software* (procedures and instructions, programs, and documentation), and (c) *personnel* needed to operate the system. Firms have found that many information-processing applications can be handled by minicomputers and microcomputers. With these smaller computers, the operational and organization problems often created by larger computers can be minimized. Small computer systems, which do not require a highly sophisticated operating staff, offer effective and efficient processing of data.

The administrative office manager must understand the potential of computers in order to provide initiative, support, and guidance for implementing computer systems. Only through a proper evaluation of the feasibility of computerized operations can the firm determine the best option to meet its needs. In addition to relying upon in-house expertise in the selection of computers and design of the systems, the office manager may seek advice from outside professional consultants as well as from equipment vendors.

## SECTION A • REVIEW QUESTIONS

**Directions:** Each of the following statements is either true or false. Indicate your choice in the Answers column by circling "T" or "F."

| | | Answers | |
|---|---|---|---|
| 1. | To be computer literate, we must be able to program a computer and know how to handle the technical aspects of managing a computer system . . . . . . . . . . | T | F |
| 2. | When a computer processes words and numbers, all of its operations are fully automated and no longer under the direction of people . . . . . . . . . . | T | F |
| 3. | Digital computers count numbers or digits while processing numeric and alphabetic data that have been converted to a numeric code . . . . . . . . . . | T | F |
| 4. | The heart of a computer system—where the computing operations are performed—is called the central processing unit (CPU) . . . . . . . . . . | T | F |
| 5. | Memory is that area in a computer system where data and programs are temporarily stored before, during, and after processing . . . . . . . . . . | T | F |
| 6. | In a personal computer, the actual processing of data takes place in its memory . . . . . . . . . . | T | F |
| 7. | A microprocessor is a microchip on which reside the control and arithmetic-logic functions . . | T | F |
| 8. | A computer program written to perform a specialized computer task, such as payroll, is known as an *application program* . . . . . . . . . . | T | F |

| | | | |
|---|---|---|---|
| 9. | The retrieval time is about 10 times faster from a floppy disk than from a hard disk ........ | T | F |
| 10. | The storage of data is less expensive on optical disks because they do not hold as much data as other media, such as magnetic disks .......... | T | F |
| 11. | A database is a central master file that contains company-wide information from the major systems of the firm .......... | T | F |
| 12. | The control unit of the CPU instructs the computer to prepare the results of processing on appropriate output devices .......... | T | F |
| 13. | A local-area network (LAN) consists of a telecommunication facility that links together various types of information-processing equipment for transmitting and receiving data ..... | T | F |
| 14. | In today's automated offices, a clerical workstation in one department has little or no access to the word processing and data processing technologies of other departments ............ | T | F |
| 15. | Executive workstations offer managers most information-handling capabilities with the exception of electronic mail .......... | T | F |
| 16. | The outcome of a feasibility study may indicate whether a computer should be purchased or leased .......... | T | F |
| 17. | To maintain the security of an automated office system, usually two copies are made of every magnetic tape .......... | T | F |
| 18. | By using the services of a data service center, a firm may realize savings in payroll taxes .... | T | F |

**Directions:** In the Answers column, write the letter of the item in Column 1 that is described by each statement in Column 2.

**Column 1**

**A** Arithmetic-logic unit

**B** Bit

**C** Floppy disk

**D** Host computer

**E** Memory

**F** Microcomputer

**G** Minicomputer

**H** Optical disk

**I** Random-access memory (RAM)

**J** Read-only memory (ROM)

**K** Source data automation (SDA)

**L** User friendly

| Column 2 | Answers |
|---|---|
| 1. A form of computer storage in which a laser-beam recorder scans a document, copies it, and transfers the image onto a metal disk .......... | 1.______ |
| 2. A computer systems term meaning "easy to operate" .......... | 2.______ |
| 3. A small computer with integrated circuits that is housed in a compact desk-size or desktop cabinet .......... | 3.______ |
| 4. The area in the CPU where data and Memory (RAM) programs are temporarily stored before, during, and after processing ...... | 4.______ |
| 5. An abbreviation of the term *binary digit*; that is, one encoded character in the binary coding system .......... | 5.______ |
| 6. The smallest and least expensive class of computers; also known as a personal computer (PC) .......... | 6.______ |
| 7. A mainframe that directs the input, processing, output, and distribution of information to, from, and among a group of small computers .......... | 7.______ |
| 8. A special type of memory that is permanently programmed with one group of frequently used instructions .......... | 8.______ |
| 9. A flexible diskette on which the data, stored in sectors, can be retrieved randomly .......... | 9.______ |
| 10. The portion of the CPU that performs computational and logical operations .......... | 10.______ |

## SECTION B • PROJECTS

# Project 16–1 • Meeting the Information Needs of Executives

The following article describes the busy executives' need for information different from their employees. In addition, many of these executives do not have the time to "figure out" the technology. After you have read the article, answer the questions at the end.

### Executive Workstations Now Feature Advanced Software

In the infancy of the office automation era, attempts were made to market single-user-oriented computer products aimed at corporate executives. These products assumed that executives had different work habits and needs than other types of computer users.

Many of the early products termed "executive workstations" combined telephones with computers because studies showed that executives spent most of their time on the telephone, in meetings or analyzing reports.

Also, according to the studies, most executives learned their work habits before computers were prevalent in the workplace. As a result, they were slightly afraid of computers and didn't have the time or desire to learn how to use them.

Early executive workstations attempted to get around this computer phobia by being menu or icon driven and extremely user-friendly.

As office automation has progressed, these specialized products have died out.

There are many reasons for their extinction. The primary ones are that easy-to-use workstation technology has advanced on many platforms, and many more of today's executives were computer literate when they took over their positions, or made themselves so.

Also, firms realized that executives need to be part of the corporate information system and network; single-user products weren't the way to go. However, as the early executive-workstation developers knew, the amount and type of information executives need is different.

#### Software Driven

Therefore, executive automation has become a subsegment of a corporate-automation plan and is basically a software-driven market.

Because corporations use a variety of platforms, networks, and hardware products to automate, each platform offers software designed to condense a variety of important information for executive decision making.

The key function of the software is to extract critical information from various departments, either in real time or in deferred reports, and then pass it over the network to the executive offices.

Today, the term "executive workstation" refers to the executive-information-system software on any workstation, PC, or terminal. Executives often have the same terminal hardware on their desks as the rest of the corporation and can run spreadsheets or word-processing packages. They also have special programs that maximize the flow of important information needed for executive decisions.

Executive reports can be presented in electronic or hard-copy form and can usually be sent back over the network to the department from which they came, with comments or action items attached. The data in the reports is designed to aid in decision making and can be imported into other programs the executive may be working in, such as a spreadsheet or word-processing document.

#### User-Friendliness

The user-friendliness or ease-of-use aspect to executive-information systems is still as critical as it was deemed to be 10 years ago. Executives don't have the time or the desire to "figure out" technology.

The typical busy executives don't want to read through 100 pages of documentation or go through 20 commands to operate their system. They want to turn on the power and know how to get the terminal working.

This means that an extremely sophisticated menu-driven system or graphical interface is necessary to provide easy access to information and easy movement from program to program. The movement should be transparent to the user. The appropriate action should occur with a minimum of commands, whether the action is importing data from program to program or sending or receiving data over a network.

Workstations with sophisticated graphical-user interfaces need to be

---

Source: Leone Johnson, "Executive Workstations Now Feature Advanced Software." Used with permission from the August issue of *Office Systems93*, 

powerful. The power necessary to drive complex graphical operations also enables the workstation to operate quickly. Speed of operation and processing is important because executives are often working in tight time spaces.

A slow system will frustrate the user and therefore not be used frequently or to capacity. The computer should help the executive work *more* efficiently, not less so.

A menu-driven system demands a keyboard as the primary means of user interface with the computer, but icon-based systems may need a mouse or incorporate a touch screen. The mouse or touch screen would be an appropriate alternative for executives who are reluctant to use a keyboard.

Keyboard operation should be function-key oriented, with single strokes for major functions. Keyboard users may also need a mouse for macro operations.

### Printers

Printers are a necessary peripheral for any executive workstation. Executives, or their assistants, more often than not need a hard copy for record keeping and for a handy paper trail in the case of system failure.

An executive may choose a laser or dot-matrix printer, depending on the company budget. If the hard-copy output from the workstation is mostly for internal files, dot-matrix printouts are sufficient.

If much of the output goes to other parties, either within the organization or outside, a laser printer makes more sense.

### Communication

Communication within the corporation is important, but executives also have to communicate with others outside the corporation. A true executive workstation facilitates this.

Early designers tried to incorporate telephones into executive-workstation terminals to assist executives in external communication. Today, the integration of voice and electronic messaging into workstations helps executives handle internal and external communication.

There are electronic messaging chips and software available that allow screen-based delivery of voice messages, as well as E-mail messages and faxes. Incorporating this capability at the workstation level in the executive suite enables busy executives to read messages and then either route them, answer them, or destroy them. Executives can decide priorities and aren't always working in an "interruption-driven mode."

Storage of information is an important issue in the designing of executive-information systems. There are three main levels of electronic storage required: the first is personal and confidential, the second is general office, and the third is corporate.

These storage levels correspond to the various types of file cabinets found in most offices. Many documents or pieces of information needed by executives are extremely confidential. Electronic storage of this information must be protected and "tamperproof." This storage has highly restricted access and is known only by chosen personnel.

Electronic office-grade storage is less restrictive and operates much as a general office file cabinet would. Those with a need to know can retrieve information from cabinets that aren't open to all. Corporate-wide storage is just that, the firm's electronic archive—the equivalent of the file cabinets in the general storage room of a corporation.

### Scheduling

Another important function of an executive-automation system is assisting the busy executive in scheduling and organizing time. Executive-information systems must have personal-information-management (PIM) software that can bring in data from other programs or other executives in the firm for meetings and E-mail transmissions.

The PIM software should also have master- and personal-scheduling functions, with broadcast capabilities for communicating new agenda items and time/place changes for meetings. The master-schedule function should communicate openly with the other executives in the organization, but access to the personal-schedule function should be more protected.

Some type of "tickler" or reminder feature is very important on PIM software. Reminding busy executives of key dates and meetings could make or break a deal.

The contact-management feature automatically follows up important meetings with letters or enters action items from those meetings onto a master schedule. Most PIM software contains an electronic-rolodex feature, keeping electronic information on executive contacts and easily merging rolodex information into correspondence generated on the system. The PIM software often comes with useful functions such as expense and contact management.

The packaging of an executive workstation is important. The bland beige or gray packaging used for most computer terminals is unsightly in many executive suites. A small unit footprint and some type of custom cabinet to hide the workstation from general view would make it less obtrusive in many plush offices.

### Sources

Many corporations don't have the expertise needed to integrate executive workstations into their management-information-system (MIS) scheme. Hardware vendors are often limited in the solutions they offer.

Systems integrators or value-added resellers (VARs) can probably offer the most creative solutions to automating the executive.

These software developers and system resellers have access to many products and the expertise to implement solutions from different vendors. By using third parties, users can often get the performance they desire, along with some custom software designed to meet specific needs.

### Convincing the Boss

Even if the MIS staff in the organization is satisfied that the executive-automation system selected will greatly assist the executives in being more efficient and productive, sometimes the executives need to be convinced.

Busy executives often rely on working in the same way they've used for years. And many of them don't have the time or inclination to find new ways of doing things.

How can MIS staff convince executives that they need to be automated?

Some executives can be convinced by seeing how the product worked for others in the company or executives in other firms. However, this "testimonial" method of persuasion may not work on executives who believe they're inherently superior to computer users.

Another tool for persuasion is a trial period with the workstation and/or intensive personal training. Executives who are open to improvement will want to try to become more efficient in the computer age. Some of these executives will try the unit out for a short period, and if the unit is easy to use, they'll use it.

For other executives, it's important to provide intensive one-on-one training. Busy executives lose patience if the learning takes too long.

There's nothing frivolous about the MIS task of executive automation; it's a necessary application in the total corporate-automation scheme.

The product chosen must integrate with the other hardware, software, and communication products used in the organization. And the software must be designed to complement the functions of the executive in question.

The task of creating these workstations may lie with corporate MIS staff, a VAR, or a systems integrator. Whoever designs the workstations must keep in mind that assisting the executives in performing their work more efficiently is the goal—not putting on features for technology's sake.

Executive workstations put in place with these goals in mind will truly be useful and frequently used.

**Directions:** Each of the following statements is either true or false. Indicate your choice in the Answers column by circling "T" or "F."

| | Answers | |
|---|---|---|
| 1. The early executive workstations caused many executives to develop computer phobia as a result of the workstation's heavy dependence upon menus and icons .................... | T | F |
| 2. Executive workstations must be equipped with terminal hardware that is different from that used by others in the organization .................... | T | F |
| 3. Executive reports may be prepared in either electronic or hard-copy form .................... | T | F |
| 4. Today there is less need for executive-information systems to be as user-friendly as 10 years ago .................... | T | F |
| 5. Executives who are reluctant to use a keyboard can work much more efficiently with menu-driven systems than with icon-based systems .................... | T | F |
| 6. If the workstation produces hard-copy output for internal files, the use of a dot-matrix printer rather than a laser printer is sufficient .................... | T | F |
| 7. The integration of voice and electronic messaging into executive workstations provides effective internal as well as external communication .................... | T | F |
| 8. Executives are concerned with only two levels of electronic storage: general office and corporate .................... | T | F |
| 9. Executive-automation systems are designed to aid executives in scheduling and organizing their time .................... | T | F |
| 10. The goal of designing workstations is to assist executives in performing their work more efficiently rather than adding new technological features to the workstations .................... | T | F |

## Project 16–2 • Field Research: Investigating the Services Provided by a Data Service Center

This project will acquaint you with the services provided business firms by a data service center. Most data service centers are organized to meet the basic accounting and record-keeping needs of businesses by providing services that include general ledger, payroll, accounts payable, and accounts receivable processing.

**Directions:** Check the yellow pages of your local telephone directory to determine if there is a data service center within your community. If not, consult your librarian to obtain the name and address of a nearby center with which you may correspond. Your instructor will ask you individually, or in groups, to contact one or more service centers to learn about the specific kinds of services rendered, costs, turnaround times, and warranties. The following checklist will aid you in obtaining a complete picture of the services provided by the center so that a report may be developed for presentation to the group.

**CHECKLIST**
**SERVICES PROVIDED BY A DATA CENTER**

1. Specific accounting services provided: general ledger? accounts payable? accounts receivable? payroll accounting?
2. Types of statements and reports provided?
3. Number of years firm has been in operation? reputation in community?
4. Number of clients?
5. Breadth and depth of program library?
6. Controls employed to ensure accuracy?
7. Controls employed to ensure confidentiality?
8. Pickup and delivery service provided? cost?
9. Turnaround time?
10. Kind of contract with client firm?
11. Input requirements by client? need for specialized equipment? need for trained personnel? need for programming personnel?
12. Price quotations? (basic program rate, transaction rate, charge for each schedule and department income statement, changes in file, etc.)

# Project 16–3 • Computer Hands-On: Automating a Payroll Accounting System

Figure 16–1 on page 184 shows how the weekly payroll is processed manually in Mario's, a small "mom and pop" operation. In addition to Mr. and Mrs. Mario, the company has two office workers, three sales representatives, and three service and repair personnel. Two pieces of office equipment—an electronic typewriter and a calculator—are used to process the biweekly payroll. Thus, the outlay for equipment and training operators is at a minimum. On the other hand, much rewriting of information is required, as you will see when tracing the following steps that make up the present payroll accounting system:

**Step 1.** The gross pay for each worker is determined by calculating the total hours (regular and overtime) worked, as recorded by the employees on time cards. After the hourly and salary rates are obtained from the employees' earnings records and recorded on the time cards, the gross pay is calculated on the calculator.

**Step 2.** The net pay for each worker is calculated and written on the face of each time card. Each employee's earnings record is consulted to determine the marital status and the number of withholding allowances claimed for federal and state income tax purposes. The file of authorized deduction slips must be inspected to make sure that no authorized deductions, such as the purchase of savings bonds, are overlooked. The appropriate wage bracket table is consulted to find the amount of federal and state income taxes to be withheld. The amount of FICA tax (social security and Medicare) to be withheld is calculated after inspecting the Cumulative FICA Taxable Wages columns in the employee's earnings record.

**Step 3.** The information appearing on the face of each time card—employee name, employee number, regular and overtime hours worked each day, gross pay, deductions, and net pay—is recorded manually in the payroll register. The columns of the payroll register are totaled to check the accuracy of the payroll entries and to obtain data to be used later in preparing the journal entries to record the weekly payroll and the employer's payroll taxes.

**Step 4.** A paycheck with a detachable earnings statement is prepared for each worker. The typewriter is used to record on each paycheck and statement the following information: employee name, gross pay, deductions, net pay, gross pay to date, and deductions to date.

**Step 5.** Each entry in the payroll register is posted manually to the appropriate employee's earnings record, and all cumulative columns (gross pay, FICA taxable wages, etc.) are updated using the calculator.

**Step 6.** The payroll entries are recorded manually in the journal, using the information contained in the payroll register.

**Step 7.** The journal entries to record the payroll and the employer's payroll taxes are posted to the appropriate general ledger accounts.

Although there is little investment in equipment and little need for machine-operator training, the present system of processing the weekly payroll is slow and involves costly duplication of effort. Further, the system lends itself to error because of the separate writing, posting, and summarizing operations. For example, the amount of gross pay for each worker is recorded four times and the amount of net pay for each worker is recorded five times. These elements, combined with the other pressing office work, cause the preparation of the payroll to be delayed at times and entail costly overtime work on the part of the office employee preparing the payroll.

**Directions:**

1. After you have studied carefully the present system, explore the feasibility of installing a microcomputer for processing the payroll. Prepare a chart similar to template file PO16-3.TEM to show how the information would flow and be processed if a microcomputer were used.
2. Prepare a report in which you indicate the benefits that can be anticipated as the result of automating the payroll system. Also, indicate those disadvantages that might be found.

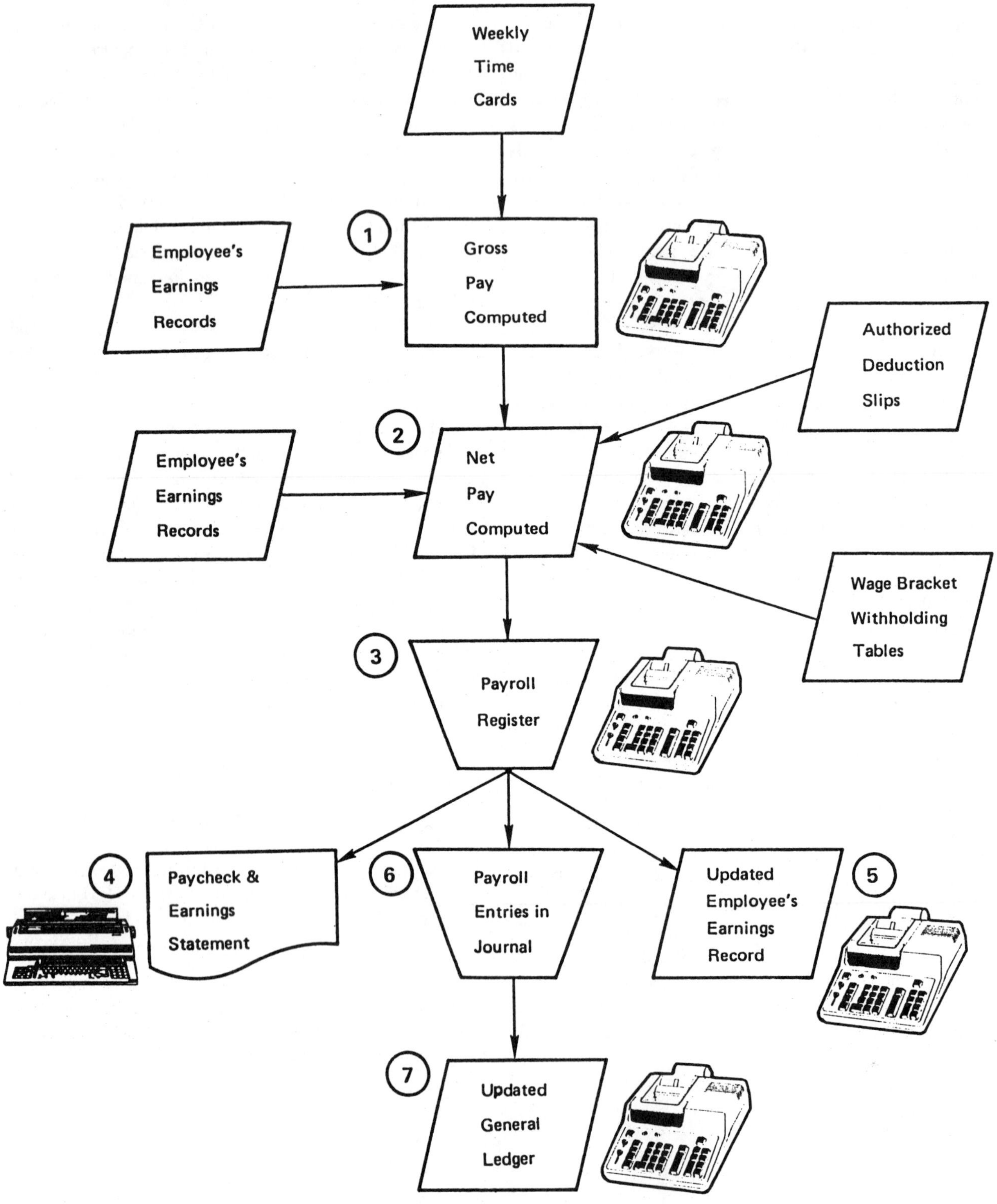


**Figure 16–1 A Manual System for Processing a Weekly Payroll**

# Project 16–4 • Field Research: Learning About a Computerized Banking System

A very effective way to learn about a computer system is to visit a business firm that uses a computer so that you can see firsthand a real system in action. For example, by visiting a bank, you can learn about its paperless methods of depositing money into checking and savings accounts (electronic funds transfer). In this field research project, you will go to a local bank that offers automated teller machine (ATM) services to its customers.

**Directions:** Follow these steps in completing this project:

1. If possible, obtain an ATM card that gives you access to the bank's computerized system. If you do not have an ATM card or cannot obtain one from a relative or friend, possibly you can observe a customer using his or her card. Or, you may ask a bank official to demonstrate a complete cycle of depositing and withdrawing funds from the bank.
2. From notes that you made during the observation period, prepare a general systems flowchart. For a model to follow, you may use Figure 16–7 in the textbook.
3. Prepare a short report that analyzes the effectiveness of the computer system when compared with the manual operations that would be necessary to perform functions such as depositing, transferring, and withdrawing funds.

# 17

# UNDERSTANDING TEXT/WORD PROCESSING SYSTEMS

In the management of written messages, one of the most important responsibilities of administrative office managers is the need to keep abreast of technological developments in automated word processing systems. To shoulder this responsibility, office managers must periodically evaluate their firms' approach to the origination of words, the conversion of those words into hard copy, and the systems by which the words are transmitted to the receivers.

In many of today's offices, we still find words being processed manually. Here, workers use dictation-transcription systems to originate the words and various kinds of typewriters to transcribe the messages. In other offices we find automated systems, where messages are transcribed, stored, and, in some cases, transmitted on electronic machines and keyboards, display screens, and logic components for storage on magnetic media. One of the latest developments in automated systems is desktop publishing (DTP), which produces professionally styled newsletters, magazines, catalogs, brochures, and books, using a system that encompasses the personal computer, a software package, and a laser printer.

## SECTION A • REVIEW QUESTIONS

**Directions:** In the Answers column, write the letter of the item in Column 1 that is described by each statement in Column 2.

**Column 1**

- **A** Administrative secretary
- **B** Central recorder system
- **C** Correspondence secretary
- **D** Desktop publishing (DTP)
- **E** Digital dictation
- **F** Discrete recording medium
- **G** Standalone word processor
- **H** Text
- **I** Text/word processing (T/WP) system
- **J** Voice-to-print system
- **K** Word origination

| Column 2 | Answers |
|---|---|
| 1. A self-contained T/WP system with one terminal . . . . . . . . . . . . | 1. ______ |
| 2. A T/WP software package that provides for writing, assembling, and designing publications by the use of computers . . . . . . . . . . . | 2. ______ |
| 3. A separate magnetic record for storing dictation that can be removed from the dictation machine for transcription after the dictation has been completed . . . . . . . . . . . . . . . . . . . . . . . . . . | 3. ______ |
| 4. A keyboard specialist who is employed to convert words into a finished communication . . . . . . . . . . . . . . . . . . . . . . . . . . . . . . . | 4 _____. |
| 5. The written communications composed and produced in the office | 5. ______ |
| 6. The process of creating messages . . . . . . . . . . . . . . . . . . . . . . . . . | 6. ______ |
| 7. A combination of people, equipment, and processes for converting words into a final product and forwarding it to the user . . . . . . . . | 7. ______ |
| 8. An office worker who is freed from large-volume keyboard responsibilities in order to handle the remaining office services in a T/WP center . . . . . . . . . . . . . . . . . . . . . . . . . . . . . . . . . . . . . . . | 8. ______ |
| 9. A dictation system where the telephone is used as a dictation instrument to access a recording device located in the T/WP center | 9. ______ |
| 10. Vocal sounds that are recorded and stored on magnetic media after being automatically converted to binary digits . . . . . . . . . . . . . . | 10. ______ |

**Directions:** Indicate your answer to each of the following questions by circling "Yes" or "No" in the Answers column.

| | | **Answers** | |
|---|---|---|---|
| 1. | Are written procedures the formal instructions that explain step by step how to complete a task? | Yes | No |
| 2. | Are office manuals used to assign responsibility for performing certain duties and to establish procedures for performing those duties? | Yes | No |
| 3. | Has the popularity of the business letter declined as a result of technological improvements in telecommunications? | Yes | No |
| 4. | Do text/word processing (T/WP) systems include simple manual systems as well as sophisticated automated systems? | Yes | No |
| 5. | Is composing at the keyboard the recommended message-creation method for executives and other administrative personnel? | Yes | No |
| 6. | Does the machine-recording method of creating messages require the presence of a secretary as well as the dictator? | Yes | No |
| 7. | Is machine recording the most widely used method of creating messages? | Yes | No |
| 8. | Do most manual systems for recording messages use a discrete recording medium? | Yes | No |
| 9. | Is the placing of a desktop recorder on every dictator's desk more cost effective than using a central recorder system? | Yes | No |
| 10. | With the advent of electronic typewriters and other forms of information technology, has there been a marked increase in the productivity of office workers responsible for written communications? | Yes | No |
| 11. | Can several standalone word processors be interconnected to share a common device such as a disk drive? | Yes | No |
| 12. | In desktop publishing (DTP), is a PC used in conjunction with page layout software and a laser printer to produce master copies close in quality to those produced by commercial typesetters? | Yes | No |
| 13. | In digital dictation, are the vocal sounds converted to binary numbers before being recorded and stored on magnetic media? | Yes | No |
| 14. | With today's storehouse of technological information, is there need for a feasibility study prior to the installation of a T/WP system? | Yes | No |
| 15. | Does the installation of a T/WP system reduce the need for an incentive system? | Yes | No |
| 16. | Is a centralized text-production plan of organization commonly found in large firms? | Yes | No |
| 17. | Is the heavy-volume keyboarding work in a centralized T/WP center usually performed by administrative secretaries? | Yes | No |
| 18. | Is the operation of the hardware the most difficult phase of machine dictation? | Yes | No |
| 19. | When analyzing the cost of creating a typical average-length letter, do we find that the most time is spent in preparing and giving the dictation? | Yes | No |
| 20. | To lower correspondence costs, does the office manager find that most savings can be realized by decreasing the salary costs of the dictator and the transcriptionist? | Yes | No |

## SECTION B • PROJECTS

### Project 17–1 • Inputting on the Dvorak Keyboard

The following article describes the early keyboard wars that involved keyboard shape, letter arrangement, and the number of keys. Today, thanks to the computer chip, the time has come to consider a keyboard speedier than the one which has been used ever since the early 1870s.

**Directions:** After you have read the article, answer the questions at the end.

### QWERTY-DVORAK: "The Keyboard Wars"

Consider QWERTY, the standard typewriter keyboard. It makes no sense. It is awkward, inefficient, and confusing. But it has withstood more than a century of criticism and has yet to find itself in danger of extinction.

Many consider the DVORAK layout, developed in the 1930s, to be the definitive typewriter keyboard, designed for maximum efficiency. With today's computer technology it now has its first real chance at success. However promising, the DVORAK system is only one of many attempts to replace the standard keyboard that dates back as far as 1880.

The QWERTY keys made their first appearance on a rickety, clumsy device marketed as the "Type-Writer" in 1874. Today, the same keyboard is a universal fixture even on the most sophisticated computers and word processors.

How could we get stuck with something so bad? In this case, the answer lies in the old proverb about the early bird catching the worm. As far as the typewriter keyboard is concerned, being first was the whole ball game.

The name QWERTY comes from the first six letters in the top alphabet row. It is also called the universal keyboard for obvious reasons. It was the work of inventor C. L. Sholes, who put together the prototypes of the first commercial typewriter in a Milwaukee machine shop in the 1860s.

#### Motives Were Pure

For years, popular writers have accused poor Sholes of deliberately arranging his keyboard to slow down fast typists who would otherwise jam up his sluggish machine. In reality, his motives were just the opposite.

When Sholes built his first model in 1868, the keys were arranged alphabetically. The crude machine shop tools available could hardly produce a finely-honed instrument that worked with precision. Yes, the first typewriter was sluggish. Yes, it did clash and jam when someone tried to operate it, but Sholes figured out a way around the problem simply by rearranging the letters. Looking inside his early machine, we can see how he did it.

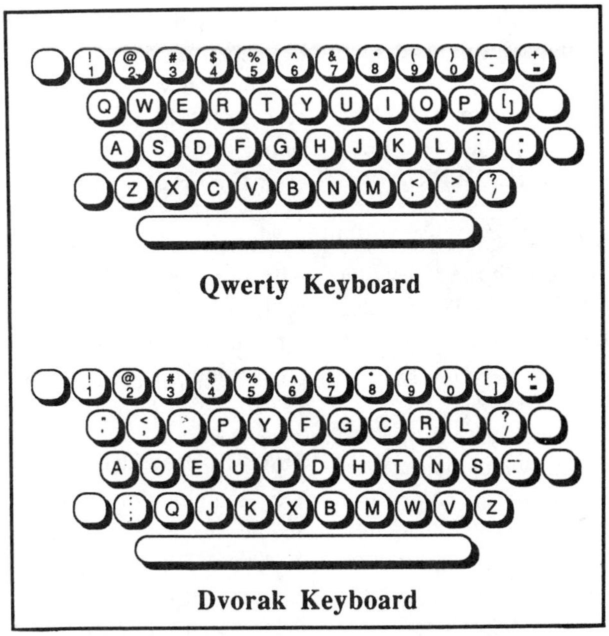


**Figure 17–1 The QWERTY and the DVORAK Keyboards**

---

Source: Darryl C. Rehr, "QWERTY-DVORAK: 'The Keyboard Wars,'" *The Office* (April, 1990), pp. 12, 14, and 19. Reprinted by permission of *The Office*.

## Typebars in a Circle

The first typewriter had its letters on the end of rods called typebars. The typebars hung in a circle. The roller which held the paper sat over this circle, and when a key was pressed, a typebar would swing up to hit the paper from underneath. The machine's clashing problem came from the typebars heading up to the paper one after another and hitting each other on the way. So, Sholes took common English letter pairs like "TH" and placed their typebars to swing up from opposite sides of the machine, thus lowering the number of clashes. The QWERTY arrangement itself was determined by existing mechanical links between the typebars to the keys on the keyboard. QWERTY's effect, by reducing most of those annoying clashes, was to actually speed up typing rather than slow it down.

The Remington Co. began producing Sholes' Type-Writer in 1874. The first models typed only capitals, but later units included upper and lower case, and had shift keys added to the keyboards. Competing companies did not begin producing typewriters until 1880. By that time, Remington had such a head start that the modern keyboard's fate was set. QWERTY was here to stay.

The first of the "Great Keyboard Wars" raged through the typewriter industry until 1915. The battles involved the shape of the keyboard, arrangement of letters and, most of all, the number of keys.

The first rival system was the double keyboard which appeared in 1880 on a Remington competitor called the Caligraph. Its chief selling point was a key for every character. This machine was a veritable monster, with 74 keys to cover every letter in both upper and lower case, as well as numerals and punctuation.

The Caligraph's makers denounced Remington's shift key as confusing. Why force a typist to make two motions for capitals when, on the Caligraph, one simple keystroke was all one needed? The argument was powerful. Most double keyboard machines copied the QWERTY arrangement, and they remained almost as popular as shift-key models until after the turn of the century.

The double keyboard disappeared about 1915, when the touch-typing technique finally became a worldwide standard. Before typists learned to use all ten of their fingers, typing was mostly a hunt-and-peck affair. Most teachers advocated using only the index and middle fingers, since all the other fingers were considered weak and awkward.

A more radical keyboard design appeared in 1884's Hammond Typewriter. With some early ergonomics in mind, Hammond's "Ideal" keyboard was arranged in two semicircular rows. A touch-typist would have had trouble finding a home position on a curved keyboard, but for the two-fingered hunt-and-peckist, it may well have been comfortable.

After ten years of moderate success with the Ideal keyboard, consumer demand forced Hammond to offer QWERTY as an option in the 1890s. Hammond's QWERTY machines, in fact, were long-lived. After a name change to Vari-Typer in the 1920s, the Hammond design remained in production on small typesetting machines until the late 1970s.

## Still Another Entry

The Blickensderfer of 1893 was another machine to offer a different keyboard. It featured a type wheel for printing similar to the IBM Selectric and a keyboard called the Scientific.

Using a letter frequency study, Blickensderfer put the ten most frequently used letters on the bottom row of the machine, that closest to the user. With fingers resting on this home row of DHIATENSOR, a typist would be doing 70% of all the work needed. The Blickensderfer sales catalog showed graphically how the same ten letters were scattered illogically all over the QWERTY keyboard.

Blickensderfer conceded to the demand for QWERTY by offering it as an option, but its literature warned "for reasons given . . . buyers are strongly recommended to use the Blickensderfer Scientific Key-board." The power of advertising was apparent even then.

## Along Came Dvorak

Hammond and Blickensderfer and the double-keyboard machines were the only serious contenders in the early keyboard wars. Then, in 1932, with funds from the Carnegie Foundation, Professor August Dvorak of Washington State University set out to develop the ultimate typewriter keyboard.

Dvorak went beyond Blickensderfer in arranging his letters according to frequency. The professor's home row uses all five vowels and the five most common consonants: AOEUIDHTNS. With the vowels on one side and consonants on the other, a rough typing rhythm is established as each hand tends to alternate.

With the Dvorak keyboard, a typist can type about 400 of the English language's most common words without ever leaving the home row. The comparable figure on QWERTY is 100. The home row letters on Dvorak do a total of 70% of the work. On QWERTY they do only 32%.

## A Niche Is Found

Despite the work done by Professor Dvorak, his system has yet to find success, although modern computer technology is giving it its best chance in more than 50 years. Converting typewriters to DVORAK is difficult and expensive, but computers and word processors are easy. There are many programs and conversion kits on the markets for all computers, as well as typing tutor programs to retrain QWERTY typists.

Randy Cassingham, a DVORAK expert, says an office with a heavy word processing load can realistically expect a 50% increase in productivity by converting to DVORAK from QWERTY. That means 50% more pages per day per typist, a considerable boost.

**Training Needed**

Not all typists are candidates for DVORAK retraining. Someone who can comfortably type on QWERTY at high speed may not necessarily improve performance with DVORAK. However, it is likely that fatigue will be reduced, which would improve the quality of working life, if not productivity, to some degree.

Mr. Cassingham suggests that an office be converted to DVORAK person by person. The first to be retrained should be the office's worst typist, with the remainder joining in, from the bottom up. The greatest improvement can be expected from the least skilled. (A comprehensive book on the DVORAK keyboard is available from Freelance Communications, Box 1895, Upland, CA 91785.)

Despite its new promise, DVORAK still faces an uphill battle. The millions of offices that require typing no faster than 40 wpm have little incentive to switch to DVORAK, as that speed is easily attained on QWERTY. So, it seems that our original typewriter keyboard, now 115 years old, will remain with us until the needs of an accelerating world reach speeds we have yet to imagine.

**Directions:** Indicate your answer to each of the following questions by circling "Yes" or "No" in the Answers column.

| | | Answers | |
|---|---|---|---|
| 1. | Were the first prototypes for a commercial typewriter designed by Sholes in the 1860s? | Yes | No |
| 2. | Did the QWERTY keyboard appear on the first model of typewriter? | Yes | No |
| 3. | Was the first typewriter model designed to type both uppercase and lowercase letters? | Yes | No |
| 4. | Did later models of the Type-Writer feature a double keyboard? | Yes | No |
| 5. | Was Hammond's Ideal typewriter the forerunner of the typesetting machine known as Vari-Typer? | Yes | No |
| 6. | Was Blickensderfer's Scientific keyboard the first to feature QWERTY on the home row? | Yes | No |
| 7. | Does Dvorak's home row contain all five vowels and the five most common consonants? | Yes | No |
| 8. | Can a typist using only the Dvorak home row type four times as many common English words as on the QWERTY home row? | Yes | No |
| 9. | Does the QWERTY home row do about one-half of the work done on the Dvorak home row? | Yes | No |
| 10. | Can computers and word processors be converted more easily to Dvorak than typewriters? | Yes | No |
| 11. | Is it estimated that word processing productivity can be increased 50 percent by converting from QWERTY to Dvorak? | Yes | No |
| 12. | When converting an office to Dvorak, is it recommended that the most skilled typist be the first to be retrained? | Yes | No |

# Project 17–2 • Computer Hands-On: Creating Input

This project gives you dictation experience as you follow up on two sensitive office incidents. Depending on the facilities available on your campus and on the time available, your instructor may ask you to:

1. Dictate your response for each situation to another class member, who assumes the role of secretary and records your words (using shorthand or a machine-dictation system).
2. Borrow a dictating machine (if available on your campus), and bring the machine to class. If your school has word processing equipment on the premises, a qualified word processing operator (perhaps one of your fellow students) may transcribe your dictation, print out your message, and copy and distribute it to the entire class. Perhaps the group can visit the word processing center, where the operator will explain the steps involved in converting your words into hard copy, a process called transcribing.

While you are dictating in front of the class, the group and your instructor will evaluate your performance using the Checklist for Improving My Text/Word Input on page 193 and on template file PO17-2.TEM. Following your dictation, the group will offer constructive criticism to help you improve your dictating skills for the future.

## Incident A

Phyllis A. Tatarinov has applied for the clerk-typist position now open in your firm's accounting department. She has been interviewed by you, as office manager, and by Denise T. Perry, head of the accounting department. Tatarinov has been given a battery of tests, including the company's own keyboarding skills test (she achieved a rate of 40 wpm). The job specifications for the clerk-typist position require a minimum of 50 wpm. The results of the aptitude test indicate that Tatarinov would be highly successful in a personal selling position and that she would perform at a less than satisfactory level in general office work.

During the interview, Tatarinov told you and Perry that she is in her early 20s, was married recently, and plans to start a family within two years.

**Directions:** Following her interview and testing, Tatarinov was told that the company would "get back to her." Today you are "getting back to her" by dictating a letter in which you give reasons for rejecting her application.

Copies of your letter are to be printed for distribution to Perry and to the human resources division. Tatarinov resides at 409 Solebury Road, Apt. 3A, Niota, IL 62358-1730.

## Incident B

Mario X. Martinez, Hispanic, age 54, has worked in your mailing department for 20 years. During this period of time, he has risen from messenger to chief mail clerk. A few months ago a vacancy arose in the credit and collections department for which Martinez thought he was qualified. He applied for the vacant position.

This opening coincides with a major overhaul in credit and collections—specifically, the incorporation of all credit and collections information into the firm's expanding database. Having "lived with the company" for 20 years, Martinez felt that he was well acquainted with all procedures and practices followed by the workers in credit and collections.

To fill the post, you have turned to the outside and hired a recent college graduate, age 25, white. Martinez sees the selection as a personal affront—a slap at his race, his age, and his years of devotion to the firm. For several weeks the situation gnawed away at him; he then presented his case to the local Equal Employment Opportunity Commission (EEOC) office, claiming that the company discriminated against him unduly on the basis of race and age.

**Directions:** You are asked by your boss, Laraine O. Tylo, to draft a memo that she can use when she talks with the EEOC. In this memo, you will want to defend your firm's position in turning to the outside to hire a person for credit and collections, rather than promoting Martinez. Your objective in drafting the memo is to convey vividly and factually the nondiscriminatory way in which your company proceeded in the selection process.

Copies of your printed memo are to be distributed to Martinez, the human resources division, and the legal department. Of course, keep a copy for your files. Template file PO17-2.TEM includes a memo format.

## CHECKLIST FOR IMPROVING MY TEXT/WORD INPUT

**Before inputting, do I:**

___ Review all operating procedures and instruction manuals?

___ Learn how to operate all equipment?

___ Familiarize myself with the duties of the transcriptionist?

___ Collect and arrange all needed information?

___ Set up a specific time slot for dictating so that I can minimize interruptions?

___ Identify the key points in letters and memos to be answered by color highlighting and marginal notations?

___ Briefly outline, with a minimum of longhand notes, what I want to say?

**As I start inputting, do I:**

___ Identify myself and, if needed, my department?

___ Indicate the kind of format—letter, interoffice memo, report?

___ Spell out, as necessary, the name, title, company affiliation, and address of the addressee?

___ Provide all special instructions—names of recipients to receive copies, extra number of copies to be printed out, enclosures, etc.?

**During inputting, do I:**

___ Indicate all needed punctuation?

___ Spell any unusual words and proper names?

___ Dictate (or manually note as instructed by the equipment manual) where corrections in the transcript are to be made?

___ Enunciate clearly and with an adequate voice level?

___ Speak naturally just as if I were talking with the recipient?

___ Avoid overly long sentences and paragraphs?

___ Use action verbs and concrete nouns?

___ Pace my dictating by speaking at a normal rate, with no fast spurts or long pauses?

___ Try to eliminate distracting noises such as coughing, clearing my throat, humming, whistling, tapping a pencil, chewing gum, and moving about in a squeaking chair?

**After inputting, do I:**

___ Turn off the equipment?

___ Arrange letters, memos, and notes in the same order as messages were inputted?

___ Turn over to a messenger or the transcriptionist all material —input medium; letters, memos, and notes; and enclosures?

___ Carefully proofread and edit the first draft by checking for form, language, and content?

___ Sign all approved outgoing messages, return all reference materials, and show appreciation for a job well done?

## Project 17–3 • Field Research: Reporting on a Text/Word Processing System

In this field research project, you will arrange an interview with the manager of text/word processing in a local company. The objective of your discussion with the manager is to study the firm's system—its organization, equipment and software used, cost effectiveness, and problems yet to be solved.

**Directions:** Either singly or along with several of your classmates, as directed by your instructor, prepare an oral or written report of your visit to a firm's text/word processing center. The following outline will help you "touch base" on some important elements to cover in your report. During your interview and observations, you are sure to detect more items to include in your report.

---

Company visited ______________________________

Product(s) or service(s) provided by company ______________________________

______________________________

No. of employees in company______________________________

Manager's name and title ______________________________

**Organization of text/word processing system**

Centralized or decentralized? hybrid? ______________________________

Organization chart showing position titles, number of employees, lines of authority and responsibility, etc. ______

______________________________

**Equipment and software used**

Manufacturer's make and model; standalone and/or computer-connected ______________________________

______________________________

No. of workstations______________________________

Type of software used______________________________

Evidence of new technology______________________________

**Cost effectiveness**

Measurement of output, development of work standards ______________________________

______________________________

Tangible savings realized______________________________

Turnaround time ______________________________

Chargeback system______________________________

Quality control over output______________________________

**Unsolved problems**

Training needs—word originators and word processors______________________________

______________________________

Equipment obsolescence______________________________

Cost-reduction measures______________________________

Computer interconnect ______________________________

Supervisory effectiveness ______________________________

Quality of service provided end-users______________________________

Promotion paths and career opportunities ______________________________

______________________________

# Project 17–4 • Field Research: Determining the Cost-effectiveness of Word Processors[1]

Organizations should periodically review their use of word processing equipment since the costs of acquiring and operating the processors are too great to be ignored once the word processing system has been installed. This project introduces you to a simple, inexpensive method for determining the cost-effectiveness of word processing equipment that is currently in use. This method, known as the *machine-in-use observation method,* involves spot checking each word processing workstation once every hour for one week and documenting whether or not the machine was in use.

**Directions:** After you have read the following description of the machine-in-use observation method, conduct a study of the word processors in your company to determine their cost-effectiveness. Prepare a report that includes your findings and your evaluation of the observation method as a technique for determining the cost-effectiveness of word processing equipment in use.

## The Machine-In-Use Observation Method[2]

As a quick and simple method of determining whether a word processor is being used sufficiently to justify its costs, an observation should be made each hour for five consecutive days. An observation consists of walking by each word processing station unobtrusively and unannounced and at varying parts of each hour and observing whether the word processor is being used at that moment. Maintain a record of the date, time of the observation, and whether or not the word processor is being used. Figure 17–2 is a sample observation log. At the end of the five days, you should have 40 entries for each word processor observed. [Eight hourly observations each day × 5 days = 40 observations.]

Before conducting these observations, you should contact the head of the department or center where the word processor is located and ask if any unusual workload fluctuations will occur in the next few days that might render the observation period atypical. Only when you have been assured that the next few days probably will be typical should you proceed with the observations.

After conducting the observations and before doing additional analysis, ask the department head if the observation period was, in fact, typical. If it was not, then the observations will have to be done again unless the head considered the observation period reflected a lighter workload than normal and the word processor was in use for more than 50 percent of the observations.

A more substantive and statistically valid approach may be used in conducting observations; note what kind of document is being produced and whether original or revision typing is being performed. Also, use a table of random numbers to determine when the observations should be made or use a different sample size that has greater statistical reliability. If you take the time to conduct the simple observations as suggested here, you will be able to weed out equipment that is clearly unproductive.

A word-processor can be assumed to be cost-effective if during 21 or more of the 40 observations (more than half) it was in use. If it was not in use during more than half the observations, then consider either replacing the word processor with an electric typewriter or modifying the workload and then conduct the typed-lines analysis.[3]

---

[1]Note: This field research project is designed for those who are employed in organizations having one or more word processors in use.

[2]Adapted from "Simplified Methods for Evaluating the Cost-Effectiveness of Word Processing Equipment," Report OIT/IMAD-85/001, Office of Software Development and Information Technology, Information Management Assistance Division, March, 1984 (Washington, DC: U.S. Government Printing Office, 20402).

[3]The typed-lines analysis method involves collecting the number of original and revised document lines produced over a sample period for each word processing workstation being reviewed; annualizing the two totals; and analyzing the cost-effectiveness of the workstation by comparing the estimated workload with a General Services Administration–derived formula. The typed-lines analysis method is described in detail on pages 7 to 22 of "Simplified Methods for Evaluating the Cost-Effectiveness of Word Processing Equipment," referenced earlier.

| | |
|---|---|
| **Machine Identification Number:** | **Location: Room ____________** |
| **Type of Machine:** | **Bldg ____________** |

| Observation Number | Date | Time | Was the word processor in use? | | Observation Number | Date | Time | Was the word processor in use? | |
|---|---|---|---|---|---|---|---|---|---|
| | | | YES | NO | | | | YES | NO |
| 1. | | | | | 21. | | | | |
| 2. | | | | | 22. | | | | |
| 3. | | | | | 23. | | | | |
| 4. | | | | | 24. | | | | |
| 5. | | | | | 25. | | | | |
| 6. | | | | | 26. | | | | |
| 7. | | | | | 27. | | | | |
| 8. | | | | | 28. | | | | |
| 9. | | | | | 29. | | | | |
| 10. | | | | | 30. | | | | |
| 11. | | | | | 31. | | | | |
| 12. | | | | | 32. | | | | |
| 13. | | | | | 33. | | | | |
| 14. | | | | | 34. | | | | |
| 15. | | | | | 35. | | | | |
| 16. | | | | | 36. | | | | |
| 17. | | | | | 37. | | | | |
| 18. | | | | | 38. | | | | |
| 19. | | | | | 39. | | | | |
| 20. | | | | | 40. | | | | |
| | | | | | TOTAL | | | | |

**Figure 17–2 Word Processing Equipment Observation Log Form**

18

# DISTRIBUTING INFORMATION: TELECOMMUNICATION AND MAILING SYSTEMS

To distribute information both internally and externally, organizations plan telecommunication systems that transmit and receive (1) *voice communication*—telephone, intercommunication, voice recognition, audio response, paging, cellular telephone, microwave, and satellite; (2) *data communication*—telephone or related wireless equipment and computer systems equipment and software; (3) *text communication*—electronic mail, facsimile, communicating word processor, computer-based message systems, and videotext; and (4) *image communication*—facsimile, video, and graphics.

With the rapid development in telecommunication technology comes the need for effective management of the systems and their costs. Expert communication staffs must be developed to use the new technology and to pass along their recommendations to managers who are faced with alternative courses of action in solving the telecommunication problems of their firms.

Despite the impact of technological advances in telecommunication tools and services, a business's mailing system continues to be indispensable to the distribution of its information. To plan and organize a cost-effective mailing system, the organization must (l) provide a trained staff, (2) develop an efficient internal mailing system, (3) design an efficient mailing center, (4) obtain efficient mailing equipment, (5) develop efficient operating procedures, and (6) use automated mailing equipment when feasible.

## SECTION A • REVIEW QUESTIONS

**Directions:** In the Answers column, write the letter of the item in Column 1 that is described by each statement in Column 2.

**Column 1**

**A** Audio-response system
**B** Cellular telephone
**C** Computer-based message system
**D** Data communication system
**E** Dumb terminal
**F** Image communication
**G** Leased line
**H** Modem
**I** Paging system
**J** Telecommunications
**K** Voice communication system
**L** Voice-recognition system
**M** Wide area network (WAN)

| Column 2 | Answers |
|---|---|
| 1. A telecommunication facility that covers a large geographic area and provides public and private channels for transmitting and receiving messages . . . . . . . . . | 1. ______ |
| 2. Messages that involve communication symbols transmitted in nonword, nonvoice, and nonnumber form . . . . . . . . . | 2. ______ |
| 3. A computer-based system in which the computer "understands" and records the human voice as input and performs operations based on these inputs . . . . . . . . . | 3. ______ |
| 4. The electronic transfer of data from one point in an information system to another . . . . . . . . . | 4. ______ |
| 5. A form of electronic mail in which a computer directs the received messages to be filed in electronic mailboxes later to be accessed by persons as their needs require . . . . . . . . . | 5. ______ |
| 6. A telegraph or telephone line between specific points made available to subscribers on a full-time basis . . . . . . . . . | 6. ______ |
| 7. A system used to locate persons who are away from their workstations | 7. ______ |
| 8. A telecommunication system in which messages originated by speakers are sent by wire or wireless methods to listeners who receive and respond to the messages . . . . . . . . . | 8. ______ |
| 9. A powerful information-transmitting system that merges the computer, the telephone, and other electronic systems to send prerecorded data over long distances . . . . . . . . . | 9. ______ |

**Directions:** Each of the following statements is either true or false. Indicate your choice in the Answers column by circling "T" or "F."

| | **Answers** |
|---|---|
| 1. The amount of space needed to transmit messages on telecommunication channels is known as *bandwidth.* | T F |
| 2. In small offices with fewer than 50 telephone users, the key telephone system (KTS) is the main form of telecommunication. | T F |
| 3. A major drawback to the dedicated intercom system is that internal calls may block incoming or outgoing telephone calls. | T F |
| 4. When entering messages in a voice-recognition system, the messages must first be converted to a written form. | T F |
| 5. Receiving and transmitting voice messages via cellular telephones are limited to a distance of 25 to 30 miles. | T F |
| 6. A local-area network (LAN) permits all PC operators in a department to share one printer. | T F |
| 7. A modem is used to convert the computer's data, stored in digital code, into analog code for transmission by telephone. | T F |
| 8. When a drawing or a graph is FAXed, only black, white, and the primary colors (red, blue, and yellow) can be transmitted. | T F |
| 9. An electronic message system (EMS) eliminates telephone tag. | T F |
| 10. A leased-line rate is substantially lower than that for an equivalent number of single telephone channels. | T F |
| 11. In a firm having Centrex, all incoming calls are routed by a central switchboard operator. | T F |
| 12. WATS is a long-distance telephone service for sending voice, data, text, and image messages at discounted rates. | T F |
| 13. The use of Telex requires an operator to type all outgoing messages. | T F |
| 14. An audio teleconference permits a sales manager in Utah to hold a meeting simultaneously with the firm's branch managers in Texas, New Mexico, and Louisiana. | T F |
| 15. With four VDTs arranged in an interconnected network, a sales manager in Utah can hold a computer conference simultaneously with the firm's branch managers in Maine, Florida, and Ohio. | T F |
| 16. In most companies today, the trend is toward a decentralized organizational plan for the mailing services. | T F |
| 17. When large amounts of paper are circulated on a continuing basis from one floor to another in a very large office building, the use of a horizontal conveyor system is recommended. | T F |
| 18. Generally, the purchase of mailing equipment is worthwhile if the value of the employee's time saved is greater than the cost and depreciation of the machine to be used. | T F |
| 19. Postage meters are leased from the manufacturer and licensed for use by the USPS. | T F |
| 20. A firm in Vermont can reduce its mailing costs by affixing airmail postage to all letters addressed to customers west of the Mississippi River. | T F |

## SECTION B • PROJECTS

# Project 18–1 • Getting Acquainted with the Telephone Directory

You have probably "let your fingers do the walking" through the Yellow Pages, but how often have you consulted the Customer Guide pages of your telephone directory? Much valuable information and cost-reducing suggestions may be obtained by studying the Customer Guide pages, which are often placed in the opening section of the directory.

**Directions:** Consult your local telephone directory to find the answers to the following questions.

1. Under what conditions is it *legal* to wiretap or otherwise intercept a telephone call?

______________________________

______________________________

______________________________

2. Explain the operation of three-way calling service.

______________________________

______________________________

______________________________

3. What steps should you take to handle obscene, threatening, or harassing calls?

______________________________

______________________________

______________________________

4. What is the meaning of telephone numbers in the directory that are preceded by *TDD*?

______________________________

______________________________

______________________________

5. What federal and state taxes and surcharges apply to your telephone calls and equipment use?

______________________________

______________________________

______________________________

6. How should you proceed to make several calling card calls in succession?

7. How would you proceed to learn the amount of time and the charge for a call you have just made?

8. What are the hours covered by (a) the Evening Time Period and (b) the Night and Weekend Time Period? Which rates are in effect on holidays?

9. If, as a residence customer, you are not interested in the product or service offered by a telephone solicitor, how should you handle the call? If you wish to reduce the number of telephone solicitation calls you receive from national companies, what steps can you take?

10. At 9:30 a.m. you decide to call a customer in Rome, Italy. The customer's telephone number is 679 93 84. (a) Give the complete number you should dial. (b) What is the time in Rome?

## Project 18–2 • Field Research: The Telephone Switchboard Operator

In this field research project, you and a group of your classmates will visit the attendant of the telephone switchboard on your campus or in a company in your community. It is recommended that you plan a definite day and time for the interview—possibly during a work break—so that the attendant is free to give you his or her undivided attention. After you have interviewed the attendant and completed the questionnaire given on pages 201 and 202, your instructor may ask your group to prepare a report of your findings or to sit as a panel during an upcoming class session to discuss telephone systems.

## INTERVIEW WITH A SWITCHBOARD ATTENDANT

1. Describe the type of telephone system your group investigated.

______________________________________________________________

______________________________________________________________

2. Is the attendant responsible for office duties other than operating the switchboard? ______________

   If so, what are these duties and what percentage of the attendant's workday is spent in performing each duty?

______________________________________________________________

______________________________________________________________

______________________________________________________________

______________________________________________________________

3. How many hours during the day does someone operate the switchboard? ______________

4. How does the company arrange for operating the switchboard during the attendant's absence for personal breaks, rest periods, lunch, etc.?

______________________________________________________________

______________________________________________________________

______________________________________________________________

______________________________________________________________

5. Ask the attendant to state three main dissatisfactions that arise from the operation of the switchboard.

______________________________________________________________

______________________________________________________________

______________________________________________________________

______________________________________________________________

______________________________________________________________

______________________________________________________________

6. What solution does the attendant have for overcoming each of the problems cited in the answer to Question 5?

______________________________________________________________

______________________________________________________________

______________________________________________________________

7. Explain what role, if any, the attendant plays in:

   a. Analyzing and checking the monthly telephone invoice.

   ___

   ___

   b. Allocating telephone expenses and equipment costs to departments within the organization.

   ___

   ___

   c. Maintaining a daily log of all toll calls made. (Obtain a sample copy of the form, if possible, to include in your report.)

   ___

   ___

   d. Completing call slips by means of which all calls are charged directly to the department involved. (Obtain a sample copy of the form, if possible, to include in your report.)

   ___

   ___

   e. Controlling the quantity and length of personal calls.

   ___

   ___

   f. Advising telephone users as to the most economical kind of call to place (such as station to station or person to person).

   ___

   ___

   ___

8. If you are able to observe the attendant on duty, "listen in" as he or she receives several incoming calls and places several outside calls. Does the attendant impart a company "personality" which you believe aids in creating a good public image and serves as an effective public relations tool?

___

___

___

___

___

# Project 18–3 • Depreciation Methods and Their Effect on Cash Flow

In Project 4–3, it was explained that when a company purchases an asset, such as office equipment, with a useful life of more than one year, the cost of the asset can be recovered over a specified number of years by taking deductions from gross income. The deductions taken during the useful life of the asset are referred to as depreciation expense.

When selecting a method for depreciating office equipment, such as telecommunication equipment, the office manager must choose the most profitable course of action. Since different methods of determining depreciation are available, the office manager should understand how each one influences the company's cash inflow. The purpose of this project is to present briefly two methods of calculating depreciation and examine their effects upon cash flow.

In calculating the annual depreciation expense, it is necessary to know the cost basis (purchase price) of the asset and its estimated life or period of usefulness. Several methods are authorized in the Internal Revenue Code for determining the annual depreciation deduction. However, for the purposes of this project, only the straight-line and the declining-balance methods are described.

Let us assume that on January 1, 1996, Strauss, Inc., acquired a new data communication system at a purchase price of $25,000. A useful life of five years was assigned the new equipment. The amount of annual depreciation determined under the straight-line and the declining-balance methods is explained below.

## Straight-Line Method

This commonly used method of calculating depreciation is described in Project 4–3, page 37. You will recall that under MACRS a half-year convention is used when calculating the depreciation for property such as a data communication system. The half-year convention treats all property placed in service during a tax year as having been placed in service on the midpoint of that tax year. Thus, the cost of the five-year data communication system is actually recovered in six years. The amount of depreciation expense for each of the six years is shown in Table 18–1.

The effect of the annual depreciation deduction upon the book value of the equipment for each of the six years is shown in the table. The *book value* of an asset is the original cost of the asset less the total amount of accumulated depreciation recorded "on the books" (the accounting records).

**Table 18–1**
**STRAIGHT-LINE DEPRECIATION**

| Year | Depr. Rate (%) | Book Value at Beginning of Year | Annual Depreciation Expense |
|---|---|---|---|
| 1996 | 10.00 | $25,000.00 | $ 2,500.00 |
| 1997 | 22.22 | 22,500.00 | 4,999.50 |
| 1998 | 28.57 | 17,500.50 | 4,999.89 |
| 1999 | 40.00 | 12,500.61 | 5,000.24 |
| 2000 | 66.67 | 7,500.61 | 5,000.66 |
| 2001 | 100.00 | 2,499.96 | 2,499.71* |

*Adjusted due to rounding in prior years.

## Declining-Balance Method

Under this *accelerated* approach to determining depreciation, the declining-balance method yields greater amounts of depreciation during the early years of life and lesser amounts during the later years. For equipment such as the data communication system, the double (200%) declining-balance method is used over the five-year estimated life along with a half-year convention. Note, however, for this class of property, we change to the straight-line method for the first tax year when the straight-line method will yield a larger deduction than the declining-balance method.

To calculate the amount of depreciation expense under MACRS, the following steps are taken:

1. Determine the declining-balance rate of depreciation by dividing the declining-balance percentage (200%) by the recovery period:

   $\frac{200}{5} = 40\%$

2. Apply the half-year convention to obtain the depreciation rate for the first year (1/2 of 40% = 20%).

3. Calculate the depreciation expense for the first year:

   20% × $25,000 = $5,000

4. Use the declining-balance rate, 40%, for the remaining years until that year when the straight-line method yields a larger deduction. At that time, change to the straight-line method.

Using the double (200%) declining-balance method, we calculate the annual depreciation expense for Strauss's data communication system as shown in Table 18–2.

**Table 18–2**
**DECLINING-BALANCE DEPRECIATION**

| Year | Depr. Range (%) | Book Value at Beginning of Year | Annual Depreciation Expense |
|---|---|---|---|
| 1996 | 20.00 | $25,000.00 | $5,000.00 |
| 1997 | 40.00 | 20,000.00 | 8,000.00 |
| 1998 | 40.00 | 12,000.00 | 4,800.00 |
| 1999* | 40.00 | 7,200.00 | 2,880.00 |
| 2000 | 66.67 | 4,320.00 | 2,880.14 |
| 2001 | 100.00 | 1,439.86 | 1,439.86 |

* Changed to straight-line method.

**Directions:** Answer each of the following questions pertaining to the discussion of depreciation methods.

1. For the equipment that Strauss purchased in 1996, which of the two methods—straight line or declining balance—produced the greater amount of depreciation over the estimated life of the equipment?

_______________________________________________

_______________________________________________

2. Assume that the data communication equipment purchased in 1996 provides a flow of services in which 20 percent of the asset's total service is consumed each year of its life. Which of the two depreciation methods provides the more appropriate matching of revenue and expenses? Explain why.

_______________________________________________

_______________________________________________

3. Suppose, as a result of technological advances, the equipment purchased in 1996 became obsolete well before its useful life of five years had ended. Which depreciation method should have been adopted? Why?

_______________________________________________

_______________________________________________

4. Assume the following operating data for Strauss, Inc., for 1997:

   - Sales, $800,000. All sales are for cash.
   - Operating expenses (excluding depreciation and income taxes), $500,000. All expenses are paid in 1997.
   - Income taxes amount to 34 percent of net income, payable in the same year the net income is earned.
   - Additional data communication equipment was purchased on January 1, 1997. Purchase price, $50,000; estimated life, 5 years.

   a. Determine the amount of net income after taxes for 1997, using each of the two depreciation methods:

      (1) the straight-line method .................... $ ________

      (2) the declining-balance method .................... $ ________

   b. What is the amount of cash flow for 1997 under:

      (1) the straight-line method? .................... $ ________

      (2) the declining-balance method? .................... $ ________

## Project 18–4 • Reorganizing the Mailing Center

Pepito Foods of El Paso maintains 10 branch offices located in key cities throughout the United States and Mexico. In the El Paso offices, there are eight departments and the corporation's executive offices. The department heads and the executive secretary have been studying the firm's handling of the incoming and outgoing mail for the past several months. The team has identified the following pressing problems:

**Incoming mail.** The mail is picked up at the main post office at 8:30 a.m. and 12:30 p.m. by Bob Hermoso, the mail clerk, since his trip from home in the morning and his return from lunch take him past the post office. The mail is very heavy, often numbering 4,000 pieces a day. For example, this morning's mail brought 1,741 pieces from branch offices, customers, job applicants, and suppliers, including 15 parcels.

When the mail reaches the office, Hermoso, the switchboard operator, and a file clerk sort the mail into two stacks—that addressed to persons and that addressed to the firm. The mail addressed to persons is sorted and delivered unopened. The mail addressed to the firm is opened by a hand-operated opener at a rate of 100 pieces a minute. Whenever there is an enclosure in a letter, it is paper clipped to the letter. After all the letters have been opened, their contents are sorted into wire baskets which are labeled for each department. When the sorting has been completed, the mail is distributed—usually not before 10:30 a.m. and 2:30 p.m.

**Outgoing mail.** The daily outgoing mail averages between 1,100 and 1,200 pieces, not including printed advertising circulars. The circulars, numbering from 20,000 to 30,000 pieces, are sent out quarterly. The daily outgoing mail typically consists of about 400 sales invoices; 100 letters to branch offices; and 600 letters that acknowledge orders, answer complaints, and enclose price lists and catalogs.

Window envelopes are used for sales invoices, while plain business-size envelopes are used for letters, except those addressed to the branch offices. The latter are sent in specially printed envelopes that require the individual affixing of stamps. There have been numerous instances of mail returned for insufficient postage, a situation that has caused delays and ill will.

Each department sends its unsealed envelopes to Hermoso's office by 4:00 p.m. He takes all outgoing mail to the post office at 4:30 p.m.

**Directions:** After carefully analyzing the facts presented, prepare a report containing your recommendations for reorganizing the mailing system. Include comments on personnel, furniture and equipment, and mailing routines. Give your reasons for any recommended changes in the routines and estimate the cost of furniture and equipment that should be purchased. (Prices may be obtained from office furniture and equipment catalogs.) Assume that two mail clerks will be employed at $380 a week and that a supervisor earning $600 a week will devote half of his or her time to the mailing work. Also, set up a schedule for handling the mail under the reorganized plan.

# 19

# MANAGING RECORDS

Like other managers in the organization, the administrative office manager requires information that is current, timely, relevant, and quickly accessible. But what about information (such as that contained on paid purchase invoices, copies of sales invoices, interim financial statements, and annual reports) that goes out of date quickly and is seldom used? Business practice demands that much of this information be retained. As a result, outdated forms and records create a mass of inactive and semiactive records that builds up, gets in the way of new business, and becomes a costly burden. Here is where the office manager must plan and organize a records management program designed to save time, space, and money.

Regardless of the medium used for storing information—on paper or invisibly within the files of the computer system—all forms containing information follow the same phases of the records life cycle:

1. **Creation**—preventing the origination of unneeded records and requiring effective design for all forms initiated.
2. **Storage**—providing for and supervising the housing of physical and electronic documents efficiently and securely.
3. **Retrieval**—aiming for speedy access to physical and electronic records.
4. **Maintenance**—surveying all records to develop a schedule for their retention, and providing for adequate protection of the records.
5. **Disposition**—transferring and storing inactive records and destroying unneeded records.

## SECTION A • REVIEW QUESTIONS

**Directions:** In the Answers column, write the letter of the item in Column 1 that is described by each statement in Column 2.

**Column 1**

**A** Bond paper
**B** Call-back system
**C** Centralized filing
**D** Data hierarchy
**E** Decentralized filing
**F** Electronic performance support system (EPSS)
**G** Files accuracy ratio
**H** Files activity ratio
**I** Filing system
**J** Ledger paper
**K** MICR
**L** OCR
**M** Records life cycle
**N** Records management
**O** Smart form
**P** Soft-copy form

| **Column 1** | **Answers** |
|---|---|
| 1. An automated form that is created with a special set of forms design and fill-in instructions stored in a computer file .............. | 1. ______ |
| 2. A scanning system used for reading numeric and alphabetic data that have been printed in a distinctive type style on business forms ... | 2. ______ |
| 3. Software that supplies functional decision-making information for completing fields on an electronic form ..................... | 3. ______ |
| 4. An organization-wide administrative service responsible for creating and maintaining systematic procedures and controls over all phases of the records life cycle ......................... | 4. ______ |
| 5. A type of paper used for letterheads, office forms, and certificates where fine appearance and durability are essential ............ | 5. ______ |
| 6. An organizational plan in which each office division maintains its own filing system ...................................... | 6. ______ |
| 7. A five-level organization stucture of information that ranges from the most basic level—the character—to the broadest level—the database ........................................ | 7. ______ |
| 8. The steps or sequential phases in the life of records that include creation, storage, retrieval, maintenance, and disposition ....... | 8. ______ |
| 9. A VDT-designed form that appears on the terminal screen for the entry of data into the computer system ...................... | 9. ______ |
| 10. A measure used to evaluate a records system in which the number of records found is compared with the number of records requested | 10. ______ |

**Directions:** Indicate your answer to each of the following questions by circling "Yes" or "No" in the Answers column.

| | | **Answers** | |
|---|---|---|---|
| 1. | Do most of the records used by insurance companies involve correspondence, reports, and operating papers? | Yes | No |
| 2. | Under the continuous transfer method, are filed materials examined at fixed intervals, such as every six months? | Yes | No |
| 3. | With the inroads made by automation, do paper records still continue to serve as the most basic medium for storing information? | Yes | No |
| 4. | Is the specialty form the most common type of record in a manual records system? | Yes | No |
| 5. | Should the physical characteristics of the paper and printing styles used in all forms be standardized? | Yes | No |
| 6. | In the manufacture of forms, is the finish of the paper determined by the manner in which the form is filled in? | Yes | No |
| 7. | Should the entire life cycle of a form be centrally controlled? | Yes | No |
| 8. | Are *both* alphabetic and numeric filing systems used in most business firms? | Yes | No |
| 9. | Under the network filing plan, are the departmental records of the organization stored in one central location? | Yes | No |
| 10. | As a rule, do open-shelf files require more space than cabinet files? | Yes | No |
| 11. | Is *archives* another name for the records center used by large offices for storing inactive records? | Yes | No |
| 12. | In the data hierarchy, does a *database* contain a *group* of related files? | Yes | No |
| 13. | When records are initially created in an electronic environment, are they considered *volatile*? | Yes | No |
| 14. | Are encryption systems a type of security safeguard in which the computer sends requested information only to authorized telephone numbers? | Yes | No |
| 15. | In the disposition of electronic records, is the transfer process the one step that cannot be automated? | Yes | No |
| 16. | Do personnel salaries represent the lowest percentage of the total costs of records management? | Yes | No |
| 17. | Are the functional costs associated with forms greater than the physical costs of the paper and print used for the forms? | Yes | No |
| 18. | Is it recommended that a records audit be conducted at least every two years? | Yes | No |
| 19. | Does a files activity ratio of 35 percent indicate that there are too many inactive records and that many should be destroyed? | Yes | No |
| 20. | A files accuracy ratio of 98 percent is determined. Is it correct to say that the files are in excellent operating condition? | Yes | No |

## SECTION B • PROJECTS

### Project 19–1 • Computer Hands-On: Designing a Combination Employee and Property Pass

While you are analyzing the use of forms in the Trent Manufacturing Company, you discover that eight different property passes and employee passes are now in use, unknown to several managers. All of these passes are shown on the template PO19-1.TEM.

Even though each pass is printed on a different color of paper stock, both visitors and employees (especiallly the security force) become confused over which pass is which.

**Assignment:** After you carefully study each of the eight passes, design one combination form that will serve as both an employee pass and a property pass. Use template file PO19-1.TEM in redesigning your form.

1. Specify the size of the newly designed form. ________________

2. What standard-size sheet of paper stock will minimize, or eliminate, waste resulting from trimming?

________________

3. What color will you use for the paper stock? ________________

4. How does your one form satisfactorily meet the needs formerly served by eight separate forms?

________________

________________

________________

________________

5. What economies do you anticipate as a result of having combined eight old forms into one new form?

________________

________________

________________

________________

6. What principles of forms management were violated when the eight different forms came into existence?

________________

________________

________________

________________

## Project 19–2 • Reorganizing the Records Management System

Soon after you accepted the position of office supervisor of Ames Farms six months ago, the following serious records problems came to your attention:

1. The 15-year-old, flimsy, paint-chipped file cabinets are difficult to operate.
2. The 30 four-drawer file cabinets are crammed with records (correspondence, accounting documents, and invoices).
3. No records retention or records disposition procedures are in effect.
4. No records management manual exists.
5. No office personnel have been specifically assigned to the records management function. Three general office workers do the filing, although all 40 office employees have access to the files. Each office worker who does the filing is currently paid a weekly salary of $320.

Company expansion and its increase in paperwork have placed a severe strain on the present records system. Further growth of the firm and a larger office staff are anticipated, and a reorganization of the entire records management system is needed soon.

One office employee, Berta Quinn, has helped you study the present records system. Because she likes records work; is a good, careful worker; knows the firm and its records problems; and has the cooperation of the office staff, you have appointed her as records supervisor at a weekly salary of $525, effective at the beginning of January 1996. In this position, she will be responsible for coordinating all records activities, procuring equipment and supplies, providing whatever systems changes and control she deems necessary, and devoting about 25 percent of her time to filing operations.

Quinn will be assigned one full-time files assistant at a salary of $350 a week, with the possibility of adding a part-time worker if the workload requires. The salary of the part-time worker will be one-half the annual salary paid the files assistant. With these appointments, centralized control can be placed over all records.

Quinn's first recommendation for managing the records involves the purchase of new steel five-drawer units that would eventually replace the old file cabinets. She has suggested the use of the duplicate equipment method of transferring records from active to inactive storage. During 1996 (the first year of operation) those records that are one year old would continue to be retained in the present four-drawer files, which would be called the "back" or inactive files. Next to these inactive files would be the active files housed in the new file units.

At the end of 1996, the contents of the "back" files would be purged and the materials would be placed in transfer cases in a storage room. The old file cabinets, having no salvage value, would be destroyed. The units purchased at the beginning of 1996, containing 1996 materials, would then become the "back" files. New file units would have to be purchased in 1997 to serve as the active files for the second year. At the end of 1997, when the "back" files are purged, their contents would be stored in transfer cases. A similar procedure would be followed at the end of each year.

For the past two months, Quinn has studied the records storage patterns of the firm. About 4,000 incoming letters and 3,000 copies of outgoing correspondence and statements are filed each week. Each 26-inch drawer in the standard-size file cabinet holds approximately 5,000 papers. To handle the storage requirements for the proposed system, Quinn has consulted several office equipment houses, one of whom has submitted the most competitive bid, as follows:

Five-drawer filing units, letter-size, 26-inch
cabinet drawers . . . . . . . . . . . . . . . . . . . . .$275 each

In addition to submitting this quotation, the equipment representative mentioned the need to consider depreciation on the equipment in the records center. The cost of the file cabinets, assuming no trade-in value, will be recovered over a five-year period under the straight-line method, as explained on page 203.

**Directions:** Calculate each of the following costs, which, along with other information you supply, are to be included in your report recommending the establishment of a new records center.

1. Calculate the present (1995) and proposed (1996 and 1997) payroll costs in the records center. Assume that, commencing in 1997, salaries in the records center increase by 6 percent. Further, assume that the services of the part-time worker are required at the beginning of 1997.

2. Project the present (1995) payroll costs for the three office workers over the five-year period 1996-2000, assuming a 6 percent salary increase each year. Compare these costs with the proposed payroll costs for the same time period. What is the amount of increase in payroll costs over the five-year period?

3. Calculate the purchase price of the new filing units required over the five-year period 1996–2000 and determine the amount of cost that will be recovered during each of these years. (In your calculation of the straight-line depreciation, ignore the midyear convention.) Assume that the paper workload increases by 5 percent each year after 1996.

4. In view of the increased payroll costs and the outlay for new filing units, what cost-reduction factors should you stress in your report?

5. Identify some of the factors to be considered as you prepare the procedures for records retention and records disposition.

6. Prepare a table of contents that identifies the topics that should be placed in the new records management manual to be developed.

# Project 19–3 • Calculating Clerical Savings Resulting from Redesigning a Purchase Order Form

In the purchasing department of El Capitan, Inc., all purchase orders are filled in manually at a typewriter by one clerk, who proceeds as follows:

1. Removes the six-part purchase order, a unit set with one-time carbons, from the shipping carton.
2. Inserts the unit set into the typewriter and fills in the form.
3. Removes the unit set from the typewriter and snaps it apart, at the same time removing the one-time carbons and placing them in a waste container.
4. Types the vendor's name and address on a regular business-size envelope.
5. Inserts the signed purchase order into the envelope and places it in the Out basket for delivery to the mailing room.

Last year 18,000 purchase orders were prepared in accordance with the procedure described above.

As a result of having studied the present procedure, you obtain the following information:

| Operation Performed | No. of Times Performed in Year | Time per Operation |
|---|---|---|
| 1. Remove unit set from box, insert set into typewriter, and align to typing position . | 18,000 | .0030 hrs. |
| 2. Remove filled-in set from typewriter . . . . . . . . . . . . . . . | 18,000 | .0004 hrs. |
| 3. Snap set apart and discard one-time carbons . . . . . . . . . | 18,000 | .0014 hrs. |
| 4. Insert, type, and remove envelope . . . . . . . . . . . . . . . . | 18,000 | .0040 hrs. |

The annual salary of the clerk for a 52-week year, 37 1/2-hour workweek is $14,500.

Your recommendation for improving the procedure includes the design of a six-part, snap-out, continuous form, with 100 forms to each roll. A pin-feed aligning device, attached to the typewriter, properly aligns and advances each form through the machine. Also, the Name and Address of Vendor section of the purchase order has been redesigned so that a window envelope may be used.

Your proposed procedure includes the operations and time allowances shown below.

| Operation Performed | No. of Times Performed in Year | Time per Operation |
|---|---|---|
| 1. Feed first form of the continuous form roll (100 form packs to each roll) into the typewriter . . . . . . . . . . . | 180 | .0028 hrs. |
| 2. Depress key to advance and align each new form . . . . . . . | 18,000 | .0002 hrs. |
| 3. Tear off each completed form | 18,000 | .0002 hrs. |
| 4. Snap form pack apart, remove stubs, and discard one-time carbons . . . . . . . . . . . . . . . | 18,000 | .0003 hrs. |

**Directions**: Answer each of the following questions.

1. What is the clerical cost of completing 18,000 purchase orders under the present procedure? . . . . . . $ ________
2. What is the clerical cost of completing 18,000 purchase orders under your proposed procedure? . . . $ ________
3. What is the amount of clerical savings as a result of adopting your new procedure? . . . . . . . . . . . . . . $ ________
4. What other kinds of savings would you expect to gain from the installation of your new procedure?

________________________________________________

________________________________________________

________________________________________________

________________________________________________

## Project 19–4 • Converting to Electronic Forms

The following article describes how forms software is displacing paper forms and shows the benefits being realized by firms that have converted to electronic forms. After you have read the article, answer the question at the end.

### PCs Start Sweeping Away Business Forms

Computers are finally starting to bend, fold, spindle, and mutilate the paper-forms business.

After years of reckless effort to reduce the flow of paper, some big organizations are concluding that getting rid of forms may be one of the most productive things they can do with their expensive computer-network systems. Instead of stuffing filing cabinets with forms for expense accounts, purchase orders, and receipts, they're storing them on computer disks.

"When you get to the idea of an electronic form . . . you're talking about a completely different office environment," says Amy Wohl, an office-automation consultant in Bala Cynwyd, Pa. "Because of the reduced human effort, time saved in processing and increased accuracy, it offers a distinct competitive advantage."

Forms software has been around for years, but in early versions, people designed forms on their computers, then printed them out and made copies so other people could fill them out on typewriters. As more people got access to high-quality laser printers, some companies distributed electronic templates of certain forms so people could fill them out on their own computers and then print them out. Many people use the tax-preparation programs that produce and fill out Internal Revenue Service forms in that way.

Now, the company networks set-up for electronic mail are making possible the next step: electronic forms that can be filled out and sent to another department by e-mail without ever being printed out. But don't expect people to stop making paper copies just yet.

Two of the leaders in the electronic-forms market, **JetForm** Corp. in Ottawa and **Delrina Technology** Inc. in Toronto, stress their ability to help users send forms over networks and store forms on central servers where users can easily get them. **Lotus Development** Corp. includes forms design and communications in Notes, its popular groupware product. And **Microsoft** Corp. unveiled forms software last week that works with its Microsoft Mail e-mail product. "The forms market will grow incredibly fast, because it's so easy to do once you have the mail infrastructure installed," says Daniel Petre, vice-president of Microsoft's Workgroup division.

Why should companies care? Organizations spend $6 billion a year on preprinted forms. The National Business Forms Association claims 83% of all business documents are forms. But one-third of all forms are thrown away before they're used, usually when they become obsolete after important information changes, such as the IRS's car-mileage allowance on expense forms.

The spread of computers has already cut into the use of paper forms, some analysts say. Merilyn Dunn of market researcher BIS Strategic Decisions, Norwell, Mass., says that the lucrative multipart forms business peaked in 1990 and is now shrinking at about 9% a year, because people prefer to process forms with computer-driven printers that can't handle multipart paper. "There's still demand for paper forms in the cut-sheet market," she says.

Some business-forms makers see the handwriting on the wall. "I'm taking our company out of the main-line business forms market, which I see maturing," says Kenneth E. Overstreet, executive vice-president of **Northstar Computer Forms** Inc. in Minneapolis. Northstar's new niche is printing bank documents with special codes on them.

The benefits of going electronic show up at Cigna Corp., the big Philadelphia-based insurer. Cigna, which has about 30,000 employees with PCs connected to networks, is trying to replace an estimated 35,000 corporate forms with electronic forms. Starting with 20 widely used internal forms, such as expense accounts and requests for training classes, the company expects to pay for the project in reduced paper costs in the first year. But the benefits go much further. "The goal is to eliminate the paper flow," says Edward F. Driscoll, assistant vice-president.

With electronic forms, Cigna doesn't have to keep branch-office shelves full of forms, often outdated. Mark Orthner, who worked on the project, says, "Forms' obsolescence is a big problem at our company. We estimate we have a 30% to 35% obsolescence rate, but people use forms that are 10 years old." When they use computerized forms, the person in charge of the form only has to change it once in a central computer—for example, every year when the IRS changes the mileage allowance. And no employee wastes an hour filling out an obsolete form only to have it sent back.

On Cigna's automated electronic forms, the computer performs calculations, dutifully adding up totals vertically and horizontally, if required. On some forms, if a salesman fills in an account number, the computer automatically fills in name, address, phone number, and even calculates special discounts. When a product number is typed, the computer fills in the name. Auditors don't have to worry about mathematical errors, and employees don't have to fill out forms again.

Mr. Driscoll predicts the benefits will mushroom. "A form is usually a very good descriptor of the way a business works," says Mr. Driscoll. "This gives us entree to look at the way we process paper. Maybe we'll say you don't need this form." Because electronic forms can be changed so easily, they aren't the impediment to innovating and experimenting that printed paper forms can be. "Now, putting it on a form isn't the critical path. You can do a major forms redesign in a day. Paper elongates the impact of change," he says.

Once an employee has completed a form at Cigna, he or she can send it to the next person or department by typing in an e-mail address, eliminating the wait for the office mail cart.

Still, Mr.Driscoll doesn't have any illusions about converting people to electronic forms overnight. Cigna chose JetForm's package in part because it creates screens that looked very much like the paper forms people were used to. "People are in love with paper," he says. "We wanted to give people something for their records they could have and hold."

**Directions:** In a short report, summarize the potential benefits that a firm may realize as it converts to electronic forms.

# 20

# MANAGING MICROIMAGE AND REPROGRAPHIC SYSTEMS

The technological advances in microimage and reprographic services have enabled the administrative office manager to strengthen the links of the information management function to satisfy the information needs of the firm. A *microimage system* refers to the total system for creating, using, and storing microrecords, which are paper documents that have been converted to microfilm. A *reprographic system* relates to the reproduction of information and records for management. In managing these two systems, the office manager is especially concerned with their cost effectiveness.

Promises of savings as a result of converting to the latest technological innovation are always tempting, but before reaching a decision in microimage and reprographic services, the office manager needs to explore alternative courses of action. For example, when is it economically feasible to convert to microrecords? What cost factors should be considered when justifying phototypesetting? Which reprographic process is best to use when 2,000 copies of an eight-page full-color report are made each month? How can office copiers be prevented from becoming an in-house printing plant?

As a result of the advances made in the field of microimage and reprographic services, a new breed of manager, often found at the corporate level, is evolving in many firms. Where formerly a company may have had a supervisor or manager of reproduction services and a supervisor of microfilming operations, each with very separate jurisdictions, today we may find an *information manager* responsible for all of the firm's information processing.

## SECTION A • REVIEW QUESTIONS

**Directions:** In the Answers column, write the letter of the item in Column 1 that is described by each statement in Column 2.

**Column 1**

**A** Computer input microfilm (CIM)
**B** Computer output microfilm (COM)
**C** Data aperture card
**D** Diffusion transfer
**E** Duplexing
**F** Microfiche
**G** Microrecord
**H** Optical disk
**I** Phototypesetter
**J** Reader
**K** Xerography

| Column 2 | Answers |
|---|---|
| 1. A machine capable of creating print on a special VDT screen from data obtained from word processing or computer systems, or from direct keyboard entry . . . . . . . . . . | 1. ______ |
| 2. The process in which a computer's output is automatically photographed and converted to human-readable images on microfilm without creating an intervening paper copy . . . . . . . | 2. ______ |
| 3. An electrostatic dry process that exposes a positively charged drum surface to light reflected through lenses from the original document . | 3. ______ |
| 4. The process of translating uncoded data on microrecords into computer language code for storage on magnetic tape as input to a computer | 4. ______ |
| 5. A paper document converted to microfilm . . . . . . . . . . | 5. ______ |
| 6. A mass memory device that captures, stores, and retrieves document images through use of laser technology . . . . . . . . . . | 6. ______ |
| 7. A microform that appears in a grid pattern on a transparent sheet of film . . . . . . . . . . | 7. ______ |
| 8. Copying on both sides of a sheet of copy paper in one operation . . . . | 8. ______ |
| 9. A device that enlarges or magnifies the microrecord to its original legible size and projects the image onto a viewing screen . . . . . . . . . | 9. ______ |

**Directions:** Indicate your answer to each of the following questions by circling "Yes" or "No" in the Answers column.

| | | **Answers** | |
|---|---|---|---|
| 1. | Does a *unitized* microform contain on the same continuous length of film unrelated items of information from many departments of a firm? | Yes | No |
| 2. | Is roll film usually considered the most economical type of microrecord? | Yes | No |
| 3. | With today's technology, is the updating of roll film a quick and inexpensive process? | Yes | No |
| 4. | Is a microfiche record retrieved by advancing the roll of film forward or backward to the desired location? | Yes | No |
| 5. | Can punched aperture cards be used to store microrecords of large documents, such as blueprints? | Yes | No |
| 6. | In the COM process, is the output of the computer transferred to a recorder to be photographed and reduced to microimage size on film? | Yes | No |
| 7. | In the CAR process, is an index of all microrecords, as well as the microrecords themselves, stored in the computer? | Yes | No |
| 8. | Does the storage of data on optical disks with the WORM format limit users to writing just once to the disks? | Yes | No |
| 9. | Is the cost per unit of optical disk storage lower than other disk systems? | Yes | No |
| 10. | In order to preserve information on microrecords, must the microrecords be periodically duplicated and replaced? | Yes | No |
| 11. | Does legislation permit microfilmed copies of business records to be admitted as evidence in courts of law under certain conditions? | Yes | No |
| 12. | In large firms, are the operational responsibilities for the microimage system supervised by the records manager? | Yes | No |
| 13. | Has the widespread use of automated copy-making processes eliminated the use of carbon paper? | Yes | No |
| 14. | Does xerography provide for reproduction of copies in only black, white, and gray? | Yes | No |
| 15. | Are *digital* copiers more commonly used in offices than *analog* copiers? | Yes | No |
| 16. | With an intelligent copier/printer, is it possible to create hard-copy images directly from the magnetic files of a computer? | Yes | No |
| 17. | Does centralized control of the reprographic services offer the advantage of reduced travel and turnaround time? | Yes | No |
| 18. | Are materials reproduced on office copiers acceptable in courts of law? | Yes | No |
| 19. | Once a firm purchases a copyrighted computer program, may it legally make as many copies of the program as needed? | Yes | No |
| 20. | Do hidden costs account for about 25 percent of the total cost of copy making? | Yes | No |

## SECTION B • PROJECTS

### Project 20–1 • Field Research: Office Copying Processes

In completing this field research project, you will investigate the copying processes in your own company, on your campus, or in a business firm within your community. You will evaluate the copying processes that are provided and determine under what conditions one process is selected in preference to another. The visit should also enable you to see some of the equipment in action and to talk with equipment operators to learn about the kinds of problems found on the job. Your instructor may assign a team of students to undertake this project and have them report back to the class orally or by means of a written report.

**Directions:** On the form on page 220, evaluate each of the copying processes according to the following factors:

1. *Appearance of Copy.* Is the copying process limited to reproduction of one color or may several colors be copied? Can pictures and line drawings be satisfactorily copied? Can pages from a bound volume be copied legibly?
2. *Length of Run.* What is the most economical range in number of copies for each process? Has a cutoff point been set with reference to economy of run for each process?
3. *Copy Size and Paper Size.* What is the maximum size of original that can be copied? What is the maximum size of paper stock that can be used for producing copies? Can copies be reduced or enlarged in size? Can a copy be printed on both sides of the sheet in one operation (duplexing)?
4. *Copy Cost.* Can plain paper be used or must special copy paper be purchased? What special supplies are required for equipment operation? (The cost per copy will vary with factors such as types of supplies and paper required, length of run, and quantity of supplies and supplies purchased. However, try to determine the approximate cost per copy for each process.)
5. *Speed of Output.* How many copies can be produced per minute? Are documents automatically fed into the copier or must they be manually inserted? Are copies automatically collated? What is the usual turnaround time for those requesting copies?
6. *Ease of Operation.* How much training is required before a worker can operate the copier satisfactorily? Is the equipment subject to frequent jamming? Is paper stock easily loaded into the equipment? Is the equipment subject to excessive downtime? Are any equipment operations messy and thus cause smudges and stains on the operator's hands and clothing?
7. *Control over Operations.* Is the copying equipment kept in one central location or do you find copiers scattered throughout the office? Is the equipment available for personal use on company time? Does the company have a chargeback system whereby reproduction costs are charged back to each department or division requesting copies? What evidence of copier misuse (personal use, reproduction of copyrighted materials without permission, excessive waste, etc.) do you find? Are operators required to keep a log of all work reproduced or do workers abide by an honor system? Are copiers kept locked with access only by authorized operators who must have a key, access card, or plug-in cartridge? What security is provided for the reproduction of confidential documents?

| FACTORS TO INVESTIGATE | OFFICE COPYING PROCESSES (Specify the Kinds of Copiers) |
|---|---|
| 1. Appearance of Copy | |
| 2. Length of Run | |
| 3. Copy Size and Paper Size | |
| 4. Copy Cost | |
| 5. Speed of Output | |
| 6. Ease of Operation | |
| 7. Control over Operations | |

# Project 20–2 • Determining the Average Rate of Return

This project explains the use of the *average rate of return,* sometimes called the *accountant rate of return,* which is another method that may be used by the administrative office manager in analyzing capital expenditures. The rate of return method measures the anticipated profitability of a proposed investment by dividing the average savings (benefits or income) to be obtained from an investment by the average amount of the investment.

Assume, for example, that the Osawa Company is contemplating the installation of an automated reprographics system, for which the total cost is $18,000. It is expected that, as a result of installing the new system, annual savings of $5,800 (before depreciation and taxes) will be realized. In this example, it is assumed that the systems equipment will have a useful life of five years. The company uses the straight-line method of calculating depreciation and is subject to a federal income tax rate of 34 percent.

The average annual savings are determined as follows:

| | |
|---|---|
| Savings before depreciation and taxes .... | $5,800 |
| Deduct: Depreciation | |
| $18,000 ÷ 5 = | 3,600 |
| | $2,200 |
| Deduct: Federal income taxes (34%) ..... | 748 |
| Savings after taxes .................. | $1,452 |

The average investment is calculated as follows:

$$\text{Average Investment} = \frac{\text{Original Cost} + \text{Salvage Value}}{2}$$

$$= \frac{\$18{,}000 + 0}{2} = \$9{,}000$$

The division by 2 is based on the assumption that the investment starts at $18,000 and is 0 at the end of its useful life. Using these amounts, the rate of return is determined to be 16 percent, as shown below:

$$\text{Rate of Return} = \frac{\text{Average Annual Savings}}{\text{Average Investment}}$$

$$= \frac{\$1{,}452}{\$9{,}000} = 16.13\%, \text{ rounded to } 16\%$$

Thus, under this proposal, a dollar of average investment results in a return of 16 percent. When using this method to evaluate capital expenditures, management usually relates the rate of return to certain conditions that must be met. For example, the company may stipulate that the cost of acquiring the capital to be tied up in the investment shall be less than 18 percent. Further, the firm may require that such an investment represent the best use of the money among a variety of alternatives. Thus, there should be no other capital expenditure proposal that can generate a return greater than 16 percent.

In relation to the payback method, which is discussed on page 170, the average rate of return method is a better tool of analysis because it measures the expected profitability of the proposed expenditure. The rate of return method is criticized, however, because it does not consider the time value of money and because in its calculation income as determined by the accountant is used rather than cash flow. In spite of these criticisms, the average rate of return and the payback methods are a combination of approaches often used by managers in their evaluation of proposals for allocating relatively large financial expenditures.

As another illustration of calculating the average rate of return, consider the Tibaldi Company, which is evaluating two different microimage systems for which the following data have been gathered:

| | System A ($50,000 investment) | System B ($43,000 investment) |
|---|---|---|
| Year | Savings after Taxes | Savings after Taxes |
| 1 | $10,000 | $1,000 |
| 2 | 9,000 | 2,000 |
| 3 | 8,000 | 3,000 |
| 4 | 7,000 | 4,000 |
| 5 | 6,000 | 5,000 |
| 6 | 5,000 | 6,000 |
| 7 | 4,000 | 7,000 |
| 8 | 3,000 | 8,000 |
| 9 | 2,000 | 9,000 |
| 10 | 1,000 | 10,000 |
| Total Savings | $55,000 | $55,000 |

Assume that for both systems there is no salvage value.

**Directions:** Prepare a report for the Tibaldi Company in which you show the average rate of return for each proposed system. Explain how your decision to recommend the installation of either System A or B would be influenced by the timing of the inflow of savings to be realized.

## Project 20–3 • Reducing the Misuse of Copiers

Reducing cost-per-copy expenses begins with the purchase of reliable copiers. However, even with the most dependable machines, copying expenses can get out of control due to unauthorized or unnecessary use of the copiers. The following article offers some help on how a company can safeguard itself against such abuse and increase revenue at the same time. After you have read the article, answer the questions at the end.

### Control Copy Costs While Increasing Revenue

Reducing expenses and increasing revenue sound like two things any business manager would be interested in. However, many businesses don't take advantage of one area where money can be saved, and made, every day. The opportunities lie in the office copiers.

According to copier manufacturers and industry analysts, more and more large corporations are beginning to take advantage of copier control systems and the even more advanced technology of copier management systems.

Copier management systems are sophisticated systems recommended for large corporations or businesses where many copiers are being used, some at off-site locations, and the company wants to manage the copiers from a central location. Since all copiers are linked via telephone wires, a manager can change personal identification numbers for the copier control system, obtain volume reports for each copier and each user, and make other changes from one location. Having this control over copier usage can save a lot of money for businesses concerned with keeping costs down.

Manufacturers see copier control systems as having three functions. Many users, such as a library or a copy shop, sell copies to walk-up customers where the copier is used as a vending machine. Another function is to control access to copiers that may be located in public areas like hallways or other open areas. Monitoring copy volume and usage is taking access control one step further. Not only can a copier control system control access to a copier by using a PIN number or access card, but the volume of copies made by an individual user can be monitored and controlled.

Many copier control systems today are built right into the copier. It is up to the user whether or not to activate the system, which is then run from the copier keypad on most units. According to several manufacturers, most companies opt not to use the system. Here are some reasons why activating the copy control system may be a good idea both as a money saver, and as a revenue builder.

A company can spend hundreds of thousands, even millions of dollars, on copying each year. This does not include the initial cost of the machines. Simply put, copy control systems reduce these costs by making the users accountable to management for the number—and nature—of copies made.

In the legal, architectural, accounting, and any industry where employees routinely charge back the client for work performed on the client's behalf, this technology can increase revenue.

"Many companies will take the copier and turn it into a profit center," says Mike Troy, product manager, Pitney Bowes Copier Systems (Trumbull, CT). "They will charge back their costs for the copies, or charge the client a set fee for copies made. Copier control sytems monitor this practice."

According to Troy, the information that Pitney Bowes gets back from the field indicates that copier control systems do cut costs because they simply cut down on the usage of the machines.

"Many people will go into a meeting with six people and make ten copies of a report," says Troy. "If you know that your copy volume is being monitored, you are more likely to make only the six you need."

According to Larry Kleuser of Oce-USA, Inc. (Chicago, IL), it is to the point copiers, in many situations, are used to see how much profit a business can make from them.

"Where our cost per copy may be two or three cents, a company who charges back to clients may charge that client 50 cents a copy. It is a cash cow for businesses that charge back," says Kleuser.

#### How Much Is Too Much?

With copier control and management systems, there are many levels of sophistication a user can achieve depending on company needs and activities.

"The obvious companies like law firms and accounting firms (those who bill back their copies) do use them," says Wilbert Verheyen, product manager, Oce. "Many companies just don't think they need them; however, we have seen that copy control devices are a tremendous benefit because they analyze where your volume is and allow you to come up with a much more efficient copy solution to reduce copy-

Reprinted from the August 1993 issue of *Managing Office Technology,* and copyrighted 1993 by Office Publications, Inc.

ing expenses. Some type of copy control device is the perfect means."

Many large corporations today are investing in elaborate copy management systems which are mainly beneficial in such companies where copiers are spread out all over the company, even in satellite office buildings.

"You have to stay realistic when it comes to these systems," says Verheyen. "If you have five copiers all in one area, and know for the most part who is making copies in the company, it really doesn't make a lot of sense to install an elaborate copy management system. A simple control device would suffice in that situation because it still can reduce copy volume, therefore controlling expenses. However, if you have more than one location and more than five copiers, it can certainly be beneficial to have an insight into how and where the copy volume is generated."

Manufacturers agree that more than two locations and more than 15 copiers constitute grounds for investigating a copy management system. The payback can be a substantial savings.

There are many points to consider beyond the obvious one of how many locations and copiers are located throughout the company. According to Dominic Pontrelli of Lanier (Atlanta, GA), several points are important to keep in mind when considering a system. However, keep in mind that any business with more than five copiers would benefit from some kind of automated control device.

"How many users? How many departments? Is the system used from 8 a.m. to 5 p.m. only? Do you authorize copier usage after hours? Do you charge clients for copies made?" asks Pontrelli. "Considering these questions will more than likely lead to some kind of automated system."

Another question regarding copier control devices is whether or not to activate the one built into the copier, if there is one, or mount a system onto the machine. First of all, there may not be a choice if the machine is older and does not have a system built in. On the other hand, the existing system may not be extensive enough to grow with the company's changing needs. Many of the devices built into the copiers cannot generate the necessary extensive reports and information on copy activity. A separate unit may be necessary.

"Once a business owns or operates at least five copiers, typically one individual spends considerable time maintaining copier operations. Large companies can operate hundreds, even thousands of copiers, and managing the fleet can grow from a one person operation into an entire staff and annual copying expenses can climb into the millions of dollars," says Chris Rickborn, Equitrac Corp. (Coral Gables, FL). "Automated copier management systems provide the management tools to reduce photocopying costs, streamline management, boost productivity, and accurately allocate photocopy expenses back to departments."

Equitrac devices are mounted on the copier units and have the capability to monitor office equipment, and then the products can be networked back to a centralized system for report consolidation or billing purposes.

According to Rickborn, automated copier management can reduce annual copy expenses by 20 percent. Also, with the information a system can provide, a company is much better informed for future purchasing decisions.

The information these systems can provide includes transaction data on each copier and user. According to Rickborn, features that a user should look for in an advanced system include the copier terminals' ability to store individual transactions with date and time, ability to network all copiers together into a central system, automated data collection capabilities, and data storage capacity of a minimum of 2,000 transactions.

With a sophisticated system, Rickborn also suggests looking for the ability for the system to fully validate user input, acceptance of magnetic code or bar code input, and the ability to provide consolidated management reports. Also important is making sure that the system has the capability to integrate data with the company's current internal accounting software.

If the sophistication of a copier management system is needed, it may be best to purchase a unit that can be mounted directly onto any brand of copier, and can be linked with any brand.

"Companies that are serious about implementing a complete copier management system, instead of just a device to keep count of copies, typically turn to specialized manufacturers," says Rickborn. "For this reason, copier manufacturers would not benefit by attempting to develop a full featured system."

Most companies, especially large corporations, do not stick with a single copier vendor for all their machines. This can be a problem when trying to link the units for better complete copier management purposes.

"Our system is in the machine but it is not designed as an extended copy control system," says Verheyen. "If you want to secure the copier completely you need outside devices and they have to be mounted outside the machine."

According to Verheyen, customers are becoming more and more conscious of copying costs as a substantial part of the budget. They are looking for ways to reduce operating expenses and one way is to get control of copy costs.

**Directions:** Each of the following statements is either true or false. Indicate your choice in the Answers column by circling "T" or "F."

| | Answers | |
|---|---|---|
| 1. A copier management system enables a company to decentralize its control over its copiers at all off-site locations . . . . . . . . . . | T | F |
| 2. Copier control systems can control the access to copiers as well as monitor the number of copies that a user makes . . . . . . . . . . | T | F |
| 3. Most companies maintain control over their copier usage by activating the control system built into their copiers . . . . . . . . . . | T | F |
| 4. Copy management systems are very cost effective in firms having fewer than five copiers located in one area . . . . . . . . . . | T | F |
| 5. A firm having more than 15 copiers in more than two locations offers fertile ground for achieving savings from the use of a copy management system . . . . . . . . . . | T | F |
| 6. Generally any business with more than five copiers can benefit from some kind of automated copier control device . . . . . . . . . . | T | F |
| 7. Most large companies use a single copier vendor when acquiring all their office copiers . . . . | T | F |

## CROSSWORD PUZZLE 3

### Across

1. Fairly stable costs
4. Contamination of program
7. Heart of computer system
9. Landlord-tenant agreement
14. Let fall in drops
17. External device that moves cursor
18. Relative hotness or coolness
20. Space needed for transmission
23. Footcandle
24. Pronoun
25. Bowlike curve
27. Shoe wiper
32. Weapon
34. Record center
35. Space controlled by worker
37. 1,000
41. Computer system equipment
43. Freight car
44. Dairy product
45. Proprietor
46. Mother of Jesus
49. Implore
50. Wanderer
51. Instructions for operating computer system
53. Personal computer
54. Long-range planning technique
55. Excessive indulgence
56. Filament bulb light
59. Microform in grid pattern
60. Indefinite article
61. Computer-assisted retrieval
63. Great quantity
64. Self-contained system
69. Computer output microfilm
70. Basic organizational unit
74. Light from tubelike lamp
78. Modulator-demodulator
79. Live animal collection
80. Local-area network
81. Alabama
82. Work (Gk.)
83. Central master file
84. Read-only memory
85. _______ optics
87. Records-protection code
88. Facsimile
90. Locating stored information
92. Computer that counts numbers
93. Small portion
94. Main workstation unit
95. Heavy, durable paper
96. No longer useful

## Down

2. Desktop publishing
3. Specially designed record
4. Video display terminal
5. Infrequent
6. Fragile
8. Expression of disgust
10. Area below a roof
11. Australian bird
12. One penny
13. Computer system safeguard
14. Decibel
15. Internal call system
16. Paid
18. Written communication
19. Smallest computer
21. Desk chair and working space
22. Simultaneous copying on both sides of sheet
26. Computer-aided design
27. 1,024K
28. _______ it were
29. Document converted to microfilm
30. Unintelligible jargon
31. Small silicon chip
33. Brightness measure
36. _______ intelligence
38. Beverage
39. Computer program writer
40. One billionth of a second
42. Random-access memory
47. Basic data character
48. Moisture in air
52. Homeless child
57. Container
58. Termination
61. Business programming language
62. Ante meridiem
65. Precut hole
66. Open plan or office _______
67. Large computer
68. WP input unit
71. Far (Gk.)
72. Written or oral evidence
73. No carbon required
74. Series of connected forms
75. Unforeseen
76. Office furniture
77. Clamor
78. Capital of Spain
80. Regulations
86. Letterhead paper
89. Binary digit
91. Private branch exchange

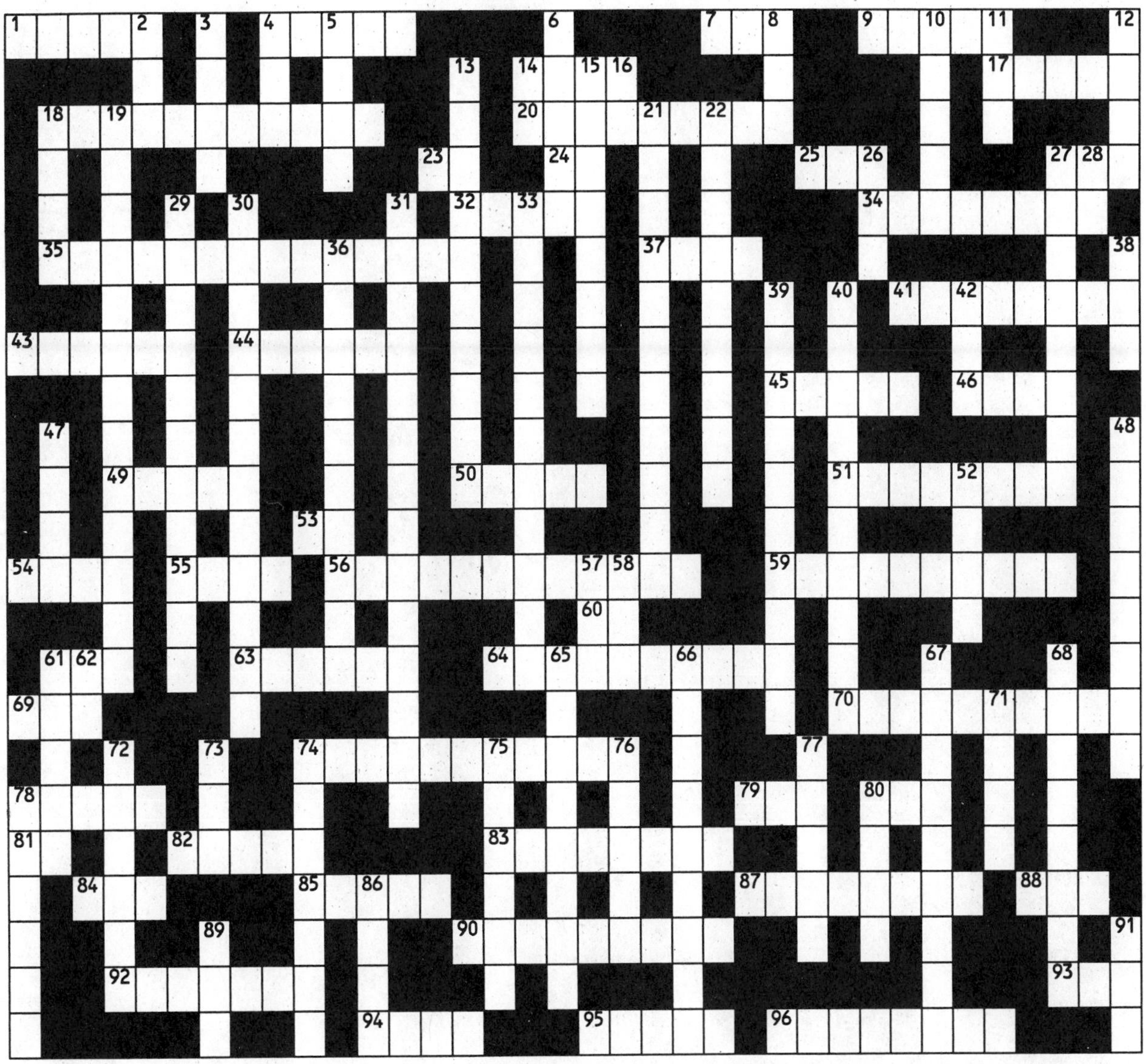

# 21

# IMPROVING ADMINISTRATIVE OFFICE SYSTEMS

Administrative office systems are evaluated to increase office productivity. After analyzing and improving systems, workflow problems are greatly lessened or eliminated; office tasks are performed more accurately, efficiently, and economically; and a greater volume of work is produced without increasing the number of office workers. As a result, operating costs are lowered.

When administrative office systems are analyzed and improved, all or only a portion of the systems elements are involved. Depending upon the availability of staff, time, and funds, one or more of the following major elements in administrative office systems may be studied: flow of work, use of office space, forms and related documents, performance of personnel, use of equipment, scheduling of work, and costs of system operations. After the systems have been studied and improvements made, the nature of the improved systems and their procedures and methods must be communicated to all users by means of (1) charts and decision tables that show the sequence, logic, and framework of the systems and (2) written narratives that provide the specific details for operating systems.

## SECTION A • REVIEW QUESTIONS

**Directions:** In the Answers column, write the letter of the item in Column 1 that is described by each statement in Column 2.

| Column 1 | Column 2 | Answers |
|---|---|---|
| **A** Decision table | 1. A technique in which functions formerly performed within the organization are contracted to be performed by an outside agent . . . | 1. ______ |
| **B** Effective system | 2. A systems technique used to determine who does what work . . . . . . | 2. ______ |
| **C** Efficient system | 3. A general model for analyzing each of the phases in an administrative office system . . . . . . . . . . . . . . . . . . . . . . . . . . . . . . . . . . . | 3. ______ |
| **D** Input-output (I/O) systems improvement model | 4. A set of general guidelines, based upon logic and common sense, for analyzing a system . . . . . . . . . . . . . . . . . . . . . . . . . . . . . . . . . . | 4. ______ |
| **E** Operations research (OR) | 5. A type of systems study that concentrates on the origination and distribution of documents and the clerical operations required to process information in an administrative office system . . . . . . . . . . | 5. ______ |
| **F** Outsourcing | 6. A graphic device used to portray an existing or a proposed system, including the flow of information and the various elements required to operate a system . . . . . . . . . . . . . . . . . . . . . . . . . . . . . . . . . | 6. ______ |
| **G** Prototype | 7. A system that is actually producing the desired quantity and quality of output; at the same time, the value of the system's output exceeds the costs of the input and transforming/processing steps . . . . . . . . . . | 7. ______ |
| **H** Systems chart | 8. A method of analysis in which advanced mathematics and scientific techniques are used to obtain the best possible solutions to decision-making problems in complex systems . . . . . . . . . . . . . . . . . . . . . . | 8. ______ |
| **I** Task | 9. A tool for presenting the logic and the sequential operations in a system by showing what action must be taken to satisfy each information-related condition . . . . . . . . . . . . . . . . . . . . . . . . . . . . . . . . . | 9. ______ |
| **J** Task analysis | 10. A system that is operating in an economical manner; that is, one that is highly reliable and minimizes the time and costs involved in its operations . . . . . . . . . . . . . . . . . . . . . . . . . . . . . . . . . . . . . . . . . | 10. ______ |
| **K** Workflow analysis | | |
| **L** Work simplification model | | |

**Directions:** Each of the following statements is either true or false. Indicate your choice in the Answers column by circling "T" or "F."

| | **Answers** | |
|---|---|---|
| 1. A properly operating system is effective and efficient at the same time | T | F |
| 2. The three factors to consider when evaluating the efficiency of a system are time, reliability, and volume of output | T | F |
| 3. In the operation of an administrative office system, most problems occur during the input and the feedback phases | T | F |
| 4. A real-world system is a utopian system in which all elements function at their most effective and efficient levels at all times | T | F |
| 5. Systems analysts approach their study of systems problems by examining all phases of a system in their entirety at the same time | T | F |
| 6. As a model for systems improvement, input-output (I/O) analysis can be applied only to a limited number of systems operations | T | F |
| 7. Simulation is a basic operations research technique in which a mathematical model of a real-world system is created | T | F |
| 8. A work distribution chart is used to trace the flow of forms and related paperwork through the departments under study | T | F |
| 9. Decision tables are used in situations where the logic and the sequential flow of data cannot be clearly represented on a chart | T | F |
| 10. The data flow diagram uses special symbols to trace the flow of data through a system | T | F |
| 11. Before-and-after layout charts are used to study the flow and frequency of movement of forms and of workers who transport records throughout the office | T | F |
| 12. In the study of an administrative office system, the highest priority should be given to the most important element in that system—the forms and records | T | F |
| 13. In analyzing tasks, the proofreading of a business document is classified as a transforming (processing) task | T | F |
| 14. A work distribution chart shows how many work units are produced and how much time is spent on each type of activity by all workers involved in a particular task | T | F |
| 15. Most studies of equipment usage start with an identification of the various tasks performed | T | F |
| 16. The main function of PERT is to determine how many workers and how much equipment is required to complete a project | T | F |
| 17. When a system is re-engineered, it is completely rebuilt from its most fundamental components | T | F |
| 18. The playscript procedure lists in sequential order the detailed steps necessary to operate a system and shows who is responsible for performing each step | T | F |
| 19. Two to three years may be required to evaluate accurately a system that operates on a once-a-year basis | T | F |
| 20. *Turnaround time* is the time that elapses before a system responds to a demand placed upon it. | T | F |

## SECTION B • PROJECTS

### Project 21–1 • Field Research: Charting the Flow of a Purchase Requisition

In this field research project, you will assume the role of a piece of paper—a purchase requisition—and trace each of the steps in your movement from the input phase through the processing phase and, finally, the output and feedback phases.

**Directions:** In your company or in some other firm in your community, or in one of the departmental offices on your campus, locate the person who initiates purchase requisitions for office supplies such as copy paper, printer ribbons, and pencils. Acquaint this person with the nature of your assignment—that you plan to study each of the steps involved in processing a requisition from its inception to the delivery of the requested materials to the person making the request.

Let us say that you are requisitioning a carton of 18 lb. computer printout paper and that this quantity is not immediately available in either the office or the stockroom. Ask the person to indicate step by step the flow of information processing in that office. Now, literally become that piece of paper—the purchase requisition—and trace each of your steps through the remainder of the processing cycle until the paper is delivered to the office in which the request originated.

1. On a blank sheet of paper, prepare a forms distribution chart that will show each of the steps involved in requesting a carton of computer printout paper.
2. Remove page 231 and make an extra copy of the flow process chart on a copying machine. This copy will be used in step 3, which follows. Using the original flow process chart, plot each of the steps involved. Calculate the distance in feet or meters and the time in minutes for each of these steps.
3. Study carefully the flow of information being processed in this system and determine where distance and time economies may be realized. On the extra copy of the chart that you made, present your proposed system for processing the purchase requisition. Approximately how much savings in dollars do you expect to gain from your proposed system? What will be the effect on turnaround time under your proposed system?

# Project 21–2 • Constructing a PERT Chart for Scheduling a Conference

Last week, Lauren Lincoln, office manager of your firm, accepted responsibility for scheduling a one-day regional conference of office managers to be held in your city 10 months from today. This conference is to be the first in a continuing series of annual conferences of the recently formed Southwestern Office Management Association (SOMA). Lincoln, a charter member of SOMA, is concerned that all details of the conference be, in her words, "done to perfection." This first conference is to be a model for all future conferences sponsored by SOMA. Other members of Lincoln's staff will be assigned to work on committees to arrange the conference.

Lincoln asks you, her assistant manager, to help in the scheduling effort. Since time permits, she requests that you develop a PERT chart with the necessary details for fulfilling all the responsibilities for this conference. Lincoln needs this information in order to estimate lead times for all future conferences.

The conference will start on a Saturday at 9 a.m. with 2 one-hour sessions interspersed with a half-hour coffee break. Spouses and friends of SOMA members will be able to participate in midmorning and midafternoon tours of your city's attractions, each tour taking three hours. There will be a keynote speaker following the luncheon. The afternoon program will commence at 1:30 with a one-hour session followed by a coffee break. The final session will begin at 3 p.m. and end at 4 p.m.

Lincoln has reviewed with you the following events that must be included in your PERT chart (others may need to be added):

1. One-day conference to be held.
2. Department secretary arranges for office staff meeting.
3. Agenda for staff meeting is prepared for discussion of committee assignments.
4. Committee on physical facilities is appointed.
5. Committee on meals and entertainment is appointed.
6. Program committee is appointed.
7. Program committee arranges for speakers from within your community.
8. Arrangements are made for physical facilities (meeting rooms, equipment, board and room accommodations, and the like).
9. Arrangements are made for luncheon.
10. Arrangements are made for tours of your city.
11. Conference program and reservation forms are mailed to all members of SOMA (the area served by this organization covers six southwestern states; potentially 250 members might attend).
12. Responses to mailed program and reservation forms are reviewed.
13. Reservations for meals are reported.
14. Reservations for hotels are reported.
15. All materials for the conference registration are prepared.
16. Registration of conference participants is held.
17. Morning sessions are held.
18. Tours of city are conducted.
19. Luncheon and after-luncheon speeches are held.
20. Afternoon sessions are held.
21. Coffee breaks are held.
22. Conference report is filed with committee in charge of next conference.

**Directions:** Working as a class or in small groups as directed, determine reasonable time estimates for completing the events outlined by Lincoln. Then prepare a PERT chart individually, giving special attention to identifying the critical path. Provide whatever explanatory information may be necessary to understand the chart.

Name ____________________ Date ____________________

# FLOW PROCESS CHART

**Chart No.** ________

**Date** ____________________

**Company** ____________________

| FORM NAME | FORM NO. | TOTAL COPIES |
|---|---|---|
| | | |

THIS IS A CHART OF System Origination ☐ Overall Procedure ☐ Copy Movement ☐

| Quantity Unit Charted | DISTANCE IN FEET OR METERS | TIME IN MINUTES | OPERATION | TRANSPORTATION | INSPECTION | DELAY | HELD FOR STORAGE | STEP NO. | DESCRIPTION OF STEP | WHO DOES IT? |
|---|---|---|---|---|---|---|---|---|---|---|
| | | | ○ | ⇨ | □ | D | ▽ | | | |
| | | | ○ | ⇨ | □ | D | ▽ | | | |
| | | | ○ | ⇨ | □ | D | ▽ | | | |
| | | | ○ | ⇨ | □ | D | ▽ | | | |
| | | | ○ | ⇨ | □ | D | ▽ | | | |
| | | | ○ | ⇨ | □ | D | ▽ | | | |
| | | | ○ | ⇨ | □ | D | ▽ | | | |
| | | | ○ | ⇨ | □ | D | ▽ | | | |
| | | | ○ | ⇨ | □ | D | ▽ | | | |
| | | | ○ | ⇨ | □ | D | ▽ | | | |
| | | | ○ | ⇨ | □ | D | ▽ | | | |
| | | | ○ | ⇨ | □ | D | ▽ | | | |
| | | | ○ | ⇨ | □ | D | ▽ | | | |
| | | | ○ | ⇨ | □ | D | ▽ | | | |
| | | | ○ | ⇨ | □ | D | ▽ | | | |
| | | | ○ | ⇨ | □ | D | ▽ | | | |
| | | | ○ | ⇨ | □ | D | ▽ | | | |
| | | | ○ | ⇨ | □ | D | ▽ | | | |
| | | | ○ | ⇨ | □ | D | ▽ | | | |
| | | | ○ | ⇨ | □ | D | ▽ | | | |

## Project 21–3 • Integrating Human Resources and Payroll into One Information System

The following article stresses that although it may be an uneasy alliance, human resources people and payroll professionals must learn to work together to prosper in the 1990s. The author of this article, Dan Harriger, is human resource product manager at AbraCadabra Software, a St. Petersburg, Florida-based company that develops PC-based HR and payroll processing software.

After you have read the article, answer the questions that follow.

### HR and Payroll

As a human resources professional, I've experienced first-hand the uneasy alliance between HR Professionals and Payroll Professionals. I've seen competition spark and grow between the two departments. With recent technological changes, I've also been fortunate enough to see the outline of solutions that will help payroll and human resources overcome their differences and work together in the coming decade.

Successful management of labor is probably the most important challenge facing business in the 1990s. And payroll is as vital to the strategic management of labor as it is to accounting. Payroll departments are becoming increasingly important in building strong employee relationships within an organization.

The new emphasis on labor in the 1990s empowers professionals in both human resource and payroll departments. Although it adds pressure to perform job tasks effectively, it also underscores the importance of these departments, giving them due recognition. Most importantly, it increases the urgency for these professionals to share information that will allow them to do their jobs more efficiently and guide management decisions better. To make it work, systems integration between HR and payroll is imperative.

#### Confession: Computers Helped Create the Conflict

All companies have three basic information systems: employee information, payroll information, and staffing information. Regardless of size, every organization tracks the names, addresses, jobs, pay rates, and emergency contacts of its staff, at the very least. All organizations also hire and fire employees.

In many respects, human resources and payroll information systems have always been integrated. We have always shared the same information; we just copied pertinent text or entered the data twice. Automation has merely replaced the filing cabinet with computers.

Unfortunately, automation (or available technology) has helped create conflicts between human resource and payroll departments. Part of the reason this occurred was because payroll functions were automated much sooner than human resource functions.

Payroll departments, which need to do multiple calculations very rapidly, have usually been assigned to mainframe computers. In the past, human resource computer systems often were designed along the lines of financial systems (if HR was automated at all). These systems did not really meet the needs of most HR departments.

The evolution of PC (personal computer) technology has helped many human resource departments automate. PC-based relational databases have made human resource information systems much less expensive, and much more obtainable, for smaller HR departments. And networking and powerful 386 technology have led to feature-rich PC-based HR systems that even the largest firms can use.

Many payroll systems run successfully on the mainframe (and who wants to argue with success?) and HR systems run well on the PC. Both are automated but separate, with no easy way to communicate from one to the other. The result: Duplicated data and interdepartmental conflict.

The good news is the development of powerful PC-based applications that encourage shared data. This makes it possible for human resource and payroll departments to share information quickly and easily. You don't even have to submit an MIS requisition. Virtually all current HR and payroll systems incorporate import and export routines that permit the exchange of at least an ASCII file for data transfer. And in many cases, PC technology is replacing mainframes altogether.

Source: Dan Harriger, "HR and Payroll," *PaytecH* (March/April 1993), pp. 30 and 31. Reprinted by permission of the American Payroll Institute, Inc, © 1993.

### Let's Learn to Live Together

Nobody can argue that to survive in the 1990s, payroll and HR departments have to become partners with line management. To have a strong, qualified, and loyal labor force, today's organizations must reevaluate employee policies, from family leave to health benefits.

A recent University of North Carolina survey of the top CEOs in the United States revealed that the top challenge for managing labor is to provide individualized productivity measurement, individualized benefits programs, and performance based compensation, all in a nontraditional workforce.

This will require a coordinated effort between payroll and HR to build strong employee relationships. These relationships could mean the difference between survival and failure for the companies. Employee relationships will determine which organizations are able to turn a profit in the 21st century.

The buzzword in many companies is TQM, Total Quality Management. It is as important to employee services as it is to product output. Payroll is on the cutting edge when it comes to operating a cost efficient, effective department that contributes to an overall TQM plan.

Survival for HR, payroll, and entire organizations will depend on TQM. One of the advantages of instituting a TQM program geared toward the labor challenges of the '90s is benefit cost containment. An organization can actually save money by restructuring medical, dental, vision, and prescription plans to meet the specific needs of the new workforce. With the right systems and the right integration between payroll and HR, an organization can tailor cost-effective plans for each kind of family in the workforce. It saves money for the company and time and frustration for the employee.

### It's Coming, So Be Prepared

Payroll *can* and *should* play a large role in providing decision support systems to guide personnel and budget decisions. At many of today's companies, payroll *already* plays this role. Linking payroll and human resources today will build the foundation for the management information systems of the future.

The next step for both HR and payroll departments is effective position control, meaning the ability to track not just people, but positions with organizations. Payroll departments will be called upon to provide up-to-the-minute reports on staffing levels, productivity needs, projected costs, time-based actual costs, and budget variances.

Managing labor and positions will undoubtedly fall under the job description of both payroll and HR departments. Payroll will be an integral part of a larger management system that includes HRMS, payroll, position control, training, staffing, and management succession.

What can you, the Payroll Professional, do to be prepared? Here are a few suggestions that will make your job easier—and make you very popular with your colleagues in HR—during the critical times ahead.

- Form a committee with your human resource counterparts. Yes, I've heard that a mule is a horse designed by committee, but it doesn't have to work that way. Accept the fact that any barriers between the organizations must come down and a spirit of cooperation must prevail. One of the biggest mistakes I ever made with payroll was to assume that the "other side" didn't really want to work together.
- Jointly identify the "customers" of your end product. Don't make the mistake of assuming that they consist only of employees. What about employees' dependents? Other staff, line, and senior management? Do benefit plan providers and administrators use your reports? Are there other vendors that depend on you to provide data to do their jobs?
- Identify the needs of your customers, then rank them by level of importance. Is an accurate paycheck delivered on time more important than the efficient handling of medical claims?
- Test your perceptions. Ask your "customers" if your list is accurate. As I learned while working for a major manufacturer, perceptions from the office do not always match realities on the shop floor.
- Reconvene and reassess your strategy. Are you spending too much time worrying about one area and not enough on another? What communication areas between payroll and human resources block your path to the joint goal of satisfying the needs of your customers? Does a form need to be redesigned? Can the problems be resolved with policy adjustments or procedural changes? Perhaps there is a hardware or software solution to make life easier.
- Most importantly, present a unified presence. Don't comment on an employee problem with "It's personnel's problem, not mine." Vice versa, I admonish any human resource professionals who are reading this article to refrain from doing the same. The responsibility for problems and their solutions must be joint efforts.

For both payroll and human resource organizations to survive the 1990s the philosophy I recommend is "Yes, I am my brother's keeper."

Name ______________________ Date ______________ 

1. In what respects have the human resource and the payroll information systems always been integrated?

______________________________________________

______________________________________________

______________________________________________

2. How has the evolution of personal computer technology helped human resource departments become automated?

______________________________________________

______________________________________________

______________________________________________

3. What is the interrelationship beween human resource and payroll systems and total quality management?

______________________________________________

______________________________________________

______________________________________________

4. How does a payroll department provide effective position control?

______________________________________________

______________________________________________

______________________________________________

5. Other than a firm's employees, who may be considered "customers" of the HR and payroll departments?

______________________________________________

______________________________________________

______________________________________________

# Project 21–4 • Installing a New System Could Put Your Job on the Line

The author of this article, William Sunderland III, is a Certified Payroll Professional with Holnam, Inc. In this article, Mr. Sunderland offers some humorous tips on how to save your neck at the time of installing a new system, whether it is designed for payroll operations or an administrative service.

**Directions:** Just read and enjoy the article—no questions at the end to be answered!

## Systems Development and Job Retention

There are two ways to make a payroll person shudder involuntarily. One is to scrape a fingernail across a blackboard, and the other is to use the word "system" in a sentence. For example, "The system just went down," or the early morning death knell, "The system blew up last night." Often, these are the result of poor system planning. Much to our chagrin, a well-known mathematician, Cletus Yentl Abercrombie, has proven by the use of differential calculus and a Nintendo power pad that poor system planning is inevitable. Hence, it becomes your duty to see to it that someone else takes the blame.

To better understand what happens during these sad times, let us define this ghastly term "systems" in connection with the payroll process. Webster's explains system in this manner (among others): "The state or condition of harmonious, orderly interaction." Those of us who have toiled in payroll view the word in a different light:

**System**—An automated operation which for no apparent reason either ceases to function or produces results which no one in their wildest dreams could have predicted.

Armed with this definition, this piece will explain the main steps of systems development as they really happen, and how you can escape the inevitable terminations which will result when the system is implemented.

### System Definition

This step defines what the system is supposed to do. For example, "This system will automatically calculate gross-ups so that I can take longer lunches," is a common definition. It is important to make the system definition as vague as possible. If someone comes back to you complaining about what the system is doing, you can always say, "Look at the system definition; that's not what I wanted the system to do." Do not spend much time on this step; you can better protect yourself in later steps.

### System Flow

This step diagrams how data will move through the system and what will happen to it as it flows. Go through your desk and find that flowcharting template you haven't used since EDP 101. Take a blank sheet of paper and use your template to draw boxes, triangles, and lines which do not connect. Label each box with titles such as 'Master File', 'Detail File', 'Work File', 'Nail File'. Label each triangle with titles such as 'Sort', 'Merge', 'Smash', and 'Fondle'. Occasionally draw numbers in circles in the margin. These are called 'off-page connectors' and are only useful if you limit your flowchart to one page. Show your creation to one of your systems people while using sentences like "This master file will be sorted in a work file and concatenated to the detail file in order to provide a smooth finish for the nail file." Believe me, they won't know what you're saying either, but will still try to perform the next step.

### System Coding

Your unwillingness to be precise in your system definition or be logical in your system flow will pay off handsomely in this step. The poor slob assigned to actually coding the programs and job streams must now coordinate two unrelated documents into a functioning system. Hah! Next we will ask him/her to balance the federal budget, no? The programmer will occasionally return with questions, which should always be answered with data processing jargon. This will make the programmer feel that you know more than he or she, and should prevent future questions. A sample answer would be "The load library and the step catalog are subject to a delete/define and the database must contain VSAM, VTAM, HISAM,

Source: William Sunderland III, CPP, "Systems Development and Job Retention," *Payroll Exchange* (May, 1989), pp. 8, 9, and 16. Reprinted by permission of the American Payroll Institute. © 1989.

HIDAM, and WHAM features." Your programmer's facial expression will remind you of someone who has just discovered they came for dinner on the wrong day.

### System Testing

It is an industry standard to play the theme from "Jaws" on your company loudspeaker while going through the testing stage. ("Taps" will come later.) This is the most crucial period of implementation. If you tell everyone that the testing phase went well without qualifying what you say, you will be the first one fired when the system fails (and it *will* fail!). You must qualify your remarks to protect your future employment. Luckily for you, we have a suggested comment which you can tailor to suit your own environment: "Within the constraints of (*your company's name*)'s corporate philosophy, bounded further by the needs of (*your division name*), restricted further still by the overwhelming budgetary limits of (*your computer department's name*), and potentially compacted by the inept capabilities of (*person you dislike in the department*), this system performed as expected." This means it didn't work.

### Live Cutover

This is it: the moment of truth. Your system, no matter how badly it is designed, no matter how poor your instructions, will defy the laws of averages and those against cruel and unusual punishment—it will work, and work well. Your superiors, peers, and subordinates (assuming you have any by this time) will be amazed. You will be smug. Checks are printing, reports are crossfooting, interfaces are balancing, and you are in control. Cherish this moment—you will need to recall it some day when the system fails.

### System Failure

After a grace period directly proportional in length to the number of things you did that your mother never would have approved of, the system will begin to experience seizures, hiccups, uncontrollable flatulence, or complete heart failure. You must act quickly to place blame elsewhere. If you have followed the procedures above, there should be plenty of other people whom you can confidently finger as the culprits. You were only directing their work, right? To be safe, shoulder a small portion of the blame by saying, "If only I had eyes in the back of my head, I could have watched them more carefully." Your boss will nod in sympathy and appoint you project leader of the team which will develop the replacement system.

### System Replacement

Take your pick; you can either go to the top of this article and begin again or you can do it right this time. As for me, I think I'll change jobs before my boss reads this. Good luck!

## Project 21–5 • Preparing a Forms Distribution Chart

**Directions:** Using the order-writing procedure given below, prepare a forms distribution chart that shows the sequence of office operations.

### ORDER-WRITING PROCEDURE

A sales order clerk receives incoming orders from customers who have prepared their own purchase orders, from customers who have FAXED or called in telephone orders, from the company's sales representatives who complete orders while visiting customers, and from letters and postal cards from customers. The sales order clerk must edit each incoming order and make any necessary corrections and substitutions. This person is also responsible for checking the customer's credit standing with accounts receivable. Accounts receivable uses *Dun & Bradstreet* and other credit reporting agencies.

After the customer's credit is approved, the incoming order is given to the data-entry operator who keys in and prints out two copies of an invoice order form (the shipping order and the packing list), which are sent to the shipping room. The customer's original order is filed alphabetically.

When the order is filled in the shipping room, the shipping clerk records the quantity shipped on the shipping order copy. The shipping clerk then sends this copy to the office. The packing list copy is completed and inserted by the shipping clerk into the package for shipment. When the shipping order copy is received in the office, the data-entry operator calls up from computer storage the invoice order form. Variable information such as date shipped, name of carrier, quantity back ordered, number of cartons or units shipped, and unit price are keyed in by the operator. The quantity shipped and unit price of each item are automatically extended and the items in the amount column are totaled. Three copies are printed out: two copies (the original invoice and one copy) for mailing to the customer and one copy (posting) that is routed to accounts receivable. In case there is a back order, this procedure is repeated, with the back order looked upon as a new order.

22

# IMPROVING OFFICE PRODUCTIVITY

Administrative office managers have an ongoing responsibility for improving office productivity through quality management. The measurement of work and setting standards, as part of this program, can prove economically feasible for many organizations and bring about a substantial improvement in productivity. However, there are many office workers—possibly 90 percent of the total workforce—over whom effective measurement control has never been extended. Why?

Reasons given for failing to establish a work measurement program include: office work is impossible to measure; the measurement of office work is difficult and too costly; there is no need for measurement in many offices since the number of workers is so few; and, unfortunately, some managers do not want to "rock the boat" on their tranquil sea of apathy. Most of the explanations offered for the lack of interest in measuring office work, like those cited, are more imaginary than real.

Work is work, whether it is done with steel or paper, whether we operate a lathe or a computer terminal. Some mental effort and physical energy are required to complete a unit of work, and the amount of productive activity needed to accomplish a job can be measured. To do so, however, a program of office work measurement and standards setting must be supported by managers at all levels—those for whom the tool has been designed. Employees must understand the program and be honestly informed as to how it will affect them and their jobs. Further, the program must be administered by first-line supervisors, truly the backbone of successful work measurement.

Finally, through quality management, supervisors and their managers systematically and continuously improve the quality of their products, services, and life using all available human and capital resources, including *time.*

## SECTION A • REVIEW QUESTIONS

**Directions:** Indicate your answer to each of the following questions by circling "Yes" or "No" in the Answers column.

| | Answers | |
|---|---|---|
| 1. Does work measurement involve *quantitative* as well as *qualitative* measurement? | Yes | No |
| 2. Are office work standards developed with the objective of obtaining at least 85 percent efficiency? | Yes | No |
| 3. Do highly routine and repetitive office tasks lend themselves to measurement and the setting of work standards? | Yes | No |
| 4. Is the grapevine an effective communication medium for informing office employees about the nature and objectives of a work measurement program? | Yes | No |
| 5. Are the techniques used to measure the output of production workers equally applicable when measuring the output of office workers? | Yes | No |
| 6. Is the weighted-line count an effective base for measuring production in a word processing center? | Yes | No |
| 7. Is the time log method of work measurement a relatively expensive technique to administer? | Yes | No |
| 8. Is the number of observations to be made in a work sampling study related to the tolerance factor? | Yes | No |
| 9. Is the major disadvantage of work sampling the need for trained analysts to set up the study and perform the required observations? | Yes | No |

| | | | |
|---|---|---|---|
| 10. | Does a quality control program aim at recognizing and removing the identifiable causes of defects and variations from the standards that have been set? . . . . . . . . . . . . . . . . . . . . . . . . . . | Yes | No |
| 11. | When predetermined times are used to set standards, can stopwatch time studies be eliminated on many job studies? . . . . . . . . . . . . . . . . . . . . . . . . . . . . . . . . . . . . . . . . . . . . . . . . . . . . . . . . . . | Yes | No |
| 12. | Can most kinds of nonroutine work be measured by traditional motion and time study methods? | Yes | No |
| 13. | Are most middle-management positions immune from a firm's downsizing efforts? . . . . . . . . | Yes | No |
| 14. | Do self-managed teams often make decisions that are traditionally reserved for management? | Yes | No |
| 15. | In the operation of a quality circle, does the facilitator select the problems that will be solved by the group? . . . . . . . . . . . . . . . . . . . . . . . . . . . . . . . . . . . . . . . . . . . . . . . . . . . . . . . . . . . . . | Yes | No |
| 16. | Does the time log method lend itself to measuring the time required by managers to complete various tasks throughout the workday? . . . . . . . . . . . . . . . . . . . . . . . . . . . . . . . . . . . . . . . . . . . | Yes | No |
| 17. | Are the manager's time wasters created only by internally created factors? . . . . . . . . . . . . . . . | Yes | No |

**Directions:** In the Answers column, write the letter of the item in Column 1 that is described by each statement in Column 2.

**Column 1**

**A** Benchmarking
**B** Historical data
**C** Motion study
**D** Performance rating
**E** Predetermined times
**F** Quality circle
**G** Quality control
**H** Time log
**I** Time management
**J** Time study
**K** Work measurement
**L** Work sampling
**M** Work standard

| **Column 2** | **Answers** |
|---|---|
| 1. A regulatory process in which the quality of performance is measured and compared with standards so that any difference between performance and standards may be acted upon . . . . . . . . | 1.______ |
| 2. The adjustment of individual differences obtained in stopwatch studies in order to obtain a theoretical normal time required by average workers to complete their jobs under standardized conditions . . . . . . . . . . . . . . . . . . . . . . . . . . . . . . . . . . . . . . . . . | 2.______ |
| 3. A work measurement method in which past production records are studied to measure what was produced in the past . . . . . . . . . . . . | 3.______ |
| 4. A work measurement method in which work is divided into its fundamental elements, which are studied and timed in order to eliminate wasteful movement and effort . . . . . . . . . . . . . . . . . . . . | 4.______ |
| 5. A work measurement method based on the law of probability in which findings representative of the universe are obtained by taking valid random samples of work done . . . . . . . . . . . . . . . . . . | 5.______ |
| 6. A work measurement method in which workers measure their output by recording the time spent and units of work produced for a stipulated time period . . . . . . . . . . . . . . . . . . . . . . . . . . . . . . . | 6.______ |
| 7. A work measurement method that determines the time required to perform each operation at an average pace . . . . . . . . . . . . . . . . . . | 7.______ |
| 8. A yardstick of performance that indicates what is expected of a worker and how the output can be evaluated . . . . . . . . . . . . . . . . . | 8.______ |
| 9. The constant time values applied to basic motions of each job element so that the time value for performing the entire job may be read from a table in order to set time standards . . . . . . . . . . . . | 9.______ |
| 10. The process of using efficiently all resources, including time, so that individuals are productive in achieving their professional and personal goals . . . . . . . . . . . . . . . . . . . . . . . . . . . . . . . . . . . . . . . . . . | 10.______ |

## SECTION B • PROJECTS

# Project 22–1 • Measuring Work and Setting Standards: Direct Observation and Wristwatch Desk Audit

This project introduces you to a relatively simple, economical approach to measuring routine, repetitive office tasks and setting standard unit times. As an analyst, you will directly observe a typical office task being performed at the worker's desk. Your instructor will select the office worker and provide all materials needed for performing the task. The only materials you will need are a wristwatch (or stopwatch), a pencil, and the Direct Observation Work Sheet, which is described later.

Before measuring the work, you must become familiar with the series of operations that comprise the "transaction." On the job, the analyst breaks down the work transaction into its component parts, known as operations, by performing a preliminary *desk audit.* During the audit, the analyst becomes familiar with the work being performed and the workflow, makes sure that each transaction can be counted, and establishes a method of counting the transactions.

In this project, the transaction to be studied and measured is one of checking, collating, and attaching, which is performed by a worker in the order processing and billing department. The operations that make up this transaction are:

1. Remove a batch of shipping orders, labeled A (Color No. 1), from the "In" basket and position on the desk. Figure 22–1 shows the location of all materials at the workstation.
2. Remove a batch of shipping orders, labeled B (Color No. 2), from the "In" basket and locate on the desk.
3. Remove from the desk drawer all supplies needed—pencils, paper clips, and a box of shipping labels—and position on the desk.
4. Place a check mark (✔) in the upper right corner of shipping order A and shipping order B.
5. Collate the two shipping orders, A over B, and staple in the upper left corner.
6. Remove a blank shipping label from the box, and paper clip the label to the shipping orders in the upper left corner.
7. Place the completed set—shipping orders A and B and label attached—in the "Out" basket.

Using only a wristwatch limits the amount of detail that can be accurately included in a measurement study. For example, basic motions such as "grasp," "reach," and "transport," and operation elements such as "position papers" and "attach paper clip" are of too short a duration to be timed successfully. Therefore, in this project the timing will include the entire transaction—checking, collating, and attaching. However, this approach should be sufficiently detailed to take into account the frequency of any irregular occurrences for which some adjustment may be necessary before standard unit times are determined.

On the job, the analyst would observe more than one person doing this type of work in the order processing and billing department. Fully trained, representative workers, selected by an operating manager on the basis

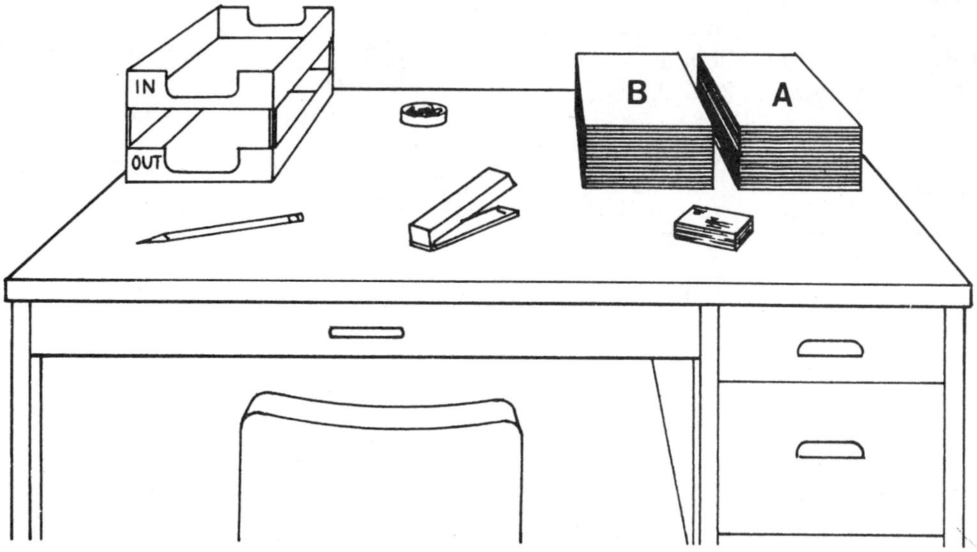


**Figure 22–1 Workstation Layout for the Transaction of Checking, Collating, and Attaching**

of the employees' satisfactory past performance, would be studied so that sufficient data may be gathered from several workers for each transaction, and the unit time for each person compared with one another. In this project, however, you will study the output of only one worker—the one selected by your instructor.

As an analyst, you have become technically competent and are able to put the employees at ease and establish personal rapport with them. You display an objective empathy in which you treat the people being studied exactly the same as if the roles were reversed.

**Directions:**

1. Situate yourself so that you can observe what the employee is doing, without disrupting the work being performed. Be prepared to note any irregularities that may occur. For example, there may be interruptions for personal time or for unrelated business reasons. Or, unusual and nonrecurring events of one sort or another may take place. Your identification of the reasons for these interruptions will be useful in analyzing the observations.

2. Using the Direct Observation Work Sheet shown on page 243, record all times (starting, excluded, and stopped) to the nearest half-minute. On the job, observations should be taken continuously until sufficient data have been accumulated. For the purpose of this project, however, your instructor will indicate the time allotted for your observations. To determine the unit time, divide the total work time by the total units processed.

3. Along with others in your class who may be called upon to directly observe the work being performed, and with the others who are "auditing" this project, discuss ways in which the quantity of output may be increased by the worker. For example, what suggestions have you for rearranging the materials on the desk to simplify the work, eliminate needless body motions, reduce employee fatigue, and increase productivity?

4. After you have discussed all suggestions for improving the workflow and layout of the workstation, ask the worker to implement your recommended changes and prepare to be studied again. After you have recorded the times again on the Direct Observation Work Sheet, determine to what extent the revisions in the workflow and layout have affected the total output and the unit times.

## Project 22–2 • Computer Hands-On: Using Work Sampling to Determine Standard Times

In using work sampling to measure output and to set standards for four data-entry clerks in the purchasing department of your company, you have obtained the summary data shown in template file PO22-2.TEM. During the study you found that each of the four clerks was available for work as shown on PO22-2.TEM.

**Directions:** Based upon the given data, prepare a report in which you:

1. Determine the unit time or standard for each activity studied.

2. Calculate whether a large enough sample was taken to provide for your planned sample size, when $T = .10$, $P = .05$, and reliability is 95 percent.

   a. If the number of observations made ($N = 3{,}500$) was not great enough to meet your specifications, how many more observations will be needed?

   b. What percentage of reliability was obtained with $N = 3{,}500$? Is this percentage of reliability sufficient for most work sampling purposes?

## DIRECT OBSERVATION WORK SHEET

**Division** Order Processing & Billing

**Section** Midwest States

**Transaction Work Code No. 1** ______________

Checking, Collating, and Attaching ______________

**Position/Name** Order Clerk/ ______________

**Date** __________ **AM PM** **Observed by** __________

| Starting Time | Minutes Excluded* | Time Stopped | Work Code | Units Processed | Work Time | Unit Time | Remarks |
|---|---|---|---|---|---|---|---|
| | | | FIRST OBSERVATION | | | | |
| | | | | | | | |
| | | | | | | | |
| | | | | | | | |
| | | | | | | | |
| | | | | | | | |
| | | | | | | | |
| | | | | | | | |
| | | | | | | | |
| | | | | | | | |
| | | | | | | | |
| | | | SECOND OBSERVATION | | | | |
| | | | | | | | |
| | | | | | | | |
| | | | | | | | |
| | | | | | | | |
| | | | | | | | |
| | | | | | | | |
| | | | | | | | |
| | | | | | | | |
| | | | | | | | |

*Nonwork Time.

# Project 22–3 • Calling Upon the TD to Monitor and Control ERT by Establishing an RTP

The following article is included solely for your reading enjoyment. But, stretch your imagination and see if you can envision policies such as the RTP making their appearance in the years ahead! Too far-fetched? Think about it!!

## Raising Your Hand Just Won't Do

**by Gary T. Marx**

As part of a research project on productivity, I recently came across the following innovative policy just adopted by a major corporation. It might serve as a model for other companies wrestling with this problem.

TO: ALL EMPLOYEES

FROM: EMPLOYEE RELATIONS DEPARTMENT

SUBJECT: RESTROOM TRIP POLICY (RTP)

An internal audit of employee restroom time (ERT) has found that this company significantly exceeds the national ERT standard recommended by the President's Commission on Productivity and Waste. At the same time, some employees complained about being unfairly singled out for ERT monitoring. Technical Division (TD) has developed an accounting and control system that will solve problems.

Effective 1 April 1987, a Restroom Trip Policy (RTP) is established.

A Restroom Trip Bank (RTB) will be created for each employee. On the first day of each month employees will receive a Restroom Trip Credit (RTC) of 40. The previous policy of unlimited trips is abolished.

Restroom access will be controlled by a computer-linked voice-print recognition system. Within the next two weeks, each employee must provide two voice prints (one normal, one under stress) to Personnel. To facilitate familiarity with the system, voice-print recognition stations will be operational but not restrictive during the month of April.

Should an employee's RTB balance reach zero, restroom doors will not unlock for his/her voice until the first working day of the following month.

Restroom stalls have been equipped with timed tissue-roll retraction and automatic flushing and door-opening capability. To help employees maximize their time, a simulated voice will announce elapsed ERT up to 3 minutes. A 30-second warning buzzer will then sound. At the end of the 30 seconds the roll of tissue will retract, the toilet will flush, and the stall door will open. Employees may choose whether they wish to hear a male or female "voice." A bilingual capability is being developed, but is not yet online.

To prevent unauthorized access (e.g., sneaking in behind someone with an RTB surplus, or use of a tape-recorded voice), video cameras in the corridor will record those seeking access to the restroom. However, consistent with the company's policy of respecting the privacy of its employees, cameras will not be operative within the restroom itself.

An additional advantage of the system is its capability for automatic urine analysis (AUA). This permits drug testing without the demeaning presence of an observer and without risk of human error in switching samples. The restrooms and associated plumbing are the property of the company. Legal Services has advised that there are no privacy rights over voluntarily discarded garbage and other like materials.

In keeping with our concern for employee privacy, participation in AUA is strictly voluntary. But employees who choose to participate will be eligible for attractive prizes in recognition of their support for the company's policy of a drug-free workplace.

Management recognizes that from time to time employees may have a legitimate need to use the restroom. But employees must also recognize that their jobs depend on this company's staying competitive in a global economy. These conflicting interests should be weighed, but certainly not balanced. The company remains strongly committed to finding technical solutions to management problems. We continue to believe that machines are fairer and more reliable than managers. We also believe that our trusted employees will do the right thing when given no other choice.

# Project 22–4 • Field Research: Examining Office Productivity Improvement Programs

Although most organizations express concern about their office workers' level of output, not all have established formal programs designed to improve worker productivity. Instead, in many instances, companies take isolated steps to boost productivity rather than inaugurate a formal productivity improvement program. In this field research project, you will investigate one or more companies in your community to identify those measures being taken to improve office productivity.

**Directions:** Either singly or in small groups, as directed by your instructor, use the following checklist to determine the existence and the nature of office productivity improvement programs among companies—large and small—in your community. Your instructor will indicate whether oral or written reporting is required.

## A CHECKLIST FOR DETERMINING OFFICE PRODUCTIVITY IMPROVEMENT PROGRAMS

Name of Company Contacted ____________________________________________

Name and Title of Person Interviewed ____________________________________________

____________________________________________

Number of Persons Employed __________________ Number of Office/Clerical Workers__________________

*Use a check mark, where appropriate*

Manufacturing ____________ Nonmanufacturing ____________

Profit-Making Organization ____________ Not-for-Profit Organization ____________

Ongoing, formal productivity improvement program? Yes_________ No _________

**Financial Incentive Plans:**

*Group*

_____ Profit-sharing

_____ Employee stock ownership

_____ Scanlon

_____ Gain-sharing

_____ Other (specify)

*Individual*

_____ Merit increases

_____ Performance bonuses

_____ Units of production (piecework)

_____ Award/recognition programs (indicate kind of programs)

_____ Other (specify)

_____ No financial incentive programs

**Nonfinancial Productivity Improvement Programs:**

_____ New training and development programs

_____ Employee participation programs

_____ Flexible work schedules

_____ Work simplification

_____ Job enlargement

_____ Employee health and fitness programs

_____ Job enrichment

_____ Rotation of work assignments

_____ Job specialization

_____ Compressed workweek

_____ Job sharing

_____ Other (specify)

**Kinds of Worker Participation Programs in Operation:**

_____ Self-managed, or self-directed, teams

_____ Employee-management committees

_____ Quality circles

_____ Supervisory training programs

_____ Employee problem-solving groups

_____ Other (specify)

**Some questions to be asked of person interviewed:**

1. What has been the effect of your firm's productivity improvement program?
2. What specific positive results can you cite that were attributable to your firm's productivity improvement program? Any negative outcomes?
3. Has any research been undertaken to measure and evaluate the specific effects of the productivity improvement program?
4. What are your firm's future plans regarding productivity improvement programs?

## Project 22–5 • To Downsize or Not to Downsize?

This reading points out that even though pink slips are still slipping and the fat is long gone, organizations are now cutting dangerously into muscle.

### When Downsizing Becomes "Dumbsizing"

Rightsizing. Restructuring. Downsizing. The terms are cold and unemotional. Yet the euphemisms of the early 1990s all mean the same thing: layoffs. Over the past five years, corporate America has been driven by a single-minded mission to gut itself of "excess workers." It was supposed to be the fastest and easiest way to cut business costs, be more competitive and raise profits—or at least that's what many top executives thought.

But there is mounting evidence that this slash-and-burn labor policy is backfiring. Studies now show that a number of companies that trimmed their workforces not only failed to see a rebound in earnings but found their ability to compete eroded even further. "What's happened shouldn't be called downsizing. It's dumbsizing," says Gerald Celente, director of the Trends Research Institute in Rhinebeck, New York. "All these firings are going to end up hurting our international competitiveness, not helping it."

Whatever it is called, its effect on the American economy has been painful and profound. More than 6 million permanent pink slips have been handed out since 1987, and layoffs are occurring at an even faster pace this year than in 1992. Despite signs of a brisker economy, at least 87 large firms announced major cuts in the first two months of 1993 alone.

What is so troubling is that while companies do trim a bloated workforce from time to time, many of the recent layoffs may not have been necessary. According to a new study by Wayne Cascio, a business professor at the University of Colorado, companies have too often assumed that if the competition was cutting costs by firing workers, then they had to follow suit. Compaq Computer, for example, announced last October that it was laying off 1,000 workers. Yet two weeks later, the company admitted that profits would double in 1992. Firms like General Electric and Campbell Soup continued to slash personnel even though they both just had highly profitable years. "There is tremendous peer pressure to get rid of workers," says A. Gary Shilling, an economic consultant. "Everybody's doing it because they think they have to."

But the deeper problem facing some companies was an inability to respond adroitly to changing markets, and decimating their workforces may have made that task even tougher when the recovery finally rolled around. "Just look at what they've done to IBM and Sears," says Celente. "They've cut the heart out of these companies. They are blaming an overstaffed workforce for bringing down profits. But that's not the real problem. These companies lost out competitively because they didn't change their products."

One of the most obvious effects of downsizing is that the employees who survive are forced to work longer and harder. In February the manufacturing workweek stretched to 41.5 hours, the longest in 27 years. The resulting increase in stress leads to discontent, lowers creativity and undermines corporate loyalty. A study by the American Management Association last year showed that of more than 500 firms surveyed that had cut jobs since 1987, more than 75% reported that employee morale had collapsed. Indeed, two-thirds of the companies showed no increase in efficiency at all and less than half saw any improvement in profits.

Not only was there often no payoff on the bottom line, but corporate chiefs who expected at least some applause from Wall Street for reducing labor costs also got a nasty shock. "Senior executives may think that a press release announcing layoffs sends a signal like, 'Look, I'm cutting costs, therefore reward me,'" says Carol Coles, president of Mitchell & Co., a manufacturing consulting firm in Waltham, Massachusetts. "But investors are a lot savvier than that. They know that firms that had major layoffs often have more significant problems. Streamlining a company does not push stock prices higher."

Coles studied 14 firms that announced major staff cuts during the 1980s and found that the rise in their stock prices lagged the overall market by 70% in the past three years. For example, Bethlehem Steel began laying off workers in 1986. Yet, its stock has fallen 50%,

Source: Bernard Baumohl, "When Downsizing Becomes 'Dumbsizing,'" *Time* (March 15, 1993), p. 55. 

in contrast to a rise of 48% by the S&P 500. Monsanto started cutting its workforce in 1985, but its stock rose a slim 30%. Clearly these were troubled companies that would probably have suffered sluggish stock prices in any event, but the study indicates that cutting labor costs did not make Wall Street forgive their more deep-seated problems.

"There is a reverential belief that during hard times, you can turn a company around, resuscitate its profitability and raise shareholder value by laying off workers," says Alexander Hiam, author of *Closing the Quality Gap.* "But that's a huge myth." For both individual companies and the economy as a whole, a true recovery may require dispelling that myth and focusing once again on real ways to increase performance and creativity.

**Directions:** Prepare a written or oral report, as directed by your instructor, in which you:

1. Interview a person (possibly yourself) who has been laid off by a company that has downsized. Collect information about factors such as (a) forewarning, if any, provided by the company; (b) outplacement services provided; (c) compensation received; and (d) attitude today toward the firm.
2. Also, contact a person (again, possibly yourself) who has survived downsizing. Report on points such as (a) effect upon the survivor's workload; (b) morale level among post-downsizing employees; and (c) tangible evidence of improved productivity, increased earnings, and firm's ability to compete.

# 23

# BUDGETING ADMINISTRATIVE EXPENSES

A company's budget and its performance reporting system form an essential management information and control system for all supervisory and management levels. An office manager relies on the budget and reports from the supervisory and department heads in order to control costs and to obtain accurate financial information quickly. After the *budget*—a planned program of estimated operating conditions for a future time period—has been developed, the office manager can periodically compare the actual operating data with the budgeted data in order to locate the differences in performance. After the differences, or variances, have been identified, the manager is able to investigate the causes of, and determine the responsibility for, variances. Thus, a program of reliable measurement and reporting of actual performance must be established so that costly delays will not prevent the manager from obtaining an explanation of significant variances and then taking the necessary corrective action.

## SECTION A • REVIEW QUESTIONS

**Directions:** Indicate your answer to each of the following questions by circling "Yes" or "No" in the Answers column.

| | Answers | |
|---|---|---|
| 1. Is the length of the budget period one year in most companies? | Yes | No |
| 2. Are budget performance reports used to compare actual operating data with budgeted data? | Yes | No |
| 3. Is the master budget usually prepared before the department budgets are submitted to the budget committee? | Yes | No |
| 4. Does a flexible budget show estimated costs at various levels of activity? | Yes | No |
| 5. Is the sales budget usually prepared before the general and administrative expenses budget? | Yes | No |
| 6. Do operating expenses, such as rent, sometimes pertain to more than one function? | Yes | No |
| 7. Should the initial responsibility for preparing budgets be assigned to top-level managers? | Yes | No |
| 8. Should a budget be flexible so that changes can be made in the event the organization is faced with an emergency? | Yes | No |
| 9. Is the administrative expenses budget prepared independently of the estimates made by those in charge of production and sales? | Yes | No |
| 10. Should administrative office managers be charged with responsibility for costs over which they have no control? | Yes | No |
| 11. On a cost-volume graph, are fixed costs represented by a line that slopes upward to the right? | Yes | No |
| 12. Do semivariable costs contain both fixed and variable cost components? | Yes | No |
| 13. Are indirect expenses often allocated among the user departments? | Yes | No |
| 14. Are chargeback accounting systems used to allocate the costs of office services? | Yes | No |
| 15. May incremental budgeting involve the addition of a given percentage of increase to the budgeted amounts of the preceding period to arrive at new figures? | Yes | No |
| 16. Does incremental budgeting effectively motivate managers to control the cost of allocating resources? | Yes | No |

17. In zero-base budgeting, are the budget figures based on a percentage of increase (or decrease) related to the previous budget period? . . . . . . . . . . . . . . . . . . . . . . . . . . . . . . . . . . Yes No

18. When comparing budgeted with actual expenses, may year-to-date cumulative figures be more significant than monthly figures? . . . . . . . . . . . . . . . . . . . . . . . . . . . . . . . . . . . . . . . . . . Yes No

19. Does the existence of a work standards program in the company impede the office manager's ability to prepare realistic budgets? . . . . . . . . . . . . . . . . . . . . . . . . . . . . . . . . . . . . . . . . . . . Yes No

20. Is the objective of cycle billing to distribute evenly throughout the month the work related to preparing and mailing the monthly statements of customers' accounts? . . . . . . . . . . . . . . . . . . Yes No

**Directions:** In the Answers column, write the letter of the item in Column 1 that is described by each statement in Column 2.

| Column 1 | Column 2 | Answers |
|---|---|---|
| **A** Budget | 1. The process of planning future business activities and expressing those plans in a formal manner . . . . . . . . . . . . . . . . . . . . . . . . . . . . . . | 1.______ |
| **B** Budgetary control | 2. A formal statement of plans for the future, expressed in financial terms | 2.______ |
| **C** Budgeting | 3. A budgeting method in which budget makers examine anew and justify each expenditure each budget period . . . . . . . . . . . . . . . . . . . . . . . . | 3.______ |
| **D** Chargeback accounting system | 4. The difference between actual operating data and budgeted data . . . . | 4.______ |
| **E** Direct expense | 5. A plan for directly allocating the costs of office services by charging each budgeting department or cost center for its actual use of the service . . . . . . . . . . . . . . . . . . . . . . . . . . . . . . . . . . . . . . . . . . . . . . . . . . | 5.______ |
| **F** Indirect expense | 6. An expense originating in and chargeable directly to one department . | 6.______ |
| **G** Variance | 7. A general expense that benefits several departments or the entire company but is not directly traceable to any one department . . . . . . . . | 7.______ |
| **H** Zero-base budgeting | | |

**Directions:** Classify each of the following kinds of office expenses by placing a check mark (✔) in either the Fixed Cost or the Variable Cost column.

| Office Expense | Fixed Cost | Variable Cost |
|---|---|---|
| 1. Rent of office space . . . . . . . . . . . . . . . . . . | ______ | ______ |
| 2. Real estate taxes . . . . . . . . . . . . . . . . . . . . | ______ | ______ |
| 3. Maintenance expense . . . . . . . . . . . . . . . . . | ______ | ______ |
| 4. Equipment repairs . . . . . . . . . . . . . . . . . . . | ______ | ______ |
| 5. Leasing of office equipment . . . . . . . . . . . | ______ | ______ |
| 6. Supervisory salaries . . . . . . . . . . . . . . . . . . | ______ | ______ |
| 7. Mailing expenses . . . . . . . . . . . . . . . . . . . . | ______ | ______ |
| 8. Depreciation expense on building . . . . . . . | ______ | ______ |
| 9. Property insurance . . . . . . . . . . . . . . . . . . . | ______ | ______ |
| 10. Stationery and supplies . . . . . . . . . . . . . . . | ______ | ______ |

## SECTION B • PROJECTS

### Project 23–1 • Preparing an Operating Budget

In the Santo Company, the text/word processing center houses all sales correspondents and word processing personnel. All written communications, except those that are highly confidential, are dictated and transcribed in this center. During the past two months, you have studied the correspondence costs and examined each of the cost items listed in Table 23–1. After talking with the workers in the center, you gained the impression that the costs and output during November and December were typical of other months of the year.

To measure output, you have adopted as your standard a one-page, single-spaced letter. During the two-month period, the output of first-class mail in the center was 9,600 one-page letters, 500 two-page letters, and 400 three-page letters. The number of form letters mailed was 10,000, but these required only the keyboarding of an inside address and inserting in window envelopes. (You estimate that this operation requires one-tenth the time a word processing operator uses in producing a one-page letter.)

You have learned from the sales department that next year's sales are estimated at $7.6 million—a 13 percent increase over this year's volume. Based on the sales department's projected volume, you anticipate that:

1. The monthly output in your center will increase 7 percent. You have taken into consideration the several vigorous sales campaigns planned for next year.
2. Salaries and benefits will increase 8 percent, on the average, next year.
3. One additional part-time operator will be hired July 1 at a cost of $9,500 for the six-month period. No additional personnel are planned for word origination, filing, and mailing.
4. The cost of office supplies has skyrocketed toward the end of the present year. You project that supplies for the next year will cost, on the average, 9 percent more than this year.
5. Recently you read that next year the USPS plans to increase the cost of first-class postage by 4 cents for the first ounce. First-class postage is now 29 cents for the first ounce.

**Table 23–1**
**COST COMPILATION**
**For November and December, 19—**

| Cost Item | Word Origination | Word Processing | Filing | Mailing |
|---|---|---|---|---|
| Salaries and benefits | $45,800 | $33,460 | $4,070 | $2,950 |
| Supplies | | 1,610 | 560 | 230 |
| Postage | | | | 5,950 |
| Depreciation: | | | | |
| Equipment | 880 | 3,800 | 330 | 290 |
| Furniture | 1,750 | 1,730 | 1,180 | 70 |
| Operating costs (rent, utilities, etc.) | 1,870 | 2,180 | 1,980 | 1,650 |
| Totals | $50,300 | $42,780 | $8,120 | $11,140 |

6. No additions are planned for equipment and furniture, with the exception of one unit of peripheral equipment to be installed in July. The purchase price of the new equipment is $6,000. The company uses the straight-line method of calculating depreciation, assuming a useful life of five years.
7. The annual operating expenses allocated to your center are to be increased as follows:

| COST ITEM | ANNUAL INCREASE |
|---|---|
| Rent | $250 |
| Telephone | 500 |
| Electricity | 800 |
| Insurance | 140 |
| Taxes | 90 |
| Maintenance | 600 |
| Miscellaneous | 250 |

**Directions**: Using the forms on page 255, prepare operating budgets for the word processing center for the next year and for the months of January and July. Round all estimated amounts to zero in the units position, as shown above in Table 23–1.

## Project 23–2 • Field Research: Investigating the Preparation of the Administrative Expenses Budget

Arrange for an interview with the person who prepares the administrative expenses budget at your place of employment, in a company within your community, or in the office of your school's business manager. The purpose of this interview is to learn about several phases of the budget-making process that are outlined below.

During your interview, obtain information that will enable you to present a written or oral report summarizing your findings. As part of your report, include a flowchart that shows each of the steps involved in the budget-making process.

1. Name of organization visited and title of person interviewed.

____________________

____________________

2. Description of the budgeting method in effect—incremental, flexible, zero base, compromise, etc.

____________________

____________________

3. Extent to which the office manager is involved in the budget-making process—responsibilities, kinds of reports prepared by the office manager, types of reports submitted to the office manager by department heads and supervisors.

____________________

____________________

4. Makeup of the budget committee, if used.

____________________

5. Listing of the major sections of the master budget. (If possible, include in your report a blank copy of the master and individual budgets.)

____________________

____________________

6. Evidence of involvement in the budgetary process by employees at the operative level.

____________________

____________________

7. How flexibility is provided in the budget in case adjustments are required in the event of emergencies such as a strike or a reduction in revenue.

____________________

____________________

8. Provisions made for periodic review of the budget.

____________________

9. Frequency of budget performance reporting; how the organization defines significant variance.

____________________

____________________

## OPERATING BUDGET FOR TEXT/WORD PROCESSING CENTER
for
Year Ended December 31, 19--

| Cost Item | Word Origination | Word Processing | Filing | Mailing |
|---|---|---|---|---|
| Salaries and benefits | | | | |
| Supplies . . . . . . . . . | | | | |
| Postage . . . . . . . . . | | | | |
| Depreciation:<br>Equipment . . . . . | | | | |
| Furniture . . . . . . | | | | |
| Operating costs (rent, utilities, etc.) . . . | | | | |
| Totals . . . . . . | | | | |

## OPERATING BUDGET FOR TEXT/WORD PROCESSING CENTER
for
January and July, 19--

| Cost Item | January | | | | July | | | |
|---|---|---|---|---|---|---|---|---|
| | Word Origination | Word Processing | Filing | Mailing | Word Origination | Word Processing | Filing | Mailing |
| Salaries and benefits | | | | | | | | |
| Supplies . . . . . . . . . | | | | | | | | |
| Postage . . . . . . . . . | | | | | | | | |
| Depreciation:<br>Equipment . . . . . | | | | | | | | |
| Furniture . . . . . . | | | | | | | | |
| Operating costs (rent, utilities, etc.) . . . | | | | | | | | |
| Totals . . . . . . | | | | | | | | |

# Project 23–3 • Computer Hands-On: Analyzing a Budget Performance Report

In the Lee Company, the office manager, Warren Williams, prepares the administrative expense budget, which is a composite of all the functional departments under his supervision. Each department head is asked to prepare on a standard form the budget figures for the next fiscal year. The budgeted and actual costs are analyzed on a monthly basis and later on a quarterly basis. Some of the costs submitted are fixed and thus are little affected by the volume of work to be done; other costs vary directly with the volume of work.

Your template file PO23-3.TEM shows the budget for the text/word processing center for the quarter ending March 31, 19--, in Table A, and the actual costs of the quarter in Table B. All costs are rounded to zero in the units position (the nearest ten dollars).

**Directions:** Prepare a quarterly comparison of the budgeted and the actual figures as follows:

1. On the performance report for the period ending March 31, show the budget year-to-date and the actual year-to-date figures.
2. On the March 31 report, show the dollar amount and the percentage of variance between the actual and the budgeted figures.
3. Indicate the possible causes of any variance of plus or minus 5 percent.
4. Compute the unit cost of each line produced during each month and the quarter, using the following output:

| | |
|---|---|
| January: | 423,600 lines |
| February: | 429,700 lines |
| March: | 459,400 lines |

5. Prepare a spreadsheet showing the budgeted costs for the next quarter. Use the actual costs for March as the basis for preparing your estimates. The estimated output for each month is:

| | |
|---|---|
| April: | 482,370 lines |
| May: | 496,152 lines |
| June: | 505,340 lines |

## CROSSWORD PUZZLE 4

### Across

1. Organization of American States
6. Old Thailand
8. Spoken
9. Italian Pie
11. Consultant to quality circle
15. Antique
17. Degree
19. Desired degree of accuracy
21. Random-access memory
22. Motion picture study
24. Filing of information
25. Productive activity
30. Given percentage of increase
32. Proofreading and checking
36. Costs responding to volume changes
37. Account
38. Journey
40. Record of work activities
41. Movement of materials
43. Some
45. Pro and
47. Try
48. Definable unit of work
50. Point in time on PERT chart
51. Representative of whole group
53. Informal communication channel
54. Operations _______
58. Doing the right thing
59. Pause in workflow
61. Yardstick of performance
63. In accordance with the law
64. Make payment
65. Ideal
68. Partly fixed and partly variable costs
69. Business document
70. Streamline
71. Generally accepted accounting principles
72. Data keyed in

### Down

1. Officer
2. Administrative assistant
3. Deceptive act
4. Two, prefix
5. Price
7. Ideal form
8. Video display terminal
9. Type size
10. ____-base budgeting
12. Find
13. General operating expenses
14. Baseball stat.
16. Make better
18. Expenses benefiting several departments
20. The whole amount
23. _______ Group Technique
26. Operating in economical manner
27. Originated motion studies
28. _______circle
29. Linear ______
31. Difference
33. New Testament
34. Basic model
35. Program Evaluation and Review Technique
39. Chart showing sequence of steps
42. Model of real-world system
44. See 9 down
45. Merge
46. Statement of future financial plans
49. Compares output with performance standards
51. Set of related elements
52. Performance rating
55. _____-world system
56. System's goal
57. Critical _____ Method
59. Short for demonstration
60. Long Island
62. Wet
65. Uniform
66. Poland
67. Automatic direction finder

# CROSSWORD PUZZLE 4

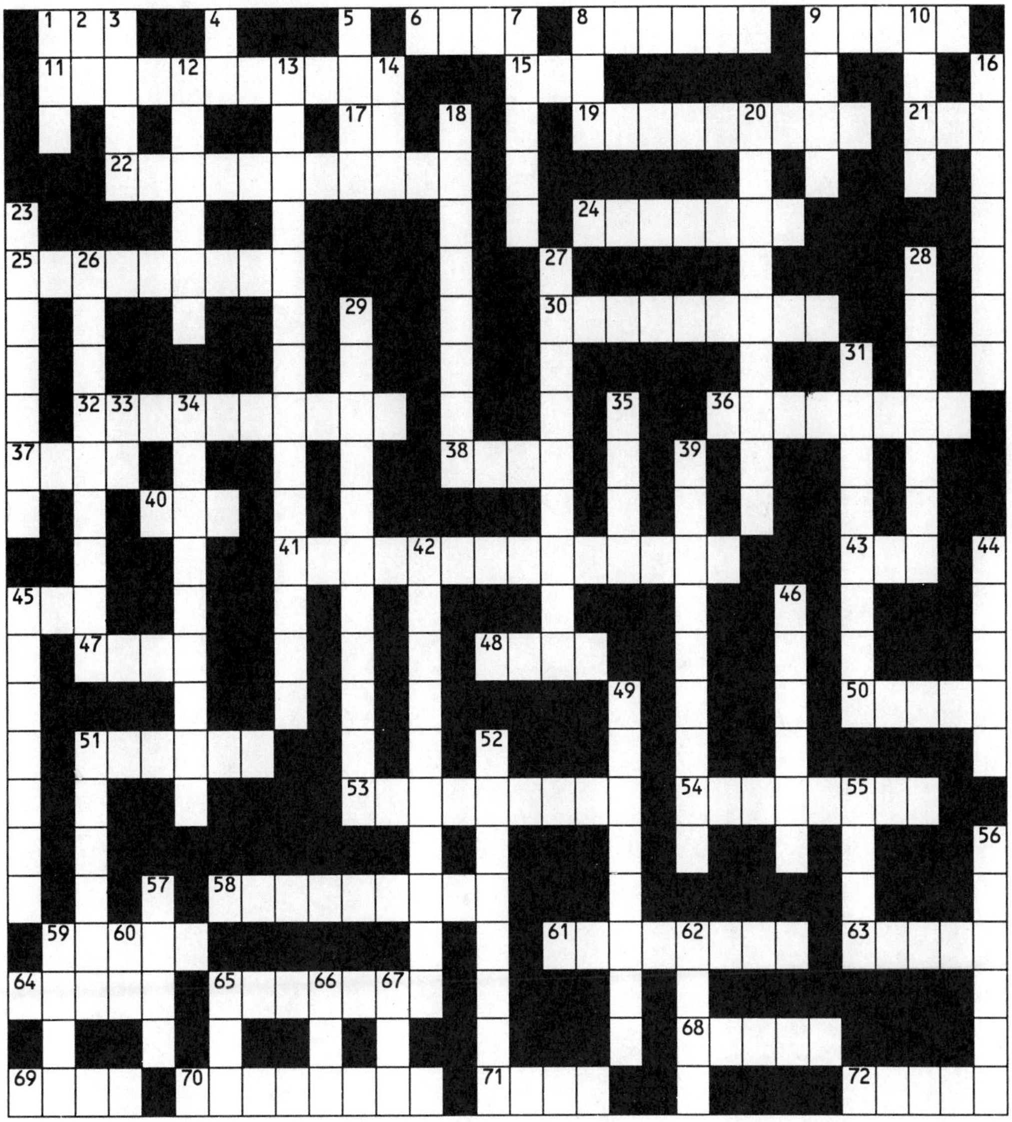

# COMPREHENSIVE CASE FOR CRITICAL THINKING

## Kidd Packing Company

Often in an administrative office management course, students are assigned a term report covering the various administrative problems faced by the office manager. This Comprehensive Case Problem presents the background of a hypothetical company to be used in developing such a term report. The case problem has been designed so that a portion of it may be completed following the reading of each of the four parts of the textbook, *Administrative Office Management,* Eleventh Edition.

In your term report, you will solve various office problems with which the company becomes involved, from the time of its reorganization and relocation until a smoothly operating office begins to function. Completion of the term report will require a good command of problem-solving skills, imaginative and creative thinking, and some supervisory knowledge. You may wish to engage in additional research and possibly interview businesspeople in the community for their reactions to the problems raised. In preparing your term report, follow the principles of report writing outlined in Chapter 5 of the textbook.

### PART A

The offices of the Kidd Packing Company are located in three buildings eight miles from downtown Chicago. The company produces and markets canned specialty meat products for wholesale warehouses, retail stores, and food service customers. All canned meats (ham, luncheon meats, sausages, and bacon) are shipped throughout the United States from the Chicago plant and seven branch distribution centers located in Trenton, New Jersey; Cincinnati, Ohio; Atlanta, Georgia; St. Louis, Missouri; Houston, Texas; Denver, Colorado; and San Diego, California. The company obtains its raw materials—such as pork, beef, and veal—from farmers, ranchers, commercial feed lots, terminal markets, and auction markets.

The company, founded in Chicago in 1897 by William Kidd, is now under the presidency of his granddaughter, Jean Kidd, age 62. Assisting Jean in managing the firm is her brother, Phil, age 58, who serves as vice president of sales. (Another sister, Carmen, age 52, is production manager for Space Unlimited, manufacturers of electronic parts for spacecraft.) A partial organization chart of the Kidd Packing Company is shown in Figure 1.

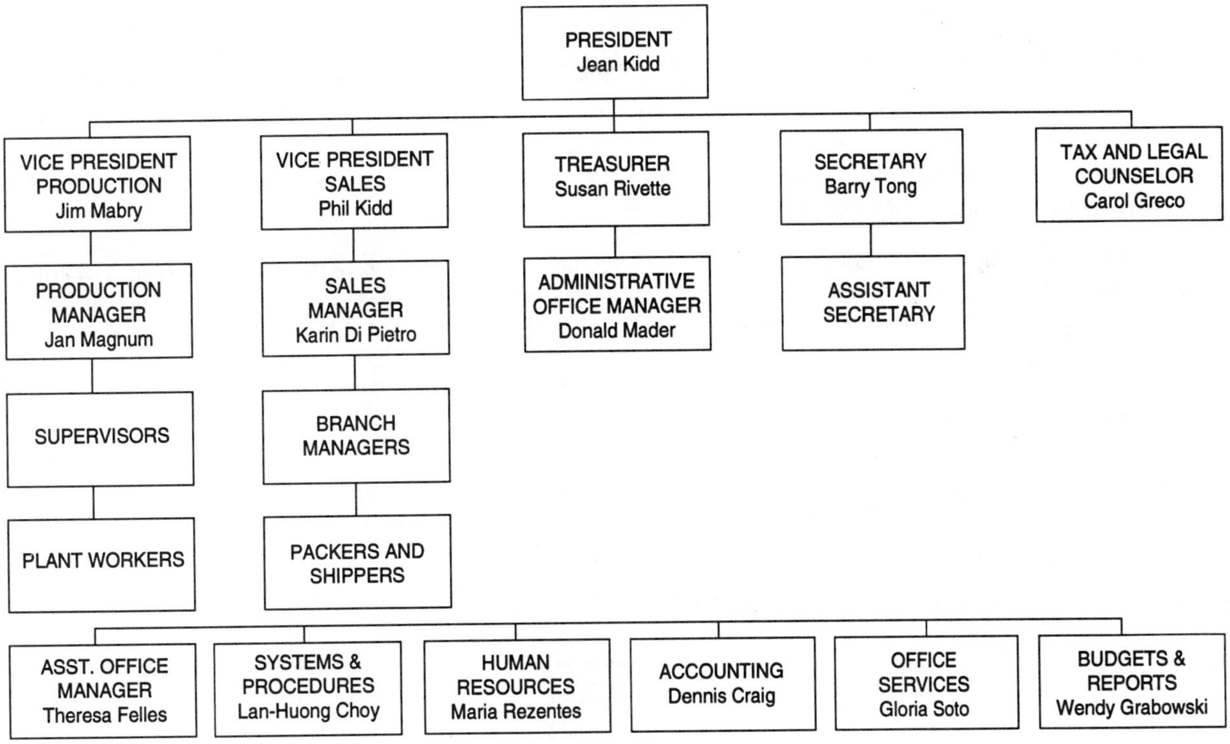


**Figure 1 Partial Organization Chart for Kidd Packing Company**

In each of the seven branch offices, only inventory and shipping records are processed and maintained. All accounting and billing are handled in the Chicago headquarters office. In charge of each branch distribution center is a manager who supervises the work of 20 to 25 packers and shippers. In the Chicago headquarters, there are 104 employees in the office and 342 workers in the plant.

The executive offices and the accounting department (64 office workers) are housed in the three-floor Building A, along with the processing and packing operations. All incoming orders are processed and billed in the accounting department. The company was originally founded in this building; but with growth over the years, the office functions have expanded and are now located as follows: Building B (one block from Building A)—systems and procedures work (4 office workers) and human resources activities (8 office workers); and Building C (across the street from Building A)—office services (20 office workers) and budgets and reports (8 office workers). The location of each building is shown in Figure 2.

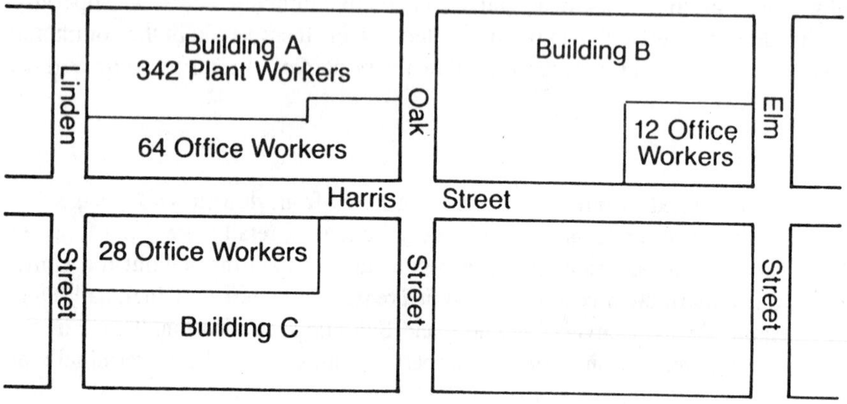


**Figure 2 Present Location of the Kidd Packing Company in Three Buildings**

Lately the company has been plagued with delays in its order processing and billing procedures. Customer goodwill has deteriorated, and sales have declined. In processing incoming orders in the Chicago office, often the orders are misplaced in one of the buildings or delivered by messengers to the wrong departments. When orders are filled by a branch, two copies of each shipping order are mailed to the Chicago headquarters for central billing. With two copies of each shipping order circulating in the offices, a customer often receives duplicate billings.

On several occasions during the past year, a few workers in the accounting department submitted ideas to the company's suggestion committee for improving order processing and billing procedures. In each instance, however, the suggestion committee took no action on the ideas submitted. Today, one of the accounting clerks, Julie Fain, had this to say to Tracy Corey, who chairs the suggestion committee:

> A few of us wonder why we never hear anything about the suggestions we turn in. We submit suggestions but never hear that they are accepted, turned down, or shelved. It looks as if the workers in the sales department have no problem in getting their suggestions approved. What gives anyway? Are you playing favorites?

## QUESTIONS FOR PART A

A–1. Following the principle that office organization should be constantly studied and improved, what is your reaction to the present organization of the Kidd Packing Company? What are your recommendations for improving the organization structure?

A–2. How might the suggestion system be strengthened to play a more effective role in company communications?

## PART B

Some of the difficulties in order processing and billing procedures can be traced to Dennis Craig, who feels that his accounting department is overworked, understaffed, and underpaid. For the past three weeks, he has been urging the administrative office manager, Donald Mader, to hire more personnel for the accounting department. Sensing that Mader is doing nothing about his request, Craig goes directly to the treasurer, Susan Rivette, expresses his dissatisfaction with how Mader is running the office, and tells Rivette to get him more accounting clerks.

Rivette listens patiently to the disgruntled Craig and then says:

> You know very well, Dennis, that I can't hire more workers for you. And Rezentes, in human resources, has no authority to recruit more people for your department unless she has an approved requisition from Mader.

Rivette goes on to say that it is difficult to get good workers not only because the market is tight at the present time but also because many high school and community college graduates can obtain better paying jobs in cleaner surroundings in the suburban offices. She ends the discussion by remarking, "We can't begin to compete and as a result, we get what's left over. As you well know, they're not the most productive workers."

Mader has not taken action to requisition more help for the accounting department because during the past six months he has been serving on a task force to investigate a new building site, with the objective of bringing together all office activities under one roof. As part of their committee work, the task force (Mader, Mabry, Rivette, and Tong) has been asked to determine the feasibility of installing new communication facilities to overcome the delay in processing orders. About 60 percent of the orders are filled by branches; 25 percent by the Chicago office from mail orders; and 15 percent by the Chicago office from telephone orders.

From Mader's preliminary study and conversations with Lan-Huong Choy and his systems staff, Mader feels there is little need for additional workers in the accounting department. The pressing need is for more microcomputers. However, Wendy Grabowski, the budget director, has shown Mader "the bare facts"—that no funds are available during the present fiscal period to purchase additional office equipment. She does point out, however, that there is an unused $225,000 that was budgeted for hiring ten more workers in the accounting department and five more in office services.

Choy and his staff have been studying the order processing and billing procedures for several weeks and have developed some specific recommendations for improving the workflow and reducing the billing time required. The staff has also been studying several data-entry operators to determine how many lines of invoice data the average operator keyboards each workday. While checking the work of Mary Owen, a data-entry operator, Choy was asked by Owen:

> Why are you doing all this checking? Why do you want to know the number of lines I am keying in? What do you want me to do—speed up my work?

Choy told Owen that he was counting the lines in order to obtain an average figure that would help management learn whether all operators were producing at a fair rate.

Owen then told Choy that she was not a data-entry operator anyway. As she explained:

> I was hired as a word processing operator, and during the first two weeks I was trained to input and edit. Then one day Mrs. Black—you know my supervisor, don't you?—told me to come over here to help out on the billing. That was six months ago and I am still here! But what really bugs me is that although I'm still considered a word processing operator, I'm being paid the beginning salary for a data-entry operator. I know the beginning word processing operators are getting about $25 to $30 more each week than I am. Mrs. Black knows that, too, but she's done nothing about it. Will you please talk with her and see what you can do for me? I think I should be doing the work I was hired for and be paid a word processing operator's salary.

Although Owen's problem was not directly related to his systems study, Choy decided to talk with Black, the supervisor in the order department about Owen's dissatisfaction. Before Choy could finish his story, Black interrupted and exclaimed:

> I've told Mary that if she has any gripes, to come to me. There was no need of her bothering you. I'll have to have a talk with her again; I can see that.

Black picked up a manual and continued:

> Here, Mr. Choy, see what it says in the procedures manual about the job of the word processing operator.

Choy read:

*Word Processing Operator:* Operates word processing equipment to input, edit, and deliver documents. Proofreads and edits own work. Jobholder is familiar with department terminology and company practices. May occasionally assist data-entry operators during the rush season.

Choy then commented:

But this says "occasionally assist" and "during the rush season." Mary tells me she's been doing the work of a data-entry operator for over six months. I don't call that "occasionally assisting." Besides, Mrs. Black, you know as well as I that our rush season never lasts more than two months at the most.

Black replied:

Well, Mr. Choy, I am shorthanded right now and I need a good operator and Mary is doing a fine job.

Choy said:

"That may be true, but Mary was hired as a word processing operator and she should be earning a higher salary right now.

Black retorted:

That's my business and I'll take care of it as I see fit. This is of no concern to you.

Upon returning to his office, Choy reflected upon his conversations with Owen and Black and decided to put his thoughts down on paper while the incident was fresh in mind. He decided to dictate a report to Rivette and send a copy to Mader, Craig, Soto, and Black.

However, before Choy was able to commence dictating, one of his staff came into the office and reported that the president's brother Phil had a severe coronary the night before and that there was little hope for recovery. Choy was told that for the time being Karin DiPietro, the sales manager, would assume most of Phil's duties. The remaining responsibilities would be handled by Barry Tong, the secretary.

At lunch that day, DiPietro was overheard talking with Tong:

Well, Barry, I'll carry on as long as Jean wants me to. But I know that Space Unlimited is going to lose a good production manager, for Jean will bring her sister Carmen in here just as quickly as the move can be made. She's determined to keep the Kidd name at the helm, and Carmen is the only one left.

Tong added:

I don't know, Karin. I think the old woman has had enough of her relatives in here. There was never any love lost between Jean and Phil, and I don't think that bringing Carmen in will help matters any. It surely won't help you. Anyway, what does Carmen know about the meat-packing business?

The conversation was interrupted by the arrival of Rivette, who excitedly reported:

Well, I knew it was just around the corner, but I didn't know it was right here on our doorstep. My secretary tells me the office workers finally got enough signatures to call for a union election. You two know what's been going on among those people in the filing department—and the shop steward always egging them on. Well, we'll have to get rid of those trouble-makers right now.

DiPietro broke in and said:

Take it easy, Susan, or you'll end up in the hospital with Phil. Things aren't so bad. The office workers have tried before to bring the union in, but we've won every time. We can do it again. All we need to do is a little educating.

Tong reacted by remarking:

Well, we've been forewarned. I have tried to get the word to Jean, but it's like hitting my head against a brick wall. Even after talking with the workers about a new office building with modern furniture and up-to-date equipment, they're still not satisfied. Always complaining that they have no one to take their problems to. They want to work overtime and when they get the chance to, they complain that they are having to work too many hours. I could go on and on, but you two know what the problems are as well as I.

Rivette added:

You're right, Barry. I hear all of this and more. Right now the big topic is "no chance to get ahead." The office people complain that there is no future with the company, that they could stay here 10 years and still be doing the same job. I'm still hearing about Mrs. Black and all the problems with her workers. There the big problem is that the workers aren't being trained for their jobs or are being shuffled about from job to job until, according to Mrs. Black, they find a niche where they seem to fit best.

Following lunch, the three managers returned to their offices. While walking through the sales department, DiPietro noticed one of the workers eating a sandwich and sipping a soft drink while operating his terminal. She stopped at the desk and declared:

> Since when did you start eating and drinking in the office? You know the regulations!

The operator retorted:

> Since today when we decided to get the union in here. Eating and drinking at our desks are two of the first things we will be getting.

DiPietro cursed under her breath, shrugged her shoulders, and stormed off to her office.

Back in the accounting department, Craig was studying the tardiness and absenteeism records of his workers during the past month. As he scanned the list, his attention was drawn to the name of a relatively new employee, Anne Schmitt, who had been 10 to 15 minutes late 15 mornings and absent 6 afternoons during the month. Angrily, Craig picked up the telephone and called the supervisor, Gilda Picca, into his office. When Picca arrived, Craig growled:

> Look at these figures on Schmitt. I've had it! I've told you before to bear down on her and if she didn't shape up, we would ship her out. Evidently you didn't bear down enough. Bring her in here and I'll show you how fast we can ship her out to . . .

Picca broke in:

> But, Dennis, I'm trying. It's a difficult situation. Anne is a little troubled right now, with her divorce and the children and all that—

Craig interrupted:

> That's her problem. She should know she can't bring her personal life into the office. This is no marital counseling service we are running here and I've told you before not to get mixed up in it. Bring her in.

When Picca went to find Schmitt, she learned from one of her coworkers that Schmitt had just gone home with a splitting headache.

---

## QUESTIONS FOR PART B

B–1. What steps should the company take to improve its recruitment of qualified office workers? Do you think this is an opportunity for the employment of temporary office workers or the establishment of a job-sharing program?

B–2. Did Choy exceed his bounds of authority and responsibility by talking with Black about Owen's dissatisfaction with her job classification? Explain.

B–3. Study the job description of word processing operator contained in the procedures manual. Is the description sufficient for use by an operator as well as by a supervisor? Did Black interpret the job description too loosely? Did Choy interpret the job description too narrowly?

B–4. What advantages would Jean Kidd obtain by bringing her sister Carmen into the business? What problems might the continuation of nepotism create for the company? Do you recommend bringing in Carmen?

B–5. Assume that the election to unionize the office is successful. What steps should Mader take to see that management's objectives are achieved?

B–6. How can the company overcome the problem of its office employees who complain that there is "no chance to get ahead?" What do you believe these employees are really looking for during their working hours with the company?

B–7. Comment on DiPietro's handling of the terminal operator who violated regulations by eating and drinking in the office. Should DiPietro have taken immediate disciplinary action?

B–8. Evaluate the supervisory ability of Craig, as evidenced by his conversation with Picca. Is Craig using the "human approach?" Is he justified in his proposed action to fire Schmitt?

B–9. Does the company have a responsibility toward Schmitt to aid her in overcoming her emotional problems? What should be the role of Schmitt's supervisor, Picca, and the department head, Craig?

---

## PART C

When mail is received in Building C of the Chicago offices, the mail clerk separates all incoming orders from the other mail and gives the orders to a messenger for delivery to the order department in Building A. Incoming telephone orders are transferred by the switchboard operator in Building A to a telephone order clerk in the same building.

When an order is received in the order department, the procedure described in Figure 3 is followed.

ORDER PROCESSING AND BILLING PROCEDURE
ORDERS TO BE SHIPPED FROM CHICAGO

1. Check the order for accuracy of stock number, description, unit price, and shipping instructions.
2. Key a six-part order form and send it to the assistant office manager, who checks the credit rating of the customer.
3. Unsatisfactory or unknown credit rating and past-due accounts:

   Assistant office manager writes letter and holds order form pending investigation.

   Approved credit rating:

   Assistant office manager okays and initials order form, removes and files one copy, and returns five copies to Order Department.
4. Remove original and one copy of the order form and attach the telephone order form or the mail order form. File these materials in the PENDING file until notification of shipment is received.

   Place the remaining three copies in the OUT basket to be picked up by messenger for delivery to Shipping Department.
5. Shipping Department returns the Notification of Shipment (NOS) copy to the Order Department when shipment is made. (At time of shipment, the Shipping Department notes on the order form quantity shipped, number of cases, and delivery charges, and attaches a copy of the freight bill for shipments sent by truck, rail, or air. The Shipping Department packs one copy of the order with the shipment and files another copy in the Shipping Department.)
6. Retrieve the original and all attached forms from the PENDING file and match against the NOS received from the Shipping Department. Discard the original and all attached forms. Key any necessary back order on a new order form and follow step Number 4.
7. Give the NOS to a data-entry operator, who prepares a five-part sales invoice, which is distributed as follows:

| | |
|---|---|
| Original and one copy: | Mailroom, to be inserted in window envelope and mailed. |
| Two copies: | Accounts Receivable |
| One copy: | Sales Statistics |

ORDER PROCESSING AND BILLING PROCEDURE
ORDERS SHIPPED BY BRANCHES

1. Separate the NOS from the second copy of the two-part branch shipping order. Send the second copy to Accounts Receivable for retention until copies of the corresponding invoice are received. (When invoice copies are received, Accounts Receivable destroys the branch order second copy.)
2. Prepare and distribute a five-part sales invoice as outlined in step Number 7.

**Figure 3 Order Processing and Billing Procedure**

In their study of the order processing and billing procedures, Choy and his staff closely examined the forms presently used. The NOS copy of the shipping order is illustrated in Figure 4. The five-part invoice prepared from this shipping order is shown in Figure 5. After analyzing the input operations of the data-entry operators, Choy reached the conclusion that the layout of information on the NOS form does not lend itself to an efficient keyboarding of the invoice data. However, time has not yet permitted him to give much thought to redesigning the forms.

**KIDD**

KIDD PACKING CO.
General Offices • 8901 Harris Street
Chicago, IL. 60629-1480
Phone: (312) 555-1930

SHIP TO
FIVE CORNERS DELI
555 HIGHWAY SOUTH
CALUMET PARK IL 60643-1555

SOLD TO
FIVE CORNERS DELI
555 HIGHWAY SOUTH
CALUMET PARK IL 60643-1555

| DATE OF ORDER | DATE SHIPPED | CUSTOMER NO. | PURCHASE ORDER NO. |
|---|---|---|---|
| 03 12 -- | 03 12 -- | 084 | 166 |

| QUANTITY ORDERED | QUANTITY SHIPPED | BACK ORDER | CODE | DESCRIPTION |
|---|---|---|---|---|
| 2 | 2 | 00 | H3 | ROLL HONEY HAM LOAF |
| 1 | 1 | 00 | S19 | TIN LIVER SPREAD |

| PACKER | SHIPPED VIA |
|---|---|
| LKH | OUR TRUCK |

NOTIFICATION OF SHIPMENT 8401

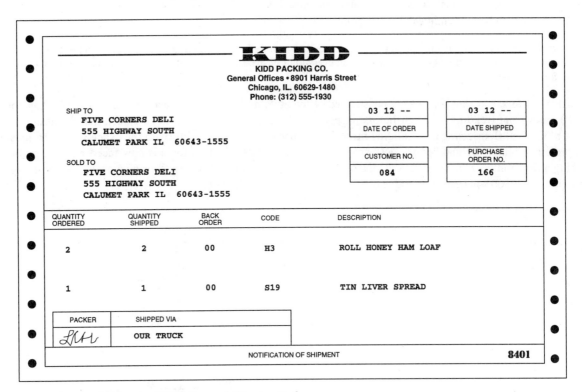

**Figure 4 Notifiction of Shipment (NOS) Copy of Shipping Order**

**KIDD**

KIDD PACKING CO.
General Offices • 8901 Harris Street
Chicago, IL. 60629-1480
Phone: (312) 555-1930

SOLD TO
FIVE CORNERS DELI
555 HIGHWAY SOUTH
CALUMET PARK IL 60643-1555

SHIP TO
SAME

CUSTOMER NO. 084

SALES PERSON 19

CUSTOMER PURCHASE ORDER NUMBER 166

PLEASE REFER TO THIS NUMBER WHEN REMITTING
INVOICE NO. 34445

DATE SHIPPED 03 12 --

INVOICE DATE 03 14 --

BRANCH CHI NOS. NO 8401

| CODE | DESCRIPTION | UNITS | UNIT PRICE | AMOUNT |
|---|---|---|---|---|
| H3 | HONEY HAM LOAF | 2 ROLLS | 13.89 | 27.78 |
| S19 | LIVER SPREAD | 1 TIN | 6.95 | 6.95 |

CASH DISCOUNT 69 TOTAL INVOICE 34.73

TERMS:
2/10 NET 30
DISCOUNT ALLOWED FROM DATE OF INVOICE, PROVIDED ALL OTHER PRIOR INDEBTEDNESS SHALL HAVE BEEN FULLY PAID. ALL PAYMENTS RECEIVED BY US WILL BE APPLIED TO THE OLDEST OUTSTANDING INVOICE.

**Figure 5 Five-Part Invoice Form**

As part of his study of the order processing and billing procedure, Choy also found a bottleneck in the methods used to obtain credit information about customers and to collect past-due accounts. For instance, it was found that Theresa Felles, the assistant office manager, and a transcriptionist spend about 30 hours each week dictating and transcribing individual letters to new customers requesting credit information and to present customers asking for payment on their accounts.

Problems also face the task force investigating the new office building site, for they seem to be getting nowhere with President Jean Kidd. Sentimentally, she points out:

> My grandfather began here in this building and it was good enough for him. I plan on staying here until I retire in a few years. I want to be near the plant so I can keep my eye on everything. If the rest of you want to move the offices out there to that God-forsaken spot, go ahead.

That "God-forsaken spot" is a newly constructed office building located on 20 acres of land in a suburban community 10 miles from Building A. After the first inspection of the new site, the task force agreed that the design and the layout of the first floor of the new building meet the company's needs very well (with the exception of the president, who prefers to remain behind her oak desk near the company plant). The task force is now faced with the problem of reaching a decision on whether to relocate the office in the new building. The first floor plan of the new building, with approximately 7,500 square feet of usable office space, is shown in Figure 6.

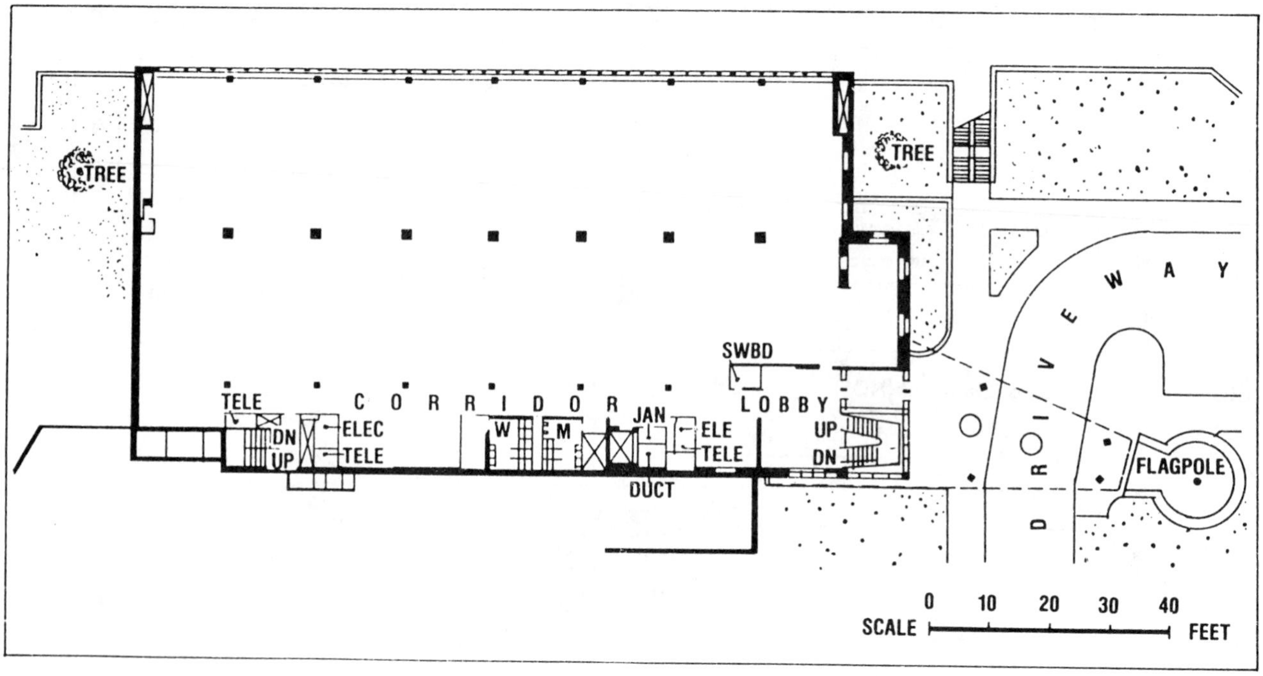


**Figure 6 First-Floor Plan of Suburban Office Building**

The task force has often called upon Choy and his staff for their recommendations on telecommunication systems that could handle interoffice communications as well as communications between the new home office, the seven branches, and the plant. Although Choy has been given the "green light" as far as funds are concerned, he is somewhat puzzled by the great variety of communication media available and the conflicting claims of the sales representatives for communications firms. At the last meeting of the task force this morning, Choy stated, "I want another week to think it over before I give a definite recommendation."

## QUESTIONS FOR PART C

C–1. Evaluate the present NOS and invoice forms used by the Kidd Packing Company. What factors should Choy consider before redesigning the forms? What specific recommendations do you have for improving the forms?

C–2. How do you recommend Felles and her transcriptionist overcome their problem of spending about 30 hours each week dictating and transcribing letters to new and present customers?

C–3. The task force has agreed that the design and layout of the new suburban building will meet the needs of the company. As part of its study on relocating, what other factors should be analyzed by the group before a decision is reached? Prepare a checklist to be used in evaluating each of these factors in relation to the suburban office site.

C–4. Do you recommend that the company move its offices to the suburban location? If so, how would you solve the problem of the president, who refuses to make the move but has given her consent for others to relocate?

C–5. The interior of the new office building has not yet been painted; nor have partitions been installed. For the most part, all that is visible is the outer shell, as shown in the floor plan in Figure 6. Thus, Mader has an opportunity to work with interior decorators, designers, and lighting engineers in selecting colors, types of partitioning, and lighting systems, and in providing for private offices. What are your recommendations in the selection of appropriate ergonomic factors?

C–6. How should the company prepare its present employees for the move? What should be the responsibility of the company toward those office employees who would like to continue working for the firm but who do not wish to commute to the new location?

C–7. Assuming that the offices are relocated, what changes do you recommend be made in the reorganization of the office support services so that the present personnel and equipment may be better utilized?

C–8. Discuss the types of interoffice communication systems that you recommend the company install in its new location. What are your recommendations for handling telecommunications between the new home office, the branches, and the plant?

C–9. How should the incoming, outgoing, and interdepartmental correspondence be handled? Do you recommend the establishment of a centralized mailing system in the new location?

## PART D

Three months have passed since the offices were relocated in the new suburban building. Sales have begun to climb, mainly as the result of Kidd's research and development department having discovered a new dry-freeze process that enables the company to market products that can be stored longer and yet retain their fresh taste. One month ago the company diversified its line by acquiring controlling interest in Striker Company, producers of canned fruits and vegetables. For the Kidd offices, this growth in sales and expansion of line have meant a staggering increase in workload.

Mader, aided by Choy and the systems staff, has made many improvements in the payroll, purchasing, and inventory control procedures. For example, today Choy handed Mader a report on the work standards to be used in measuring the output of data-entry operators who key in payroll data. Choy plans to meet with the operators tomorrow morning and explain the results of his study that led to the setting of new standards.

Because of budgetary constraints, however, Mader has been unable to implement the changes in the order processing and billing procedures that were recommended by Choy. Thus, for the most part, the order processing and billing procedures remain pretty much the same as when they were developed a few years ago in the former location. In his last conversation with Grabowski, Mader learns that shortly after relocation, three new workers were hired for the accounting department and five for office services. As a result, with only one month remaining in the current fiscal period, $100,000 remains unused in the budget allocations for accounting and office services. Grabowski still remains adamant in refusing to transfer this amount to Mader to be used for buying additional PCs.

At an office management seminar last month, Mader discussed his budget problems with Doris Voltano, manager of information services for Sundown Products. Voltano related some of her similar experiences during the installation of a mainframe. She indicated to Mader that he might want to study the feasibility of bringing in a large computer rather than adding more PCs to handle his order processing and billing operations. However, Voltano cautioned Mader:

> Watch out for those people at the top. Our president and one of the VPs felt that we had to have this new computer just to keep up with what our competition was doing. Our officers never really studied the problem but instead plunged headfirst into the installation, talking about how much prestige we would have. Well, prestige doesn't pay the bills and it doesn't answer the questions now as to what happened to all those savings we were told we would be making.

After the meeting ended, Mader was approached by Hank Tyson, the local sales representative for A1A1 computers, who said:

> Hello, Don. Just wanted to catch you before you left. You know, Don, it's about time you got underway with your computer study. Let me drop by tomorrow morning and talk with your people about what our A1A1 computer can do for your company.

---

### QUESTIONS FOR PART D

D–1. Assuming the role of Choy, how would you proceed to communicate to the data-entry operators the new work standards and the objectives of the work measurement program? What points would you specifically stress regarding productivity improvement when you meet with the workers?

D–2. Analyze the flow of paperwork and personnel involved in the order processing and billing procedure outlined in Figure 3. What opportunities are there for eliminating, combining, or simplifying the forms and the information recorded on them?

D–3. Mader sees as a prime need the installation of more microcomputers to handle the order processing and billing operations. According to Grabowski, there is an unused $100,000 in the budget for employing more workers in the accounting department and in office services. Should this money be made available for the purchase of office equipment? Would Grabowski violate any principle of budget making if she were to allocate the funds differently than originally planned? Looking ahead to the first year's operations in the new offices, what principles of budget preparation should be especially adhered to?

D–4. Outline the program of action that Mader should follow in studying the feasibility of installing a mainframe in the Kidd Packing Company. Who should be represented on the team to undertake the feasibility study? What help can Mader expect to receive from a computer manufacturer's representative such as Tyson?

---

# ANSWERS TO SECTION A • REVIEW QUESTIONS

## Chapter 1

1. No
2. Yes
3. No
4. No
5. No
6. Yes
7. Yes
8. No
9. Yes
10. Yes
11. No
12. Yes
13. No
14. No
15. Yes
16. No
17. Yes
18. Yes
19. Yes
20. No

### Part I

1. D
2. E
3. B
4. D
5. A
6. E
7. F
8. C

### Part II

1. F
2. E
3. B
4. A
5. H
6. G
7. C

## Chapter 2

1. K
2. F
3. E
4. H
5. G
6. B
7. C
8. I
9. J
10. D

1. Yes
2. Yes
3. Yes
4. No
5. No
6. Yes
7. No
8. Yes
9. No
10. No
11. No
12. Yes
13. No
14. Yes
15. Yes
16. No
17. Yes
18. No
19. No
20. Yes
21. Yes
22. Yes
23. No
24. No
25. Yes
26. No
27. No

## Chapter 3

1. Yes
2. Yes
3. No
4. Yes
5. No
6. No
7. No
8. Yes
9. Yes
10. No
11. Yes
12. No
13. No
14. No
15. No
16. Yes
17. Yes

1. H
2. C
3. I
4. D
5. E
6. B
7. A
8. F

*(Chapter 3 questions continued)*

### Steps in the Problem-Solving Process

4
6
3
2
5
8
7
1

## Chapter 4

1. L
2. G
3. D
4. E
5. I
6. J
7. F
8. A
9. B
10. C

1. Yes
2. Yes
3. No
4. Yes
5. Yes
6. No
7. Yes
8. Yes
9. Yes
10. No
11. No
12. Yes
13. No
14. No
15. Yes
16. Yes
17. Yes
18. No
19. Yes
20. Yes
21. No
22. Yes

## Chapter 5

1. I
2. D
3. K
4. F
5. E
6. J
7. L
8. B
9. G
10. C

1. No
2. Yes
3. No
4. No
5. Yes
6. Yes
7. No
8. No
9. No
10. Yes
11. No
12. Yes
13. No
14. Yes
15. No
16. Yes
17. No
18. No
19. Yes
20. No

## Chapter 6

1. No
2. Yes
3. No
4. No
5. Yes
6. Yes
7. No
8. No
9. No
10. No
11. Yes
12. No
13. Yes
14. Yes
15. No
16. Yes
17. Yes
18. Yes
19. Yes
20. No
21. No
22. No

*(Chapter 6 questions continued)*

| | | | | | |
|---|---|---|---|---|---|
| 1. | C | 4. | G | 7. | F |
| 2. | E | 5. | J | | |
| 3. | D | 6. | A | | |

## Chapter 7

| | | | | | |
|---|---|---|---|---|---|
| 1. | J | 5. | F | 9. | D |
| 2. | H | 6. | B | 10. | A |
| 3. | C | 7. | L | | |
| 4. | E | 8. | G | | |

| | | | | | |
|---|---|---|---|---|---|
| 1. | Yes | 7. | No | 13. | No |
| 2. | Yes | 8. | No | 14. | Yes |
| 3. | No | 9. | Yes | 15. | Yes |
| 4. | Yes | 10. | Yes | 16. | Yes |
| 5. | No | 11. | No | | |
| 6. | No | 12. | Yes | | |

## Chapter 8

| | | | | | |
|---|---|---|---|---|---|
| 1. | D | 4. | B | 7. | E |
| 2. | I | 5. | H | 8. | G |
| 3. | C | 6. | A | 9. | F |

| | | | | | |
|---|---|---|---|---|---|
| 1. | T | 8. | T | 15. | F |
| 2. | F | 9. | F | 16. | F |
| 3. | F | 10. | T | 17. | F |
| 4. | T | 11. | T | 18. | T |
| 5. | F | 12. | T | 19. | T |
| 6. | T | 13. | F | 20. | T |
| 7. | F | 14. | F | 21. | F |

## Chapter 9

| | | | | | |
|---|---|---|---|---|---|
| 1. | T | 8. | F | 15. | F |
| 2. | T | 9. | T | 16. | F |
| 3. | F | 10. | T | 17. | T |
| 4. | T | 11. | F | 18. | T |
| 5. | F | 12. | F | 19. | F |
| 6. | F | 13. | F | 20. | F |
| 7. | F | 14. | T | | |

| | | | | | |
|---|---|---|---|---|---|
| 1. | G | 3. | A | 5. | F |
| 2. | E | 4. | H | 6. | D |

## Chapter 10

| | | | | | |
|---|---|---|---|---|---|
| 1. | T | 8. | T | 15. | F |
| 2. | F | 9. | T | 16. | T |
| 3. | F | 10. | T | 17. | T |
| 4. | F | 11. | F | 18. | T |
| 5. | F | 12. | F | 19. | T |
| 6. | T | 13. | F | 20. | F |
| 7. | F | 14. | T | | |

*(Chapter 10 questions continued)*

| | | | | | |
|---|---|---|---|---|---|
| 1. | F | 5. | N | 9. | E |
| 2. | M | 6. | G | 10. | D |
| 3. | H | 7. | B | | |
| 4. | I | 8. | C | | |

## Chapter 11

| | | | | | |
|---|---|---|---|---|---|
| 1. | H | 4. | A | 7. | E |
| 2. | J | 5. | I | 8. | C |
| 3. | G | 6. | B | | |

| | | | | | |
|---|---|---|---|---|---|
| 1. | F | 8. | T | 15. | F |
| 2. | T | 9. | F | 16. | T |
| 3. | T | 10. | F | 17. | T |
| 4. | F | 11. | F | 18. | T |
| 5. | F | 12. | F | 19. | F |
| 6. | T | 13. | T | 20. | T |
| 7. | F | 14. | F | | |

## Chapter 12

| | | | | | |
|---|---|---|---|---|---|
| 1. | No | 10. | Yes | 19. | Yes |
| 2. | No | 11. | No | 20. | Yes |
| 3. | Yes | 12. | Yes | 21. | No |
| 4. | Yes | 13. | No | 22. | No |
| 5. | No | 14. | Yes | 23. | Yes |
| 6. | Yes | 15. | Yes | 24. | No |
| 7. | Yes | 16. | No | 25. | No |
| 8. | No | 17. | No | | |
| 9. | No | 18. | No | | |

## Chapter 13

| | | | | | |
|---|---|---|---|---|---|
| 1. | C | 4. | A | 7. | F |
| 2. | J | 5. | K | 8. | G |
| 3. | E | 6. | I | | |

| | | | | | |
|---|---|---|---|---|---|
| 1. | T | 8. | F | 15. | T |
| 2. | T | 9. | T | 16. | F |
| 3. | T | 10. | T | 17. | T |
| 4. | F | 11. | T | 18. | T |
| 5. | T | 12. | F | 19. | F |
| 6. | T | 13. | F | 20. | F |
| 7. | F | 14. | F | 21. | T |

## Chapter 14

| | | | | | |
|---|---|---|---|---|---|
| 1. | B | 4. | A | 7. | F |
| 2. | C | 5. | H | 8. | G |
| 3. | E | 6. | D | 9. | I |

*(Chapter 14 questions continued)*

| | | | | | | | | |
|---|---|---|---|---|---|---|---|---|
| 1. | | No | 10. | Yes | | 19. | | No |
| 2. | Yes | | 11. | | No | 20. | Yes | |
| 3. | Yes | | 12. | Yes | | 21. | | No |
| 4. | | No | 13. | | No | 22. | | No |
| 5. | | No | 14. | | No | 23. | Yes | |
| 6. | Yes | | 15. | | No | 24. | Yes | |
| 7. | | No | 16. | Yes | | 25. | | No |
| 8. | | No | 17. | Yes | | | | |
| 9. | Yes | | 18. | | No | | | |

## Chapter 15

| | | | | | |
|---|---|---|---|---|---|
| 1. | A | 3. | C | 5. | A |
| 2. | D | 4. | D | 6. | C |

| | | | | | | | | |
|---|---|---|---|---|---|---|---|---|
| 1. | | No | 9. | Yes | | 17. | Yes | |
| 2. | Yes | | 10. | Yes | | 18. | | No |
| 3. | Yes | | 11. | | No | 19. | | No |
| 4. | Yes | | 12. | Yes | | 20. | Yes | |
| 5. | | No | 13. | | No | 21. | Yes | |
| 6. | Yes | | 14. | Yes | | 22. | | No |
| 7. | Yes | | 15. | | No | | | |
| 8. | | No | 16. | Yes | | | | |

## Chapter 16

| | | | | | | | | |
|---|---|---|---|---|---|---|---|---|
| 1. | | F | 7. | T | | 13. | T | |
| 2. | | F | 8. | T | | 14. | | F |
| 3. | T | | 9. | | F | 15. | | F |
| 4. | T | | 10. | | F | 16. | T | |
| 5. | T | | 11. | T | | 17. | | F |
| 6. | | F | 12. | T | | 18. | T | |

| | | | | | |
|---|---|---|---|---|---|
| 1. | H | 5. | B | 9. | C |
| 2. | L | 6. | F | 10. | A |
| 3. | G | 7. | D | | |
| 4. | E | 8. | J | | |

## Chapter 17

| | | | | | |
|---|---|---|---|---|---|
| 1. | G | 5. | H | 9. | B |
| 2. | D | 6. | K | 10. | E |
| 3. | F | 7. | I | | |
| 4. | C | 8. | A | | |

| | | | | | | | | |
|---|---|---|---|---|---|---|---|---|
| 1. | Yes | | 8. | Yes | | 15. | | No |
| 2. | Yes | | 9. | | No | 16. | Yes | |
| 3. | | No | 10. | | No | 17. | | No |
| 4. | Yes | | 11. | Yes | | 18. | | No |
| 5. | | No | 12. | Yes | | 19. | | No |
| 6. | | No | 13. | Yes | | 20. | Yes | |
| 7. | | No | 14. | Yes | | | | |

## Chapter 18

| | | | | | |
|---|---|---|---|---|---|
| 1. | M | 4. | J | 7. | I |
| 2. | F | 5. | C | 8. | K |
| 3. | L | 6. | G | 9. | D |

| | | | | | | | | |
|---|---|---|---|---|---|---|---|---|
| 1. | T | | 8. | | F | 15. | T | |
| 2. | T | | 9. | T | | 16. | | F |
| 3. | | F | 10. | T | | 17. | | F |
| 4. | | F | 11. | | F | 18. | T | |
| 5. | | F | 12. | T | | 19. | T | |
| 6. | T | | 13. | T | | 20. | | F |
| 7. | T | | 14. | T | | | | |

## Chapter 19

| | | | | | |
|---|---|---|---|---|---|
| 1. | O | 5. | A | 9. | P |
| 2. | L | 6. | E | 10. | G |
| 3. | F | 7. | D | | |
| 4. | N | 8. | M | | |

| | | | | | | | | |
|---|---|---|---|---|---|---|---|---|
| 1. | | No | 8. | Yes | | 15. | | No |
| 2. | | No | 9. | | No | 16. | | No |
| 3. | Yes | | 10. | | No | 17. | Yes | |
| 4. | | No | 11. | Yes | | 18. | Yes | |
| 5. | Yes | | 12. | Yes | | 19. | | No |
| 6. | Yes | | 13. | Yes | | 20. | Yes | |
| 7. | Yes | | 14. | | No | | | |

## Chapter 20

| | | | | | |
|---|---|---|---|---|---|
| 1. | I | 4. | A | 7. | F |
| 2. | B | 5. | G | 8. | E |
| 3. | K | 6. | H | 9. | J |

| | | | | | | | | |
|---|---|---|---|---|---|---|---|---|
| 1. | | No | 8. | Yes | | 15. | | No |
| 2. | Yes | | 9. | Yes | | 16. | Yes | |
| 3. | | No | 10. | | No | 17. | | No |
| 4. | | No | 11. | Yes | | 18. | Yes | |
| 5. | Yes | | 12. | Yes | | 19. | | No |
| 6. | Yes | | 13. | | No | 20. | | No |
| 7. | | No | 14. | | No | | | |

## Chapter 21

| | | | | | |
|---|---|---|---|---|---|
| 1. | F | 5. | K | 9. | A |
| 2. | J | 6. | H | 10. | C |
| 3. | D | 7. | B | | |
| 4. | L | 8. | E | | |

*(Chapter 21 questions continued)*

| | | | | | | | | |
|---|---|---|---|---|---|---|---|---|
| 1. | T | | 8. | | F | 15. | T | |
| 2. | | F | 9. | T | | 16. | | F |
| 3. | T | | 10. | T | | 17. | T | |
| 4. | | F | 11. | T | | 18. | T | |
| 5. | | F | 12. | | F | 19. | T | |
| 6. | | F | 13. | | F | 20. | | F |
| 7. | T | | 14. | T | | | | |

## Chapter 22

| | | | | | | | | |
|---|---|---|---|---|---|---|---|---|
| 1. | Yes | | 7. | | No | 13. | | No |
| 2. | | No | 8. | Yes | | 14. | Yes | |
| 3. | Yes | | 9. | Yes | | 15. | | No |
| 4. | | No | 10. | Yes | | 16. | Yes | |
| 5. | | No | 11. | Yes | | 17. | | No |
| 6. | Yes | | 12. | | No | | | |

| | | | | | |
|---|---|---|---|---|---|
| 1. | G | 5. | L | 9. | E |
| 2. | D | 6. | H | 10. | I |
| 3. | B | 7. | J | | |
| 4. | C | 8. | M | | |

## Chapter 23

| | | | | | | | | |
|---|---|---|---|---|---|---|---|---|
| 1. | Yes | | 8. | Yes | | 15. | Yes | |
| 2. | Yes | | 9. | | No | 16. | | No |
| 3. | | No | 10. | | No | 17. | | No |
| 4. | Yes | | 11. | | No | 18. | Yes | |
| 5. | Yes | | 12. | Yes | | 19. | | No |
| 6. | Yes | | 13. | Yes | | 20. | Yes | |
| 7. | | No | 14. | Yes | | | | |

| | | | | | |
|---|---|---|---|---|---|
| 1. | C | 4. | G | 7. | F |
| 2. | A | 5. | D | | |
| 3. | H | 6. | E | | |

| | Fixed Cost | Variable Cost |
|---|---|---|
| 1. | ✔ | |
| 2. | ✔ | |
| 3. | | ✔ |
| 4. | | ✔ |
| 5. | ✔ | |
| 6. | ✔ | |
| 7. | | ✔ |
| 8. | ✔ | |
| 9. | ✔ | |
| 10. | | ✔ |

## Solution to Crossword Puzzle 1

| | | | | | | | | | | | | | | | | | | | | | | | | |
|---|---|---|---|---|---|---|---|---|---|---|---|---|---|---|---|---|---|---|---|---|---|---|---|---|
| N | E | E | D | S | | | | | | | P | R | O | B | L | E | M | | | I | N | P | U | T |
| E | | | | U | N | C | L | E | | | O | A | K | | | | B | | | | Y | | | A |
| A | L | | | D | | P | | | C | | L | I | | | | M | A | N | U | A | L | | | B |
| P | A | P | A | S | | A | | D | E | M | I | N | G | | | O | | | | | O | P | A | L |
| | T | | U | | | | C | | O | | C | | | | | D | | L | | | N | | | E |
| | E | | T | A | Y | L | O | R | | H | Y | P | O | T | H | E | S | E | S | | | | D | D |
| | R | | H | | | | B | | | | | E | | I | | L | | F | | L | I | N | E | |
| F | A | Y | O | L | | | R | | | D | E | N | | K | | | | F | | | | | L | |
| E | L | | R | | | J | A | R | G | O | N | | K | I | N | E | S | I | C | S | | | E | |
| A | | F | I | V | E | | | | | W | | | | | O | | | N | | | | N | G | T |
| S | P | I | T | | | B | R | A | I | N | S | T | O | R | M | I | N | G | | O | | | A | |
| T | I | N | Y | | | U | | B | | S | | R | U | B | | | | W | | P | E | A | T | |
| | | | | | O | R | G | A | N | I | Z | A | T | I | O | N | | E | | E | | | I | |
| H | O | G | | | | E | | T | | Z | | | | | B | | S | L | A | N | T | I | N | G |
| A | | I | | G | R | A | P | E | V | I | N | E | | | J | O | W | L | | | | | G | R |
| W | | L | | R | | U | | S | | N | | L | | | E | | A | | O | | | O | | O |
| T | | B | | A | | C | | | | G | O | L | D | | C | O | M | P | U | T | E | R | | O |
| H | E | R | Z | B | E | R | G | | | | A | S | | | T | | P | | T | | | A | O | M |
| O | | E | | S | | A | | O | | | S | | | B | I | A | S | | P | U | L | L | | S |
| R | A | T | S | | | C | A | M | | | I | | | | V | | | | U | | | | | |
| N | | H | O | L | L | Y | | I | | | S | Y | S | T | E | M | | | T | A | I | L | O | R |
| E | | | D | | | | | T | A | X | | R | O | D | S | | A | A | | L | E | A | R | N |

## Solution to Crossword Puzzle 2

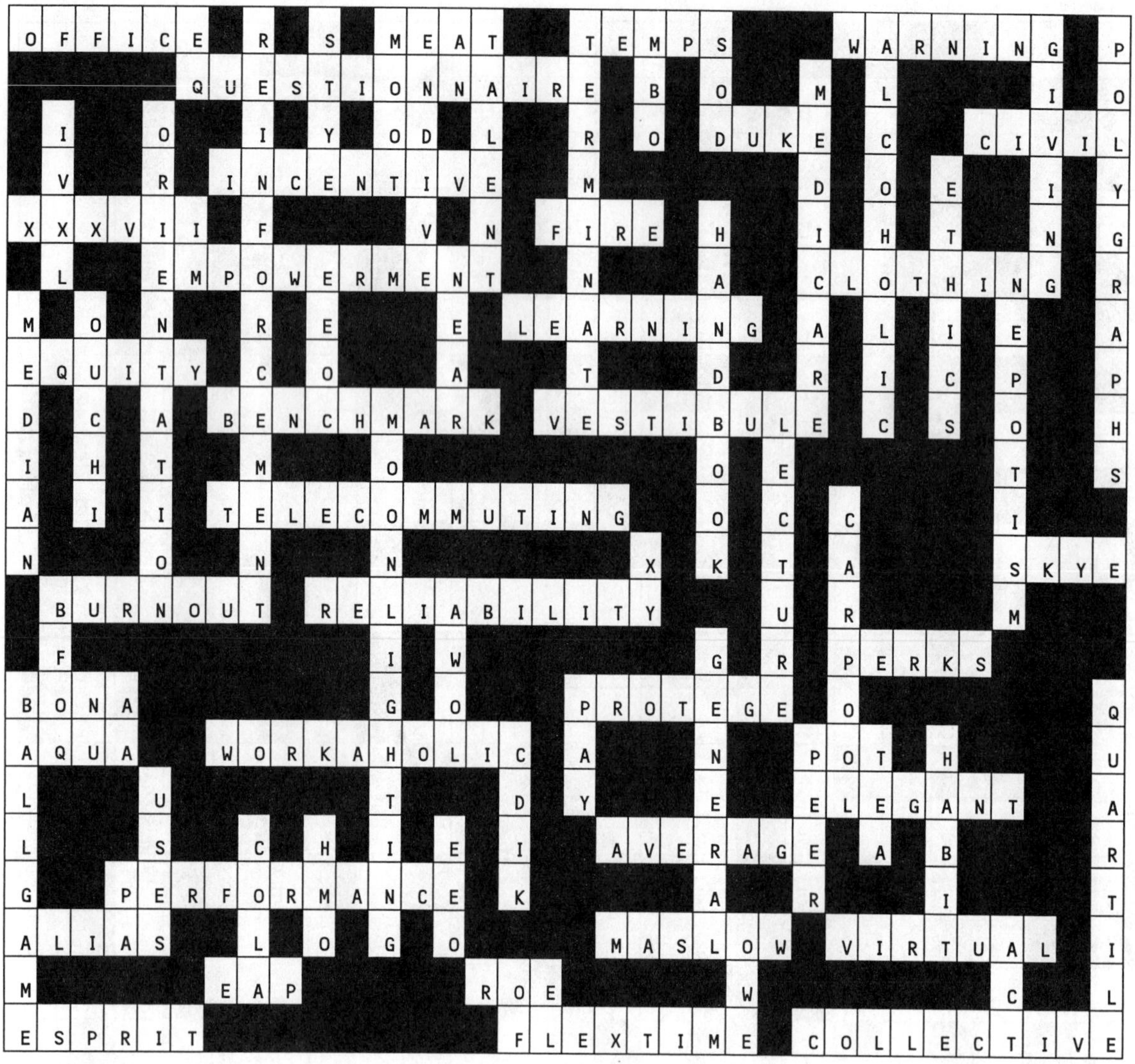

## Solution to Crossword Puzzle 3

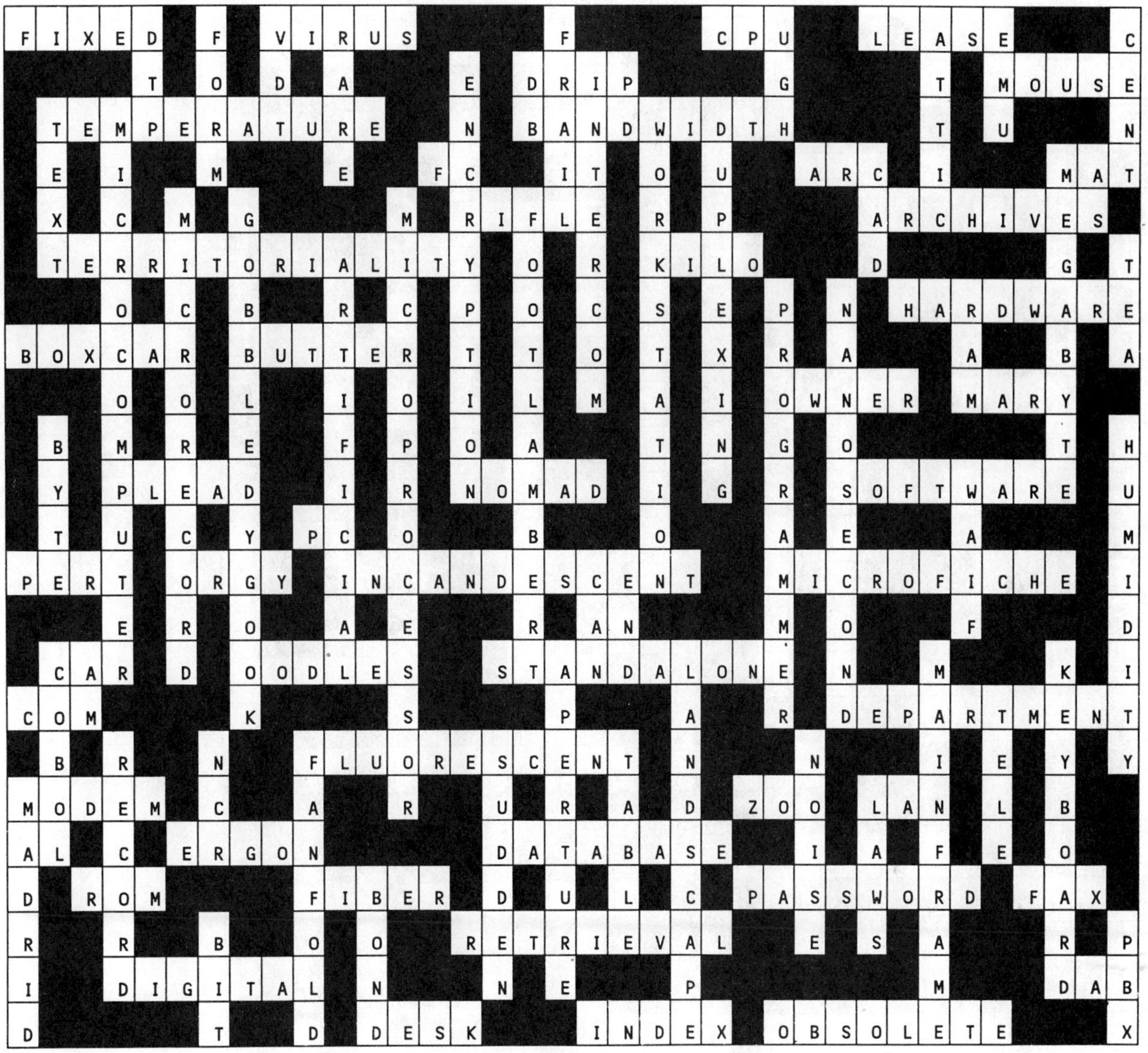

## Solution to Crossword Puzzle 4